SOUTHERN BIOGRAPHY SERIES

GENERAL WILLIAM J. HARDEE

Nathaniel Cheairs Hughes, Jr.

GENERAL
WILLIAM J. HARDEE

Old Reliable

LOUISIANA STATE UNIVERSITY PRESS
Baton Rouge and London

Copyright © 1965 by Louisiana State University Press

Manufactured in the United States of America

ISBN 0-8071-1802-8

Louisiana Paperback Edition, 1992
01 00 99 98 97 96 95 94 93 92   1 2 3 4 5

Maps prepared by Blake A. Magner and reprinted with the permission of
Broadfoot Publishing Company.

The paper in this book meets the guidelines for permanence and durability of the
Committee on Production Guidelines for Book Longevity of the Council
on Library Resources. ∞

To the Faithful,
Nat and Celeste Hughes

Contents

Maps

Preface

MARK TWAIN, with his incomparable gift for expressing what others dared not say, contended that a biography provided "but the clothes and buttons of the man." Every biographer or would-be biographer, I suppose, shares Twain's misgivings to some extent. Captain Irving A. Buck certainly did, in the case of William J. Hardee. Although he had served under Hardee and had had a close personal relationship with him, Buck hesitated to undertake his biography, feeling that there were others, closer to the general, who were better qualified.

Two biographers, both of whom met Buck's standard, failed. Colonel Thomas B. Roy, Hardee's chief of staff and later his son-in-law, limited himself to defending Hardee's operations in one controversial campaign. Another of Hardee's staff officers, William D. Pickett, succeeded only in compiling a short and superficial pamphlet.

The task of attempting to portray the long-neglected Confederate commander has fallen, then, to a member of a later generation, one who has never heard the voice of Hardee nor the firing of an angry six-pounder, and who is fully aware of Buck's misgivings.

Viewed across the years since his death in 1873, Hardee's most marked characteristic is that he was, and remained, a professional soldier. The story of his career as an officer in the pre–Civil War United States Army is a full one. He emerged from the Mexican War as a minor hero; he won acclaim for his light-infantry tactics manual; and he was recognized as an able disciplinarian and administrator while serving as commandant of cadets at the United States Military Academy. His career of some twenty years in the United States Army had brought him distinction as a military man.

In 1861 Hardee linked his fate with that of the Confederacy. Like the Army of Tennessee that he was to serve and love, he had to subsist on a long diet of failures, leading at last to surrender. In the end not only his career was gone but, to a large degree, his prewar personality. His story is significant in more than a personal sense, however. It is felt by many that the Civil War was decided in the West; the West was the responsibility of the Army of Tennessee; and William J. Hardee was one of the key figures of that army.

But he had an even larger importance. His book on tactics influenced a whole generation of soldiers before the war and during the war. Whether read in the original form or in an abridged or pirated edition or under the name of another officer, it became the great instructor of all officers of the war, Northern or Southern, professional or civilian. To paraphrase a tribute paid to the great Jomini, it might be said that every officer of the war went into battle with a sword in one hand and a copy of Hardee's manual in the other.

As will be seen in the Bibliography, there were special problems in locating material about Hardee, and I am indebted to numbers of persons for their assistance. For their part in making their material available and for making historical research a pleasure, I wish to thank the staffs of the Southern Historical Collection, University of North Carolina Library; the Manuscript Division, Duke University Library; the Georgia Department of Archives and History; the United States Military Academy Archives and Museum; the Alabama State Department of Archives and History; the Tennessee Historical Society; the National Archives; the Division of Manuscripts, Library of Congress; the Department of Archives, Louisiana State University; the Howard-Tilton Memorial Library, Tulane University; the Emory University Library; the North Carolina State Department of Archives and History; the Florida Historical Society; the St. Augustine Historical Society; the Tennessee State Library and Archives; the Henry Huntington Library and Art Gallery; the Mississippi Department of Archives and History; the Arkansas Department of Archives and History; the New York Public Library; the Southern Railroad System; the Barker Texas History Center, University of Texas; the Houston Public Library; and the Western Reserve Historical Society.

The author is also indebted to the following individuals for their suggestions, assistance, and encouragement: Dr. John G. Barrett,

Virginia Military Institute; Miss Margaret Bierschwale, Mason, Texas; Mrs. Thomas H. Bowles, Little Rock, Arkansas; Peter A. Brannon, Alabama Archives; Mrs. Mary G. Bryan, Georgia State Archives; Dr. T. Conn Bryan, North Georgia College; Arthur Ben Chitty, University of the South; Hardee Chambliss, Jr., Fairfax, Virginia; Colonel de Cosse-Brissac, Saumur, France; Miss Marguerite Drennen, New Smyrna, Florida; Mrs. T. E. Dudney, Sewanee, Tennessee; Miss Flora England, Marion, Alabama; Dr. Sidney Foreman, United States Military Academy Archives; Gilbert Govan, University of Chattanooga Library; Mrs. Connie G. Griffith, Tulane Library; Albert Hardee, Bronson, Florida; Miss Harriet Hardee, Savannah, Georgia; Pearson Hardee, Haverford, Pennsylvania; Walter P. Hardee, Durham, North Carolina; Mrs. Telfair Hodgson, Sewanee, Tennessee; Stanley F. Horn, Nashville, Tennessee; Mrs. Sara Jackson, National Archives; Mrs. Anna C. Johnson, Daytona Beach, Florida; Mrs. Chambliss Keith, Selma, Alabama; Dr. Frank Klingberg, University of North Carolina; Miss Beatrice F. Lang, Woodbine, Georgia; Mrs. William B. Lawton, Savannah, Georgia; Dr. Grady McWhiney, Northwestern University; Mrs. Alfred C. Miller, Homestead, Florida; Mrs. Lindsay Neville, Chapel Hill, North Carolina; Dr. James W. Patton, Southern Historical Collection; John R. Peacock, High Point, North Carolina; Milton F. Perry, Harry Truman Library; Robert Quarles, Jr., Tennessee Historical Society; Mrs. W. W. Rainer, Selma, Alabama; Dr. James I. Robertson, State University of Iowa; Dr. Charles P. Roland, Tulane University; Miss Mattie Russell, Duke University Library; Dr. Arnt M. Stickles, Bowling Green, Kentucky; Colonel Frederick H. Todd, United States Military Academy Museum; Dr. Caroline Wallace, Southern Historical Collection; Lee Wallace, National Park Service; Dr. Bell I. Wiley, Emory University; and Mrs. O. S. Wynn, Selma, Alabama.

I wish particularly to acknowledge the assistance rendered by Mrs. Howard Bowen, who worked long hours with me in the attempt to reconstruct faithfully the life of her grandfather. My professor, Fletcher M. Green, witnessed the birth of Hardee's biography and carefully guided its development. T. R. Hay graciously provided indispensable advice, material, and encouragement.

To my wife Bucky—typist, researcher, and critic—should go the lion's share of credit for transforming an idea into a book.

N. C. HUGHES, JR.

GENERAL WILLIAM J. HARDEE

I

"It Is My Most Earnest Wish"

LIGHTHEARTED FESTIVITIES ruled the day as the citizens of Little Satilla Neck, Georgia, gathered in 1820 for the annual Fourth of July celebration. The president of this assemblage, Major John Hardee, rose and proposed the initial toast: " 'Let the commerce of our country suffer its worst by a war than submit to further negotiations with the government of Spain.' 3 guns, 3 cheers." [1]

The lively toasting and merrymaking continued while the Major threaded his way through the crowd, greeting and conversing with his fellow planters and their families. The tall, corpulent Hardee enjoyed the friendship and respect of the community and with its support had repeatedly been elected state senator from Camden County since 1808. Later in the evening he gathered his family and embarked for the short voyage home. The four slaves who manned the oars of the Hardee boat bent to their tasks and, ignoring the rival wakes occasioned by the gleefully dangled fingers of young George and William, soon brought the welcome lights of "Rural Felicity" into view.[2]

Giant cypress trees festooned with Spanish moss sheltered a beautiful and comfortable home. Stout walls of tabby, with a watertight

---

1 Savannah *Daily Georgian*, July 22, 1820. Little Satilla Neck, or "Hazzard's Neck," lies ten miles due south of Brunswick, Georgia, and one hundred miles south of Savannah.

2 "Rural Felicity" no longer exists. The inhabitants of the extreme point of Little Satilla Neck, where the home once stood, are limited to the stray pig and the Georgia redbug. The only visitor is an occasional hunter. Only a few scattered pieces of tabby and a briar- and cane-entangled area, devoid of large trees, suggest the location of the house. The Hardee wharf site has been confiscated by the encroaching marshland, and the canopied boat, fashioned from a single cypress, probably lies submerged beneath tons of mud.

stucco finishing layer, rose twelve feet from the ground and supported
two stories of well-constructed cypress or oak planking. A piazza
ran the length of the southern side of the building, and the northern
side overlooked vast expanses of marshland, trammeled intermittently
by the glistening, unpredictable Little Satilla River. Breezes from the
river refreshed the entire home through a central breezeway. The
interior of the home was dominated by an ancient and rather majestic
grandfather clock at the first bend of the great staircase.[3]

"Rural Felicity" and its household were recent additions to the life
of Little Satilla Neck. Major Hardee himself was a relatively new
settler, having arrived in Camden County shortly after the close of
the Revolutionary War. He had immigrated to Georgia during the
Revolution as a boy of seventeen or eighteen, accompanying his father,
Captain Joseph John Hardy of Pitt County, North Carolina.[4]

Joseph Hardy, who had acquired military experience as an ensign
in the Pitt County militia, secured a lieutenant's commission in the
Georgia military establishment. In May, 1776, Georgia employed him
in withdrawing cannon to the interior from the exposed fort at
Frederica. Three months later Governor Archibald Bullock authorized him to undertake a more ambitious task. After procuring the
necessary boats and crewmen, he was to reconnoiter the sounds and
inlets along the southern coast of Georgia, determining the presence
and strength of British warships and privateers. His galley, the *Washington*, he outfitted and manned with his own funds and Negroes and
stationed it near Savannah. For three years he conducted reconnoitering missions, drove off enemy privateers, and attacked small parties
engaged in raiding or in reprovisioning the British troops at Savannah.[5]

3 Charles Seton Henry Hardee, "Reminiscences and Recollections of Old
   Savannah," in the C. S. H. Hardee Papers (Southern Historical Collection,
   University of North Carolina Library).
4 The names "Hardy," "Hardee," and "Hardie" are used interchangeably in
   the Georgia and North Carolina colonial, revolutionary, and early state
   records. Major Hardee himself inserted his name spelled "Hardy" in a deed
   but signed the document "John Hardee."
5 Roster of the Pitt County militia, 1766, in Pitt County Miscellaneous Papers
   (North Carolina State Department of Archives and History, Raleigh); Allen
   D. Candler, *The Revolutionary Records of the State of Georgia*, 3 vols. (Atlanta, 1908), I, 130, 188; Walter Clark (ed.), *The State Records of North
   Carolina* (Winston, N.C., 1895), XXII, 915–16; Revolutionary Pay Rolls, in
   Liberty County Records (Georgia State Department of Archives and His-
   tory, Atlanta); Phillip Cook, Secretary of State of Georgia, to Mrs. Peter W.
   Godfrey, June 21, 1899, in possession of Miss Harriet Hardee, Savannah, Ga.

Hardy's most notable military accomplishment occurred in 1778, when he joined a squadron of galleys that attacked and captured two British brigs and a sloop. Captain Hardy was commended in the official report of the action. He also received recognition from the British government two years later, when "John Hardy Capt. of rebel Galley" was listed under the British Disqualifying Act of July 6, 1780, and was thus deprived of citizenship and reduced to criminal status. One hundred and fifty-one other "rebels" also appear on this list, including other names that were to reappear significantly in Georgia history: Bowen, Bullock, Habersham, Houston, McIntosh, Middleton, and Telfair.[6]

The state of Georgia, which regarded Hardee's services differently, rewarded him with 1,360 acres on Little Satilla Neck. Captain Hardee settled on this land soon after the close of the war and built "Rural Felicity." He became a slaveholding cotton planter and figured prominently in the political activities of Camden County, representing the county in the Georgia General Assembly from 1783 to 1786 and serving as a Justice of the Peace for Glynn, Liberty, and Camden counties in 1784. He died at "Rural Felicity" on April 3, 1809.[7]

John Hardee followed his father's career closely. At an early age he became one of the most active of Camden County's citizens. His military career began in 1793, when he served as ensign, and he was later made a lieutenant in the Georgia militia. In the War of 1812 he held the rank of major, commanding a battalion of Georgia military cavalry. In business activities his management of "Rural Felicity" proved profitable, and the number of his slaves increased. Because of the salt marshes around the property, "Rural Felicity" did not offer favorable conditions for rice planting unless numerous dikes and drainage

---

6 Will Bacon Stevens, *A History of Georgia* (Philadelphia, 1859), II, 134; Joseph Clay to Josiah Smith, Jr., n.d., in Joseph Clay, *Letters of Joseph Clay* (Savannah, 1913), 70; Col. Samuel Elbert to Gen. Robert Howe, April 19, 1778, quoted in Charles C. Jones, Jr., *The Dead Towns of Georgia* (Savannah, 1878), 130–31; Charles Oscar Paullin (ed.), *Out-Letters of the Continental Marine Committee and Board of Admiralty, August, 1776–September, 1780* (New York, 1915), I, 263–64; George White, *Historical Collections of Georgia* (New York, 1854), 98.

7 Cook to Mrs. Godfrey, June 21, 1899, in possession of Miss Harriet Hardee; James T. Vocelle, *History of Camden County, Georgia* (Jacksonville, Fla., 1914), 40, 147; Savannah *Gazette of the State of Georgia*, 1783–86; *American Ancestry* (Albany, 1887–99), V, 130; Mrs. Howard H. McCall, *Roster of Revolutionary Soldiers of Georgia* (Atlanta, 1941), 195.

ditches were built. Since none are in evidence or are known to have existed there, one may conclude that Hardee's income came primarily from cotton, supplemented with limited crops of sugar cane.[8]

Major Hardee's political career is easier to trace than his military and business activities. He held the office of state senator from Camden in the following years: 1808–11, 1813, 1815–17, 1821, and 1825. For a short period he also held the position of overseer of the poor for the Thirty-third District.[9]

In 1797 Hardee married Miss Sarah Ellis of Savannah. They had seven children: Thomas Ellis (1798), Sarah (1800), John Hais (1803), Noble Andrew (1804), Caroline (1808), George Washington (1812), and William Joseph (October 12, 1815).[10]

Most of the sons pursued business and professional activities successfully, and the youngest, William Joseph, projected the military tradition of his ancestors to a significant conclusion.

From his earliest childhood young Hardee listened to the accounts of Camden County's violent and colorful history. Throughout the county were the overgrown ruins of Spanish missions and the crumbling forts of the Oglethorpe era, the Revolutionary War, and the War of 1812. Continuous warfare had marked the history of the area long before and since the county was officially created. The Indians had driven out the Spanish priests and administrators in 1680, and the following eighty-five years witnessed intermittent conflict among the English, the Spanish, the Indians, and the local inhabitants. Numerous great swamps such as the Okefenokee surrounded this section and served as a refuge for depredating Indian bands, escaped slaves, and outlaws.

---

8 Cook to Mrs. Godfrey, March 5, 1903, cited in letter from Hardee Chambliss, Jr., to author, July 19, 1956; Julia King to "Miss Blair," September 26, 1933, in Julia King Papers (Georgia State Department of Archives and History); Hardee, "Reminiscences and Recollections of Old Savannah"; Fourth, Fifth, and Sixth Censuses of the United States, Camden County, Georgia (photostatic copies), in Record Group 29, Records of the Bureau of the Census (National Archives and Record Service, Washington, D.C.); author's interviews with Henry Berry, resident of Hazzard's Neck, Ga., and with Miss Beatrice Lang, secretary of the Board of Registrars of Camden County, Ga., June 15, 1956, in Woodbine, Ga.

9 Georgia *Senate Journal*, 1808–25; Savannah *Georgian*, September 17, 1822; Minutes of the Court of Ordinary, Camden County, Ga., 1818, p. 200.

10 Hull-Hardee Family Bible (photostatic copy, Georgia State Department of Archives and History).

The historic area proved to be a romantic and exciting place in which to grow up. The older settlers added color to Hardee's boyhood surroundings with their stories of Arcadia, Santa Domingo, and Minorca. Within the vicinity lived several men of military prominence who delighted in passing on stories of their exploits: Brigadier General Duncan L. Clinch, Major Archibald Clark, and the famous Indian fighter Captain William Cone. Major General John Floyd made his home for many years at "Bellview," close to "Rural Felicity"; and "Dungeness," once the home of General Nathanael Greene and the last resting place of General "Light-Horse" Lee, stood just southeast of Little Satilla Neck on Cumberland Island.[11]

There were no schools in the immediate vicinity for the plantation children, but the families engaged tutors, who lived in the great houses and imparted to their pupils a firm foundation in at least the essentials of grammar, literary expression, and reading.[12] William Joseph Hardee's tutor must have succeeded in his undertaking, for in 1830 William J. Gipson, a local attorney, examined the fourteen-year-old youth in the fundamentals of English, education, reading, writing, grammar, arithmetic, "moral philosophy," and "the elements of Euclid." Gipson reported: "I have no hesitation in saying that I find him much farther advanced than could have been expected in any young man of his age. He also acquired the art of stenography after Gould's most approved system, has some knowledge of the Latin Language, and has made considerable progress in that of French, the study of which with that of the higher branches of English education he is now pursuing." In addition to reporting on Hardee's academic fitness, Gipson also commented: "By actual measurement his height is five feet four inches, and I believe him to be free from any bodily defect." [13]

Doubtless influenced by his family background and his environment, young Hardee decided prior to March, 1830, that he wanted to enter the United States Military Academy. His father heartily con-

11 Vocelle, *History of Camden County,* 41 and *passim.*
12 Author's interview with Miss Harriet Hardee, June 16, 1956, in Savannah, Ga.; Hardee, "Reminiscences and Recollections of Old Savannah."
13 William J. Gipson to John H. Eaton, March 4, 1830, in Application Papers of Cadets, 1814–66, Record Group 94, Adjutant General's Office (National Archives and Record Service); hereinafter cited as Application Papers of Cadets, 1814–66.

curred with his son's choice, aware that even if his son later abandoned his military career, he would have had an excellent education. John Hardee, with the assistance of his friend Major General John Floyd, prevailed upon Judge James M. Wayne, one of Georgia's representatives in Congress, to use his influence with the Secretary of War so that William might be appointed. Judge Wayne complied with these requests and urged Hardee's appointment in preference to any other that he had previously recommended. Hardee reinforced Judge Wayne's letter with requests of his own. To Secretary of War John H. Eaton he wrote: "Among many other wishes it is my most earnest one, to be admitted as a cadet to the U.S. military academy at West Point." [14]

The "most earnest" wish of a fourteen-year-old boy, however, often remains unfulfilled. Thus it was with William J. Hardee's desire to be a West Point cadet. No vacancies appeared in 1830 nor in the years immediately following. As the door to his preferred profession closed, Hardee evidently determined to begin a career in business and joined his older brother Noble Andrew Hardee, a cotton factor, on his cotton plantation near Sandersville, Georgia.[15] He did not give up his hopes, however, and continued his studies.[16]

In March 1833, Hardee drafted another letter to the Secretary of War:

In the spring of 1830, I made application through Judge Wayne our Representative in Congress for admission into the Military Academy at West Point: but as all the places were then filled, my application was dismissed, until a vacancy should occur, at which time *mine* was to have been taken into consideration. Whether any vacancy has occurred since that time I am unapprized, but I understand that there is now, two or three, which you are desirous of supplying. And supposing my claims from their priority to be superior to any other applicant that may now apply, I thought it best to inform you of it, that they may not be entirely overlooked. If any further recommendations should be deemed necessary, they can be easily obtained, and from persons with whom you are acquainted. The length of time which has intervened since the date of my former application has not lessened my desire for admittance, nor neither has age, physical power, or mental imbecility disqualified me.[17]

14 John Floyd to James M. Wayne, March 5, 1830; Wayne to Eaton, March 17, 1830; and William J. Hardee to Eaton, March 6, 1830, *ibid*.
15 William J. Hardee to Lewis Cass, March 6, 1883; and Governor Wilson Lumpkin to Lewis Cass, March 22, 1833, *ibid*.
16 Hardee to Cass, March 30, 1833, *ibid*.
17 *Ibid*.

The War Department evidently replied either negatively or eva-
sively, so Hardee went to nearby Milledgeville and personally pressed
his case with Governor Wilson Lumpkin. Lumpkin, impressed with
his dogged determination, endorsed him in a letter to the Secretary of
War, Lewis Cass.

Nor did Hardee let matters rest with his series of letters. After persistent urging, he enlisted the help of his brother, Noble Andrew, who
wrote George R. Gilmer and Judge Wayne, requesting them to renew William's application, and they did.

On March 15, 1834, Hardee received his answer. He had been
accepted as a cadet in the United States Military Academy and was to
report at West Point by June, 1834. He joyfully penned his letter of
acceptance.[18]

West Point in 1834 was still a young institution, though already
enjoying a reputation for the thoroughness of its training. Sylvanus
Thayer, superintendent of the Military Academy from 1817 to 1833,
introduced French methodology in scientific military subjects, greatly
strengthened the mathematics courses, made class rank dependent
upon scholastic achievement, and lowered the student-teacher ratio,
thereby affording greater opportunity for individual instruction.
Thayer's rigid code of discipline and his system of mathematical and
military studies had taken root by 1834, but years of careful con-
solidation were necessary before the full flowering of his concepts.
He had appointed young, vigorous, and stimulating faculty members, such as Jacob W. Bailey, William H. C. Bartlett, and Dennis H.
Mahan,[19] but as yet they lacked the experience and the accumulation

18 Lumpkin to Cass, April 30, 1833; Noble A. Hardee to George R. Gilmer,
January 30, 1834; Wayne to Cass, January 6, 1834; Gilmer to Cass, February
14, 1845; and William J. Hardee to Cass, April 14, 1833, *ibid.*
19 Dennis Hart Mahan (1802–71) was probably the most significant American
military theorist and author of the nineteenth century. His works included
Complete Treatise on Field Fortifications (1836), *Elementary Treatise on
Advance-Guard, Out Post, and Detachment Service of Troops* (1847), and
various books on engineering, geometry, and drawing. Although he was
sharply restricted to the concepts of static and positional warfare by the
supreme military authorities, he indoctrinated many of his students with the
principles of fluid and mobile warfare. He emphasized particularly the value
and necessity of speed in offensive maneuvers. Mahan formed the popular
Napoleon Club at West Point and encouraged his students to undertake the
serious study of military history, for it is there "that we are to look for the
sources of all military science . . . [and the] exemplifications of failure and
success by which alone the truth and value of the rules of strategy can be
tested." For an appreciative treatment of Mahan's career, see R. Ernest
Dupey, *Where They Have Trod* (New York, 1940).

of knowledge that benefitted their students in the 1840's and 1850's.[20]

From 1834 to 1838 the number of cadets enrolled in the Military Academy ranged between 211 and 240. Seven civilian professors and thirty United States Army officer instructors composed the faculty. The reins of discipline, administration, and overall control of military and academic instruction remained in the hands of the superintendent, Brevet Lieutenant Colonel René E. De Russy, a veteran of the War of 1812 and a capable engineering officer and administrator. The office of superintendent also absorbed the functions of the commandant during the 1834 to 1838 era.[21]

A few days after Hardee's arrival at West Point the Academic Board of the Academy examined him, pronounced him academically qualified, and admitted him conditionally. His military training in his first year stressed the simple duties of a private soldier. The plebe's academic program consisted of French and "pure mathematics." Grammar, pronunciation, and translation were emphasized in French, and "pure mathematics" included algebra, geometry, trigonometry, application of algebra to geometry, and mensuration of planes and solids. Hardee ranked thirty-fourth in a class of 57 academically, but sixty-ninth out of 240 in conduct, accumulating the impressively low figure of 35 demerits.[22]

Duties of the corporal and the school of the company replaced the duties of the private soldier in Hardee's second year. These third-classmen received their first artillery course, and drawing was added to more advanced French and mathematics courses. The Military Academy stressed drawing, to enable army officers to provide their own maps in emergencies and to perform the functions of a topographical officer when engaged on reconnaissance or expeditions into uncharted areas.[23]

20 William A. Ganoe, *The History of the United States Army* (New York, 1924), 151; author's interview with Col. Frederick P. Todd, curator, United States Military Academy Museum, West Point, on March 29, 1956; author's interviews with Dr. Sidney Forman, archivist, United States Military Academy, West Point, March 26–30, 1956.
21 New York *Times*, June 7, 1854; Staff Records No. 2, 1835–42 (United States Military Academy Archives), 16 ff.; Register of the Officers and Cadets of the U.S. Military Academy, June, 1835 (United States Military Academy Archives), 3.
22 Battalion Order No. 40, May 25, 1834, and June 1, 1834, entry in Post Order Book No. 6, 1833–37 (United States Military Academy Archives); *Regulations of the U. S. Military Academy at West Point, New York* (New York, 1832), 13–14; Register of the Academy, 1835, pp. 16, 22.
23 *Regulations of the Academy*, 1832, pp. 13–14. For evidence of the profitable

In February, 1836, Hardee was promoted to corporal in the corps of cadets, although his deportment mark dropped his relative position in the cadet corps to one hundred fifth out of 216, with 87 demerits. In his academic studies Hardee fell to forty-first out of fifty-one. This can be attributed to a poor record in mathematics.[24]

It is worthwhile to examine Hardee's reading during his cadet days. Unlike his classmate P. G. T. Beauregard, who indulged heavily in classic military treatises, Hardee never ventured far beyond the required course reading. The number of books that he borrowed from the library during the four years is unimpressive. He seems to have been interested in American history, reading several standard books on the subject. The writings of Dr. William Robertson also apparently struck a sympathetic and romantic chord, for Cadet Hardee completed his three-volume *History of Scotland* and his biography of Charles V.[25] Robertson, an eighteenth-century Scottish writer, evoked the pageantry of history, painting his characters and settings in bold, picturesque, and romantic colors.

Hardee again won a promotion in his third year, being appointed sergeant in June, 1836. His relatively advanced age may explain why he continued to advance in spite of his mediocre academic record, but more probably these promotions represented recognition of his interest and ability in military duties and subjects.[26]

In his third year Hardee progressed to the study of the school of the battalion, the duties of the sergeant, and a second course in artillery. Advanced drawing, chemistry, and "natural and experimental philosophy" constituted the academic curriculum. He met with little success in these courses. Primarily because of wretched marks in "natural and experimental philosophy" his academic rating was declared deficient. This deficiency is somewhat offset by the fact that he had a good conduct record, receiving only forty-six demerits. Al-

---

drawing instruction the cadets received at West Point, the reader may examine the Kirby Smith reconnaissance journal in the Southern Historical Collection, University of North Carolina, and the assorted drawings by the cadets deposited at the United States Military Academy Museum.

24 Battalion Order No. 15, February 6, 1836, in Post Order Book No. 6; Register of the Officers and Cadets of the U.S. Military Academy, June 1836 (United States Military Academy Archives), 14, 22; Staff Records No. 2, p. 33.

25 Library Circulation Records, 1831–36 and 1836–41 (United States Military Academy Library).

26 Battalion Order No. 52, June 15, 1836, in Post Order Book No. 6. In his military subjects Hardee excelled, receiving either above average or good ratings, particularly in artillery. Staff Records No. 2, pp. 107 ff.

though he ranked thirty-sixth out of forty-six academically, he moved
to the top twenty-five per cent of the cadet corps in deportment.[27]

As a cadet, Hardee matured into a tall, lean, and sharply erect individual. He won the distinction of being appointed a lieutenant in
the cadet corps during his senior year at the Military Academy and
was given the supervision of a barracks wing. Five days after his appointment was announced, however, Hardee embarrassed himself and
his superiors by being placed under arrest for leaving his post as
officer-of-the-day without proper authorization. He received the light
penalty of one additional tour of guard duty and still retained his
position.[28] The light penalty indicates perhaps that Hardee's infrac-
tion resulted not from a flagrant violation of orders but from his inexperience in his new role as officer-of-the-day.

The curriculum for the first-classman offered the academic desserts
of rhetoric, mineralogy, moral and political science, and engineering
and the science of war, ably taught by Dennis Hart Mahan.[29] The
military subjects included evolution of the line (tactics), duties of
orderly sergeants and commissioned officers, a third artillery course,
and swordsmanship. Hardee encountered difficulty in his engineering
course and was reported deficient at midyear.[30] On the whole, however, his academic and military marks showed improvement, enabling
him finally to rank twenty-sixth out of forty-five in merit in the class
of 1838.[31] His yearly conduct rank dropped seriously during his final

27 *Regulations of the Academy*, 1832, pp. 13–14; Register of the Officers and
    Cadets of the U.S. Military Academy, June, 1837 (United States Military
    Academy Archives), 11, 21; Staff Records No. 2, p. 63.
28 Battalion Order No. 60, June 14, 1837; Battalion Order No. 65, June 19, 1837;
    and Battalion Order No. 69, June 28, 1837, all in Post Order Book No. 6.
29 The engineering course concentrated primarily on military engineering,
    teaching defensive systems for positional warfare. Carmontaigne's system of
    fortifications received detailed examination, as did the general methods
    of constructing and defending field and permanent fortifications. One part of
    the course was devoted to civil engineering, however, introducing the cadet
    to road building, bridge construction, railroad construction, development of
    natural and artificial harbors, and surveying. The science of war supplement
    to the engineering course dealt with composition, employment, and organiza-
    tion of armies; conduct of campaigns; castramentation (choosing sites and
    erecting camps); and principles of strategy.
30 *Regulations of the Academy*, 1832, pp. 13–14; Staff Records No. 2, p. 90.
31 The two best-known personalities in the Class of 1838, other than Hardee,
    were Irvin McDowell, later to be the ill-fated Union commander at First
    Manassas, and P. G. T. Beauregard. Beauregard graduated second in the
    Class of 1838, with an outstanding record. Hardee's cadet record pales by

year. He was awarded 101 demerits and fell to the lower half of the cadet corps in conduct rankings.[32]

In a final appraisal of Hardee's West Point career, it should be pointed out that his academic record was mediocre at best. Perhaps the only positive and reassuring observation that can be made, in light of the inadequate and impersonal information available, is that Hardee salvaged his performance at the Military Academy by determined and evidently enthusiastic self-application in the military courses. His record of promotions in the cadet corps indicates that he at least succeeded in winning the confidence of his classmates and superiors.

Although he did not utilize his opportunity to the fullest, he received a sound military education and familiarized himself with the tools and principles of his profession. In eighteen years he was to return to the Military Academy as one of its highest officials.

---

comparison, although in fairness it should be pointed out that Beauregard's marks were always cushioned with perfect grades in French. It is lamentable that the accounts of the period do not reveal any personal relationship between the future Confederate leaders who were to work together so closely.

32 Register of the Officers and Cadets of the U.S. Military Academy, June, 1838 (United States Military Academy Archives), 7, 22.

II

"Before the Wedding Cake Was Cool Enough to Cut"

"RURAL FELICITY" welcomed home her glistening West Point hero. Hardee, after exhausting the glories of the family's attention, made the rounds of the neighboring plantations, probably thrilling the Hull children [1] with tales of metropolitan New York and impressing the old campaigner General Floyd with the latest military technological developments.

After the expiration of his leave Hardee prepared to join his regiment, the Second Dragoons, in Florida. Before he left for Florida, however, he received orders detaching him from the dragoons and directing him to report to General Winfield Scott in north Georgia. Scott's men were engaged in the removal of the Cherokee tribes to the West from northern Georgia and Alabama and from southeastern Tennessee. [2]

Hardee's duties during these summer months entailed occasional expeditions into the mountains and hilly country of northern Georgia in quest of small, cleverly concealed Cherokee bands which had eluded the searching parties. His few months in this mountainous country familiarized him with the terrain over which his forces struggled in 1864 against decidedly more formidable opponents.

In October, 1838, General Scott ordered that the Indians who had been gathered in the Chattanooga area should be conducted to the new Indian Territory. When the main body of the Cherokees departed, the services of such officers as Hardee, who had been detached from

1 Sarah Hardee, William's oldest sister, married Joseph Hull in 1818. They made their home with their twelve children at "Little York" plantation, located only a few miles from "Rural Felicity."
2 War Department General Orders No. 18, June 28, 1838, cited in *Niles' National Register*, July 7, 1838.

their commands, were no longer needed. In November, 1838, Hardee returned to his unit in Florida.[3]

In Florida the United States Army confronted the Seminoles, unquestionably a less tractable group than the Cherokees. The Seminoles had been strengthened by great numbers of refugees from the upper Creek tribes and sizable elements of runaway slaves. The scattered Seminole bands, restricted to inadequate and unproductive land by the American government in 1823, recognized no common chieftain, and any warlike Indian leader could find a considerable group of followers among the dissatisfied young braves. Although Seminole activity increased appreciably during the late fall of 1838, when several raiding parties crossed the state line of Georgia into Camden County, General Zachary Taylor, the American commander, still entertained hopes that the Seminole War would not burst forth again.[4]

The Second Dragoon Regiment formed the nucleus of the American cavalry force in Florida. This relatively new unit had established by 1838 a reputation for effectiveness under the vigorous leadership of its colonel, David E. Twiggs. Several years' experience in swamp warfare, which demanded rapid and sustained maneuverability, had shown the feasibility of employing dragoons in Florida.[5] Tandems of small, lightly defended forts speckled the map of territorial East Florida. These posts provided easily accessible supply depots for the dragoons and served as springboards from which these troops might launch sudden raids deep into the Indian country, without fear of precariously overextending their lines of communication.

Second Lieutenant Hardee joined the Second Dragoons on November 21, 1838, but because of illness was ordered to the Government Hospital at St. Augustine, where he remained until December 4.[6] He

---

3 November, 1838, entry in Regimental Returns, Second Dragoon Regiment, 1838–61, Record Group 94, Adjutant General's Office (National Archives and Record Service); hereinafter cited as Regimental Returns.

4 Grant Foreman, *Indian Removal, the Emigration of the Five Civilized Tribes of Indians* (Norman, Okla., 1932), 315 and *passim*; Capt. Richard F. Floyd to Gen. John Floyd, August 19, 1838, quoted in Isaac F. Arnow, "History of St. Marys and Camden County," in intermittent issues of the *St. Marys Camden County Tribune*, April 21, 1950–January 30, 1953.

5 The first dragoons were French horsemen, raised by Marshal Brissac about 1600. They played upon the superstitions of their contemporaries by engraving dragon heads on the muzzles of their short muskets. In Hardee's day dragoons were mounted infantrymen, capable of fighting in the saddle or on foot. They formed a highly effective body of rapidly maneuverable infantry.

6 December, 1838, entry in Regimental Returns.

returned to active service as an officer in Company B, which occupied Forts Peyton and Call during the months of December and January.[7] In late January Colonel Twiggs moved most of his regiment near Volusia, located midway between Lake George and Lake Monroe in central Florida, where they remained throughout the spring. The dragoons passed these months cutting roads through the swamps, constructing causeways and bridges, and conducting scouting missions into the interior and to the south of St. Augustine.[8]

On one of these missions Hardee, with a detachment from Company B, was sent to investigate a report from an escaped Indian slave that a small marauding party of Seminoles had encamped in the vicinity. He followed the slave to the edge of the Okalwakee Swamp and, after prolonged urging, persuaded him to guide the dragoons to the Seminole camp. The small group of soldiers struggled through the sucking quagmire, stumbled through the tangled undergrowth, and thrashed about in the large stream bisecting the swamp. To no one's surprise the Indians heard them coming and after facing one volley, hastily delivered by the dragoons, disappeared into the remote regions of the swamp.[9]

Such seemingly insignificant raids, occasionally interspersed with petty military engagements, characterized the conduct of the Second Seminole War (1836–43) until late April, 1839, when General Alexander Macomb superseded General Taylor in command. General Macomb determined to end this frustrating contest by offering the Seminoles an acceptable peace. The Indians accepted Macomb's terms at once, and within a month tranquility prevailed.[10] The Seminoles crept out from their hiding places in the swamps and presently thronged about the government posts seeking shelter and food.

The army now allowed several large military units to withdraw from Florida. Six companies of Hardee's regiment departed with this group in May, 1839, but Company B remained. Hardee was assigned

---

7   Theodore F. Rodenbough, *From Everglade to Cañon with the Second Dragoons* (New York, 1875), 449; December, 1838, and January, 1839, entries in Regimental Returns.
8   Washington *Army and Navy Chronicle*, November 15, 1838, and February 14, 1839; February–July, 1839, entries in Regimental Returns; Franklin H. Churchill, *Sketch of the Life of Bvt. Brig. Gen. Sylvester Churchill, Inspector General U.S. Army* (New York, 1888), 41.
9   Washington *Army and Navy Chronicle*, August 8, 1839.
10 Foreman, *Indian Removal*, 371 ff.

to various minor staff duties during the summer, including those of acting assistant commissary and subsistence officer and acting assistant quartermaster. These additional duties, together with the routine drilling, instruction, and administrative functions required of every company officer, evidently did not overtax the young lieutenant's energies, for he made at least one visit to St. Augustine to relieve the "so small, so unchanged, so unexcited, so *same*" social life of the army post.[11]

The regiment granted Hardee a leave of absence in July, 1839, and he returned to Camden County. He was still there the following month, when a family tragedy occurred. William's older brother, Thomas Ellis Hardee, was murdered in the streets of St. Marys on August 30, and the assailant was never apprehended.[12]

Meanwhile, the peaceful state of affairs in Florida underwent a drastic change. A band of Seminoles ambushed Colonel William S. Harney and twenty-eight dragoons. Only the colonel and a few others managed to escape. The army immediately alerted the countryside, and once again volunteers from the southeastern states were recalled to duty. Bloodhounds were imported from Cuba, and presently expeditions equipped with these "dogs of war" penetrated the hinterlands, destroying every village and every stand of grain that they discovered.

Hardee's activities in the opening months of the new phase of the Second Seminole War consisted of commanding temporarily F Company at Fort Shannon in September and October and assisting with the training of new recruits at Fort Fowler in November. December, 1839, found him still detached from his company and engaged on an extended reconnaissance along the Georgia-Florida border and into the Okefenokee swamp. By the time he returned, Company B had established a new station, Fort Fulton, near St. Augustine. Hardee joined his company there in early February, 1840, and received the welcome news that he had been promoted to first lieutenant.[13]

During March and April Hardee took part in raids against the Seminoles but in May, because of illness, did not engage in the usual activities of Company B. From June to October he left the company on

11 Washington *Army and Navy Chronicle*, May 9, 23, June 6, 13, 20, August 8, 1839, April 9, 1840; July, 1839, entry in Regimental Returns.

12 July, 1839, entry in Regimental Returns; Savannah *Georgian*, September 4, 6, 9, 1839.

13 September, 1839–February, 1840, entries in Regimental Returns.

sick leave, either staying at the Government Hospital in St. Augustine or in one of the houses in town, perhaps the Thomas Henery Dummett home.[14]

The Dummett family had moved to Florida in the fall of 1825 after leaving Barbados in the West Indies in 1817 and residing in New Haven, Connecticut, for approximately six years. In February, 1825, Thomas Dummett purchased two large plantations in Florida, one on the Tomoko River and the other on the Mesquito River.[15] He turned at once to sugar production as a means of livelihood and met with striking success. The immediate sugar yield and the considerable profit that he achieved gained him wide publicity as a pioneer in Florida sugar development.

Thomas and Mary Dummett had eleven children. Two of these, Elizabeth (born April 11, 1820) and her older sister, Anna, figured prominently in Hardee's life, and Douglas, the eldest son, became a person of some historical importance.[16]

In 1835 the Dummett family fled from their Tomoko home to St. Augustine, shortly before a Seminole raiding party plundered and partially destroyed their plantation in December. Thomas Dummett at that time purchased the "governor's palace," on the corner of St. George and St. Francis streets in St. Augustine. The home was located close to Trinity Episcopal Church, to which the family belonged. Hardee had probably met twenty-year-old Elizabeth during the planters' gay social season of the preceding winter, and he must have enjoyed many pleasant times in the Dummett home during the summer of 1840, while he recovered from his illness.[17] His friendship with Elizabeth ripened and resulted in their engagement that fall.

14 May–October, 1840, entries, *ibid.*
15 Anna Maria Dummett, "Remembrances of the Old Plantation . . . the Old Dummett Grove," in *Literary Florida,* V (February, 1949), 9.
16 Born in the British West Indies in 1806, Douglas Dummett emigrated with his father to Connecticut, and then to Florida in 1825. Dummett pioneered Florida orange cultivation, founding the famous orange grove on Indian River in Brevard County. He strongly supported the Florida policy of promoting the welfare of the region by luring laborers and other new settlers into the state. He raised a company of Florida militia at the personal request of General Scott in 1836 and served as captain of it. Dummett represented St. Johns County in the state legislature in 1843 and was listed as one of the original members of the St. Augustine Historical Society in 1857. He died in 1873.
17 St. Augustine *Florida Herald,* January 13, 1836; Dummett, "Remembrances of the Old Plantation," *loc. cit.,* 13; List of Parishioners, 1821–54, in Trinity Parish Registers, Trinity Parish, St. Augustine, Fla.

Hardee rejoined his regiment on October 29, 1840, and took temporary command of Company C at Picolata, twenty-five miles due west of St. Augustine. A week later he received orders directing him to proceed to France for a year's study at the Royal Cavalry School at Saumur.[18] A dilemma now faced the lieutenant of dragoons. He had long been waiting for just these orders, but his eagerness to study in France was now subordinated to thoughts of Elizabeth Dummett. As he told his daughters in later years, he "could not leave his beautiful sweetheart until she became his wife." After hasty preparations the two were married on November 16, 1840, by the Reverend R. H. Rutledge.[19] A family saying remains concerning that wedding: "Grandfather had to leave for France before the wedding cake was cool enough to cut." Only a week after the wedding the bridegroom was en route to France.[20]

Hardee's appointment to study in France came not so much because of his outstanding service record or his entreaties, but because of his influential sponsors and the needs of the service.

One of his fellow officers in Company B, Second Dragoons, was Lieutenant Washington Irving Newton. Evidently he and Hardee became good friends, for in March, 1840, Newton's father, Thomas Newton of Norfolk, a former Congressman and an influential figure in Virginia politics, recommended that the Secretary of War designate Lieutenant Hardee as one of the Second Dragoon officers to be sent to France.[21] The other two Second Dragoon officers selected by the War Department to accompany Hardee were Captain Lloyd J. Beall and Lieutenant Newton. The three men probably received their instructions from the Secretary of War himself, who ordered them to

18 October, 1840, entry in Regimental Returns; Washington *Army and Navy Chronicle*, November 19, 1840; War Department to Capt. L. J. Beall, Lt. W. I. Newton, and Lt. W. J. Hardee, November 26, 1840, in Military Book XXII, Record Group 107, Office of Secretary of War (National Archives and Record Service); hereinafter cited as Military Book XXII.
19 Marriage Records, 1821–45, in Trinity Parish Registers. The wedding seems to have been conducted quietly, without any elaborate social preparations. Although the marriages of army officers to local women usually merited St. Augustine newspaper notices, the Hardee-Dummett wedding apparently was an exception. Probably when Hardee's orders came, sending him to France, they hastily made up their minds to marry before his departure.
20 Washington *Army and Navy Chronicle*, December 3, 1840; Charlotte (N.C.) *Observer*, August 7, 1932; author's interview with Mrs. Howard Bowen, granddaughter of William J. Hardee, August 5, 1957, in Birmingham, Ala.
21 Joel R. Poinsett to Thomas Newton, March 4, 1840, in Military Book XXII.

proceed to the Royal Cavalry School at Saumur for a twelve-month period, "during which time you will avail yourselves of the entire course of instruction in riding and cavalry tactics."

Joel R. Poinsett, the Secretary of War, had observed the European armies in action in the closing years of the Napoleonic wars and was determined to bring the American Army up to European standards. His decision to send three officers from the Second Dragoons to the Royal Cavalry School at Saumur may be traced back to an unfavorable inspection report concerning the regiment by the army's Inspector-General in the summer of 1839. The officers were to complete the course of instruction offered at Saumur in one year and, upon their return, were to introduce the French practices into the American service, thereby modeling the cavalry service after that of France, which Poinsett considered "the finest in the world." [22]

After giving the young officers their instructions, Poinsett filled their pockets with four months' advance pay and directed them to call on Lewis Cass, now the American Minister in Paris, upon their arrival. On December 8, 1840, they boarded the *Louis Philippe* in New York and sailed for Le Havre. [23]

The Royal Cavalry School, founded by Louis XV in 1768, was located on the left bank of the Loire at the town of Saumur, seventy-five miles southwest of Paris. Two types of students usually attended the Royal Cavalry School—the graduates of St. Cyr Academy destined to enter the cavalry service after two years of postgraduate studies and exercises, and experienced cavalry officers who had returned to refresh their formal knowledge of the science of war. [24] At the time of Hardee's attendance, new and rather unorthodox cavalry methods were being introduced into the French cavalry service by veterans of the Algerian campaigns. New tactics emphasizing elastic formations and rapidity of movement resulted from the irregular character of the war that the French had conducted in Algeria since 1830. The effectiveness of dragoons in this type of mobile warfare had been demonstrated conclusively. [25]

22 *Senate Documents*, 26th Cong., 1st Sess., Doc. 1, p. 49. Thomas Kearny, *General Phillip Kearny* (New York, 1937), 49.
23 Washington *Army and Navy Chronicle*, December 3, 24, 1840; War Department to Capt. L. J. Beall, Lt. W. I. Newton, and Lt. W. J. Hardee, November 26, 1840, in Military Book XXII.
24 *Senate Miscellaneous Documents*, 36th Cong., 2nd Sess., Doc. 3, p. 33.
25 From 1840 to 1845 a significant number of modified French tactics manuals poured from the French presses, as all branches of the service hastily conformed to the demands of the fluid warfare being waged in Algeria. Hardee's *Tactics* was later adapted from one of these manuals.

The year spent at Saumur had a significant impact on Lieutenant Hardee. It broadened his military perspective; it taught him by association the refinement that comes from being a member of a capable, confident, and institutionalized class of military devotees; it showed him the weaknesses inherent in a rough, semitrained, semidisciplined citizen army, such as the United States possessed in the early nineteenth century; and it demonstrated clearly the wonders that could be wrought through intensive military instruction, rigorous discipline, and a professional attitude toward military affairs. Above all, Saumur taught Hardee what a model army officer could be and should be.[26]

The Council of Instruction at the Royal Cavalry School granted Hardee his certificate of merit on January 28, 1842.[27] The American minister, Lewis Cass, forwarded the certificate in a letter to the new Secretary of War, John C. Spencer. Cass remarked in his letter that he was greatly pleased by the very favorable impression that the American officers had made. Also appended to this letter was a communication from the commandant of the Royal Cavalry School, expressing his satisfaction with the conduct of Lieutenant Hardee and saying that France would always be glad to receive any such officers that the United States desired to send.[28]

After receiving his certificate from the Royal Cavalry School, Hardee went to England for a few weeks. In March he embarked aboard the steamer *Columbia* at Liverpool and arrived in Boston on March 27, 1842. After enjoying a leave of absence, he rejoined, on May 17, the Second Dragoon Regiment, which had been transferred from Florida to Louisiana. Three weeks after this return, Hardee

26 One incident that reputedly occurred in Europe proved fortunate for Hardee in later years. While crossing the Alps with a group of American sightseers, he saw a carriage being carried away by two unmanageable horses. He managed to seize the horses and get them under control. One of the ladies in the carriage happened to be the wife of William H. Seward. Seward expressed his indebtedness to Hardee and stated that "if at any time he could be of service to him in any way, he stood ready to cancel the great debt he owed him." Unidentified newspaper clipping in possession of Mrs. Howard Bowen.

27 Certificate signed by the Conseil d'Instruction signifying that Lieutenant William Joseph Hardee had completed the course of instruction at the École Royale de Cavalerie satisfactorily, January 28, 1842, appended to letter of Cass to John C. Spencer, February 20, 1842, in Letters Received, Record Group 94, Adjutant General's Office; hereinafter cited as Letters Received, Adjutant General's Office.

28 Marshal Prevost to Cass, January 29, 1842, appended to letter of Cass to Spencer, February 20, 1842, in Letters Received, Adjutant General's Office; Spencer to Cass, April 20, 1842, in Military Book XXII.

evidently prevailed upon his regimental commander to permit him to go to St. Augustine so that he might bring Mrs. Hardee to his station at Baton Rouge. They returned late in August and established their home at the military post. Three years of routine, though happy, life on garrison duty in frontier posts awaited them.

III

Mexican War Service
and Frontier Duty

ELIZABETH HARDEE found garrison life on the Louisiana frontier quite different from the merry social whirl at St. Augustine. There were only a few permanent buildings in Baton Rouge, and the dirt streets crumbled into suffocating powder beneath one's feet in the summer and turned into mud that sucked at one's shoes in the winter. The town was "inhabited with few exceptions by a most immoral and god forgetting population." Murders occurred more frequently than dress balls, and "congenial society" could be found only in the company of other officers' wives.[1]

Lieutenant and Mrs. Hardee remained at Baton Rouge until May, 1843, when Hardee received orders to join the main body of the Second Dragoons at Fort Jesup, strategically located in northwest Louisiana between the Sabine and Red rivers.[2] It was here at Fort Jesup that Hardee's first two children were born: Anna Dummett in 1843 and Sarah Florida ("Sallie") in 1845.[3]

Lieutenant Hardee once again served with Company B, but in 1844 Colonel Twiggs assigned him to the special duty of training the five companies at Fort Jesup in the latest French methods. Hardee established and conducted an intensive training program emphasizing saber drills and precision movements of company and squadron formations. He selected two squadrons, armed them with lances that he had had made at the post, and drilled them to a degree of near perfection. They would serve as models for the regiment.

1 Mrs. Frances Webster to Mrs. Frances Kirby Smith, June 2, 1851, in Edmund Kirby Smith Papers (Southern Historical Collection).
2 May, 1843, entry in Regimental Returns.
3 Eighth Census of the United States, St. Johns County, Florida (microfilm copies in P. K. Yonge Library, University of Florida).

A visiting officer who saw the Second Dragoons charge in line with lances said that the "compactness and precision of their alignments at a gallop . . . were equal to the performances of the best mounted troops in England or France." [4]

Largely because of his success as regimental drillmaster, the War Department promoted Hardee to captain on October 21, 1844.[5] Hardee's rate of promotion had not been phenomenal, but no other members of the Class of 1838 assigned to dragoon duty had yet gained their captaincy. To emphasize the point, Hardee now shared the rank of captain with Robert E. Lee, Class of 1829. Since the position of company commander of Company C stood vacant at this time, Twiggs assigned Hardee to command, a position that Hardee would retain until 1853.

As the Second Dragoons drilled hard to become an accomplished cavalry unit, events moved rapidly elsewhere. Relations between the United States and Mexico had deteriorated during the early 1840's, and on April 23, 1844, General Zachary Taylor was ordered to Fort Jesup to assume command of the First Military District. In February, 1845, the War Department directed Taylor to hold his command in readiness to defend the Texas frontier, once the Texas Congress consented to annexation. In compliance with further orders in June, Taylor and the major portion of his small army embarked from New Orleans for Corpus Christi, Texas. The Second Dragoons, however, made the journey overland.[6]

Taylor's army remained in Corpus Christi throughout the fall and winter of 1845, and the omens of an impending war grew more pronounced.[7] When Mexico refused to receive the American minister, John Slidell, in January, 1846, the Secretary of War ordered Taylor to advance his "Army of Observation" to the Rio Grande. On March 8, the dragoons, accompanied by Major Samuel Ringgold's battery of "flying artillery," set out toward the town of Matamoras, followed by the First Brigade of Infantry on the ninth, and the Second Brigade on the tenth.

The general's force arrived at the Rio Grande opposite Matamoras

4 Rodenbough, *From Everglade to Cañon*, 83–84.
5 November, 1844, entry in Regimental Returns.
6 When the dragoons left Fort Jesup, Mrs. Hardee and her children departed for St. Augustine.
7 For Hardee's activities during this period see Nathaniel Cheairs Hughes, Jr., "William Joseph Hardee, U.S.A., 1815–1861" (M.A. thesis, University of North Carolina, 1956), 80–90.

on March 26, 1846. While Taylor fortified his position on the north bank and established a secure line of communications to Point Isabel, the Mexicans on the far bank augmented their forces with fresh reserves. General Pedro de Ampudia arrived on April 11, 1846, with 2,000 men and warned Taylor to return to the Nueces River; Taylor replied by blockading the Rio Grande. General Mariano Arista arrived on April 24 to take command of the Mexican forces and decided to take prompt and positive action to thrust the American Army back to the Nueces. He ordered General Anastasio Torrejon, with approximately 1,600 cavalry and infantry, to cross the Rio Grande above the American position.

Military authorities regarded the Mexican cavalry at that time as superior to the American mounted force, not only in numbers, but also in training. The impending war would be fought in terrain advantageous for the use of cavalry, and many thought that the Mexican superiority would be decisive.

The opening event of the war justified this opinion. Surgeon Robert C. Wood, attached to Taylor's command, recorded the news of an American cavalry disaster on Sunday, April 26, 1846. The American camp was startled when a Mexican guide "came in and reported the capture of 2 [companies] of Dragoons . . . Captain Hardee and Lt. Kane prisoners at Matamoras—Captain Thornton and Lt. Mason killed." [8] General Torrejon, who had no field hospital, sent a wounded dragoon back to the American camp later in the day, and this man confirmed the report.[9]

General Taylor had ordered Captain Seth Thornton, with Hardee as second in command, to take a squadron of dragoons composed of their two companies to reconnoiter some twenty-two miles along the banks of the Rio Grande west of the American encampment to ascertain what force, if any, had crossed the Rio Grande and the position of that force. Accompanied by a Mexican guide the command left on April 24, and between 8 A.M. and 10 A.M. on April 25 reached the Carricitos ranch, near the Mexican village of La Rosia. The ranch appeared to be a good place to halt, as it was protected on one side by the river and its land boundaries were defined by a high chaparral

---

8 Robert Crook Wood Diary, April 26, 1846, in Trist Wood Papers (Southern Historical Collection).

9 Nathan S. Jarvis, "An Army Surgeon's Notes of Frontier Service, 1833–1838," in *Journal of the Military Institute of the United States,* XXVII (July, 1906), 8.

fence. Thornton led the advance into the ranch, neglected to post sentries, and allowed the command to scatter about, procuring water, peering into the Mexican dwellings, and even sleeping. Suddenly an immense enemy force appeared and surrounded the ranch. Thornton leaped to his horse and immediately ordered the troops to charge. He raced ahead of his men toward the Mexican position, but their gunfire evidently excited his mount, because it became unmanageable. Struggling with his horse, Thornton next ordered his men to tear down the fence and finally in desperation ordered every man to "look to his own safety." The squadron rapidly disintegrated.

Captain Hardee, realizing that the situation was serious, collected twenty-five members of Company C and led them to the river bank, where he directed several men to ride out into the water to determine if it was passable. These men reported that they could not make their way down the boggy banks to the water, so Hardee formed the small group, joined by a few stragglers, into a line of battle. However, when he then urged them to fight, they replied that they did not possess the means, as most of them had lost their firearms in the confusion. Hardee thereupon sent a flag of truce to the enemy commander, asking whether the Mexicans would grant his force "honorable terms"; if not, he proposed to charge the enemy "and to sell their lives as dearly as possible." General Torrejon gave the honorable terms, however, and Hardee surrendered the portion of the squadron that he commanded.[10]

A few days after the skirmish at the Carricitos ranch, General Taylor received Hardee's report from Matamoras, where he was being held captive. General Arista had quartered him "in the most gracious manner." Arista maintained "that his nation had been regarded as barbarous and that he wished to prove to us the contrary." Hardee lodged at General Arista's quarters, ate at his table, and evidently enjoyed himself.

In his report Hardee said that Thornton had led the command into an ambush after the guide had warned him of the probability of the enemy's presence. He stated that Thornton was prepossessed with the idea that the Mexican forces had not crossed the river and that, if they had, they would not engage the American forces. Thornton neglected, upon entering the ranch, to take security precautions and allowed the

10 Court of Inquiry in the Case of Captain W. J. Hardee, E. E. No. 248, Record Group 153 (National Archives and Record Service); hereinafter cited as Hardee Inquiry.

column to disperse within the enclosure while he sought someone to interrogate. When the Mexican forces appeared, Captain Thornton lost control of his mount, issued conflicting orders, and finally galloped into the enemy's ranks astride his unmanageable horse. Hardee also stated in his report that he was convinced that Captain Thornton had "died bravely." [11]

Captain Seth Thornton, however, was very much alive. He had been captured after his horse had thrown him, on the route back to the American camp. His version of the skirmish differs greatly with that of Hardee. He stated that throughout the reconnaissance every precaution had been taken against surprise and that "if the command had obeyed his instruction, they would not have entered the field in which they were afterwards captured." Thornton believed that two factors primarily contributed to his failure. First, the commanding general had given him an impossible mission to perform, for he had ordered him to investigate too wide an area and allowed him only fifteen hours to accomplish the task. Second, his guide had proven untrustworthy and had deserted as soon as he felt that the column was cut off. Both charges proved damaging to Thornton. The first incurred General Taylor's displeasure, and the second implied that Thornton exercised poor judgment in allowing the command to be drawn into an ambush.[12]

American officers were soon discussing the two versions of the skirmish around their campfires. "I have heard, as every officer in the Army must have heard, different opinions expressed upon the subject of the capture of Capt Thornton's command. . . . It was a subject of common camp talk, and had not a difference of opinion existed, I presume it would not have been discussed." [13]

By May 10, 1846, Taylor had administered two stunning defeats upon Arista's forces at Palo Alto and Resaca de la Palma, and the Mexicans had withdrawn to a position south of the Rio Grande. These two victories gave Taylor a sufficient number of prisoners to exchange for Thornton's command, and on May 10, 1846, the Mexicans released their captives. By May 11 Hardee had once again assumed command of his company.[14]

Captain Hardee returned to the familiar campfires, only to find that some once-friendly faces were now hostile. Imputations against his

11 *House Executive Documents,* 29th Cong., 2nd Sess., Doc. 119, pp. 19 ff.
12 *House Executive Documents,* 30th Cong., 1st Sess., Doc. 60, p. 290.
13 Hardee Inquiry.   14 May, 1846, entry in Regimental Returns.

conduct were "whispered, and dwelt upon, by those among whom I would have expected to find my warmest defenders—the officers of my own Regt." Colonel Twiggs himself felt that Hardee should be censured in that "when Capt Thornton gave orders for a charge Capt Hardee gave different orders." Captain C. A. May concurred with his colonel's opinion and believed that Hardee had assumed a "commission to which he was not entitled," when he formed the twenty-five men on the riverbank.[15]

Two weeks of ridicule and censure convinced Hardee that he must vindicate himself in the eyes of his fellow officers. He therefore requested an investigation into the conduct of the affair of April 25 and into "my own conduct and bearing from first to last in the whole transaction." He said: "My motive in asking for the investigation . . . is twofold, first from the character and unfortunate issue of the affair itself which renders it proper for all concerned that the circumstances should be well understood and clearly established and the second from the fact that imputations of an unworthy and injurious nature have by some individual at least been made with more or less publicity against me, and parts of my official report have been said to contradict that of Capt. Thornton, my comdg. officer." [16]

On May 26, 1846, the Court of Inquiry convened at the camp of the Fifth Infantry, near Matamoras, and remained in session for a week. The court called dozens of witnesses, including Colonel Twiggs, Captain May, Captain Thornton, and numerous members of F and C companies. Hardee skillfully conducted his own case and systematically demolished Captain Thornton's official report.[17] When the question of Hardee's personal conduct arose, the court handled the interrogation of the witnesses, for Captain Hardee, at his own request, withdrew before the witnesses testified.

During a later phase of the trial Hardee defended himself against the stinging accusation that he had "surrendered too soon and before a sufficient number of men were killed and wounded." Hardee declared:

15 Hardee Inquiry.   16 *Ibid.*
17 The findings of Hardee's court of inquiry, which substantiated Hardee's report, consequently condemned Captain Seth Thornton to a court-martial for negligence. The court-martial was held on July 11, 1846. Thornton, stoutly defended by Hardee, was acquitted, but his professional career had been blighted.

The evidence proves that we were surrounded by a party of some two thousand men; that we were shut up within an enclosure which our horses could neither leap nor break down; that an effective charge was therefore impractical, and that the enemy by lining this hedge with his Infantry could have picked us off at leisure and with scarce a possibility of resistance on our part. When I had rallied the twenty-five men upon the bank of the river, I had no doubt that all the remainder of the squadron were killed or wounded, and that [surrender under such circumstances] would have been a proposition with which the most blood-thirsty fire-eaters could scarce find fault, and might surely justify the survivors, half-armed as they were, all retreat cut off and all resistance hopeless, in rendering themselves as prisoners of war.

The many witnesses who testified before the Court of Inquiry substantiated Hardee's contention that his official report was accurate in every particular. Perhaps the most interesting testimony concerns Hardee's personal behavior during the skirmish. Every witness defended Hardee, and even the men of Thornton's company sided with him and implied that Thornton was guilty of rashness. Lieutenant Kane stated that Hardee "appeared to be cool and collected and not at all excited" and that Hardee "wanted to fight" but the men did not possess sufficient arms or will. A trooper from Company F maintained that "by trying to collect the men in going to the river, and in surrendering I thought he saved our lives. He was cool, and his conduct was good. He wanted us to fight." Another Company F sergeant said "I thought Capt. Hardee behaved like a courageous man, and if we had followed his advice we would have been better off." Still others remarked, "He was cool and collected, and he behaved like a brave man, and like an officer"; "he acted as a soldier should." [18]

After Hardee rested his case, the court deliberated briefly and announced its decision:

1st. That the conduct of Captain W. J. Hardee ... was in all respects that of an intelligent and gallant soldier; that he did all in his power, by word and deed, to sustain his commanding officer in the discharge of his duty; and that any imputations against his character, growing out of his conduct as connected with that affair, are utterly without foundation.

2d. That the official report of Captain Hardee to the commanding general of the army of occupation ... is correct in all its particulars.[19]

18 Hardee Inquiry.
19 *House Executive Documents,* 30th Cong., 1st Sess., Doc. 60, pp. 491–92; *House Executive Documents,* 29th Cong., 2nd Sess., Doc. 119, p. 202; Hardee Inquiry.

Regardless of the court's findings, Captain Hardee emerged from the La Rosia skirmish and the subsequent controversy with a tarnished reputation. He grimly resolved to blot out this damaging episode with distinguished service in the coming campaigns.

The capture of Hardee and Thornton had had wider repercussions than a court of inquiry. Taylor had promptly sent the news of their capture to Washington, and Polk had quickly convened his cabinet and presented the information. The cabinet members agreed that Polk should ask Congress for a declaration of war. In his speech before Congress Polk's reference to "American blood being shed on American soil" marked the La Rosia affair as one of those small events in history that has far-reaching consequences. On May 13, 1846, Congress declared war on Mexico.

The summer of 1846 denotes the low-water mark of Hardee's career in the United States Army. His first encounter with the enemy had proven a fiasco; he had incurred the animosity of many of his fellow officers during the court of inquiry, and now the illness that had plagued his activities in Florida returned to remove him from his regiment. On July 25, 1846, only a few days after assuming command of a detachment of recruits, Hardee again fell ill, probably from dysentery. General Taylor learned of Hardee's illness and inquired about his health in a letter to Surgeon Wood.[20]

Taylor had lost a precious opportunity in May, when he allowed Arista to withdraw from Matamoras to the interior unmolested. While Taylor regrouped and reprovisioned at Matamoras, Arista situated his broken army at Linares, strategically located within easy supporting distance of Taylor's two possible objectives, Victoria or Monterrey. Taylor, once convinced that the victories north of the Rio Grande and the occupation of Matamoras would not suffice to break the Mexican resistance, determined to overcome the most formidable obstacle in northern Mexico, Monterrey.

On August 16, 1846, the advance guard of Taylor's army moved west toward Monterrey. General Twiggs placed his dragoons at the head of the massive column. Company C moved forward under the command of Hardee, but only for a short distance, for Hardee became ill once again on August 24 and was confined at Camargo. The United

20 Zachary Taylor, *Letters of Zachary Taylor from the Battlefields of the Mexican War* (Rochester, 1908), 36.

States Medical Corps probably had a case of mental depression to treat as well as dysentery, for while he lay on a hospital cot, his regiment continued to advance toward the enemy. Once Hardee learned that another engagement with the Mexicans at Monterrey was imminent, he left the hospital, perhaps prematurely. He assumed command of his company on September 3.[21]

En route to Monterrey the dragoons cleared small pockets of enemy resistance and acted as escorts to the pioneering parties who were repairing the road to the city. During the siege of Monterrey (September 20–25, 1846) the dragoons engaged in "reconnoitering, collecting the dead and wounded, and guarding the passes through which the enemy was likely to retreat." [22]

In November, Taylor, prodded by Polk, advanced to Saltillo. The Americans encountered negligible resistance, and during the following weeks the army enjoyed a period of relaxation. Captain Hardee and his fellow officers went sightseeing. They examined Mexican cotton mills, marveled at the beauty of the churches, and took long excursions into the neighboring countryside. Lieutenant Daniel Harvey Hill recorded one of the trips in his diary: "Went today with Captain Hardee of Dragoons to try the practicality of becoming acquainted with these families that seclude themselves so carefully. We had a most laughable time of it and were completely unsuccessful." [23]

Hardee and Company C left Saltillo in December and helped escort Taylor's army to Victoria. Late in the month they were transferred to the operational control of General Scott. At Scott's order the Second Dragoons, now commanded by Colonel W. S. Harney, proceeded to the coast to await Scott's transports.[24]

The dragoons embarked during the first week in March on "small coasting vessels" at Brazos Santiago. A destructive storm caught them on March 14, scattering and damaging the invasion fleet. The waves swept so many horses overboard that during the siege of Vera Cruz, many of the dragoons found themselves in the trenches alongside the infantry.[25]

---

21 August–September, 1846, entries in Regimental Returns.
.22 Rodenbough, *From Everglade to Cañon*, 117.
23 Daniel Harvey Hill Diary, December 5, 1846 (Southern Historical Collection).
24 *Ibid.*, December 30, 1846; Rodenbough, *From Everglade to Cañon*, 131.
25 Rodenbough, *From Everglade to Cañon*, 134; Hill Diary, March 18, 1847.

When Scott moved up to besiege Vera Cruz, the Mexican cavalry launched attacks from the vicinity of the village of Medellín south of Vera Cruz. Colonel Harney with a small force of dragoons set out to find and, if possible, to destroy this Mexican force. On March 25 at the stone bridge, Puente de Moreno, Harney encountered stubborn resistance, and he sent back for reinforcements. Captain Hardee, engaged in disembarking his horses, quickly gathered the dismounted dragoons and hurried to Harney's support. The Americans pinned down the Mexicans at the bridge and "then, with a wild yell, that resounded far and near, we rushed toward the bridge in an irregular manner, the men . . . becoming all mingled together." Hardee, with his dragoons, and "the volunteers, headed by Colonel Haskell and Captain Cheatham . . . ,[26] rushed upon it with fearless intrepidity. The fortification opposed no obstacle. It was immediately leaped." The Mexicans "retreated, run, broke, *vamosed*,—the infantry taking to the thick chaparral in every direction. Some were overtaken and killed, and we pushed on in a trot after the main body of lancers." Once the pursuit began, Hardee mounted and served as one of Harney's staff. For Hardee's "gallant and meritorious conduct in the affair with the enemy at Medellín," the War Department promoted him to brevet major.[27]

Vera Cruz capitulated on March 27, 1847, and General Scott moved quickly inland toward Mexico City. The dragoons led the advance, gathering intelligence and clearing the obstacles that threatened to impede the army's progress.

On April 8, 1847, the Americans fought their first major battle of the campaign at the pass of Cerro Gordo, on the seaward slope of the mountain range separating them from Mexico City. During the battle Scott held the dragoons in reserve until the opportunity for pursuit arose. Aided by a skillful reconnaissance by engineering officers, the American infantry enveloped the Mexicans and threw them back in

26 Benjamin Franklin Cheatham, who commanded a body of Tennessee volunteers in the Mexican War, later became one of Hardee's division commanders in the Army of Tennessee. Next to Patrick Cleburne, he was probably Hardee's ablest and most renowned lieutenant.

27 *Senate Executive Documents*, 30th Cong., 1st Sess., Doc. 1, pp. 251–52; George C. Furber, *History of Mexico* (Cincinnati, 1848), 543; Fayette Robinson, *An Account of the Organization of the Army of the United States* (Philadelphia, 1848), 131; George W. Cullum, *Biographical Register of the Officers and Graduates of the U.S. Military Academy* (Boston, 1891), I, 718; the original brevet commission is in the possession of Mrs. Howard Bowen.

disorder. At this moment Scott unleashed his dragoons for the pursuit, and they pressed the retiring Mexicans mercilessly until the exhausted conditions of their horses forced them to halt. An army correspondent passing over the route a few days later remarked: "All along the road were the bodies of Mexican lancers and their horses, cut down by Colonel Harney's dragoons when these fire-eaters chased Santa Anna and his retreating forces beyond Jalapa. Almost every man's skull was literally split open with the sabres of our horsemen and they lay stretched upon the ground in ghastly groups." [28] Hardee's saber drill at Fort Jesup had rectified the discrepancies noted by General Wool at Camp Washington in 1839.

Scott halted his army and reorganized it at Puebla. He advanced again on August 7, passing unmolested through the mountain range and into the Valley of Mexico. Santa Anna disputed the Americans' passage at Churubusco, a carefully prepared position only a few miles from the walls of Mexico City.

While the battle of Churubusco was in progress, Company C of the Second Dragoons remained at the village of San Augustín, protecting the flank of the attacking forces. On August 20 a "large band of guerrillas" appeared on the outskirts of the village and approached to sweep Hardee's company back upon the main army. Hardee formed his company into line, withstood the Mexican attacks, and contrary to expectation, swept them from the field, capturing "between thirty and forty horses with arms and accoutrements." For his performance at San Augustín Hardee was promoted to brevet lieutenant colonel. Meanwhile, at San Antonio, another small village engulfed by the fighting, the discredited but valiant Seth Thornton was struck and killed by a sixteen-pound cannon ball. The disaster at the Carricitos ranch was growing dimmer.[29]

The defeats around Churubusco compelled the Mexican army to withdraw into the inner defenses of Mexico City, which hinged about a supposedly impregnable fortress, Chapultepec. The Americans invested the city but were handicapped by a precarious line of communications, extending to their base of supplies at Vera Cruz. Following the battles at Churubusco this line had been virtually

---

28 Rodenbough, *From Everglade to Cañon*, 140.
29 Report of Major E. V. Sumner, quoted in L. V. Revis, *The Life and Military Services of Gen. William Selby Harney* (St. Louis, 1878), 233; Hardee's brevet commission; Cullum, *Biographical Register*, I, 718; Rodenbough, *From Everglade to Cañon*, 151.

severed by irregular Mexican cavalry detachments, and provisions were short. To relieve the situation, Colonel Harney sent Hardee out with a foraging party to locate some corn. D. H. Hill commented, "Captain Hardee, 2d Dragoons, went out some days ago in command of an escort for a train of wagons in search of corn. Great fears were entertained at one time for his safety, but he has returned without a mishap and brings a thousand bushels of corn." [30]

Scott delayed the final attack on the defenses of Mexico City, while General William J. Worth conducted an attack on El Molino del Rey, a building supposedly housing a Mexican cannon foundry. This fortification, however, constituted a stronghold at one of the extremities of the inner defense and was protected with enfilade fire by the guns of Chapultepec. As Worth's command deployed for the attack, "an immense body of lancers, with a considerable force of infantry, made their appearance in the valley . . . and moved steadily forward." Scott realized the danger to Worth's vulnerable flank and ordered Major E. V. Sumner, with two squadrons of dragoons, to act jointly with General Franklin Pierce's brigade and Captain John B. Magruder's battery in repulsing this threat. The American flank guard moved into position under heavy fire from the enemy fortifications and repulsed the enemy attack with "considerable loss." Major Sumner in his official report commended Hardee: "They all did well; but I must mention in particular the successful efforts of Captain Hardee in maintaining order in his squadron during the many evolutions that it was necessary to make with great rapidity." The costly and disheartening assault by Worth's division was fruitless, however, because once within the walls of El Molino del Rey, the Americans learned that the foundry that forged cannon from church bells existed only in General Scott's imagination. Chapultepec fell, as the American infantry, equipped with scaling ladders, swarmed the fortress. Organized Mexican resistance collapsed. [31]

On September 14, 1847, the dragoons escorted the victorious American commander, General Scott, into Mexico City. The dragoons enjoyed General Scott's favor, and the entire brigade reveled in the choice facilities provided for them in the National Palace. The officers, however, found their quarters elsewhere. Many of them congregated

---

30 Hill Diary, September 3, 1847; G. W. Kendall, "Letters from the Army," in *Littel's Living Age*, XV (November, 1847), 24.
31 *Senate Executive Documents*, 30th Cong., 1st Sess., Doc. 1, pp. 374, 400; September, 1847, entry in Regimental Returns.

in the mansion of Señor Boca Negra, the former Mexican minister to the United States. The close association of these officers during the campaign was cemented here by the Aztec Club, organized on October 13, 1847. Originally composed of Scott's veterans, the initial roster included names destined for greater distinction: Beauregard, Harney, Hooker, Grant, Lee, Joseph E. Johnston, Magruder, McClellan, Twiggs, Wilcox, Ewell, Pemberton and Hardee. Franklin Pierce was the first president of the club. Hardee cherished the memories of these associations and in later years always "wore a very handsome badge of that club." [32]

The Georgia senate wishing to commend Hardee for his services, passed a resolution proposing that Brevet Lieutenant Colonel Hardee be awarded a ceremonial sword for "his brilliant achievements in Mexico." The Georgia House of Representatives concurred with this resolution and directed that the governor procure and present a sword suitable for the purpose. In November, 1847, accordingly, Governor George W. Townes requested Noble Andrew Hardee to come to Milledgeville to receive the sword for his brother. A New Orleans newspaper gave its readers a description of the sword:

The Sword for Col. Hardee—A Dragoon Sword, Blade of finest Steel. The hilt silver guilt [sic] with gold. The pummel represents a horse's head, the neck forming the grip and chased representing the mane—a chased scroll in the mouth rounding to the guard, the shield being the coat of arms of the State of Georgia and on the guard above, a small eagle. The scabbard of steel with silver gilt mountings. The bands silver gilt, and trophies etched on each. Just below the first band is the inscription, "The State of Georgia to Lt Col Wm J Hardee, USA, as a tribute to his gallantry in Mexico." Below the next two bands on the Scabbord are engraved a dragoon skirmish, and a dragoon engagement.[33]

Medellín, San Augustín, and El Molino del Rey restored and enhanced Captain Hardee's professional reputation, so badly tarnished by the surrender at La Rosia. During Scott's campaign he had dis-

32 Hill Diary, September 19, 1847; Mrs. Anna C. Johnson to author, July 11, 1956; Cadmus Marcellus Wilcox, *History of the Mexican War* (Washington, 1892), 710–11; DeLancey Floyd-Jones, *Proceedings and Addresses Attending the Presentation of a Silver Centre-Piece to the Aztec Club* (New York, 1892) 6–8.

33 Georgia *Senate Journal*, November 30, 1847; Georgia *House Journal*, December 22, 1847; *Acts of the State of Georgia*, 1847 (Milledgeville, 1848), 313; George W. Townes to Noble Andrew Hardee, November 17, 1849, in Governor Townes' Letterbook (Georgia State Department of Archives and History); New Orleans *Weekly Delta*, September 17, 1849.
    Hardee's sword is in the possession of Hardee Chambliss, Jr., Fairfax, Va.

played initiative, courage, and excellent disciplinary control over his forces—command qualities which held promise for the future. Most of the engagements in which the Second Dragoons participated envinced the effectiveness of Hardee's training program at Fort Jesup. Many of his fellow officers now regarded him as an authority on cavalry training. Furthermore, the Mexican War afforded him the opportunity to serve in large-scale military operations and to witness the employment of infantry. This experience would fortify his judgment in later years when he, a cavalry officer, compiled a system of light-infantry tactics. The knowledge accumulated during 1846 and 1847 would also contribute significantly to his distinguished performances as leader of a corps of infantry in the Confederate Army of Tennessee. Perhaps of most importance was the fact that the Mexican War brought William J. Hardee to the attention of Jefferson Davis.[34]

No sooner had Nicholas Trist hastily tucked the freshly signed treaty of Guadalupe Hidalgo into his portfolio than Brevet Lieutenant Colonel Hardee departed from Vera Cruz aboard the steamer *New Orleans.* Hardee arrived in New Orleans on February 14, 1848, but sailed as soon as possible for Savannah, where he "received a warm and enthusiastic reception . . . and left . . . , after one day's stay for his home in St. Augustine, Florida." [35] In St. Augustine he experienced a joyous reunion with his family. Doubtless he marveled at the size of his daughters Anna and Sallie, whereas they in turn clutched uncomfortably at their mother's skirts, suspiciously and timidly regarding this gigantic, weatherbeaten, bearded stranger. The War Department allowed Hardee to remain with his family until May, 1848, when he was ordered to Baltimore for duty as a recruiting officer. He served in this capacity until late summer, replenishing the depleted ranks of his regiment, then returned to St. Augustine for a short leave of absence.[36]

Hardee spent the next few months at Carlisle Barracks, Pennsylvania, engaged in training four newly recruited companies of the Second Dragoons. At the close of the year the War Department decided that the dragoons had achieved a satisfactory degree of perform-

---

34 Letter from Jefferson Davis, n.d., quoted in the *Veteran* (Columbus, Ohio) II (January, 1882), 16.
35 New Orleans *Bee,* February 14, 1848; *Daily American Star* (City of Mexico), April 1, 1848.
36 March–August, 1848, entries in Regimental Returns; Special Order No. 75, July 26, 1848, in Special Orders.

ance and dispatched them to Texas. While the troops were en route, Hardee went to St. Augustine for his family, which now included a son, William Joseph, who had been born while he was in Pennsylvania. The Hardees left St. Augustine in February, 1849, sailed through the Florida Keys and across the Gulf of Mexico to Corpus Christi. They exchanged their steam packet for jolting army ambulances and proceeded up the Nueces River to San Antonio, where Hardee settled his family. He then rejoined his old command, Company C, at Ringgold Barracks on the Rio Grande.[37]

After enjoying the luxury of Ringgold Barracks for a month, Hardee and his men journeyed north to Fort Inge, "pleasantly situated in a grove of small elms on the Leona River, three miles below its fountain head." [38] Fort Inge would be the permanent base of operation for Hardee's command during the following two years.

The task of Company C and the other units scattered about Texas was to dominate the region. They had to control the unruly Texas citizenry, to protect the fringe areas from Indian molestation, and to be on the alert for any encroachment on the part of Mexico.

Generally, the years passed uneventfully. Occasionally, however, small bands of Indians would be tempted by the supplies and horses at Fort Inge and would raid the fort itself, providing temporary excitement.

In August, 1849, an Indian party raided the fort and stole a few horses. Hardee dispatched a party in pursuit the following morning. The dragoons discovered only three Indians; they killed one and badly wounded another. The stolen horses were recovered, along with three Indian ponies. The success of his men pleased Hardee. "Lieutenant Neill's party was armed with Colt's revolvers, and I gave him orders to take no prisoners. I wish he had met thirty instead of three." [39] Hardee's ruthless sentiments were typical of his contemporaries on the frontier. His attitude can be understood as the logical

---

37 September, 1848, entry in Regimental Returns; Adjutant General to Charles A. May, October 11, 1848, in Letters Sent, Adjutant General's Office; Thomas Berry to Edward Porter Alexander, February 3, 1858, in Edward Porter Alexander Papers (Southern Historical Collection); Rodenbough, *From Everglade to Cañon*, 245 ff.

38 New York *Times*, June 7, 1854; November, 1848–January, 1849, entries in Regimental Returns.

39 Hardee to Adjutant General, Eighth Military District, August 27, 1849, quoted in Rodenbough, *From Everglade to Cañon*, 165.

outgrowth of his childhood on the troubled Georgia-Florida border and his service in the Second Seminole War, in which frustrated searching parties of soldiers finally used bloodhounds to combat their wily foes.

The small Indian raids of 1849 became intensified in 1850, and in June of that year Hardee was given the opportunity to conduct a sizable operation. Brevet Major General George M. Brooke, the commander of the frontier district, issued a warning order to the dragoons. They were to conduct "a vigorous campaign against the Savages who are and have been for some time past infesting the country between the Rio Grande and the Nueces." Every "disposable" dragoon at Forts McIntosh, Inge, Merrill, and Lincoln, plus a detachment of Texas Rangers, were to be assembled under the command of Brevet Lieutenant Colonel Hardee, who would commence a campaign to discover the Indians in their "lurking places" and "severely chastise" them.[40]

Hardee wasted little time in assembling his new command. By June 23 he had four companies of dragoons and several companies of Texas Rangers—in all about three hundred men—assembled at Fort Inge ready for offensive operations. To rid southern Texas of the marauding Indian bands posed quite a complex problem; Hardee proposed a simple plan of operation, consisting of four distinct movements in the region between the Nueces and the Rio Grande. Collectively these movements would provide a dragnet that, if it did not ferret out most of the Indians, promised at least to harass them and restore operational initiative to the Americans.

Hardee kept his men in the saddle for two months. Marching and counter-marching, they combed valleys and riverbanks, probed every suspicious area, and relentlessly pursued groups of Indians whom they saw or heard about. The results were conclusive. The Indian marauding parties in the territory were scattered and their numbers badly depleted. The principles of frontier warfare underlying Hardee's campaign may be found in his report. Indeed, the report itself could be studied profitably by those interested in the problems of modern counterguerrilla warfare:

It is difficult, nay, impossible, to overtake and punish any of these parties, when they become aware of pursuit. If in danger of being overtaken, they scatter and, each pursuing a different route to some remote point, they

40 Washington *National Intelligencer*, July 13, 1850, quoting New Orleans *Weekly Delta*, July 2, 1850.

effectually baffle the skill of the most experienced trailers. My object has been, as far as circumstances would permit, to push my scouts through unfrequented parts of the country, to take up the trails where Indians least expected to be pursued, to follow these trails cautiously and quietly, and in this way take them by surprise.[41]

The success of this 1850 expedition caused Hardee to be assigned command of the next major expedition the following year. This time Hardee led his men into the Comanche country, not to fight, but to negotiate and secure intelligence. Again he succeeded, obtaining not only the needed information but "the only Mexican prisoners delivered up by the Indians, since the establishment of the Eighth Military Department." [42]

When he returned from this expedition, Hardee found his wife Elizabeth in a critical state of health and took her back to St. Augustine.

Elizabeth Hardee had lived in San Antonio while her husband served at Fort Inge. Her presence was recorded by another army officer's wife, who found that she was "delightfully situated with every comfort around her—but with the exception of San Antonio, all other posts in Texas and New Mexico are wretched in the extreme." [43]

The Hardee's fourth child, Elizabeth Douglas, had been born in San Antonio in August, 1850. There seem to have been no complications regarding the birth, but within a year Mrs. Hardee contracted tuberculosis and declined in health rapidly.[44]

The return to St. Augustine did not help, and Elizabeth continued to grow weaker. In November, 1851, Hardee wrote Washington from St. Augustine requesting an extension of his leave, and again on April 21, 1852, he prevailed upon his superiors for more time to remain with his wife. The War Department granted these requests and allowed Hardee still another extension in June. In July, 1852, how-

41 W. J. Hardee's Official Report of Indian Operations in the Summer of 1850 to Adjutant General, Eighth Military District, September 14, 1850, quoted by M. L. Crimmins, "The Second Dragoon Indian Campaign in Texas," in *West Texas Historical Association Year Book*, XXI (October, 1945), 51–56. For a detailed account of Hardee's Indian fighting, see Hughes, "Hardee, U.S.A."

42 Hardee to Adjutant General, Eighth Military Department, August 29, 1851, quoted in *House Executive Documents*, 32nd Cong., 1st Sess., Doc. 2, p. 123.

43 Mrs. Webster to Mrs. Kirby Smith, August [n.d.], 1851, in Kirby Smith Papers.

44 Eighth Census, St. Johns County, Florida; St. Augustine *Ancient City*, June 11, 1853.

ever, the War Department refused Hardee's request for assignment in Florida and ordered him to report to his regiment as soon as his extension ended.[45]

Hardee returned to Texas in October, 1852. During his absence Company C had been transferred to Fort Graham, equidistant from Austin and Fort Washita. Hardee remained at Fort Graham through the closing months of 1852, commanding a squadron.[46]

Urgent letters from home compelled Hardee to apply again for a leave of absence in February, 1853. He returned to St. Augustine and found Elizabeth dying of tuberculosis. To accommodate Hardee the War Department gave him a nominal command as pay officer for several Florida militia companies.[47]

Elizabeth Hardee's suffering continued through the spring, finally ending on June 10, 1853. As befitted the wife of a regular army officer, she was buried not with her family but in the National Cemetery amid the hundreds of unknown soldiers who had fallen in the Second Seminole War.[48]

Following the death of his wife, Hardee put his children in the care of their aunt, Anna Maria ("Dena") Dummett. She would keep them in St. Augustine until he could provide a suitable home for them. These were to be pleasurable years for the Hardee children, and all of them recalled with fondness the times spent with Dena and their horde of cousins in St. Augustine.

Late in October Hardee completed the last of his pay accounts and reported for duty. To his surprise his new orders did not mention Texas; they stated simply: "The Secretary of War directs you to report to Washington for temporary special duty." [49]

---

45 Hardee to Adjutant General, April 21, June 19, 1852, in Letters Received, Adjutant General's Office; Special Order No. 81, June 17, 1852, in Special Orders; Adjutant General to Hardee, July 27, in Letters Sent, Adjutant General's Office.
46 M. L. Crimmins (ed.), "W. G. Freeman's Report on the Eighth Military Department," in *Southwestern Historical Quarterly,* LIII (April, 1950), 462; February, 1853, entry in Regimental Returns.
47 Hardee to Adjutant General, March 8, 1853, in Letters Received, Adjutant General's Office; Special Order No. 69, May 16, 1853, in Special Orders.
48 Tombstone inscription, National Cemetery, St. Augustine, Fla.; St. Augustine *Ancient City,* June 11, 1853.
49 Hardee to Adjutant General, October 22, 1853, in Letters Received, Adjutant General's Office; Adjutant General to Hardee, November 2, 1853, in Letters Sent, Adjutant General's Office.

IV

Hardee's Tactics

THE UNITED STATES ARMY knew relatively little about William J. Hardee in November, 1853. His colleagues and the officials in the War Department regarded him as one of many proficient and promising officers. His services in the Mexican War had caught the eyes of a few; his interest and talent in matters pertaining to drill and organization had been recognized by his immediate superiors. The American public hardly knew that he existed. Yet two years later Hardee's *Tactics* was a popular topic of discussion in the generals' offices and in the privates' tents. And eight years later Hardee's name had become a household word throughout most of America. This remarkable rise from obscurity was the result of his work on the light-infantry manual. How did he come to be singled out to prepare it? And to what extent was the manual his own?

In late November, 1853, Hardee wrote his family from Washington that the War Department had assigned him a more ambitious task than he could have hoped for, and that he would be stationed in Washington for some time.[1] Working closely with the Secretary of War, Jefferson Davis, he was to prepare a new army tactics manual.

The War Department during the 1850's was characterized by a progressive, enlightened outlook, particularly during the tenure of Jefferson Davis. Davis recognized the significance of recent military developments, especially those in the French army, and wanted to modify the tactical system of the American Army to take them into account. A new manual was needed, he felt:

In anticipation of an increased, if not exclusive use of rifle arms by the regular Army, and because of the belief that the rifle or light infantry sys-

1 Mrs. Kirby Smith to Edmund Kirby Smith, November 28, 1853, in Kirby Smith Papers.

41

tem of instruction . . . is best adapted to the foot militia; I have caused inquiries to be instituted into the systems used by the light troops of other countries, that complete light infantry or rifle tactics [2] might be introduced into the service with such improvements as the experience of other armies has shown to be valuable. A work on this subject is now in the course of preparation. . . . With the recent improvements in small arms, it is probable that the distinction in the armament of heavy and light infantry, and riflemen, will nearly cease, especially in our service, where the whole force is liable to be employed as light troops.[3]

New means of communication, transportation, conscription, and even finance had changed methods of waging war; since the French Revolution the precision of formal warfare had been replaced by a process of constant shifting and adaptation. In fact, the dazzling tactical formations devised by the French military minds of the Napoleonic era became obsolete before the Americans learned to use them.

Moreover, military innovations were numerous—the rifled cannon, the delayed-action fuse and the Borman fuse, shrapnel, the revolver, the percussion cap. Perhaps the most significant innovation was the Minié bullet, which extended the range of accurate fire for a rifleman to fifteen hundred yards. The new bullet had other advantages, as well. Its design enabled him to reload and fire more rapidly, and it could be made by the soldier himself, using a hand mold.

Surely, the nature of warfare had been drastically altered. Heavy columns of infantry were doomed; once within the zone of the enemy's fire, troops must be able to move rapidly. The individual soldier, acting more independently and armed with his deadly weapon, now became the basic element in tactical employment.

The French army had learned its lesson in Algeria during the 1830's

2   The term "tactics" as employed in the mid-nineteenth century was a more comprehensive term than in present-day usage. Tactics included basic foot drill, instruction in elementary small arms, and maneuvers of bodies of troops. Bülow defines tactics as "the science of movements which are made in the presence of the enemy, that is, within reach of his artillery." Scott, Hardee, and the other tacticians accepted this definition. As deployments and attacks were carried out in drill formations, the mid-nineteenth-century military mind did not differentiate between formal foot drill and field maneuvers. Foot drill served a double purpose for the commanders of that day: not only did it inculcate discipline and precision of movement, but skill in foot drill meant mastery of the science of maneuver when troops were in contact with the enemy.

3   *Appendix to the Congressional Globe for the Second Session, Thirty-third Congress* (Washington, 1855), 17–18.

and early 1840's. There Bonaparte's heavy, formal columns had struck like a fist, only to sink harmlessly into the Algerian pillow. Untrained French skirmishers had been picked off by the Moorish cavalry, for the French heavy cavalry could not afford the infantry the necessary protection. All the while, the Algerians subjected the exhausted French regulars to ambushes. Casualty figures mounted, and the French mission remained unaccomplished. Recognizing that Algerian warfare demanded a major change in tactics, the French began to accentuate the tactical concept of skirmishing.

"Comrades in battle" were also developed, a tactical formation that grouped the skirmishers in self-sustaining units of four men. The light-infantrymen were armed with long-range, accurate rifles, their conspicuous uniforms were changed to a drab bottle green, and they were put through a program of intensive training in fencing, bayonet drill, and gymnastics. Perhaps the most significant feature of the new drill was that the old cadence of 90 steps a minute was increased to 110 and 165 steps a minute, so that the infantry could maneuver more rapidly and effectively. After these changes were introduced, casualty lists became shorter, and losses were relatively light in Algeria and in the Crimea.

This shift in French infantry tactics did not go unnoticed in America. Hardee and his fellow officers who journeyed to France to study cavalry tactics during the 1840's undoubtedly saw it occurring and reported their observations to their superiors. It had special relevance for the Americans: not only was France the recognized center of military science, having supposedly the world's finest army, but the new fluid warfare developed by the French could be employed with great effectiveness on the American frontier, where combat conditions closely resembled those of Algeria.

Davis was probably aware of Hardee's training at Saumur and of his knowledge of French. He probably knew also that Hardee had instructed the Second Dragoons in the latest French cavalry methods in 1842–45. Davis is known to have been impressed by Hardee's Mexican War service and his record of professional accomplishments, and Hardee may have been further recommended by influential friends. His commanding officers, Harney and Sumner, were good friends of Jefferson Davis. At the time of Hardee's selection, Sumner was traveling throughout Europe investigating Continental cavalry developments, and could easily have influenced Davis' decision during consultations prior to his departure.[4] In addition to Hardee's record and recommendations, he possessed the distinct advantage of being detached from duty and therefore immediately available.

Hardee began his new duties with a trip to Harpers Ferry Arsenal in late December, to confer with the superintendent and to examine the army's new rifle designed for the Minié bullet.[5] He spent most of the spring of 1854 meeting with a board of officers at the Washington Arsenal, analyzing, translating, and adapting the French tactics manual, *Ordonnance du Roi sur l'Exercice et les Manoeuvres des Bataillons de Chasseurs à Pied*.

By July 28, 1854, Hardee's manuscript was completed. He submitted it to the Adjutant General, who in turn forwarded it to the Secretary of War. Davis, who had worked closely—indeed, daily—with Hardee on the manual, gave his approval at once and directed that a testing board be assembled. This board convened at West Point on August 15, and Hardee joined the board to furnish information and to make suggestions. Davis put the cadet corps at the board's disposal, thereby providing an intelligent, well-disciplined group for use as an experimental unit. By late October the board felt that the cadets had mastered the drill well enough to display it before the Secretary of War. Davis thereupon came to West Point and observed the French drill used by Americans.[6]

While Hardee's manual was being prepared for publication, Colonel Ethan Allen Hitchcock was also writing a manual, which he believed would be much more useful than Hardee's. He claimed, in fact, that Hardee's manual was not adapted to the new rifle being issued by the War Department. A heated controversy was resolved by the intervention of Jefferson Davis, who supported Hardee.[7]

As soon as the first proofs of Hardee's manual had been proofread and corrected, Hardee decided to take a long-postponed trip to St. Augustine. He remained there for a month, returning in June to supervise the printing of his light-infantry manual and of a cavalry tactics manual.

4 Adjutant General to Edwin V. Sumner, May 23, 1854, in Letters Sent, Adjutant General's Office.
5 Adjutant General to Hardee, December 20, 1853, *ibid*.
6 J. Davis to Adjutant General, July 29, 1854, S. Casey to Adjutant General, in Letters Received, Adjutant General's Office; *Veteran*, II (January, 1882), 16; Special Order No. 131, August 2, 1854, in Special Orders.
7 E. A. Hitchcock to Adjutant General, April 2, 1855, Hardee to Adjutant General, April 11, 1855, in Letters Received, Adjutant General's Office.

The cavalry manual is a reprint of the 1841 *Cavalry Tactics* and does not bear Hardee's name, but it owes much to his careful revisions and modifications. For example, Hardee was responsible for its supplement dealing with the Colt revolver, a new feature that made the manual particularly desirable and practical for the dragoon regiments. Hardee had displayed great interest in the Colt revolver throughout his service as an officer in the Second Dragoons, and the supplement was compiled, probably with his encouragement by Samuel H. Starr, a lieutenant in Hardee's Company C. Hardee's own mark is upon it, moreover, for he revised it at will before including it in the cavalry manual.

The publisher of the two manuals was Lippincott, Grambo, and Company, but publication was subsidized by the government. During June, Lippincott printed more than two thousand copies of the two manuals, and soon more than eighteen thousand copies of *Light Infantry Tactics* had been printed and delivered to the government, for one dollar a copy.[8]

Now that Hardee's manual had been completed, American infantry officers had to discard their old manuals and familiarize themselves with the new work. Changes in American tactics had been relatively few. In colonial days American militiamen had used a drill derived by British tacticians from the Prussian drill introduced in the time of Frederick the Great. During the Revolutionary War, Baron von Steuben compiled a manual to instill discipline and uniformity into the poorly trained Continental army, and this manual remained in use until 1812. The old system was modified in 1827 by a French officer, Guibert, and this, in turn, was used as a basis for Winfield Scott's manual, which appeared in 1835.

Scott's system had been described as "complicated," "wearisome," "tedious," and "imposing," but the transition to Hardee's *Tactics* did not come easily to those who had drilled under the other system for years. Militia units in several states balked at having to learn the new

---

8 William Joseph Hardee, *Memorial to the Congress of the Confederate States, December 14, 1863* (Mobile, 1863), 1.

Although the *Tactics* was authorized by the War Department, Hardee received royalties on each copy, as was customary at the time. These royalties continued until the beginning of the Civil War. The publishers did not copyright the work, however, because publishing costs had been high, and they believed that sales would be poor. Their failure to do so ultimately cost them as well as Hardee, for many publishing houses brought out unauthorized editions during the war.

drill. To a New York militia officer Hardee wrote, "I think under the circumstances, you have acted wisely in not attempting to force the new tactics on the Militia. It is with many of them as with many old officers in our services. They don't wish after learning one system to be compelled to learn another. In time they will be brought to see the advantages of the new drill and will also discover that after all there is not much new to learn & that it is easy to pass from one system to the other." [9]

In later years professional jealousy, sectional hatred, financial considerations, and personal animosity occasioned many attacks on Hardee and his manual. One individual maintained, "I have compared it with the [French] original and it is word for word a *translation* and nothing but a *translation*." [10] Another claimed that "Hardee was Chief of a Board 'to translate a system of Light Infantry Tactics' from the French. Lieut. Bennett [*sic*] of Ordnance did the work, every word of it; and Hardee's name was attached to the translation! He never, in all probability, saw or read one word of it, until called upon to 'study it' for the purpose of learning how to drill the cadets at West Point. . . ." [11]

Such allegations must be answered, for there is a kernel of truth in both statements. Hardee's work did follow the French version closely and did incorporate literal translations in many instances. (Perhaps the most noticeable examples are the chapter headings: "Titre Premier, Article Premier" becomes "Title First, Article First.")

No record as yet discovered substantiates the contention that someone else "did the work," although Lieutenant Stephen Vincent Benét, probably an old St. Augustine friend of Hardee and a capable translator, was in the area of Washington at the time.[12] The fact remains that Hardee assumed responsibility for the manual and headed the board assembled to revise the French text. He never denied translating sections of it, and it is certain that he added the modifications necessary to adapt it for the American army.

The differences in French and American organization occurred in

9 Hardee to F. Townsend, December 1, 1859, in William J. Hardee Letters, 1859–62 (Historical Society of Pennsylvania).
10 Benjamin F. Evans to William P. Miles, May 20, 1861, quoted in Rembert W. Patrick, *Jefferson Davis and His Cabinet* (Baton Rouge, 1944), 23n.
11 Frank Moore (ed.), *The Rebellion Record*, 11 vols. (New York, 1861–68), I, 111.
12 Adjutant General to Stephen V. Benét, March 20, April 4, 1854, in Letters Sent, Adjutant General's Office.

the lower echelons of command. The basic tactical unit of the American army was the regiment, whereas that of the French was the battalion. The United States had ten companies in its regiments, the French battalion, only eight; the American company was comprised of two platoons, the French company, of seven platoons and a platoon of *carabiniers*. These distinctions were carefully observed by Hardee.[13]

Hardee's work also includes several features omitted in the French manual, such as a lesson on loading and firing procedures in the kneeling and prone positions.[14]

Comparison of the two works further reveals that Hardee's instructions are more detailed:

Ordonnance du Roi	Hardee's *Tactics*
§ 36. Each year, at the period when one will begin instruction, the school of the soldier and the school of the platoon will be taught in each company under the direction and responsibility of the Captain. (Vol. I, p. 7.)	§ 43. Captains will be held responsible for theoretical and practical instruction of their non-commissioned officers, and the adjutant for the instruction of the non-commissioned staff. To this end they will require these tactics to be studied and recited by lesson; and when instruction is given on the ground, each non-commissioned officer, as he explains a movement should be required to put it into practical operation. (Vol. I, p. 11.)
§ 27. The buglers, formed in four ranks, will be posted twenty paces from the file closers, behind the fifth platoon, the bugle-major in front, the bugle corporal to the right. (Vol. I, p. 5.)	§ 34. The buglers will be drawn up in four ranks, and posted twelve paces in rear of the file closers, the left opposite the centre of the left centre company. The senior principal musician will be two paces in front of the field music, and the other two

13 France, Ministre Secrétaire d'Etat de la Guerre, *Ordonnance du Roi sur l'Exercice et les Manoeuvres des Bataillons de Chasseurs à Pied*, 3 vols. (Paris, 1845), I, 2, 11; William Joseph Hardee, *Rifle and Light Infantry Tactics*, 2 vols. (Philadelphia, 1855), I, 5, 19.

14 *Ordonnance du Roi*, I, 11; Hardee, *Tactics*, I, 19.

Ordonnance du Roi   Hardee's *Tactics*

paces in the rear. (Vol. I, p. 9.)

§ 35. The regiment band, if
there be one, will be drawn up
in two or four ranks, according
to its numbers and posted five
paces in rear of the field music,
having one of the principal musi-
cians at its head. (Vol. I, p. 9.)

The manual was divided into two volumes, *School of the Soldier
and Company, Instruction for Skirmishers*, and *School of the Battalion*. These volumes were subdivided into particular phases of training, each with a series of lessons progressively leading to mastery. An
example of this system may be seen in Part Second of *School of the
Soldier*:

Lesson 1 Principles of shouldered arms

Lesson 2 Manual of arms

Lesson 3 To load in four times, and at will

Lesson 4 Firings, direct, oblique, by file, and by rank

Lesson 5 To fire and load, kneeling and lying

Lesson 6 Bayonet exercise

The manual specified that an "instructor never requires a movement
to be executed until he has given an exact explanation of it; and he
executes, himself, the movement which he commands, so as to join
example to the precept." Hardee explained in intelligible terms the
reason for many movements that the individual soldier was required
to make. For example, Von Steuben simply states that when a soldier
is at the point of attention, the "heels will be placed together." Hardee
explains: "Heels on the same line; Because if one were in rear of the
other, the shoulder on that side would be thrown back or the position
of the soldier would be constrained."

Hardee reduced the steps in loading a rifle from twelve to nine,
and ultimately to four, enabling a proficient recruit to increase his
rate of fire to three rounds per minute. He emphasized precision and
gave great emphasis to exercise in the massing of firepower: fire by
battalion, fire by company, fire by wing, fire by file, and fire by
rank.[15]

15 Hardee, *Tactics*, I, 16–18, 36 ff.; II, 224.

Although he permitted soldiers to practice at 90 steps a minute (the standard used in Scott's work) until they "acquired steadiness," he thereafter required training only at "quick time" (110 steps) or "double-quick time" (165 steps). These troop maneuvers were soon labeled the "Shanghai drill." [16] The cumbersome facing movements detailed in Scott's manual were replaced by marching flank and oblique movements, so that no halts were required during deployments. Hardee also provided that countermarching could be done by files rather than by massive bodies.[17] Every effort was made to cut drastically the time required for deployment, because within the range of the deadly new weapons, time was life.

The light-infantry concept embodied in Hardee's *Tactics* stressed two French features—"comrades in battle" and skirmishers. The concept of "comrades in battle" represented a positive step in the direction of effective small tactical formations. No longer did an individual soldier need to fear being isolated from the main body of troops. Men were trained in groups of four, "careful to know and to sustain each other." Properly schooled in the many, lengthy bayonet and rifle exercises of their manuals, these men could act together to ward off attacks by small groups of cavalry and could defeat attacks made by larger groups of infantry. Hardee used Bonaparte's concept of skirmishing but also provided the skirmish lines with local reserves and directed that circumstances should regulate the size of the group. He taught that skirmishers should never sacrifice flexibility or their great asset of elasticity: "A chain of skirmishers ought generally to preserve their alignment, but no advantage which the ground may present should be sacrificed to obtain this regularity."

Hardee's *Tactics* was designed only for the lower echelons of command, stating that "when a battalion, instructed in this drill, shall be required to maneuver in the evolutions of the line, its movements will be regulated by the instructions contained in the third volume of the Tactics for Heavy Infantry, approved by the War Department, April 10th, 1835"—that is, by Scott's manual.[18] Civil War veterans would often criticize their tactics manual because it had

16 *Army and Navy Journal*, February 11, 1888; R.E.C., "Modern Tactics," in A. W. Ward, G. W. Prothero, Stanley Leathes (eds.), *The Cambridge Modern History*, 13 vols. (New York, 1902–12), X, 504–505.
17 Hardee, *Tactics*, I, 17, 26, and *passim*; Winfield Scott, *Infantry Tactics*, 3 vols. (New York, 1835), I, 7, and *passim*.
18 Hardee, *Tactics*, I, 175.

not provided instruction for the deployment of bodies larger than the regiment. When the brigade replaced the regiment as the basic tactical body, a new manual was indeed desperately needed.

Before the Civil War, however, Hardee's manual became "the authoritative guide of our army drill, and by that means his name [was] familiar to every officer and man among us." [19] One of his contemporaries commented on the utility of his work for the American Army: "The effect of the new system of instruction, as taught in Hardee, is nearly to double the efficiency of the troops so taught. The celerity of movement, the facility of minishing distances by moving on the shortest lines, and the rapidity with which changes from column to line, and the reverse, can be made without halting, enable a body of troops to multiply itself on the field of battle." [20]

Having been a simple practical guide for the company and regimental infantry commanders in the regular army of the 1850's, the manual became the pocket-size text for Union and Confederate officers during the Civil War. Hardee's lessons in how to mass and increase firepower and to increase accuracy, together with new weapons that had been introduced, were utilized so effectively at Malvern Hill and Fredericksburg that tactics in Virginia during the closing months of the Civil War became a matter of positional warfare.

The ultimate significance of Hardee's *Tactics* can be seen when it is contrasted with Scott's manual. Although it retained the formations and the general terminology of the Scott era, it broke sharply with the old emphasis on precision and mass. For the first time in American tactics, it demonstrated the importance of speed and flexibility, heralding the tactics of Sherman, Guderian, and Patton.

---

19 Jacob Dolson Cox, *Military Reminiscences of the Civil War*, 2 vols. (New York, 1900), II, 525.
20 *Senate Miscellaneous Documents*, 36th Cong., 2nd Sess., Doc. 3, p. 87.

V

Commandant of Cadets

WHILE HARDEE had been arranging for the publication of his manual, events far removed from Washington had affected the course of his career. In 1855 the slavery controversy in Kansas erupted into civil war, and army units from Texas were dispatched to the trouble area. Simultaneously, the Sioux staged an uprising in western Kansas, and more troops had to be sent from Texas. The military force that remained in Texas proved inadequate, and the Indians quickly exploited their advantage. Indian raids increased in frequency and intensity; so did the pleas of the Texas legislature for help from Washington.[1]

Congress and the War Department met the situation by creating four new regiments. Such action, of course, meant promotion for the rank-starved regular officers. Hardee requested a position in one of the new regiments, the Second Cavalry, commanded by Colonel Albert Sidney Johnston.[2] The War Department not only complied with Hardee's request but promoted him to major.[3]

Major Hardee remained in Washington during the summer of

1 St. Louis *Daily Missouri Republican,* July 2, 1855.
2 Hardee to Adjutant General, March 2, 1855, in Letters Received, Adjutant General's Office.
3 General Orders No. 4, March 26, 1855, in General Orders; Hardee to Adjutant General, March 12, 1855, in Letters Received, Adjutant General's Office.
   With the assurance of increased pay, Major Hardee purchased the Dummett home in St. Augustine from Anna Dummett on May 21, 1855, thereby providing ample housing for his children and relieving "Dena" of the burden of tax payments on a home filled with her sister's children. This purchase gave Hardee a sizable amount of property in St. Augustine, for he already owned two lots and a small house adjacent to the Dummett home. Deed Book P, 416–17, in St. Johns County Court Record Collection (St. Augustine Historical Society).

1855, serving as a member of a cavalry equipment board. The War Department accepted nearly all of the board's recommendations and thereby virtually revolutionized American cavalry equipment. The adoption of these new items supported the contention of many of the cavalry officers that Jefferson Davis intended the new regiments to be agents of experimentation as well as instruments of defense for the trans-Mississippi area.[4]

Among the numerous War Department novelties was the "Hardee hat." Major Hardee apparently interested himself in the design of this felt hat and promoted its use in the cavalry, where it replaced the commonly used cap. Although probably not as comfortable to wear as the old cap, it certainly provided better protection against the prairie sun. The hat remained a provisional part of the cavalryman's uniform until 1858, when it was authorized for general use throughout the army.[5]

As soon as the cavalry equipment board adjourned, Hardee proceeded to join his regiment in Missouri, purchasing en route some eight hundred mounts to be used by the command. Hardee arrived at Jefferson Barracks, Missouri, on September 20, 1855.

The officer corps of the regiment consisted of "the greatest aggregation of fighting men that ever represented the United States Army in the Old West." [6] Jefferson Davis had hand-picked these officers, most of whom he had observed from his experience in the Mexican War or through his capacity as Secretary of War. Albert Sidney Johnston commanded the regiment, with Robert E. Lee as his executive officer and with William J. Hardee and George H. Thomas as majors. Among the captains were Earl Van Dorn, Edmund Kirby Smith, and George Stoneman. Nathan G. ("Shank") Evans, Richard W. Johnson, and John B. Hood served as lieutenants.[7]

---

4 For an account of Hardee's activities on various boards in Washington in the summer of 1855, see Hughes, "Hardee, U.S.A."

5 Author's interview with Colonel Frederick P. Todd, Curator, United States Military Academy Museum, March 29, 1956, at West Point, N.Y. The War Department prescribed that "Hardee hats" would be "black, trimmed with gold cord, . . . to be looped upon the right side, and fastened with an eagle, the eagle being attached to the side of the hat; three black feathers on left side; the number of the regiment to be in front. The hat will be worn instead of the *cap* now used by the other troops." General Orders No. 13, August 15, September 16, 1855, in Letters Received, Adjutant General's Office; Hardee to A. S. Johnston, September, 1855, in Albert Sidney Johnston Papers, 1803–1900 (Howard-Tilton Memorial Library, Tulane University).

6 John P. Dyer, *The Gallant Hood* (Indianapolis, 1950), 37.

7 Severyn H. Middagh (comp.), "The History of the Fifth U.S. Cavalry," unpublished manuscript, in Oversize Document Collection, Record Group 94.

No other regimental roster bore so many names destined to become famous during the next ten years.

Captain Kirby Smith was enthusiastic over the prospects of the newly created regiment under such leadership. Colonel Johnston showed outstanding ability and inspired the rank and file by stating that he was determined to mold the Second Cavalry into "the best regiment in the Army." Kirby Smith considered Lieutenant Colonel Lee "the most accomplished officer and gentleman in the army," and regarded Hardee as "the model drill and duty officer of the mounted service." [8] Another member of the regiment thought that "Hardee was a man of less stability of character than Albert S. Johnston or Robert E. Lee, but he was better fitted than either to 'set up' a regiment or a large command. He was a man of affairs, of talent and industry, and temperate in his habits. There were old officers who considered him overambitious." [9]

An organizational problem immediately faced Major Hardee upon his arrival at Jefferson Barracks. The regiment must be quickly trained and properly equipped so that it could be moved to Texas in the fall, and Johnston and Lee could not assist Hardee, for they were at Fort Leavenworth sitting as members of a general court-martial.[10]

The undertaking was made more difficult, because cholera had swept through the ranks causing several deaths and lowering morale. Hardee, as temporary regimental commander, proceeded with his task, however, and soon succeeded in making the regiment quite proficient in its drill.[11] Hardee "was thorough in his knowledge of the tactics, and seemed to take great delight in teaching others," a soldier wrote. "A position under him was not a sinecure, for when the officers were not drilling their own troops, he had officers drill." [12] To equip the regiment for field service, Hardee also had to procure adequate field transportation from the War Department. Although his days were spent on the parade field, most of Hardee's nights were spent writing a stream of letters to Washington for more wagons.

8   Edmund Kirby Smith to Mrs. Kirby Smith, October 20, 1855, in Kirby Smith Papers.
9   George F. Price, *Across the Continent with the Fifth Cavalry* (New York, 1883), 273.
10 Endorsement by Adjutant General on letter of Hardee to Adjutant General, October 1, 1855, in Letters Received, Adjutant General's Office.
11 John B. Beall, *In Barrack and Field* (Nashville, 1906), 87; St. Louis *Daily Missouri Republican*, October 27, 1855.
12 Richard M. Johnson, *A Soldier's Reminiscences in Peace and War* (Philadelphia, 1886), 98.

This proved to be of little avail, and the regiment consequently suffered on its march to Texas.[13]

The order for the march to Texas came on September 27. The regiment, about seven hundred fifty strong, left Jefferson Barracks on October 27 and proceeded southwest toward the Ozark Mountains. By November 14 they reached Springfield, Missouri. As the regiment went on, they closely paralleled the route of the Pacific Railroad surveys.[14] They passed through the Indian Territory in November and reached their destination, Fort Mason, Texas, during the first week in January. Major Hardee, however, had been left with four companies on the Clear Fork of the Brazos. Hardee established a semi-permanent camp nearby, in the center of a large Comanche reservation, naming it in honor of Samuel Cooper, the adjutant general.[15] Camp Cooper later became one of the central bases of operations on the southwestern frontier.

Captain Kirby Smith, stationed there shortly before the outbreak of the Civil War, explained the establishment and permanence of Camp Cooper: "Coln. Hardee with four companies of our Regt. first camped here seeking shelter in the winter of '55 from a severe norther —and with that magnificent inertia which characterized some of our army movements—here we've stuck." [16]

The four companies at Camp Cooper passed two highly uncomfortable months before adequate supplies, proper shelter, and usable mounts could be provided. The commanding general of the Department of Texas appears to have done little or nothing in preparation for the arrival of the Second Cavalry. A captain who arrived in the spring found that "the men had nothing to eat but *ground corn & starved beeves—without any small rations whatsoever; they were without clothes . . . and several in consequence have died,* and the horses had *no shelter,* and *no forage,* so that when corn *was* procured, they *died by hundreds* of *blind staggers,* and on the first appearance

13 Hardee to Adjutant General, October 3, 1855 (enclosing reports of Captain Kirby Smith, Lieutenant McArthur, and Lieutenant Garrard), in Letters Received, Adjutant General's Office.
14 Johnson, *A Soldier's Reminiscences,* 105 ff.; for an interesting firsthand account of the march see "The Diary of Mrs. Albert Sidney Johnston," in *Southwestern Historical Quarterly,* LX (1956).
15 Washington *National Intelligencer,* March 15, 1856, quoting St. Louis *Republican,* n.d.; Hardee to Adjutant General, January 7, 1856, in Letters Received, Adjutant General's Office.
16 Edmund Kirby Smith to Mrs. Kirby Smith, November 1, 1859, in Kirby Smith Papers.

of grass they *continued dying* of *scours.* I passed through Fort Mason in the latter part of March, and I saw several horses die under my own eye." [17]

The condition of Hardee's command improved rapidly during the spring, however, and after his men and animals had sufficiently recovered, he was relieved by Lieutenant Colonel Lee and departed for Fort Mason, where, in turn, he took command from Captain Kirby Smith on April 24.[18] Hardee remained at Fort Mason until June 17, 1856, when he received orders from the War Department to report for duty "at the Military Academy as Commandant of the Corps of Cadets . . . with as little delay as practicable." [19] On June 21 he turned over the command of Fort Mason to Major George H. Thomas and headed eastward, brimming with anticipation and enthusiasm.[20]

Service with the Second Cavalry Regiment had provided Hardee with a bracing episode of field experience. His organizational experience derived at Jefferson Barracks equipped him for the massive reorganizational task that was to come in Mississippi in 1863. Furthermore, the practical lessons that he learned during the arduous march from Jefferson Barracks to Texas could be applied in 1865. From raw Charleston garrison troops he would create, and effectively maintain by forced marches, a deadly deterrent to Sherman's march through the Carolinas.

The duties of the commandant at West Point changed significantly with the appointment of Hardee. Prior to 1856, the precedent had been that the commandant, a line officer, commanded the cadet battalion, was responsible for the discipline of that body, and *might* instruct in the Department of Infantry Tactics. Junior officers of

17   Captain Charles Radziminski to Colonel William H. Emory, May 18, 1856, in private collection of Thomas R. Hay, Locust Valley, N.Y.

18   M. L. Crimmins (ed.), "Colonel J. K. F. Mansfield's Report of the Inspection of the Department of Texas in 1856," in *Southwestern Historical Quarterly,* XLIII (April, 1939), 357.

19   Edmund Kirby Smith to Mrs. Kirby Smith, June 17, 1856, in Kirby Smith Papers; Special Order No. 55, May 26, 1856, in Special Orders.

20   Crimmins (ed.), "Mansfield's Report," *loc. cit.,* 357. It is only fair to allow one of Hardee's severest critics, Albert Brackett, to give his interpretation of Hardee's service with the Second Cavalry: "His career in the regiment was unmarked by a single thing which could go to show that he was anything more than a vain and conceited martinet, who had been pushed forward to the manifest injustice of braver and better men. He was a man of mediocre talent, joined to sobriety, and an industry carried on at the expense of others." *History of the United States Cavalry* (New York, 1865), 147–48.

infantry, cavalry, and artillery headed the various tactical departments and possessed no disciplinary responsibility over the cadets except in the classroom.[21]

Secretary of War Jefferson Davis had a different concept of the office of the commandant and brought Hardee to the Military Academy to implement the new policy.[22] Davis wanted the commandant to retain disciplinary control over the corps of cadets, but he also wished to consolidate the tactical branches of instruction into one department headed by this officer. Thus, in July, 1856, Davis issued the order giving the commandant these duties. He also provided him with six junior officers as assistants.[23]

The implementation of Davis' order brought Hardee into open conflict with the superintendent, Major John G. Barnard. Barnard maintained that Hardee had misunderstood the Secretary of War's order, that no fusion of the departments of military instruction was intended, and that officers heading those departments under no circumstances were to be regarded as the commandant's subordinates.[24] The controversy moved through proper command channels until it reached the desk of the Secretary of War. As Barnard previously had made known his objections to Davis' plan, and as his actions and sentiments clearly defied the spirit and the letter of Davis' July order, Davis decided to remove Barnard. He did so on August 25, 1856, and assigned the experienced Lieutenant Colonel Richard Delafield to the superintendency.[25]

Hardee, meanwhile, had begun to drill the cadets with his usual thoroughness, and within two months he had them ready for an important review. On September 12, nine years to the day after the battle of Chapultepec, Winfield Scott, the hero of that day, reviewed the heroes of battles to come. Beside him stood "a tall man with solid, gray eyes, a low forehead, heavy grizzled moustache and imperial," who had also witnessed the storming of Chapultepec. In 1847, however, he had not stood beside the commanding general.

21 *Regulations for the U.S. Military Academy* (New York, 1853), 2; Adjutant, U.S.M.A., to Hardee, August 8, 1856, in Adjutant's Letterbook No. 2 (United States Military Academy Archives).
22 Letter from Davis, n.d., quoted in the *Veteran,* II, 16.
23 Special Order No. 117, August 6, 1856, in Post Order Book No. 4.
24 *Ibid.;* John G. Barnard to Joseph G. Totten, August 8, 1856, in Superintendent's Letterbook No. 3 (United States Military Academy Archives); Adjutant, U.S.M.A., to Hardee, August 8, 1856, in Adjutant's Letterbook No. 2.
25 Adjutant General Special Orders No. 101, August 25, 1856, in Post Order Book No. 4, September 8, 1856.

Brevet Lieutenant Colonel Hardee justifiably felt proud; Scott approved of the review, saying that the cadets "acquitted themselves like veterans." [26]

The following year the functions of the commandant, as set forth in Davis' order, became formalized in the 1857 *United States Military Academy Regulations*, and Hardee was given the rank of temporary lieutenant colonel.[27] By 1859 the commandant's duties had expanded, ripping the heart out of D. H. Mahan's Department of Engineering by transferring "the subjects of Strategy, Grand Tactics, Army Organization . . . to the Department of Tactics . . . under the supervision of the Commandant of Cadets."

The new role of the commandant, defined by Davis and implemented and amplified by Hardee, was reflected primarily in two phases of the West Point program—discipline and military instruction. Hardee the disciplinarian remained a shivering memory for many of his cadets. Their reminiscences bear witness to his impressive bearing, his unusually stern features, and the vigor with which he sustained his demanding code. Hardee described his concept of proper discipline: "As commandant I have the entire charge of the discipline. All reports come to and are examined by me. The system is as follows: When a cadet is reported for an offense the report is shown to me, recorded in a delinquency book, and read at evening parade; the next morning, if the young man pleases, he may submit to me a verbal excuse. If this is satisfactory I remove the report; if not, I ask for a written excuse, which is referred to the reporting officer. If this reference is satisfactory I remove the report; if not, it is referred to the Superintendent, and passes beyond my control." [28]

Although Hardee's administration was characterized by forceful discipline, the cadets gained many benefits. Hardee substituted two five-week vacations for the one ten-week furlough that had been granted to the cadets once during their four years. Hardee also instituted Cadet balls, held three nights a week during the summer en-

26 Washington *National Intelligencer*, September 18, 1856.
27 Hardee to Adjutant General, August 22, 1858, in Orders and Endorsements; Hardee to Mrs. Jefferson Davis, August 15, 1858, quoted in Dunbar Rowland (ed.), *Jefferson Davis, Constitutionalist. His Letters, Papers, and Speeches*, 10 vols. (Jackson, Miss., 1923), III, 282; *Regulations of the U.S. Military Academy at West Point* (New York, 1857).
28 Morris Schaff, *The Spirit of Old West Point* (Boston, 1907), 37; Oliver Otis Howard, *Autobiography of Oliver Otis Howard*, 2 vols. (New York, 1907), I, 101; *Senate Miscellaneous Documents*, 36th Cong., 2nd Sess., Doc. 8, pp. 95–96.

campments. These "hops," held usually at Cozzen's Hotel and managed by the more socially inclined cadets, such as Stephen D. Ramseur and Nathaniel R. Chambliss, merited attention throughout New England. "These gay parties are justly famed among the fair sex; for better or more indefatigable dancers than the cadets are not to be found even in New York." During the winter months Hardee dispensed with the rigorous military exercises and permitted the cadets to "resort to the gymnasium, or to a room where music is provided, and where those who wish can dance." [29]

Hardee, furthermore, pleased the cadets immensely by accepting many of their suggestions for changes, some of which had broader implications than merely amusement and relaxation. Among other organizations, he encouraged a group under a young lieutenant, Oliver Otis Howard, who led the assembled cadets in prayer and gave them personal guidance.[30]

Howard, later a capable Union corps and wing commander, was only one of a large group of junior officers who served as Hardee's assistants. Other prominent members of the group were John Pegram, John M. Schofield, Andrew J. Donelson, Charles W. Field, Cadmus M. Wilcox, Richard K. Meade, E. Porter Alexander, and Alexander McD. McCook. Although Hardee preferred assistants who had served for at least five years with a line regiment, he appreciated natural ability and sometimes retained exceptional cadets as instructors. E. Porter Alexander, who would be Longstreet's chief of artillery officer in the Civil War, was one of the cadets so favored.[31] The assistant instructors assumed the responsibility for their respective tactical departments, while the commandant supervised the entire practical military course of instruction and visited the section rooms regularly, "putting questions to the cadets." As a department head Hardee proved as hard a taskmaster as he had been on the drill field at Jefferson Barracks. He set high standards for the quality of instruction

29 Stephen Dodson Ramseur to David Schenck, April 6, 1857, in Stephen Dodson Ramseur Papers (Southern Historical Collection); *Harper's Weekly*, September 3, 1859; *Senate Miscellaneous Documents*, 36th Cong., 2nd Sess., Doc. 3, p. 201.
      Nathaniel Rives Chambliss, a member of the class of 1861, would marry Hardee's daughter Anna and serve as a member of Hardee's staff during the Civil War.
30 Edward Porter Alexander to Alan Leopold Alexander, December, n.d., 1856, in Edward Porter Alexander Papers (Southern Historical Collection); Howard, *Autobiography*, I, 91.
31 Hardee to Joseph E. Brown, January 21, 1860, in Hardee-Zacherie Papers (Southern Historical Collection).

and required that each instructor submit a syllabus periodically for his inspection.[32]

During Hardee's tenure several new courses were instituted in the Tactical Department, including military law, equitation, and veterinary science.[33] Hardee further facilitated instruction in the cavalry branch by supervising the construction of a new riding hall. Bayonet exercises became a portion of the first-class man's required program, as Hardee wished to indoctrinate the future officer in the use of that weapon, which was emphasized strongly in his tactics. Excellence of performance in Hardee's light-infantry drill was expected, of course, and one may judge the success of his training program by an observation made by a member of the 1858 Board of Visitors: "Nothing can be more perfect, striking, and beautiful, than the exercises of the infantry in the system of tactics introduced by the present commandant at this point. There are no soldiers in the world who perform with more beauty and skill than the cadets at this institution." [34]

Hardee also may have been responsible for the addition of history to the general curriculum, and he probably facilitated the inclusion of Spanish. "As a matter of practical importance to our officers, I consider the Spanish language of greater value than the French," he commented.[35]

Although importance of his service as commandant can best be tested by the Civil War performance of his students, his contribution was realized at the time by his colleagues: one wrote, "the commandant of the corps exercises a more important influence on the military character and opinions of the junior officers of the Army than any other individual. . . ." [36]

It should not be overlooked, however, that Hardee's opportunity for this service appears to have resulted directly from his relationship with Jefferson Davis. The formal relationship of a progressive, imaginative superior like Davis and an enthusiastic and gifted subordinate like Hardee often produces a feeling of mutual respect and understanding, particularly when the backgrounds of the two seem to have been in relative harmony. While at West Point, Hardee cultivated

32 *Senate Miscellaneous Documents,* 36th Cong., 2nd Sess., Doc. 3, p. 95; Hardee to Adjutant General, October 16, 1857, in Letters Received, Adjutant General's Office.
33 *Regulations of the Academy,* 1857, p. 12.
34 *Senate Documents,* 35th Cong., 2nd Sess., Doc. 2, p. 840.
35 *Senate Miscellaneous Documents,* 36th Cong., 2nd Sess., Doc. 3, p. 98.
36 *Ibid.,* 174.

the friendship of Davis. He invited Davis and his wife to visit at the Military Academy and went so far as to name one of the annual summer camps after his benefactor.[37] Morris Schaff, one of Hardee's cadets and the biographer of Jefferson Davis, witnessed the growing bond between the two. "I always associate Mr. Davis with Hardee ... and in my mind's eye see them loitering in friendly intercourse under the elms at West Point." [38] Schaff, prejudiced by four years of sectional animosity towards Davis, and perhaps with his "mind's eye" filmed by a cadet's memory of an awe-inspiring Hardee, ventured to make an impulsive comparison. William J. Hardee was "a greater man than any one of the professors, greater even than Jefferson Davis." [39]

A warm and human account of the Davis-Hardee friendship exists in connection with Davis' illness in the early winter of 1858. Davis suffered from an acute attack of laryngitis and lost the sight in his left eye. When Hardee was in Washington, he often came to visit and sat for hours "reading and writing ... for Davis," to let Mrs. Davis relax.[40]

Hardee delighted in Washington social life, and there, during his leaves, he became a veritable social lion. A stimulating and witty conversationalist, he "was eminently a social man and very fond of society." Furthermore, the handsome widower was "a great favorite with the ladies." [41] He was invited to important social events and even dined with President Buchanan and his family. Hardee recorded this dinner in a letter to his young friend Clara Paige: "I was present

---

37 Hardee to Mrs. Davis, August 15, 1858, quoted in Rowland (ed.), *Jefferson Davis*, III, 282.
38 Schaff, *West Point*, 95.
39 *Ibid.*, 39. Unfortunately, Schaff does not substantiate his opinion.
40 Hardee to R. Delafield, February 26, 1858, in Superintendent's Letterbook No. 3; [Varina Howell Davis], *Jefferson Davis, Ex-President of the Confederate States of America*, 2 vols. (New York, 1890), I, 578.
    Another visitor at the bedside of Jefferson Davis during this winter was Colonel E. V. Sumner. Sumner, like Hardee, remained with his ill friend for hours, recapturing bygone days. Sumner's presence, however, involved Hardee in a very delicate situation. Sumner and General Harney, whose professional feud can be traced back to the winter of 1846, had renewed hostilities, and Sumner had come to Washington "seeking satisfaction for a discourtesy and affront from . . . Harney . . . and had sent him a challenge through his friend Colonel Hardie [sic]." The duel never materialized, as Harney forwarded the challenge to the Secretary of War and requested that Sumner be court-martialed. The position of Hardee and Davis must have been uncomfortable, for they seem to have been fond of both of the fiery-tempered old soldiers.
41 Benjamin Perley Poore, *Perley's Reminiscences*, 2 vols. (New York, 1886), I, 523; Mrs. Anna C. Johnson to author, July 11, 1956; Marian Campbell Gouverneur, *As I Remember* (New York, 1911), 120–21.

at the reception of the Japanese Embassy, as at Miss Ledyard's and dined, en famille, with the prest; which by the way, & with all due respect to comd'g officer, I do not consider any great honor. I would rather dine with your father and mother any day, not to speak of their charming daughter." [42]

One member of the President's family was quite impressed by Hardee, however; Harriet Lane, the President's niece and acting "first lady," reported the same activities differently. "The Japanese have come. [Lily] went out this morning at 10—for a romantic stroll with Mr. Woodbury & I know not *when* they will return. Col. Hardee is also here & is so agreeable that I almost regret the deep impression Lily has made there—for it excludes *me* from *all* hope. . . ." [43]

Miss Lane was not the only lady attracted to the tall and graying widower, as many contemporary accounts record. He often escorted a group of young ladies to West Point summer parades, afterward entertaining his guests in his "commodious, richly furnished marquee, overlooking and lording over the whole scene." [44] One of these young ladies was Miss Kate Lewis of Savannah, whose aunt had married Hardee's older brother, Noble Andrew. As she lived nearby in New York, Hardee invited her to the Military Academy occasionally. He "taught her to call him '*Uncle William*' & she always said she cared more for him than any of her uncles." [45]

The letters Hardee wrote to Clara Paige while he was commandant form one of the most substantial bases for an understanding of Hardee's personality. Hardly any of these letters are written in a serious tone; most are teasing, tantalizing notes, revealing a side of Hardee's character foreign to the distilled official accounts.

My Dear Miss Clara,
You have not written, I believe, to any one since you left. Where are you and what are you doing? . . . In the name of Diana I pray you answer at once. . . .

---

42 Hardee to Clara Paige, May 22, 1860, in Clara K. Paige Papers (New York Public Library). Clara was the daughter of Hardee's friend Alonzo Paige, of Schenectady, N.Y. Almost all that is known about her is that she was a close friend of Clara French (daughter of Chaplain French at West Point) and that she visited the Military Academy periodically, going out with the Junior officers and some of the older cadets.

43 "Letters of Presidents of the United States and Ladies of the White House," in *Pennsylvania Magazine of History and Biography*, XXVI (1902), 123.

44 Schaff, *West Point*, 45; J. M. Wright, "West Point before the War," in *Southern Bivouac*, I (June, 1885), 20.

45 Julia King to Miss Russell, August 10, 1933, in King Papers (Georgia Department of Archives and History).

West Point was never more pleasant (except when you are here) than it is at present. The weather has been beautiful and the company charming. I spent the two last evenings at Cozzen's Hotel where I have two or three sweet-hearts, Miss B of Philadelphia is decidedly the most attractive girl (save one) I have met this summer. (Miss P., Miss C., & Miss R of New York are also lovely.) You see however, that notwithstanding the attractions of the place that you are not forgotten, but that I am faithful to the last.[46]

Hardee continually and mockingly scolds Miss Clara in his letters, and although the language often poises delicately on the line of familiarity, it never violates Hardee's pronounced sense of propriety. A vein of vanity is also noticeable.

Write soon or I will cut your acquaintance, no I will inflict a greater punishment than that. I will come to see you so often when in Albany that you will vote me above. I shall bring my full uniform when I come.[47]

What are you doing with yourself? How is your heart? Puzzling questions to a young lady of your vacillating turn of mind. I want to get to Schenectady before it gets cold so that we may have some more agreeable drives. Perhaps, on some of these excursions, you may let me see beyond the exterior crust of your character. To me you have been somewhat of an enigma.[48]

[Writing jointly to Misses Clara Paige and Clara French] What do you mean treating us in this way? Mr. Chambliss & myself are in despair. You have disappointed us & my most cherished hopes are crushed. . . . You are both friends and if I were with you I would tell you but as I am not, I'll subscribe myself yours till death.[49]

Hardee constantly flirted with the subject of marriage in his letters to Miss Paige, but he does not appear to have been serious. Indeed, in the light of Hardee's practice of "courting" Miss Paige while on visits to his good friends her parents, with his children and Miss Dummett along, such an idea seems ludicrous (which is probably exactly what Hardee intended). Nevertheless, Clara Paige undoubtedly relished attentions of such a distinguished older man. Hardee continued to appease Miss Paige's desire for attention, not only by pledging exaggerated oaths of fidelity, but also by feigning jealousy, and by denouncing and mocking her suitors in lively terms. "So McCook . . . saw you off—did McCook say unutterable things? I should like to see him making love! Sir Jno Falstaff must be a fool to him. However,

46 Hardee to Clara Paige, September 12, 1858. This and the following passages are from letters in the Paige Papers.
47 Hardee to Clara Paige, January 5, 1859.
48 Hardee to Clara Paige, October 10, 1859.
49 Hardee to Clara Paige (probably written in the late fall of 1859).

he is a clever fellow & would make a good husband. Tell me if you are engaged to him. Is the coast clear? It is well to know one's rivals." [50]

The light-hearted, irresponsible tone of Hardee's notes to Clara Paige suggest that he utilized his social activities and correspondence as an outlet for a convivial personality repressed and restrained by the demands of his office and by his own concept of the proper bearing of a soldier. Some of his other personality traits were noticed and recorded, however, by interested and observant contemporaries. The deeply religious Oliver O. Howard noticed Hardee's courtesy and his sense of fair play; one cadet carried an indelible memory of his fiery temper and lashing tongue; others remembered him for his "pleasing address, which did much to relieve the natural harshness of his features when in repose," still another recalled Hardee's meticulous regard for the proper wearing of the uniform: "Hardee was, to use a current expression, a good deal of a dude. He thought more of his shape than his books." His daughter Anna never forgot her father's courtly manners and his punctiliousness. She "once came out of her room putting on her gloves. He said in effect, 'Your room is the place to complete your dress. Do not leave it until you have done so.' He was a dear, though, and my mother was devoted to him." [51]

While Hardee served at the Military Academy, one of his favorite social diversions was the "Saturday afternoon dinners" at Gouverneur Kemble's at Cold Springs, New York. With such guests as Scott, Davis, Mahan, Lee, William Bartlett, and Martin Van Buren often present, the conversation ranged over wide fields of interest and proved intellectually stimulating.[52] Hardee's background of general knowledge, based on the shaky foundation of his West Point cadet reading and academic endeavors, and largely neglected by his years of duty on the intellectually barren frontier posts, definitely needed strengthening before he could participate effectively in such discussions. Hardee appears to have realized his weakness, for during his four years at the Military Academy he read over a hundred volumes, mostly military works, biography, and history. His military reading centered about the Napoleonic epoch. He read several biog-

---

50 Hardee to Clara Paige, July 2, 1860.
51 Howard, *Autobiography*, I, 101; Wright, "West Point before the War," *loc. cit.*, 20; Price, *Across the Continent*, 274; Mrs. Anna C. Johnson to author, July 11, 1956.
52 Margaret Leute Raoul, "Gouverneur Kemble and the West Point Foundry," in *Americana*, XXX (July, 1936), 461, 471.

raphies of Bonaparte, André Masséna's *Memoirs*, and three works by
the Swiss military theorist, Henri Jomini. He also studied several
military atlases and cavalry and ordnance manuals. His biographical
reading adhered principally to the lives of the great military chieftains
such as the Duke of Marlborough, Alexander the Great, and his two
favorites, Washington and Bonaparte. Plutarch's *Lives*, Sparks's
American Biography, and *The Queens of England* constituted his
collective biographical reading. Hardee also read every biographical
work written by Prescott. His general history reading had a broad
base and he selected the books with care. They included Goldsmith's
Rome, Hume's *History of England*, Thiers' *History of the Consulate
and the Empire*, Alison's *History of Europe*, Macauley's *Essays*, and
Arnold's *Lectures on History*. His diet of general reading contained
several of Shakespeare's plays, Defoe's *Robinson Crusoe*, Griswold's
Poets and Poetry, Tennyson's works, Burton's *Anatomy of Melancholy*, Ruskin's *Modern Painters*, and various works by Byron and
Poe.[53]

Hardee's two favorite authors were Sir Walter Scott and Washington Irving. He borrowed some of the volumes written by these
men and evidently reread them as many as three times over the four
years. It is easy to visualize Hardee seated at his desk in his bedroom
or at the commandant's office poring through these works.

Hardee's home at West Point still stands, quartering the present-day
commandant and his family. The great veranda stretching across its
front has been removed, but otherwise much is the same. If one faces
the home from the West Point parade field, one may envision the days
of 1857–60, when Anna and Elizabeth sprawled over its lawn in the
summer and Willie and Sallie placed their warm faces against the cold
windowpanes in the winter, peering out over the "Plain" to the
turbulent and icy Hudson.

William J. Hardee the family man differs distinctly from Hardee
the commandant, and Hardee the party-loving widower. By 1856
Hardee had been separated from his children for almost three years,
and he determined to bring them to West Point at the first opportunity. In January, 1857, he returned to St. Augustine and made
arrangements for the family to move to West Point early in the sum-

---

53 Library Circulation Records, 1854–60 (United States Military Academy
    Library).

mer.[54] Hardee was well aware that his children needed a mother, and it seems that he endeavored to find a suitable wife. One of his prospects was "Miss Crane" of Newark, New Jersey. To Mrs. Kirby Smith this lady seemed to have all of the requisite charms, despite her "advanced" age of twenty-five: "She is amiable, sensible, *well educated*, of good family and has a *pretty fortune* of some 25 or 30,000. Your gallant Major or Col. Hardee tried . . . to get her into a correspondence with him, but she gave no encouragement to his advances, I am told. I think Col. H. has intentions towards one of Col. Delafield's daughters at West Point." [55] Mrs. Kirby Smith also remarked at the time that Hardee "looks fine and in manners is quite a man of the society of the world." [56]

The Hardee children did not suffer from the lack of a mother as much as they might have, for they had "Dena." Anna Maria Dummett, Hardee's sister-in-law, not only cared for his children but also raised the children of her other two sisters, Mary Nauman and Sarah Jane Madison. The house that she kept for these children in St. Augustine was a "merry establishment," and the name "Dena" lives on in family tradition as a symbol of noble selflessness. The relationship between Hardee and Dena is obscure. In his letters to Clara Paige, she is mentioned frequently in respectful although affectionate terms. It has been maintained that Hardee was in love with Dena and failed to marry her only because she was an English citizen (and remained one until death), and the English common law forbade her to marry her brother-in-law. This may or may not be the case, but the facts remain that Dena loved Hardee's children, lived close to him for several years, traveled frequently with him, and remained a spinster for life.[57]

Dena brought the children to West Point in the summer of 1857, and there they remained until the fall of 1860. The Hardee children differed in their attitudes toward life at the Military Academy. Sallie loved her "dear old West Point," Anna remained homesick for St.

54 While in St. Augustine, Hardee was consulted by state military officials in regard to a series of Seminole uprisings. Washington *National Intelligencer*, February 15, 1858; Mrs. Kirby Smith to Edmund Kirby Smith, May 21, 1856, in Kirby Smith Papers; Special Order No. 13, January 15, 1856, in Post Order Book No. 5.
55 Mrs. Kirby Smith to Kirby Smith, May 21, 1856, in Kirby Smith Papers.
56 Mrs. Kirby Smith to Kirby Smith, March 7, 1856, *ibid.*
57 St. Augustine *Record*, July 4, 1937; Mrs. Anna C. Johnson to author, July 11, 1956; *Army and Navy Journal*, March 25, 1899; Hardee to Clara Paige, October 20, 1858, in Paige Papers.

Augustine for quite some time, Elizabeth did not prevail upon her father to record her sentiments, and Willie used his home as a base of operations against the cadets.[58] Willie and his friends among the faculty members' children made life unbearable for the plebes, "shouting after them 'Hep! Hep! imitating their awkward ways (and what in this world is *so* awkward as a Plebe?) and generally making [themselves] disagreeable at the expense of the 'animals' or 'things.' " The cadets, of course, retaliated on their mite-sized tormentors, rubbing their faces in the snow or mud if they could catch them unaware and unaccompanied by their fathers.[59] Cadet Sergeant Kingsbury brought matters to a head, however, when he lodged an official complaint against Willie and Professor Bartlett's son: "I beg leave most respectfully to complain of the annoyances to which the files of my company are exposed when marching from parade. Last evening they were hit with knotted handkerchiefs and screamed at by the officers' children. . . . There were at least a dozen children in the crowd. Those conspicuous for their actions were the sons of Col. Hardee & Prof Bartlett." [60] Willie overreached himself with this antic and assuredly incurred the wrath of his embarrassed father, for no further incidents involving Willie and the cadets were recorded. Willie Hardee was the acknowledged favorite of the family and the "idol of his father." Although Hardee's cadets would have thought the idea was preposterous, Willie's ambition was to be a soldier just like his father.[61]

In 1860 Hardee knew that his tour of duty at West Point would soon end. He wrote one of his last letters to Clara Paige, telling her of his plans. "I am going to leave West Point in the summer or fall. Do you know who would be willing to accompany me into the wilds of Texas? I am open to proposals, it is leap year. Can you recommend any one?" [62]

Hardee received an opportunity to leave the army in 1860. On a trip to Virginia in July, 1860, he attended the annual examination of the Virginia Military Institute cadets. He drilled the cadet corps, and many of the cadets' letters refer to the "spectacular sight." V.M.I. not

58 Hardee to Clara Paige, October 20, 1858, October 10, 1859, in Paige Papers.
59 Bailey, "My Boyhood at West Point," *loc. cit.,* 17.
60 Hardee to Richard Delafield, September 29, 1859, in Superintendent's Letterbook No. 3.
61 W. D. Pickett, *Sketch of the Military Career of William J. Hardee, Lieutenant-General, C.S.A.* (Lexington, Ky., 1910), 44.
62 Hardee to Clara Paige, undated (probably March or April, 1860), in Paige Papers.

only named its summer encampment after Hardee, but the school officials approached him about a position on the faculty. Hardee declined, apparently because of the modest salary that the school offered.[63]

Shortly after his return from Virginia Hardee received his orders. He was promoted to lieutenant colonel in the First Cavalry regiment and was authorized by the War Department to take a leave of absence until February 1, 1861, at which time he would join his new command in Texas.[64] Hardee passed the remainder of the summer working with Jefferson Davis and the Military Academy Commission, and getting his family ready for the trip to St. Augustine. Finally, on September 8, 1860, he was succeeded as commandant by Brevet Major John F. Reynolds of the Third Artillery.[65]

Hardee left his mark upon West Point. He drastically altered the practical military courses, introduced and taught the new system of tactics, and permanently established the role of commandant as second in importance only to that of superintendent. Many of his students achieved distinction in the Civil War and provided both armies with alert, well-trained, and energetic leadership. One of these students maintained that Hardee was "the best commandant the corps of cadets ever had. . . . Whatever control I have of myself I attribute to the relentless teaching of that unbending disciplinarian." [66]

Samuel B. McIntire's thoughts probably represented the sentiments of many of his classmates.

[I] stood in the presence of Colonel Hardee . . . as he sat at his desk, pen in hand, dressed in uniform, his handsome face turned toward me, his dark eyes seemingly full of kindness. I thought I never beheld a finer specimen of manhood: tall and slender, he looked every inch a soldier. He spoke words of encouragement, and when I "passed," he was pleased, and asked me how I was "getting on," thereby showing the contrast in kindness toward me, as between the commandant and the superintendent, yet the one was from the North, the other from the South. When Colonel

---

63 Superintendent of V.M.I. to James L. Kemper, July 9, 1860, and General Richardson to Colonel Smith, August 30, 1860, quoted in William Couper, *One Hundred Years at V.M.I.*, 4 vols. (Richmond, 1939), II, 37–38, 67; John Letcher to John B. Floyd, May 25, 1860, in Letters Received, Office of Secretary of War (National Archives and Record Service).
64 Hardee to Clara Paige, July 2, 1860, in Paige Papers; Tallahassee *Weekly Floridian*, November 18, 1873; Special Order No. 108, September 18, 1860, in Special Orders.
65 Special Order No. 126, September 8, 1860, in Post Order Book No. 5.
66 Wright, "West Point before the War," *loc. cit.*, 20.

Hardee left the Point for other duty I felt as though I had lost my best friend.[67]

The six months following his departure from West Point proved as tumultuous for Hardee personally as for his country. He traveled widely during this period, and as the months passed, he became more and more involved with the secessionists of his and other states. Like other Southerners in the United States Army, he recognized that a hard choice would soon be necessary.

During the latter half of 1860, he served the state of Georgia as well as, or indeed, instead of, the United States government. Governor Joseph Brown prized his services and offered Hardee the position of state adjutant general. When Hardee declined, Brown employed him to purchase munitions and weapons for Georgia. Hardee spent weeks in New York examining and purchasing armaments and would have traveled to Europe to procure weapons if the War Department had allowed him to do so.[68]

January 1, 1861, found him in Savannah advising Governor Brown and the Savannah officials on the feasibility of seizing Fort Pulaski. When Georgia seceded on January 19, Hardee knew that he would follow. Four days later Hardee revealed his sentiments to his colleague Edmund Kirby Smith:

> I returned three days ago from St. Augustine where I saw your mother with whom I had several conversations respecting you and your future.... Florida & Georgia our native states have both seceded and I feel confident that we are destined to have a Southern Confederacy. I do not think there is any probability of a compromise being made which will cause the scattered fragments to reunite again. Under these circumstances an all important question presents itself, at what time shall we resign? The State of Florida has passed a Resolution inviting the officers of the Army & Navy to return to the service of the State with the same rank and same pay which they at present receive [from] the general government. A similar resolution has been introduced into the Georgia Legislature but it has not yet been acted on, it may or may not pass. Whether it does or not I consider that Georgia has a paramount claim on my allegiance, and I have written to the Governor of the state to say that I am ready to resign whenever he may need my services, or whenever in his judgement it may be proper for me to do so. I am awaiting his reply, & shall be governed by what he recommends.

67 Samuel B. McIntire, "Echoes of the Past," in *Army and Navy Journal*, June 14, 1902.
68 For a detailed account of Hardee's activities during the fall of 1860 and the early winter of 1861, see Hughes, "Hardee, U.S.A.," 227–42.

I am sure you feel as I do about sustaining the South, but your case is somewhat different from mine. The Florida resolution required all officers desirous of serving the state to signify their intentions to do so within thirty days, this with you is impossible. Unless therefore a collision of arms takes place before a southern confederacy is organized I don't think I would resign. There is no immediate need of your services, you are out of the way, and you will not be forgotten when a Southern Army is organized. [To remain on] the frontier I think . . . would be my course of action, but much must depend on the state of your feelings. [There] is no probability that you will be called on to act against the South, & this should be duly considered in making up your decision. If I thought your failure to resign now would interfere with your appointment in the southern confederacy, I would recommend you to resign immediately, but I don't believe it will. Cole Huger altho pressed by S. Carolina refused to resign until a southern confederacy should be organized. I don't approve his conduct, for called on by the state he should have resigned at once. I mention this to show the state of feeling among some of our officers.[69]

Six days after composing the letter to Captain Kirby Smith, Hardee followed the dictates of his conscience and resigned his commission as lieutenant colonel of the First Cavalry.

The following day he received Special Order No. 21 from the War Department, requiring all officers to return to their units immediately. He replied at once, saying that he had resigned his commission prior to the receipt of the order and asking that his resignation be accepted without delay.

On February 7 the War Department telegraphed the reply: "Resignation accepted January 31, 1861." [70]

---

69 Hardee to Kirby Smith, January 23, 1861, in Kirby Smith Papers.
70 Hardee to Adjutant General, January 29, 1861, in Letters Received, Adjutant General's Office.

VI

A New Uniform

THE STATE of Georgia lost little time in acquiring a military establishment. The Secession Convention authorized two regiments of infantry on January 25, and Governor Brown chose Hardee to command the First Regiment and W. H. T. Walker, the Second Regiment.[1] Hardee received his commission on February 7 and immediately began organizing his regiment at Savannah. In addition he had to perform numerous tasks fundamental in the organization of the Georgia armed forces. During February he presided over a board "to determine the uniform, dress, and equipment" of the Georgia forces. He also served on a board to screen officer appointments, helped to establish the Georgia Navy, and assisted in procuring armament for Fort Pulaski.[2]

Hardee's duties at Savannah filled the interlude while the Confederacy was being organized. Two weeks after the election of Jefferson Davis, Hardee offered his services to that government.[3] The Confederate War Department quickly made use of him, summoning him to Montgomery to assist in the formulation of the Army Bill. From February 27 through March 1 Hardee worked with Secretary of War Leroy Pope Walker and with Beauregard, laying the groundwork for a regular army. The "Act for the Establishment and

1 H. C. Wayne to Hardee, February 7, 1861, in Adjutant General's Letterbook, February 1, 1861–October 8, 1864 (Georgia Department of Archives and History); Joseph B. Cumming War Recollections, 1861–65 (typed copy in Southern Historical Collection).
2 General Orders No. 1, February 9, 1861, Wayne to A. Iverson, February 16, 1861, Wayne to C. M. Morris, February 14, 1861, and Wayne to F. S. Bartow, February 19, 1861, in Georgia Adjutant General's Letterbook.
3 Hardee to L. P. Walker, February 26, 1861, in William Joseph Hardee Military Service Record, 1861–65, Record Group 109 (National Archives and Record Service).

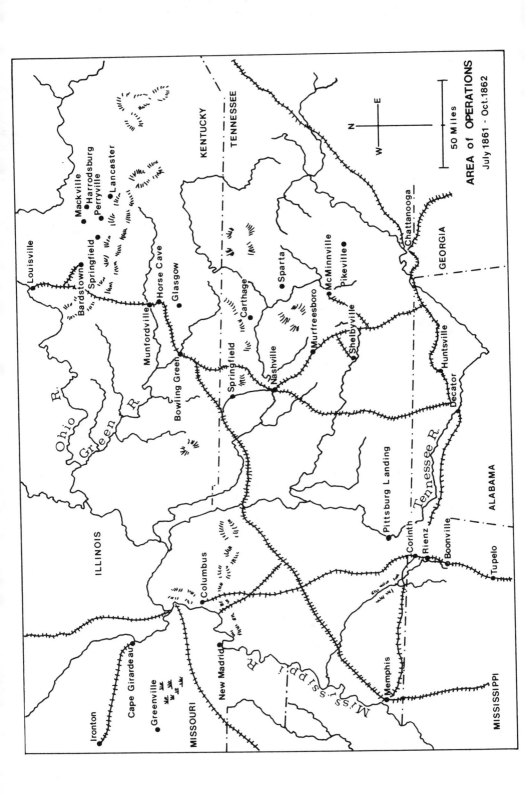

AREA of OPERATIONS
July 1861 - Oct. 1862

50 Miles

Organization of the Army of the Confederate States of America" called for one corps of engineers, one corps of artillery, six regiments of infantry, and one regiment of cavalry. The bill provided for such things as the appointment of officers, rank, promotion, and pay. Modeled closely upon the United States Army, the Confederate Army would be governed by the identical code of military law and the same articles of war. The Confederate Army Bill was deliberately conservative, proposing a less ambitious military establishment than that of the United States but adhering rigidly to the principles of military organization to which Davis, Hardee, and Beauregard were accustomed. The bill proved satisfactory to the Confederate Congress and was approved on March 6, 1861.[4]

Colonel Hardee remained in Montgomery for several weeks assisting and advising Secretary of War Walker on the many technicalities inherent in establishing an army. On March 7 Walker offered Hardee an appointment as colonel in the Confederate Provisional Army. Hardee accepted and resigned from the Georgia Army on March 13.[5]

For his first assignment the War Department gave Hardee command of the First Regiment of Infantry. For the nucleus of this regiment Hardee wanted the five infantry companies that he had already organized at Savannah. These troops, however, had not been offered to the Confederacy by Georgia, so the War Department decided to send him to take charge of the garrison at Fort Morgan, Alabama.[6]

Fort Morgan had been seized by Alabama troops early in January, 1861. The Southern states regarded it as one of the sweetest strategic plums obtained during the frenzied winter. Built on the classic pentag-

---

4 Walker to Hardee, February 26, 1861, in Letters sent, Office of Secretary of War; Pierre G. T. Beauregard Diary, 1861–62 (microfilm copy in Joint Universities Library, Nashville, Tenn.), February 27–March 1, 1861; Confederate States of America, *Laws for the Army and Navy of the Confederate States* (Richmond, 1861), 12–19.

5 *The War of the Rebellion: A Compilation of the Official Records of the Union and Confederate Armies*, (73 vols. Washington 1880–1901), Ser. I, Vol. LII, Pt. 2, p. 24; LIII, 137; hereinafter cited as *Official Records* (unless otherwise indicated, all citations are to Series I). Hardee to J. E. Brown, March 13, 1861, in possession of the Abraham Lincoln Bookshop, Chicago, Ill. Hardee to S. Cooper, March 13, 1861, in Letters Received, Adjutant General's Office.

T. B. Roy, Hardee's chief of staff, contends that Davis offered Hardee the position of adjutant general, but that Hardee refused it, preferring a field command. No evidence has been found to corroborate Roy's statement, however.

6 Hardee to J. E. Brown, March 13, 1861; *Official Records*, LII, Pt. 2, p. 24; LIII, 137.

onal design, the fort was located at the tip of Mobile Point, about forty miles from Mobile. Its guns commanded the entrance to Mobile Bay.

By the latter part of April, 1861, Hardee had increased the armament of Fort Morgan from 71 to 107 guns and had added powerful eight- and ten-inch columbiads, plus mortars and fieldpieces. Men who were not active on gun crews joined the labor gangs that were removing every tree within range of the lighter cannon or aided in the enormous task of leveling the dunes. Construction began on floating batteries, and Hardee procured a steamship to increase the flexibility and firepower of his defenses.[7]

Hardee's command consisted of nine companies of volunteers. As the fort's facilities could not accommodate so many, most of the men camped on the hot, windswept beach. This not only alleviated the billeting problem but minimized the threat of yellow fever. However, the punishing glare of the sun, the itching salt, and the monotony of felling trees and leveling sand dunes burst the bubble of enthusiasm for many. Their "sand-hill" bored them; military restraint frustrated them, and the continuing lack of an enemy enraged them.

For an officer conditioned by twenty-five years in the regular army and the example of West Point, discouragement was inevitable— Hardee reported: "I should dislike to fight this command in its present condition; indeed I should not like to see the face of an enemy for three months. . . . The material is good, but officers and men are deplorably ignorant. I am doing all in my power to instruct and discipline them, but where so much is to be done, one person, however zealous, can do but little. . . . I have instituted a regular course of instruction for the officers and non-commissioned officers, . . . but am embarrassed for the want of instructors." [8]

To assist Hardee in training the artillerists, the War Department assigned two capable artillery lieutenants, Francis A. Shoup and Charles P. Ball. Infantry instruction depended primarily upon Hardee himself and a few Mexican War veterans. Nevertheless, by late spring the Fort Morgan garrison began to resemble a military organization. The acquisition of an experienced artillery captain and a once-upon-a-time West Point cadet strengthened the officer corps. The beneficial

---

7 Report of Samuel H. Lockett to General Goldthwaite, February, 1861 (Southern Historical Collection); *Official Records,* LII, Pt. 2, pp. 47–48, 60, Ser. IV, Vol. I, 227.
8 *Official Records,* LII, Pt. 2, p. 31.

blend of a few capable junior officers, incessant drill, and exhausting labor hardened the pulpy volunteer organization. An official Confederate observer reported: "Colonel Hardee's command is now in a condition to be easily managed, and I left him yesterday in a better temper than he has been for some weeks. I will continue to arrange everything as near as I can to his wishes. He is one of the best officers in America, and I want him to have a fair chance." [9]

Shortly after this communication reached the War Department, the weary men manning the creaky wheelbarrows at Fort Morgan received the long-awaited news—war had begun with the United States. For junior officers and men, drilling and construction work continued at an even more insistent pace. Beyond the strengthening of Fort Morgan, activities consisted of reconnaissance expeditions to procure intelligence information. In addition to these routine duties, Colonel Hardee sought to exploit the opportunity provided by enemy ships in Mobile Bay. He wired the War Department for permission to seize these ships, but the request was denied and the opportunity passed. [10]

On April 17 the War Department extended Hardee's command to include Fort Gaines and all of the approaches to Mobile. As Hardee began to secure troops and armaments for the defense of this area, Major General David E. Twiggs, Hardee's old commander, was placed in charge of Department Number One, which included Louisiana and the coastal regions of Mississippi and Alabama. [11] With the defenses of Mobile now under the control of a departmental commander, Hardee's independent command was liquidated. A new assignment came shortly.

While the Confederates were strengthening and consolidating their coastal defenses, the situation in the border states had deteriorated. Matters in Missouri were alarming. Unionists, encouraged and led by Francis P. Blair, Jr., had seized St. Louis, depriving Southern sympathizers of its great arsenal. The Unionists then defeated the Missouri state forces and drove them into the fringe areas. Presently they controlled the transportation network, most of the military potential, and

9 *Ibid.*, 34–35. Another observer did not share Clemens' respect for Colonel Hardee. London *Times* correspondent William H. Russell recorded, "The Colonel is an agreeable, delicate-looking man, scarcely of middle age, and is well known in the States as the author of 'The Tactics'. . . . He does not appear to be possessed of any great energy of capacity, but is, no doubt, a respectable officer."

10 *Official Records*, I, 454, 458; LII, Pt. 2, p. 42.

11 *Ibid.*, LII, Pt. 2, pp. 45–46, 53; LIII, 960; Ser. IV, Vol. I, 251.

the liquid assets of the state. By the end of June the Confederate leaders appeared desperate, General Sterling Price was ill; his headquarters was unknown; and no one knew what, if any, plan of campaign he contemplated.[12] In Arkansas the picture was equally gloomy. Factional controversy paralyzed resistance efforts, and the military leaders failed to inspire confidence. One Arkansas citizen wrote to the Confederate Secretary of War, "My belief and conviction is that little can be done among these factions, and that a military leader from without the State is needed . . . [around whom] the bold and brave men can rally . . . without disturbance from leaders of any faction. . . ." [13] The Confederate War Department responded to these demands on June 17 by appointing Hardee to an Arkansas command, with the rank of brigadier general.

Hardee's territory comprised "that portion of Arkansas lying west of the White and Black rivers and north of the Arkansas River to the Missouri line. The general purpose of this assignment is to watch over and protect the country within the limits referred to and also that part of the State of Missouri contiguous thereto." The Confederacy supplied him with the regiment of Thomas C. Hindman and promised to furnish him three thousand additional troops.[14]

By July 3, 1861, Hardee had arrived in Memphis and could wire the Adjutant General that he would be leaving for Little Rock as soon as Hindman's regiment could be equipped. Colonel Hindman had been gathering his regiment since May, and by the time Hardee arrived, he had mustered seventeen companies, thus expanding his regiment to the size of a legion.

The sojourn in Memphis proved personally profitable to General Hardee. He enjoyed a series of charming parties and discovered, and delighted, Felicia Shover, the widow of one of his old army friends. She came to be his faithful correspondent and his provisioner of delicacies during the next year.[15] Perhaps through Mrs. Shover he met Samuel Tate, President of the Memphis and Charleston Railroad and an influential Memphis figure, who proved to be one of Hardee's staunchest supporters.

12 *Official Records*, III, 601; Stanley Fitzgerald Horn, *The Army of Tennessee* (2d ed., Norman, Okla., 1952), 16 ff.
13 *Official Records*, III, 589–90.
14 S. Cooper to W. J. Hardee, June 17, 25, 1861, in Letters Sent, Adjutant General's Office.
15 Hardee to Felicia Shover, July 4, 1861, in Felicia Shover Letters (Library of Congress).

On July 10, 1861, Hindman's regiment left Memphis; Hardee followed on July 11.[16] Prior to his departure he attempted to confer with Major General Leonidas Polk, the commander of the Mississippi River defenses, but the conference could not be arranged, and Hardee left, after explaining his plans to Sam Tate. Hardee wanted to co-ordinate his movements with Polk's or, if need be, to place his command under Polk's control. Furthermore, Hardee urged that Polk occupy New Madrid, Missouri, as a defensive move to block one of the logical invasion routes into Arkansas.[17]

Hardee proceeded directly from Memphis to Little Rock, where as the representative of the Confederate Government, he met Governor Henry M. Rector and the Arkansas Military Board, to arrange for the transfer of the Arkansas state troops to the Confederacy. After about a week's deliberation Hardee and the Military Board signed an agreement whereby "the troops, arms, and munitions now in service of the State of Arkansas are to be transferred to the Confederate States." Seven infantry regiments, one cavalry regiment, and five batteries of artillery came under Hardee's control, as well as "such other arms and munitions as may hereafter be deemed necessary to be transferred." Hardee was to inventory the Arkansas supplies, give a receipt for the same, and promise that the Confederacy would reimburse the state. This formal agreement appeared to be a signal measure in the cause of Southern military unity.[18]

The execution of the agreement proved more difficult than its formulation. Factional differences within the state came close to sabotaging Hardee's efforts. Several of the state military figures knew that they might well lose their newly won rank and privileges if the state force was integrated into the Confederate Army. Others felt quite reasonably that these regiments would be whisked off across the Appalachians, as so many in the Mississippi Valley had been, and the people of Arkansas would be left unprotected. As a result of these and other reasons, obstructionists such as General Nicholas B. Pearce and the state Adjutant General, arose to plead with the Arkansas

16 Edward Bourne, "The Young Guard," in *The Military Annals of Tennessee,* ed. John Berrien Lindsley (Nashville, 1886), 600.
17 S. Tate to L. Polk, July 12, 1861, in Leonidas Polk Papers (microfilm copies in Southern Historical Collection).
18 *Official Records,* III, 609; Contract between the Military Board of State of Arkansas and Brigadier General W. J. Hardee, C.S.A., for transfer of troops, arms, munitions, & c from State of Arkansas to the Confederate States, July 15, 1861, in Letters Received, Office of Secretary of War.

soldiers not to join Hardee's force. These men were remarkably successful. For instance, out of the three thousand potential Confederates on the northwestern frontier only eighteen agreed to transfer; most of the remaining men departed from the state camps with their weapons. "In Northeastern Arkansas nearly half of the first regiment approached on the subject decided to go home." Armed and organized troops were precious in Arkansas, and the absence of these men might influence the decision in the coming Missouri campaign. Embarrassed and frustrated, Hardee hurried the popular and politically influential Hindman to the remaining regimental camps before the obstructionists appeared, and Hindman succeeded in saving for the Confederacy a considerable number of troops in these isolated camps.[19]

While Hardee held conferences with the Military Board, his brigade assembled at Pitman's Ferry, Arkansas. Hardee chose this position as his base of operations because it poised his tiny army just short of the Missouri line, and the navigable Current River provided a reliable line of communications. Offensively, Pitman's Ferry could be utilized as a springboard into the interior of Missouri; defensively, it blocked a primary avenue of approach into Hardee's assigned district.

General Hardee assumed direct operational control of his brigade on July 22, 1861. Few of the troops had seen Hardee before, and "all were on the *qui vive* to see a live brigadier who had been in the old [army]. . . . Hardee on his arrival was dressed in a very plain, faded uniform, which looked rather seedy in the eyes of those who thought he would be covered with buttons and gold lace." He rode up to the encampment and nodded approvingly at the tandems of guard posts surrounding the area. The sentry directly to his front typified the "backwoods specimen of humanity" from the Arkansas swamps. "The sentry paced his post backward and forward [whistling, with] his gun slung across his shoulder in a devil-may-care style, and with an impudent strut that denoted that he felt the importance of his duties." Hardee decided to conduct an experiment. He moved his horse up close to the sentry, but the man ignored him. Thereupon Hardee nudged his mount toward the forbidden line. Around wheeled the guard, up came the rifle, and out came the rustic challenge: "Stop thar, stranger! and don't you cross that line or I'll blow your head off!" Hardee quickly established his identity. "Oh!" said the guard,

19 *Official Records*, III, 715–16; VIII, 31; David Yancey Thomas, *Arkansas in War and Reconstruction* (Little Rock, 1926), 94.

and the rifle was lowered immediately. "How are you, General Hardee? Glad to see you . . . my name is Tom Simkins. Come down, general, and I'll give you a good dinner!" Hardee politely refused and rode on.[20]

To be sure, more Tom Simkinses awaited Hardee in camp—in fact, the stronger and more articulate composed his officer corps. In all there were five regiments of infantry, one battalion of cavalry, and four batteries of artillery. Among these enthusiastic Arkansas units Hardee found the unique Ninth Arkansas, the "regiment of preachers," whose colonel and major, together with several company commanders and over forty of the men, were frontier spiritual leaders. As a counterweight the ungodly could point to the "Shamrock Guards," a company of rowdy types, predominantly Irish, complete with their foremen from the railroads who now were officers rather than straw bosses.[21]

There was another Irishman in camp. At least, he had come from Ireland, but he was an educated, articulate Anglican, at variance with the expected norm. This man, Patrick Ronayne Cleburne, capably commanded the First Arkansas and soon outstripped all of his fellow regimental commanders. Indeed, he joined with Hardee to produce a team that was the pride of the Army of Tennessee. The two men worked together with remarkable harmony and became devoted friends.

Men such as Cleburne were needed at Pitman's Ferry, for Hardee maintained that "it will require energy and dispatch to place this command in condition to take the field." [22] The troops needed all types of equipment and arms. They also suffered from the diseases common to newly organized bodies of men. Measles, for instance, incapacitated over two hundred within a few weeks.

With Hardee at Pitman's Ferry, a Confederate offensive opportunity was at hand, for southeastern Missouri was thinly held by Union forces. Confederate strategy, though dimly defined, called for General Pillow to move into Missouri with a column of six thousand men, there to be joined by three thousand Missouri volunteers. Hardee

20 [Anonymous,] *The Greyjackets* (Richmond, 1867), 402; for another anecdote of Hardee's experience with the Arkansans see *Army and Navy Journal,* XXI (February 9, 1884), 563.

21 Basil Wilson Duke, *Reminiscences* (New York, 1911), 60; Clement Anselm Evans (ed.), *Confederate Military History,* 12 vols. (Atlanta, 1899), X, 305.

22 D. C. Govan to wife, July 28, 1861, in Daniel C. Govan Papers, 1861–1908 (Southern Historical Collection).

would move north with seven thousand men and unite with Pillow at Ironton. Meanwhile, Price and McCulloch would advance toward Lyon, in southwestern Missouri. The objectives of the converging columns were to cut off Lyon, take St. Louis and then progress up the Missouri River, raising swarms of volunteers. This strategic concept never became formalized in an order, however. The responsibilities or discretion of any one of the individual commanders could nullify it. For success, the efforts of Price, McCulloch, Hardee, M. Jeff Thompson, and Pillow would have to be closely co-ordinated. Collectively they had a good chance to penetrate Missouri deeply; individually they did not.

On July 27 General Price requested that Hardee join with him and McCulloch in a movement against Lyon. Hardee refused, using a dozen creditable excuses; but when he learned that Pillow had arrived at New Madrid, Missouri, and was within supporting distance, he unilaterally decided to advance into Missouri toward Ironton. Defying maxims he had stressed at West Point, he plunged ahead with only half of his force.[23]

By August 4, 1861, Hardee had reached Greenville, Missouri. The uncontested advance bred confidence; perhaps an immediate attack on Ironton would succeed. Before Hardee could attack, however, he had to get support from Pillow. Pillow refused to assist Hardee, believing that their objective should be Cape Girardeau, not Ironton. He would not leave New Madrid to assist Hardee, and Hardee would not go to his assistance. Without the other's help, each was powerless. On August 12 Polk finally intervened and ordered Pillow to unite with Hardee, but Pillow had already commenced an abortive attack along the Mississippi. The exasperated Polk, after pen and patience had been exhausted, ordered Hardee to pull back from Greenville and Pillow to abandon his Cape Girardeau ambitions.[24]

Recriminations followed Polk's decision to discontinue the offensive. Pillow, in a letter to the Secretary of War, blamed both Hardee and Polk. Hardee maintained that he could not "have cooperated with [Pillow] in his foolish enterprise. He desired I should abandon Arkansas and my base of operations to assist him in an attack where his

23 *Official Records,* III, 612–13, 616, 619, 629.
24 For a detailed account of the confused pattern of events and communications during the latter part of August, 1861, see Nathaniel Cheairs Hughes, Jr., "William Joseph Hardee, C.S.A., 1861–1865" (Ph.D. dissertation, University of North Carolina, 1959), 36–50.

flank and rear were exposed and the enemy could bring two or three times our combined forces to meet us at the point of contact." [25] Hardee went so far as to write President Davis about the controversy. Davis reacted quickly, demanding a full explanation from Polk and hinting that the popular Tennessean Benjamin F. Cheatham might replace Pillow.[26] Polk replied that he believed that the real source of difficulty was the lack of a unified command system in the West, and he suggested that Albert Sidney Johnston be appointed to general command.[27]

Thus the Confederate invasion of eastern Missouri ended. Cross-purposes and incredibly bad co-ordination had wrecked the effort. Polk and Pillow had, if anything, clouded their military reputations. Their bickering and failure to co-operate had destroyed the confidence of many citizens and had confused and disheartened subordinate officers.[28]

Following the battle of Wilson's Creek on August 10, the Confederates held the strategic initiative. With the tide turning, a countermovement back into central Missouri might have produced material results. To succeed, this countermovement needed the combined forces of Pillow, Hardee, Price, and McCulloch. McCulloch, however, distrusted Price's state guard and the people of Missouri. Hardee and Pillow could not agree on any plan, and neither seemed willing or able to unite with the forces in southwestern Missouri. It all amounted to one of the costliest failures the Confederacy experienced, for these Confederates left unfulfilled an offensive opportunity the like of which would never appear again. The critical factor seems to have been the lack of a supreme Confederate commander on the spot. Polk, the only military figure available with the necessary rank, never left Memphis. His efforts to control and direct Hardee and Pillow were completely ineffectual.

Meanwhile, at Hardee's camp in Greenville the nucleus was formed for the famous Hardee-Cleburne division. The men were rigidly disciplined and were allowed few idle moments. Hardee personally supervised regimental instruction, first drilling Cleburne's regiment and

---

25 *Official Records*, III, 685; G. J. Pillow to L. P. Walker, September 1, 1861, in L. P. Walker Papers, 1861–68 (Duke University Library).
26 Davis to L. Polk, September 2, 1861, in Leonidas Polk Papers, 1860–64 (Duke University Library).
27 *Official Records*, III, 688.
28 *Ibid.*, 396; J. F. Henry to G. A. Henry, August 31, 1861, in G. A. Henry Papers (Southern Historical Collection).

then Hindman's. Following the war General Basil W. Duke maintained that during the weeks at Greenville the rough Arkansas volunteers developed into excellent fighting material. Moreover it was here that

I first saw and made the acquaintance . . . of two, who were subsequently ranked only a little below the ablest and most famous of the Confederate leaders. The two were Hardee and Cleburne.

General Hardee was a thoroughly educated and exceedingly accomplished soldier. No one in the old army, perhaps, was more perfectly versed in either the more important or the minutest details of professional knowledge. I believe that it is admitted that he had no superior as a corps commander, and his capacity for handling troops on the battlefield and his skill as a tactician were unsurpassed. . . . I have sometimes heard General Hardee characterized as a martinet. This is not just to him. He believed in careful discipline and was sometimes strict in enforcing its essentials. But he was never harsh, and was not only solicitous for the comfort of his men, but entertained the kindest feeling for them. He was a handsome man of a very striking figure, and extremely courteous and pleasant in manner.[29]

Hardee broke camp at Greenville on August 28 and began the retrograde movement to Pitman's Ferry, which he reached on September 2. Pitman's Ferry proved a more profitable encampment than Greenville, in that men began to join Hardee's command in large numbers. By September 16 he had five thousand infantry and eight hundred cavalry. With his twelve artillery pieces he had "a good corps d'armee complete within itself. I have just mustered a regiment into service and will soon muster another." On another occasion he wrote, "We labor under great difficulties but don't dispair of accomplishing some good."

The opportunity to do so seemed much better east of the Mississippi, however. In a letter to Mrs. Shover he expressed his desire to transfer his brigade to the neighboring theater: "I am, entre nous, particularly desirous to bring my command to the other side of the Mississippi. It is there, in my opinion, the great battles for our independence must be fought and in these I wish to participate. I am desirous, also, that Gen'l Sydney [sic] Johnston should be sent to command in the valley of the Mississippi, he has more experience than Gen'l Polk & will inspire greater confidence." [30]

Events soon gratified General Hardee's desires. On September 6

29 Duke, *Reminiscences*, 67–68.
30 Hardee to Mrs. Shover, September 4, 6, 1861, in Shover Letters.

Grant seized Belmont, Missouri, directly across the Mississippi from Columbus, Kentucky. Polk considered this an act of aggression and dispatched a force to hold Columbus, conceded to be the strongest natural position on the river. Polk was soon superseded by General Albert Sidney Johnston, who had been Hardee's commanding officer in the Second Cavalry. Johnston, who probably possessed the greatest military reputation of any Southerner in 1861, had been assigned to the Western Department of the Confederacy with extensive powers. He decided not to withdraw Polk's forces from Kentucky and quickly dispatched General Simon Bolivar Buckner to occupy Bowling Green, Kentucky, a critical railroad junction and a strong defensive point.

The race for position and possession was on. Grant captured strategic Paducah, the Confederates moved through Cumberland Gap, and from every direction troops poured into the demoralized state.

The Confederacy required Hardee's brigade in Kentucky, and General Polk lost little time in ordering Hardee to cross the Mississippi. Hardee's brigade began its movement toward the Mississippi on September 19. Cleburne's regiment preceded the main body, repairing the roads to permit the passage of the wagon train. Hardee decided not to transport his command by water, preferring to use the overland march as a training exercise.

In Kentucky General Johnston hurriedly made preparations to meet the enemy. The line of defense extended completely across Kentucky. Bowling Green, the center of this line, dominated central Kentucky south of the Green River. Located in a natural amphitheater, the town could be supplied and reinforced easily from Tennessee by road, rail, and water. To the front of Bowling Green stretched the Barren and Green rivers, formidable obstacles for an advancing enemy. Although this position in central Kentucky offered defense in depth, two segments of Johnston's line promised opportunities to the attacker: eastern Kentucky and the Tennessee-Cumberland line, which bisected the theater vertically.

On October 4, 1861, General Buckner, commander at Bowling Green, reported the advance of about fourteen thousand Union troops. As Buckner had less than six thousand men, he pressed for reinforcements. With his center threatened, Johnston decided to weaken his left flank at Columbus. He had to do this, because he could count only on a negligible number of effective troops to be brought up in time from Tennessee. For the reinforcements to be transferred from Columbus to Bowling Green, Johnston chose Hardee's brigade.[31]

Hardee arrived in Columbus on October 6. He allowed his men two days' rest and then began the movement to Bowling Green by rail. Because of incompetent railroad management and a treacherous river crossing, the transfer took two days longer than anticipated, and all of Hardee's personal baggage was lost. In addition to these annoyances, Hardee suffered a more serious blow, for a regimental commander was drowned.[32] When the train reached Russellville, Kentucky, the citizens "called lustily for Hardee. He appeared upon the platform of the cars. He spoke to them thus: 'I am . . . no speaking man; if I were, the time for speaking has passed by. The sword is the only argument. I believe you are in earnest in the cause, and hope to see every one of you up the road soon, with your knapsacks on your back and your gun on your shoulder.' Such is the gallant Hardee."

Hardee's arrival in Bowling Green also stirred up interest. People turned out to see him, "his brave and daring toothpick boys," and the large Indian scouting party that he had recruited in Arkansas. A reporter for the Nashville *Republican Banner* describes Hardee as "about fifty years old, has strong marked features, and possesses an air of decisive command. . . . His manner, though stern, is restless. . . . He is about medium size, with a singularly fine muscular development, which can withstand the varying vicissitudes of any sort of a campaign." [33]

General Hardee found the streets of Bowling Green flooded by streams of refugees. Kentucky political figures jammed the boarding houses, and newly enlisted messengers galloped furiously hither and thither carrying messages of the enemy's movements. On October 11 Hardee went forward to the advanced line at Green River. He positioned Hindman's regiment along the river, and he tried to determine the nature of the reported enemy advance against Bowling Green. Reliable scouts soon confirmed Buckner's information about the enemy. Hardee thereupon wired Johnston in Nashville that his presence was needed, but Johnston took no action. Reinforcements were also needed, for Hardee's and Buckner's forces together numbered

---

31 *Official Records*, IV, 412–13, 449.
32 G. K. Miller to Celestine Miller, October 8, 1861, in George Knox Miller Papers (Southern Historical Collection); Hardee to Mrs. Shover, October 11, 1861, in Shover Letters.
33 Nashville *Republican Banner*, October 15, 28, 1861.

less than twelve thousand.[34] Furthermore, the troops at Bowling Green lacked arms and supplies. The equipment they did have was so varied that logistics became a nightmare. Secretary of War Judah P. Benjamin compounded the problem by refusing to allow Johnston's army to draw upon the stores stockpiled at their natural supply point, Nashville, because these supplies were needed for the Confederacy's first army in Virginia.[35]

Despite the fact that the Confederates lacked men and supplies, Hardee decided to counter the enemy advance with an offensive movement. He wired Johnston for permission, but Johnston vacillated, first consenting, then refusing, then consenting. When Johnston finally agreed, Hardee pushed Hindman's regiment forward on October 15. Hindman's men soon encountered rain and the roads turned to mud. By the time the column reached the Barren River, it was impassable. With the element of surprise lost, Hardee stopped the advance. Disappointed, he wrote, "The enemy fled, but for the rise I would have been on them before daylight & captured the entire party. . . . What a charming introduction to Kentucky!" The movement did have positive results, however, for the Federal force under General Ward discontinued its advance and retreated to Muldraugh's Hill.

Even though Hardee had failed to snip off the exposed Federal advanced elements, he was compensated personally on October 21 with his promotion to major general. "As it was unsolicited by myself or friends, it was gratifying," he wrote. With the promotion to division commander, Hardee set about organizing his division. For his brigade commanders he chose three of his regimental commanders, Cleburne, Hindman, and R. G. Shaver. The three new brigades contained eight Arkansas, two Tennessee, and one Mississippi regiments.[36]

To capture the fancy of his men and to signalize their new organizational loyalty, Hardee designed a flag for his division. It had a blue field with a silver full moon in the center, and with "crossed cannon

---

34 Little Rock *Arkansas True Democrat*, October 12, 1861; Official Records, IV, 412–13, 444.
35 Hardee to W. W. Mackall, October 29, 1861, in Hardee Military Service Record; Edwin Porter Thompson, *History of the Orphan Brigade* (Louisville, 1898), 49; *Official Records*, IV, 444.
36 Hardee to Mrs. Shover, October 23, 1861, in Shover Letters; *Official Records*, IV, 336, 448; Raleigh *North Carolina Standard*, October 23, 1861; Wilmington (N.C.) *Daily Journal*, October 22, 1861; D. C. Govan to wife, October 15, 1861, in Govan Papers.

inverted" within the moon. Later in the war when Cleburne commanded the division, it was permitted "at its urgent request" to retain its unique emblem. "This was the only division in the Confederate service allowed to carry into action other than the national colors, and friend and foes soon learned to watch the course of the blue flag that marked where Cleburne was in the battle." [37]

To assist him in organizing and training his command, Hardee sought out former United States regular army officers or West Point cadets who had resigned and who happened to be in the state regiments. Sometimes when he found a capable young officer, Hardee had him appointed to his staff either as a drillmaster or an inspector general.[38] Several talented but inexperienced men, such as Jason M. Fairbanks, were also given opportunities in staff positions, but usually in the assistant adjutant general's office. Fairbanks, who served as Hardee's secretary, found the work much more demanding than he had anticipated.

I am not obliged to go to work at the Papers & Business before 9 o'clock in the morning but from that time until 11 at night there is a constant arrival and departure of couriers, orderlies and messengers. The papers have to pass through my hands first for examination and assortment. The genl is occupied every moment giving audience, hearing grievances, regulating irregularities etc. He never denies himself not even to the humblest private in the Ranks, and by consequence he is very much beloved by all the soldiers, high and low, and can count on them with confidence when the conflict comes.
                                        . . . . . .
Great regularity and system pervades every department—and everything goes on like clock work.[39]

During this period of organization Hardee remained on the Green River, constantly sending out reconnaissance patrols and raiding parties. He directed his subordinates to conduct frequent marches to harden the men and give them experience. These excursions had the desired effect and also kept the enemy off balance.

Hindman's screening force also succeeded in its assignment, for Sherman complained about the scantiness of information that filtered

37 William Joseph Hardee, "Biographical Sketch of Major-General Patrick R. Cleburne," in *Southern Historical Society Papers*, XXI (1903), 162; Thomas Benton Roy, "Odds and Ends of Reminiscences," in Thomas M. Owen Collection (Alabama State Department of Archives and History).
38 T. Claiborne to wife, November 23, 1861, in Thomas Claiborne Letters and Reminiscences, 1849-1929 (Southern Historical Collection).
39 J. M. Fairbanks to G. R. Fairbanks, January 18, 1862, in Jason Massey Fairbanks Letters, 1855-68, in possession of Mrs. T. E. Dudney, Sewanee, Tenn.

through concerning Johnston's strength and position. As November opened, however, Johnston and Hardee grew apprehensive about Hindman's position and ordered him to draw nearer to Bowling Green. Hindman did so, destroying the railroad and telegraph lines as he retired. Hardee positioned him at Rocky Hill Station, where he could still mask the main Confederate force and protect the avenues of approach from Green River. Hardee's other brigades remained close to Bowling Green: Cleburne occupied a valley five miles away, and Shaver snuggled cozily within the town's fortifications.

Bowling Green appeared safe at the moment, but anxiety existed about East Tennessee, where the steady approach of General George H. Thomas threatened Johnston's flank. Hardee proposed to strike this force: "My own feeble voice if called on will be to pursue and fight, march rapidly, whip the enemy, then turn back and give battle to the foe which may be in front. In war much is gained by activity. Napoleon used to say he gained more victories by the legs of his soldiers than by their bayonets. I am glad the responsibility does not rest with me, it is weighty and I would not bear it if I could." [40]

Hardee found himself to be more comfortable in preparing his division to fight. He did this in the careful, systematic manner that became synonymous with his name. The regiments drilled daily, and the division held reviews almost every week. The new brigade commanders experienced difficulty in adjusting to the difference between regimental and brigade drill. Although Hindman studied his manual intently, he still had to acknowledge his inability to drill his command and asked Hardee to drill it until he felt more confident. Cleburne fared better, winning Hardee's approval as a drillmaster and organizer. [41]

Hardee also carefully rotated the field training of his brigades. Shaver's and Cleburne's brigades made routine forced marches to nearby towns to toughen the men and also to deceive the enemy. He added to the effect of the training marches by disseminating false information. In November Hardee sent one force to Morgantown and Cleburne to Jamestown, and the repercussions surprised even Hardee. Sherman thought that Cleburne's command represented the advance guard of a sweeping movement toward Louisville and Cincinnati.

40　Hardee to Mrs. Shover, November 9, 1861, in Shover Letters.
41　J. M. Fairbanks to G. R. Fairbanks, January 31, 1862, in Fairbanks Letters; Hardee to Mrs. Shover, November 9, 1861, in Shover Letters; Hardee, "Cleburne," *loc. cit.*, 152; *Official Records*, IV, 531.

Even General Henry Halleck in St. Louis thought that Hardee intended to cross the Ohio. As a result Thomas was recalled from southeastern Kentucky. General Albion Schoepf, advancing in eastern Kentucky against General Felix Zollicoffer, feared a flank attack and fell back precipitately, in a retreat generally referred to as the "Wild Cat Stampede." A Northern newspaper remarked that the retreat was worse than that following Bull Run. "The stampede was the result of General Hardee's expedition from Bowling Green, having been reported as advancing with one hundred thousand men. . . . We have no heart to comment upon such imbecility." [42]

Schoepf's stampede, coupled with Sherman's failure to take aggressive action and reports that he was suffering from nervous disorders, contributed to the appointment of a new Union commander in Kentucky, Don Carlos Buell. Buell stepped up the offensive. He intended to use his main force in central Kentucky to check Johnston's army while a column penetrated East Tennessee. Another column would move on Gallatin, two flotilla columns would advance up the Tennessee and Cumberland rivers, and a fifth force would demonstrate before Columbus. To oppose this projected offensive by nearly 100,000 Federals, Johnston had 13,000 men at Columbus under Polk, a few thousand along the Tennessee and Cumberland under Tilghman, his own force of about 20,000 at Bowling Green, 3,000 under Zollicoffer advancing into eastern Kentucky, and 2,800 under Humphrey Marshall in the extreme southeastern corner of the state.

As the Union forces gathered for the offensive, matters in Bowling Green remained quiet. The first snow had fallen by November 24, and the thousands of recruits felt the need for adequate clothing. Hardee labored unsuccessfully to provide them. In desperation he enlisted the help of Felicia Shover in Memphis in converting blankets into overcoats. Mrs. Shover and her friends found hundreds of blankets, but even so, many more were needed. Finally Hardee abandoned the idea, declaring that blankets were more necessary than overcoats.[43]

Hardee also worried about his children in St. Augustine. Enemy forces threatened the town, and it appeared that his family would be uprooted at any time. "What are [we] to do should this atrocious war

42 *Official Records,* IV, 350, 444; VII, 444; Tarboro (N.C.) *Southerner,* November 30, 1861, quoting Cincinnati *Commercial,* November 18, 1861; Edward Alfred Pollard, *The First Year of the War* (2d ed., Richmond, 1862), 176.
43 Hardee to Mrs. Shover, November 21, December 4, 1861, in Shover Letters.

continue fifteen months longer, unless the blockade be raised?" he wrote to Mrs. Shover. "I dislike to look the future full in the face, it looks to me lowering & dark. God in his mercy may bring us deliverance and I hope will."

Hardee's concerns increased in December. On December 4 General Johnston gave him command of the Central Army of Kentucky and that part of Tennessee and Kentucky north of the Cumberland River. Johnston "found the labor greater, with his other duties than he could well perform. I was well satisfied with the command I had and did not desire the additional responsibility of comd'g an Army. You will think me very unambitious and I believe it is so." Hardee was not granted complete operational control over the army, however; Johnston still issued a few orders and also directed that sudden enemy movements be reported directly to himself.[44]

On December 7 Hardee received an opportunity to strike at the enemy. Buell had ordered the division of A. McD. McCook to take a position near Green River. As McCook moved up, Hardee decided to embarrass his old West Point subordinate. He sent a promising Kentucky cavalry captain, John Hunt Morgan, to burn the Bacon's Creek bridge, which Morgan did successfully. To threaten McCook's flank and to seal off East Tennessee from invasion, Hardee wished to attack swiftly the enemy force in eastern Kentucky. He proposed to send Buckner's division to feint toward McCook and then march rapidly to Columbia. Once Columbia fell, Zollicoffer could come forward and occupy it. As to the defense of Bowling Green, Cleburne and Shaver could hold it until Buckner returned.

While Johnston deliberated this plan of operations, McCook advanced. On December 17 one of his brigades crossed the river. In accordance with Hardee's orders to be aggressive, Hindman struck at once. He attacked, however, with only a fraction of his command, and after sharp fighting, he was repulsed. Buell quickly reinforced his Green River bridgehead and secured a permanent lodgement. The situation alarmed Johnston, and he requested reinforcements. The War Department complied, sending the brigade of the ex-Secretary of War, John B. Floyd.

General Zollicoffer also contributed to Johnston's anxiety by reporting an enemy advance and calling for reinforcements. To remedy the situation, Johnston turned to Hardee's proposed attack on Colum-

44 Hardee to Mrs. Shover, December 5, 1861, in Shover Letters; *Official Records*, VII, 734.

bia. He modified it by increasing the attacking force by one brigade and by shifting the objective from Columbia to Skegg's Creek. This operational blueprint never materialized, however, and joined the growing file of stillborn Confederate offensives. Meanwhile, Zolli-coffer's position grew more perilous.[45]

Christmas temporarily relieved the uneasiness in Kentucky. General Hardee spent the day with his staff, who prepared dinner at headquarters. Mrs. Shover provided the delicacies, salad and Old Harmony sherry, which made the dinner a success.[46] During the Christmas season Hardee's headquarters became famous as a social center:

Last evening Genl. H. was here & we were teasing him about the number of lady visitors he was honored with at his house—(for you must know he is the ladies' man among the officers here)—when he told us quite an amusing incident, or rather "smart speech" of a Miss Bang of Nashville who was here a few days ago. It seems Hardee & other officers at his Head Quarters had been very attentive to her and the party that was with her. . . . When she was going away and taking leave of all . . . he kissed her hand—when she said, "Genl. you did that so sweetly you should teach your aide"! The idea with her being probably this—that such gallantry would better become younger men—but he did not so understand her.[47]

Hardee's Christmas would have been tinctured with misgivings if he had known of his children's plight in St. Augustine. His old friend, Frances Kirby Smith, was a neighbor of Anna Dummett and the Hardee children and was aware of the difficulties that confronted them: "Poor Anna, has the charge of a large family and is much perplexed as to what to do—her mother so infirm, so many children—the Madisons & Hardees—and quite a number of young darkies. She says what shall I do, I am *out of corn*,—have been all around, can find only a small quantity at two dollars a bushel. . . . She told me the Aunt & Cousins did not think the Federals could take Savannah, yet they had their trunks packed, and held themselves in readiness to move at short notice to the upper Country. They are better off than we are—for we must cross the St. Johns to get any where." [48]

As the year 1862 opened, the Federals seemed to be preparing to attack in every section of Kentucky. The Green River line had been

45 *Official Records*, VII, 14-21, 758-59, 781, 786; LII, Pt. 2, p. 238.
46 Hardee to Mrs. Shover, December 25, 1861, in Shover Letters.
47 J. F. Gilmer to wife, January, 1862, in Jeremy F. Gilmer Papers, 1769-1895 (Southern Historical Collection).
48 Mrs. Kirby Smith to Kirby Smith, December 2, 1861, in Kirby Smith Papers.

punctured at several points, Halleck threatened Polk at Columbus, and Thomas menaced Zollicoffer in eastern Kentucky. Johnston believed that if he could hold on a little longer, winter would put an end to these activities. The troops from Tennessee would come up in the spring and restore the military situation. Heavy weather set in, as Johnston had hoped. In January the roads became "one continuous quagmire," and the streams became swollen and virtually impassable. Johnston believed the vulnerable sector of his line of defense to be in central Kentucky, and when both the Union and Confederate armies in that area became mired in the mud, he drew a breath of relief.[49]

General Buell, however, realized the significance of the Tennessee-Cumberland line and together with Halleck formulated movements up these water courses. "The center, that is, the Cumberland and Tennessee where the railroad crosses them, is now the most vulnerable point. I regard it as the most important strategic point in the whole field of operations," he wrote.[50] General Hardee agreed. "We are at a loss to know their next movement. From indications I do not believe it is designed to march on us in front, we have put so many obstructions in the way he will not attempt it, but will approach by coming up the Cumberland and Tennessee rivers. This I have always thought their safest and most practicable route. A movement up the Tennessee would now seem to be their objective to be followed by Buell's advance up the Cumberland. The plot is thickening and we shall have heavy work on this line." [51]

On January 19 the winter respite ended suddenly, when the Confederate right collapsed. Thomas administered a crushing blow to the forces of Zollicoffer and G. B. Crittenden at Mill Springs. Reinforcements were needed at once in that quarter, but Polk at Columbus also cried out for assistance, for some forty to fifty thousand Federals, he believed, were ready to assault his position. The stunned Confederates received the next and heaviest blow not at Columbus, however, but at Fort Henry on the Tennessee. Grant had maneuvered up the river and had found Tilghman's handful incapable of real resistance. In the meantime Halleck sent forward every available man to exploit this advantage. Fort Henry fell on February 6. Its fall precipitated a chain of events that cleaned the Tennessee of Confederate river traffic, destroyed the shipbuilding facilities, deprived Johnston of great stock-

49 *Official Records*, VII, 792–94, 812–13.
50 *Ibid.*, 521.
51 Hardee to Mrs. Shover, January 23, 1862, in Shover Letters.

piles of provisions and equipment, and implanted Union soldiers in north Alabama.

To meet this crisis President Davis sent the "Hero of Manassas" to Bowling Green. Beauregard arrived on February 4, fell ill, and confined himself to his quarters. The day after the fall of Fort Henry, Hardee, Johnston, and Beauregard conferred, to decide their course of action. The three officers concluded their meeting unanimously resolved that "preparations should at once be made for the removal of this army to Nashville." The troops under Floyd at Clarksville were to be moved to the south side of the Cumberland. The forces under Johnston and Polk would be separated if Fort Donelson fell, and the two commands were to be operated independently, Polk on the west side of the Tennessee, Johnston on the east. Columbus would be abandoned, although Island No. 10 and Fort Pillow were to be defended to the "last extremity." The three generals planned a line of retreat for the Columbus force as far south as Jackson, Mississippi.[52]

The decision reached by Hardee, Johnston, and Beauregard was sound in the light of the situation as they knew it. The entire western line of defense had been shattered by the collapse on the right at Mill Springs and the puncture at Fort Henry. If Fort Donelson fell, the entire army in central Kentucky would be cut off. The fluid state of events, however, required powerful corrective measures. Hardee, Johnston, and Beauregard answered this crisis negatively, although one must bear in mind that they did not know the enemy's immediate objectives.

Hardee set to work to evacuate the Central Army of Kentucky and its supplies. He sent a confidential dispatch to Hindman disclosing the decision and ordering him to draw nearer Bowling Green and to send immediately to the rear all of the sick and the baggage. He also advised Hindman to "talk loudly of an advance as the only means of extricating us, that is, if you talk at all." [53]

General Johnston had directed Floyd to the vicinity of Clarksville as a precautionary measure. At Clarksville Floyd could aid either the river forts or Bowling Green, whichever was threatened. Hardee controlled Floyd's movements at this time, and both Johnston and Hardee

---

52 Alfred Roman, *The Military Operations of General Beauregard*, 2 vols. (New York, 1884), I, 213; John Beatty, *Memoirs of a Volunteer, 1861–1863*, ed. Harvey S. Ford (New York, 1946), 85; *Official Records*, VII, 861–62; Hardee to Mrs. Shover, February 25, 1862, in Shover Letters; Beauregard Diary, February 4, 7, 1862.

53 *Official Records*, LII, Pt. 2, p. 265.

agreed to allow Floyd to make the disposition for the defense of Clarksville, Fort Donelson, and the Cumberland River at his own discretion.[54]

The army at Bowling Green began retiring in echelon on February 11. Hardee hurried the removal of stores, hoping that the cavalry screen and Hindman's obstructions would give him sufficient time. He also worried about crossing the Cumberland River. If the enemy captured Fort Donelson and sent their river fleet upstream, a crossing could be hazardous.

At noon on February 14, Hardee's time ran out. Although the enemy could not cross the Barren River, they brought up artillery and began to shell Bowling Green. Most of the shells exploded near the depot, where Hardee was feverishly loading one last train. After destroying the supplies that he could not take, Hardee and the rear guard evacuated the town at 3:30 P.M. The Federals who occupied Bowling Green found a great many burned supplies, a few damaged locomotives, and a considerable supply of beef and pork. Hardee maintained that the loss was "unimportant for if we had taken them to Nashville we would have lost them there." [55]

Buell allowed Hardee's men to withdraw in peace while his men reveled in the abandoned Confederate stores. The Confederates should have retired to Nashville by rail, but the overloaded railroad system broke down, and most of the troops had to march. On the road to Nashville the men suffered greatly. The temperature dropped as rapidly as had Confederate morale, and the mercury hovered near the bottom of the thermometer.

Buell decided to pursue and prodded his men forward. Johnston ordered Hardee to speed up the retreating column, "as rapidly as is consistent with an orderly march." Finally the Army of Central Kentucky reached the Cumberland, crossed the river with difficulty, since the bridge had been destroyed, and moved through the city. Crowds pressed close to the soldiers, taunting them for their cowardice, and begging them to turn on the enemy. Hardee marched his men out the Murfreesboro Pike and encamped. Rain poured down

54 W. J. Hardee to J. B. Floyd, February 6, 1862, in John Buchanan Floyd Papers, 1836–62 (Duke University Library); endorsement by Hardee on letter from C. Clark to S. Cooper, January 24, 1862, in Office of the Secretary of War, Letters Received; *Official Records*, LII, Pt. 2, p. 269.
55 *Official Records*, VII, 419, 432, 881; J. M. Fairbanks to G. R. Fairbanks, February, 1862, in Fairbanks Letters; Beatty, *Memoirs*, 85; Hardee to Mrs. Shover, February 25, 1862, in Shover Letters.

upon the soldiers, and irritated and frustrated, they turned on their officers. They demanded to be allowed to fight the enemy and implored the generals to halt the retreat. "They threatened to mutiny if not allowed to meet the enemy; but this spirit was overcome by speeches from Gens. Pillow, Floyd, and Hardee." [56]

Back in Nashville chaos prevailed. The state and city officials had lost control, and Johnston decided to send Hardee back to the city to supervise the evacuation of government stores. The enormity of the task at Nashville can hardly be compared with that at Bowling Green, however. Nashville factories produced considerable quantities of many different types of equipment and munitions. For example, the Claiborne Machinery Works supplied the Confederacy with fifteen guns and ten tons of shot and shell per week.[57] Precious, but heavy, rifling tools and machinery had to be saved. The government warehouses filled with equipment had to be emptied. All of this had to be accomplished while mobs of civilians and soldiers were pillaging warehouses and obstructing attempts to remove government stores.

Hardee did more than attempt to rescue the military treasures. He also received reports and sent orders to local commanders on the Cumberland and in middle Tennessee. These telegrams show Hardee in the role of a central co-ordinator. Johnston, as far as can be determined, remained outside of the city. He issued only a few orders, and several of his subordinates did not know where to locate him.[58]

Matters grew worse in Nashville after the news of the surrender of Donelson. A mob came to Hardee's headquarters and shouted for the generals to come out. Only after Hardee and Floyd had made speeches to the citizens did the mob disperse.[59] The dissatisfaction degenerated into panic as it became evident that the Confederates were not going to defend Nashville. Refugees clogged the roads leading south. After the rifling machinery and most of the other supplies had been shipped to Chattanooga, the rear guard moved to Murfreesboro to join the rest of the army.

56 *Official Records,* VII, 881; John M. Taylor, "Twenty-Seventh Tennessee Infantry," and D. J. Noblitt, "Forty-Fourth Tennessee Infantry," in *Military Annals of Tennessee,* 417, 530.
57 *Official Records,* IV, 481.
58 *Ibid.,* VII, 890; J. W. Fisher to Hardee, February 19, 1862, T. C. Hindman to Hardee, February 19, 1862, V. L. Stevenson to Hardee, February 19, 1862, G. J. Pillow to Hardee, February 19, 1862, in Floyd Papers.
59 William Preston Johnston, *The Life of General Albert Sidney Johnston* (New York, 1878), 496.

Here at Murfreesboro Johnston attempted to consolidate and sta-bilize his command. To strengthen the department as a whole, he brought the remnants of Crittenden's battered brigade to Murfrees-boro, ordered the evacuation of Columbus, and granted high-ranking officers the right to appropriate civilian property for military use. Johnston's immediate command totaled about seventeen thousand men, with the addition of Crittenden's brigade and the Fort Donelson survivors. Within this army Johnston created three divisions, assign-ing Hardee the first, Crittenden the second, and Pillow the third. Hardee's division contained ten regiments of infantry, two regiments of cavalry, and three artillery batteries. Hindman and Cleburne com-manded Hardee's two brigades.[60]

Johnston's army remained at Murfreesboro for about two weeks. Hardee spent most of this time drilling his division and re-equipping his men. He dispatched scouting parties to the front, ranging from Nashville to Carthage, Tennessee. He also sent Captain Morgan out on numerous combat patrols and intelligence missions. He directed Morgan to remain close to the Federals at Nashville and to keep him informed as to what they were doing. Hardee also had Morgan send spies into Nashville and had him supply him with enemy newspapers, from which he often gleaned much information.[61]

In the latter part of February Johnston decided to move his army farther south to unite with Beauregard's retreating forces across the Tennessee River. On February 28, just prior to the departure from Murfreesboro, teenage Alice Ready watched a review of Hardee's division. After the review her father asked Generals Hardee and Breckinridge to pass the evening at their home, and Alice recorded the event in her diary: "They accepted, Gen. H. came into town with us, we have seen a great deal of him, . . . his evenings are always spent with us, and we have found him charming—he is a tall fine looking man, quite militaire, between 45 & 50 years of age, he is very unas-suming and affable in his manners, perfectly at home here, calls for whatever he wants, pets Ella [her older sister] and me a good deal seems to regard me as a child. Sister as a young lady."

The next day Hardee returned and dined with the Readys. He re-vealed that the army was leaving and invited them out to his camp.

60 Bromfield Lewis Ridley, *Battles and Sketches of the Army of Tennessee* (Mexico, Mo., 1906), 68.
61 Hardee to W. W. Mackall, February 26, 1862, in Hardee Military Service Record; Hardee to J. H. Morgan, February 28, 1862, in John Hunt Morgan Papers, 1840–70 (Southern Historical Collection).

The girls accepted, and Alice tumbled into the carriage behind her sister.

We drove up to [the General's tent]. . . . There was a large log fire in front of the door; we went in the tent to see how things were arranged, found a goods box inverted for a table, with dishes on it, the General's bed rolled up in a bundle—and one large arm chair completed the furniture. We took our seats by the fire and had a delightful time, the scene was picturesque in the extreme. . . . The band play[ed] . . . a beautiful, heart stirring piece. It was . . . just growing dark, all around far as we could see were bright camp fires. With figures standing round, distinguishable as men from the light thrown out from the fires. . . . The General went to his trunk and brought forth, as a trophy of our visit . . . an elegant blue satin Mouchoir case with his initials embroidered in white, we only waited then for a cup of thin coffee, which I must confess was not worth waiting for. . . .

The general soon escorted the girls home and then returned to camp. He again stopped by the Readys' the next morning. Following breakfast the feminine section of the Ready household was thrilled when Captain Morgan rode up and gave the report of his latest raid to General Hardee. Then Hardee announced that he must leave them. "Before the General left he took the comforter from his neck, which he had worn during the bombardment of Bowling Green and tied it around my neck, asking me to 'wear a Soldier's comfort.' Bless his old heart. I love him dearly."

Hardee did not forget Alice Ready. During the following week he sent her several "very sweet and precious" notes. These made Alice's mind wander: "I believe he came to the conclusion that I would do very well to fill a place on his staff. . . . Oh! that the Soldiers were back again." [62]

Many loyal Confederates shared Miss Ready's sentiments, which she demonstrated by sending General Hardee a "geranium leaf with some violets." A number of Southerners denounced Albert Sidney Johnston, but generally they did not include Hardee in their attacks. The criticism of Johnston was severe and widespread. One observer claimed that "no other general of the Confederate armies, except General Polk, suffered so much at the hands of the press and the politicians, who assumed to speak for the people." [63] One of Hardee's

62 Alice C. Ready Diary, 1860–62 (Southern Historical Collection), March 3, 5, 1862.
63 J. M. Keating, "Tennessee for Four Years the Theater of War, 1861–1865," in *Annals of Tennessee*, 28.

colonels, according to Alice Ready, "said he had defended [Johnston] as long as he could, but believed now that he was either a fool or a traitor, left Gen. Hardee to bring up the rear of the retreat blind-folded, took no notice of the many and important dispatches which were sent to him." [64]

A defense of Johnston's actions lies beyond the scope of this study, and would involve speculation on many variables that Johnston seems to have misjudged. Colonel Munford probably came close to the real reason for Johnston's failures when he stated that Johnston "had no army." [65] One might suggest that some of the blame could be laid upon those Confederates who demanded the security of hundreds of nonstrategic positions. If the garrisons frozen at these scattered points had been concentrated, Johnston would have had an adequate instrument with which to defend the South. Johnston himself accepted the criticism of his countrymen with equanimity: "The test of merit in my profession with the people is success. It is a hard rule, but I think it right." [66]

Hardee defended Johnston against personal attacks. He asked his friends particularly to kill the ugly lie that Johnston drank too heavily. One must infer what Hardee thought of Johnston as an army commander, for he did not record his sentiments and quieted one of his staff officers who was "excessively denunciatory" of Johnston, "as anything coming from him would be regarded as coming from me." However, there appears to have been friction between Hardee and Johnston. Hardee, discouraged and distraught, wrote to Mrs. Shover from Murfreesboro: "I forbear to write about our movement from Nashville and our present condition. In my judgment nothing can save us except the presence of the President, who ought to come here, assume command, and call on people to rally to his standard. We have lost Kentucky and may lose Tennessee. I don't despair of our cause. If we can make head against the villians [sic] until May, we are safe. . . . I have been more broken down in the last ten days than at any other time in my life. . . . This is the darkest hour of my fortune." [67]

The Confederates began their retreat from Murfreesboro on Feb-

---

64 Ready Diary, March 13, 1862.
65 W. P. Johnston, *Johnston*, 328.
66 *Official Records*, VII, 259.
67 Hardee to Mrs. Shover, February 25, March 22, April 3, 1862, in Shover Letters.

ruary 28. Grant's army, on the Tennessee, roughly paralleled their course. Whereas Grant's men traveled by water, the Confederates used the railroads as far as they could and marched the rest of the way. The Confederate line of retreat, running through Shelbyville, Tennessee, to Huntsville and Decatur, Alabama, enabled them to save their provisions and to protect southeast Tennessee from any ambitions Buell might have had.

When Hardee reached Shelbyville, he halted his division in a defensive position, remaining for over a week to guard the great quantity of supplies gathered at that point. In Shelbyville Hardee encountered the fiery Tennessee Unionist "Parson" William G. Brownlow. Although Brownlow had a pass from the War Department to Nashville, Hardee ordered him to go to Alabama or Mississippi, because "his presence at Nashville . . . would have been extremely prejudicial to our cause." [68] Brownlow, of course, did not appreciate Hardee's position and blamed his detention on the influence of Tennessee secessionists on "the already corrupt and poisoned mind of this humbug of an officer, Hardee." [69]

As commander of the rear guard Hardee demonstrated his knowledge of the proper employment of cavalry. Johnston had ordered him to destroy every bridge over which the enemy might follow. According to General Buell, Hardee thoroughly accomplished this task. Hardee also had his cavalry conduct reconnaissance and harassing raids, with John Hunt Morgan as his chief instrument. During this period Morgan made some of his most spectacular raids in fulfilling Hardee's assigned missions, although each mission seemed a degree more difficult than the previous one. Morgan's raids were successful militarily, but more than this, they kindled a light of enthusiasm in middle Tennessee, a section that felt that it had been forsaken by the Confederacy. Hardee became Morgan's champion and urged the War Department to promote him. Basil Duke, one of Morgan's ablest lieutenants, declared that Hardee "was very partial to this use of cavalry and was an intelligent, firm believer in its efficacy. He became an ardent friend and advocate of Morgan, so soon as the latter began to develop his remarkable efficiency in this service, warmly encouraged and commended him, and constantly

---

68 Hardee to W. W. Mackall, March 13, 1862, in Hardee Military Service Record.

69 William Gannaway Brownlow, *Sketches of the Rise, Progress, and Decline of Secession* (Philadelphia, 1862), 374–76.

urged his promotion." [70] This attention to the cavalry arm and to enterprising cavalry leaders characterized Hardee's service throughout the war. In 1862 he would have a significant part in the preparation of Joseph Wheeler for responsible cavalry command.

As the rear guard moved south into Alabama, an event occurred in Florida that would have depressed Hardee, yet given him cause to be proud, had he known of it. Federal forces occupied St. Augustine on March 12, and the town capitulated at once. That is, the men capitulated. Sallie Hardee led a group of young women to the center of town and there proceeded to cut down the flag staff. Sallie "struck the first blow, . . . saying that the *Stars & Stripes* should *not* float from that Staff." Soon even Sallie despaired of further resistance, however, and the Hardees, accompanied by Anna Dummett, fled to Orange Springs, Florida.[71]

After the Army of Central Kentucky entered Alabama, their objective became apparent. Corinth, Mississippi, located near the south bank of the Tennessee and midway between Johnston's and Beauregard's armies, seemed the logical place for a junction of the Confederate forces in the West. Furthermore, Corinth was a vital concourse for the remaining bands of steel that bound together the eastern and western sections of the Confederacy. General Hardee stressed Corinth's strategic value: "[it is] important [to the Confederacy as] the center of the railroad communications passing southwardly from the Ohio River, through Western Tennessee, to the Gulf of Mexico, and from the Mississippi River eastwardly to the Atlantic. Marshes and muddy streams in its vicinity rendered it difficult to approach and make it strong and defensible." [72]

Grant was aware of the importance of Corinth and hoped to occupy the town before the Confederates appeared. Although he took Pittsburg Landing on March 17, Grant seemed cautious, probably because of restrictive orders from Halleck. While the Grant of March reacted differently from the Grant of February, the Confederates hurried on—Johnston from the east, Beauregard from the west, and Braxton Bragg and his fresh Pensacola troops from the south.

The Army of Central Kentucky became strung out across northern

---

70 *Official Records*, VII, 679, 911; X, Pt. 2, pp. 6–7, 302; T. Claiborne to wife, March 4, 1862, in Claiborne Letters; Duke, *Reminiscences*, 71.
71 Hardee to Mrs. Shover, April 3, 1862, in Shover Letters.
72 *Official Records*, X, Pt. 1, p. 566.

Alabama as the urgency of the situation drove every unit to exert maximum effort. Hardee remained in Huntsville, hurrying the troops forward. He also sent Morgan out on a major raid into middle Tennessee to retard Buell's march to join Grant at Pittsburg Landing.[73]

Anxious to join the army at Corinth, Hardee was nevertheless detained at Iuka with a highly unpleasant assignment. General Bragg, accustomed to the sight of his Pensacola garrison troops, was distressed by the appearance of Johnston's army. He thought that they could not succeed "against a well-organized foe." Notorious among Johnston's troops were Crittenden's and Carroll's men from east Tennessee. Bragg, who had become Johnston's chief of staff as the Confederate forces consolidated, sent Hardee to Crittenden's camp at Iuka to investigate. Hardee's findings shocked the army. The prominent Crittenden "was ordered to consider himself under arrest for drunkenness. . . . I arrested Brigadier-General Carroll for drunkenness, incompetence and neglect of his command." [74]

Another thing worried Hardee: Johnston had kept Hindman's reliable brigade with him at the head of the column, and Hardee felt that his commander might deprive him of the command of his own division in case of battle. He wrote, "I trust Genl. Johnston will not do me the injustice of separating me from my Division. I have labored hard to discipline and instruct it, and having succeeded well, I would justly complain if not permitted to fight it." [75]

Johnston allayed Hardee's fears when he arrived in Corinth. Moreover, with more professional officers present, such as Beauregard and Bragg, the lax tone of the army gave way to one of stringent regulation. With the Confederate command system tightening, with masses of troops concentrating at Corinth, and with Confederate forces under "Frank" Cheatham and Randall Gipson crowding Grant's army at Pittsburg Landing, the skies seemed to be clearing in the western Confederacy. One smashing victory could set things aright.

73 S. D. Morgan (Hardee staff officer) to J. H. Morgan, March 18, 1862, in Morgan Papers.
74 Don Carlos Seitz, *Braxton Bragg, General of the Confederacy* (Columbia, S.C., 1924), 98; *Official Records*, X, Pt. 2, p. 379.
75 Hardee to Mrs. Shover, March 22, 1861, in Shover Letters.

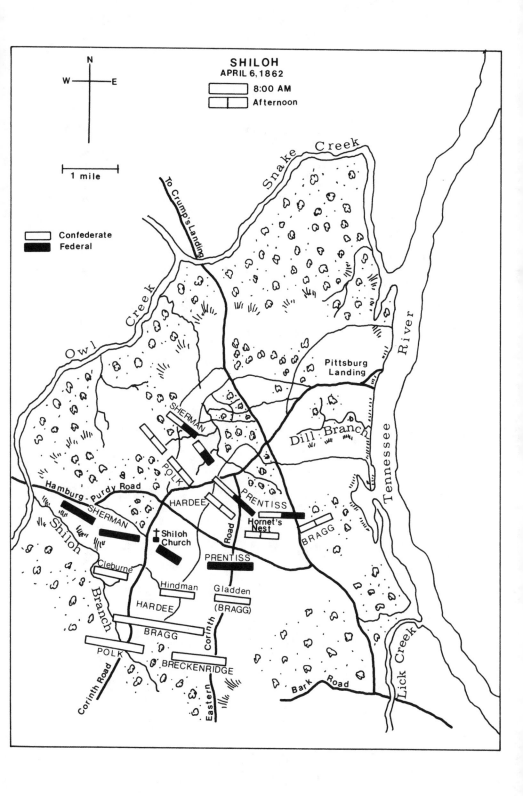

VII

"Thro' Slippery Pools of Blood"

DURING THE last days of March, 1862, the long-awaited concentration of Confederates in the West became a reality. Boxcars filled with
Johnston's and Bragg's men unloaded at Corinth or at nearby points
on the Memphis and Charleston Railroad. Many of the Confederates
who were disgorged from the trains wandered about staring at the
masses of men—more people than most had ever seen before.

Johnston promptly set to work to organize the thousands of arriving soldiers. He entitled his forces the Army of the Mississippi and
divided the army into three corps and a reserve. Polk commanded the
First Corps, Bragg, the Second, and Hardee, the Third. John C. Breckinridge commanded the reserve. Beauregard acted as second in command, and Bragg assumed the duties of chief of staff in addition to
leading his own corps. The entire army numbered about 38,000.[1]

General Bragg and Polk commanded the largest corps, consisting
of six and four brigades respectively. Breckinridge and Hardee led
corps composed of three brigades each. Hardee's Third Corps included seventeen infantry regiments and five batteries of artillery.
Hardee did not formally divide his corps into divisions. Instead, he
organized his men into three brigades commanded by Hindman,
Cleburne, and Sterling A. M. Wood.

The newly created army was destined for an early battle. Across
the Tennessee, Buell began to move southward from Nashville to
unite with Grant at Pittsburg Landing. The Confederates learned
of Buell's approach, and Johnston decided to strike Grant's forces
at Pittsburg before Buell arrived, even though the Confederate preparations were "incomplete and imperfect." On April 1, 1862, John-

---

1 *Official Records*, X, Pt. 2, pp. 370–71, 382; Hardee to Mrs. Shover, April 3,
1862, in Shover Letters.

ston issued a warning order to the army. The three corps and the reserve were to "be placed in readiness for a field movement and to meet the enemy within twenty-four hours." [2]

At 10 P.M. the following day news arrived that transformed the warning order into a battle order. General Cheatham at Bethel, twenty miles away, reported that one of Grant's divisions under General Lew Wallace now confronted him. With Wallace detached, General Beauregard urged Johnston to avail himself of the opportunity and strike Grant's weakened force. Johnston hesitated, but agreed when Bragg supported Beauregard's views. Beauregard quickly sketched out a plan of operations and handed the notes to Colonel Thomas Jordan to be drawn up in a formal order. Jordan first composed a rough march order. It directed the corps commanders to be ready to advance at 6 A.M. the following morning with five days' cooked rations and one hundred rounds of ammunition per man. Jordan then began a draft of the battle order; as a guide he used a copy of Napoleon's order of battle for Waterloo beside him. [3]

Colonel Jordan's messenger awoke Hardee at 1:40 A.M. and delivered the initial order. The immediate preparation of five days' cooked rations presented a problem for Hardee, for he had an insufficient supply of hard bread. He procured more bread, and while the rations were being prepared, he waited for the order to march. By 8 A.M. the expected order had not yet arrived. Hardee wondered about the fate of the order and also about Johnston's intentions: "I suppose if we go at all we shall move to the Tennessee river, where it is supposed the enemy must be in force, the object I take it will be to attack & whip him before he is reinforced by [Buell]." [4]

After breakfast Hardee proceeded to Beauregard's quarters, where he met Johnston, Bragg, and Polk. Beauregard then spread maps before them and outlined the plan of battle. Grant's forces occupied a position with strong natural defenses. He had encamped his five divisions in an irregular perimeter backed against a "range of bold, wooded hills" on the southwest bank of the Tennessee. Pittsburg itself was the shipping point for nearby Purdy and consisted of one house and a grocery at the foot of the bluffs. The terrain in the vicinity was characterized by "rolling uplands, partially cultivated, interspersed with

2 *Official Records,* X, Pt. 2, p. 381.
3 Thomas Jordan, "Notes of a Confederate Staff-Officer at Shiloh," in Robert U. Johnson and Clarence C. Buel (eds.), *Battles and Leaders of the Civil War,* 4 vols. (New York, 1884–87), I, 594–95; hereinafter cited as *Battles and Leaders. Official Records,* X, Pt. 2, p. 283.
4 Hardee to Mrs. Shover, April 3, 1862, in Shover Letters.

copses, and forests, with small fields cultivated or abandoned." [5] Generally, the Union position rested on a plateau rising some ninety feet above the river. Numerous unpredictable creeks crisscrossed the plateau with ravines. Owl Creek to the north and Lick Creek to the south enclosed the position. The only large opening, which was two or three miles wide, faced to the southwest.

Beauregard next pointed out factors to be weighed before launching the attack. The Federals at Pittsburg Landing numbered about thirty-seven thousand after Wallace's division had been subtracted. Reconnaissance reports revealed that the Federals had not thrown up extensive defensive works, and it appeared that the Federal division camps were not aligned in a compact, defensive formation. Although Federal patrols had been active, the Confederates might achieve a tactical surprise. The terrain would impede the maneuver of troops, however. It would render cavalry useless, would limit the role of artillery, and would complicate the control of units larger than regiments. Owl and Lick creeks benefited the attackers by interdicting the battlefield, but they also prohibited a flank attack. Therefore the attack must be made through the opening to the southwest.

This fact influenced the Confederate attack formation. Hardee's corps had operated as a unit in the field for a longer period of time than the other corps, so his corps was selected to deliver the first blow. Upon their arrival at the battlefield the army would deploy in the following manner: Hardee's corps would form the first line. He would rest his left flank on Owl Creek and extend his right toward Lick Creek. A brigade from Bragg's corps would fill the gap between Hardee's right and Lick Creek. Bragg would deploy his corps in a line to the rear of Hardee with a five-hundred-yard interval between them. Breckinridge and Polk would form their corps behind Bragg on either side of the Bark Road, which bisected the area. The general plan was to attack, drive the enemy back from the entrance of the position, then endeavor to turn their left flank, cut them off from the river, and pin them against Owl Creek.

Following the meeting Hardee returned to his headquarters and prepared to advance. He received an order from the chief of staff designating the route of advance and intermediary objective points. Bragg directed him to "move as soon as practicable . . . by way of Ridge and Bark road in the direction of Pittsburg, halting the head of your column to-night at a point beyond the sand hill known as

---

5 *Official Records*, X, Pt. 1, p. 567.

Mickeys." Hardee would then advance at 3 A.M. and deploy before the enemy's positions.[6]

By noon Hardee had put his corps in motion on the Monterey road.[7] The two other corps soon followed on the same or parallel roads. It was a beautiful day. The roadside was "gay with peach blossoms and the perfume of wild flowers." The corps marched on and on, narrowing the twenty-five miles between themselves and the enemy. At the Tennessee border Hardee sent staff officers hurrying back along the ranks to announce the crossing. "The air was rent with cheer after cheer—as we were in our native state again." Hardee halted the corps near Mickey's as planned and moved his men off the road to a nearby spring. That night Polk's column passed by on the same road and encamped farther ahead.

The next morning, April 4, Hardee's men formed on the road and proceeded toward Pittsburg. A short distance up the road they encountered Polk's corps, which blocked the road. Polk's troops had to be moved to one side to allow the passage of Hardee's men, and the wagon train had to be removed from the road. This slowed the advance and caused some confusion. Even with this interruption, Hardee advanced too rapidly. Bragg, tangled in traffic problems at Monterey, ran behind schedule. His large command extended over several roads, his rear division had not appeared at the designated point, and his temper grew short. "Bad roads, insufficient transportation badly managed, and the usual delays of a first move of new troops caused the delay." "These delays will render it necessary to hold General Hardee in check until we can be ready in the rear." [8]

By afternoon of April 4 Hardee approached the enemy position. The Federals soon appeared, and by 3 P.M. an active skirmish commenced. Hardee's covering force had attacked the Union pickets.

6 *Ibid.,* 392–94; Pt. 2, p. 387; T. Jordan to Hardee, April 3, 1862, in Army of the Mississippi, Orders and Circulars, 1861–65, Record Group 109.

7 *Official Records,* X, Pt. 1, pp. 400–401. Secondary accounts have censured Hardee for delaying the advance on April 3, largely because of Beauregard's statement that Hardee was "dilatory" in starting. The evidence does not seem to bear this out. Hardee did not receive the warning order until 1 A.M.; the march order came after 8 A.M., at which time he was conferring with the commanders of the army. Furthermore, Bragg's order did not have an urgent tone. Hours later regarded as precious were wasted on that morning, but the army, rather than one corps commander, bears the responsibility for squandering them.

8 Henry H. Wright, *A History of the Sixth Iowa Infantry* (Iowa City, 1923), 81; Taylor, "Twenty-Seventh Tennessee Infantry," in *Military Annals of Tennessee,* 418; Roman, *Military Operations of General Beauregard,* I, 529–30; *Official Records,* X, Pt. 2, p. 391.

They had been repulsed and pursued by four companies of Federal infantry and a cavalry force. These units struck Hardee's lines and were, in turn, easily repulsed.[9] Certainly, any element of surprise had vanished by now, for the returning Federals reported at least two regiments to their front.

During the night of April 4 a heavy rain fell. Hardee's orders stipulated that he would advance at 3 A.M., but the rain-swollen rivulets and water-filled ravines caused the advance to be suspended until dawn. At daybreak Hardee's corps advanced. About 10 A.M. they encountered opposition, and Hardee deployed the corps. This deployment took place approximately one and a half miles from a crude log structure known as Shiloh Church. Sporadic but light firing occurred first on the left of Hardee's line, then on the right. Actually, his brigades had only been brushed by small enemy patrols. Time passed, and the men tired of waiting for the word to advance. To relieve the tension and to boost his men's morale, Hardee asked his West Point classmate Beauregard to ride in front of his lines so that his men might see the "Hero of Manassas." Beauregard complied and received cheers as he passed in front of Hardee's corps.[10]

Meanwhile, General Johnston became exasperated with the delay. He had come to the line of departure at 6 A.M. Hardee was in position, but the second line had not appeared. Soon Bragg's right wing came up but not the left. Johnston fretted and periodically sent back messengers; yet by 11 A.M. Bragg's left had still not appeared. Johnston "looking first at his watch, then glancing at the position of the sun, exclaimed, 'This is perfectly puerile! This is not war!' " He mounted, rode to the rear, and found Bragg's men blocked by Polk's corps. By the time the confusion had been rectified and the troops placed in position, it was 4 P.M. At that time the senior Confederate commanders held a council of war and decided to make the attack the following morning.[11]

Hardee's men slept on their arms during the night of April 5, 1862. Shivering on the wet ground, they envied the men to the rear who

---

9 Pickett, *Hardee*, 8–9; W. J. Hardee to B. Bragg, April 4, 1862, in Albert Sidney Johnston Papers.
10 *Official Records*, X, Pt. 1, pp. 400–401, 403, 567; J. Thompson to P. G. T. Beauregard, April 14, 1862, in Alfred Roman Papers, 1824–92 (Library of Congress).
11 W. P. Johnston, *Johnston*, 563, 568; William Mecklenburg Polk, *Leonidas Polk, Bishop and General*, 2 vols. (2nd ed., New York, 1915) II, 98–104; *Official Records*, X, Pt. 1, pp. 406–407; Jordan, "Notes of a Confederate Staff-Officer," in *Battles and Leaders*, I, 597.

were allowed to light fires. The two days of marching and the two nights of bivouacking on cold rations had slackened their enthusiasm. Their enemy, however, was near, and during the evening stimulating patriotic tunes drifted from the unsuspecting Federal camp over the tangled woodland to the silent Confederate line.

Just before dawn Johnston's senior officers gathered again at his headquarters. "They ate thin crackers and sipped coffee—some talking, General Johnston, mainly a listener." Even at this late time a discussion arose about whether to make a general attack or not. The debate ended abruptly with "an ominous sound, and apparently not far off. All knew what it meant." Johnston said, "Gentlemen the 'ball has opened' no time for argument now; or words to that effect. . . . How well do I remember the mien and manner of Gen'l Hardee, as he quitted the group and made for his horse. . . . His form was erect —his stride long but regular, and as he walked he gathered up his trailing sword that had hung loosely by his side, and tucking it under his left arm, so reached his horse, and at a gallop went in the direction of his command. . . ." [12]

Sunday morning, April 6, had opened bright and cheery. The cloudless sky and warm sun gave "every promise of a fine day." From 5 o'clock until 6 o'clock intermittent musket fire rippled across Hardee's line, as his men thrust back a Union reconnaissance party. At 5:45 Hardee dispatched aides with watches to the extremities of his line, to synchronize the corps' time of departure.[13] The troops waited silently in line. In the ranks of the Sixth Arkansas, seventeen-year-old Henry Porter fidgeted, then discovered some violets near his feet. He nudged his buddy, Henry Stanley, and said, "It would be a good idea to put a few in my cap. Perhaps the Yanks won't shoot me if they see me wearing such flowers, for they are a sign of peace." "Capital," Stanley replied, "I will do the same." About 6 o'clock the line started forward. Stanley thought as he marched along that this would be a perfect setting for a picnic; ". . . strange that a Sunday should have been chosen to disturb the holy calm of these woods." [14] At 7:05 came the first discharge of a cannon. The pace quickened.

12 Isaac Barton Ulmer, "A Glimpse of Johnston through the Smoke of Shiloh," in Isaac Barton Ulmer Papers, 1838, 1855–65, 1907–27 (Southern Historical Collection).
13 Pickett, *Hardee*, 10.
14 Dorothy Stanley (ed.), *The Autobiography of Sir Henry Morton Stanley* (New York, 1909), 187. Although this private was captured at Shiloh and lost to the Confederacy for the rest of the war, he reappears in history as the famous nineteenth-century journalist and African explorer.

By 7:30 Hardee's corps was within half a mile of the enemy camps.[15] The musketry grew heavier. Adley H. Gladden's brigade from Pensacola, which extended Hardee's right, wearied at the pace of the Arkansans, for unlike Hardee's men they had missed their breakfast.

Lieutenant Eustace H. Ball, of the Fifty-third Ohio, had been awakened by the staccato of musket fire. He and his regiment quickly drew up in a defensive line on high ground. From this vantage point Ball watched the Confederates approach. The scene, he said, "was one never to be forgotten. In front were the steadily advancing lines of Hardee's corps marching in perfect order and extending until lost to sight in the timber on either flank." Colonel C. C. Marsh of the Twentieth Illinois saw "column after column moving on us with a steadiness and precision which I had scarcely anticipated. . . . The enemy opened on us with a most terrible and deadly fire. . . ." Marsh's regiment broke with the shock of the initial attack and rushed to the rear. Ball's unit held its position, largely because of the defensive piece of terrain they occupied. Ball noticed that to his front "there was a group of mounted officers and a peculiar flag, dark blue with a white centre." [16]

By 8 o'clock the ground shook from the heavy cannonading all along the front. The gaily bedecked woods shrieked with ricocheting Minié balls, and the new green leaves fluttered crazily to earth as if it were fall. General Gladden on Hardee's right rolled along throwing back enemy opposition before it could be jelled into a stable defense. On the left of Hardee's line things progressed in a like manner as Cleburne pushed on unhampered. In the center Hindman advanced rapidly. His brigade had the advantage of attacking over a road leading directly through the Union position. For a mile the brigade shoved forward, striking enemy skirmishers and brushing them aside. Hindman had captured the first line of enemy camps before 8 o'clock. His men crossed one ridge and continuing, encountered opposition at the second ridge. "Through the lurid haze the contours of their pink faces could be seen, but their gappy, hesitating, . . . and sensitive fire revealed their mood clearly." [17] The Confederates halted, fired, and prepared to rush the Union line. The Federals retired. The Confederates quickly pursued. A scream startled young Henry Stanley, and

15 Roman, *Military Operations of General Beauregard*, I, 524.
16 Ephraim C. Dawes, "The Battle of Shiloh," in *Papers of the Military Historical Society of Massachusetts*, 10 vols., ed. Theodore F. Dwight (Boston 1895-1912), VII, 140-41; hereinafter cited as *Massachusetts Military Papers: Official Records*, X, Pt. 1, p. 133.
17 Stanley (ed.), *Autobiography of Stanley*, 190-91.

he looked behind. There lay Henry Porter writhing in agony. His foot had been crushed. Stanley hesitated, then continued. Perhaps they could catch the Federals before they reached the next ridge. At the third ridge Hindman's brigade received a destructive fire and the skirmish line fell back on the main body. Bragg's corps now moved up to join Hardee's men on the front line.

With a line over two miles in length to control, Hardee moved about constantly. During the initial phase of the attack he supervised the employment of Hindman's brigade. Seeing that Hindman had the situation well in hand, Hardee proceeded to the extreme right, where General Johnston personally directed Gladden's brigade. About 9 o'clock Hardee joined Johnston at the Wisconsin camp, which Gladden had just captured. Hardee and Johnston then went ahead of Gladden's troops to make a reconnaissance of the next line of enemy camps, six to eight hundred yards ahead. While conducting this reconnaissance, the group was shelled by an attentive enemy battery but escaped injury.[18]

After the reconnaissance heavy firing on the extreme left of the Confederate line attracted Hardee's attention. With Gladden prepared to attack and with General Johnston present, Hardee decided to move to the left. Here Hardee found Cleburne in serious trouble. Cleburne's brigade had advanced without difficulty until it encountered a morass. Cleburne pushed on, but this natural obstacle split his command. Behind the morass and on higher ground Sherman's men waited, with the advantage of superior numbers and enfilading fire. The Sixth Mississippi and the Twenty-third Tennessee launched the attack but met the heavy fire. "Under the terrible fire much confusion followed, and a quick and bloody repulse was the consequence." The repulse shattered Cleburne's brigade. The Sixth Mississippi, for example, lost 300 out of 425 men. At this time the second line came up.[19] Hardee gathered Cleburne's command plus some of the newly arrived regiments and placed them in a ravine under cover. He ordered up Francis A. Shoup's battery, and a furious artillery duel ensued.

Morgan's cavalry rode up at this time, and Hardee also held them in reserve, waiting until a break occurred in the Federal line. "The General sat on his horse near Shoup's gallant battery, which was replying, but ineffectually, to the vicious rain of cannister and shell

18 *Official Records*, X, Pt. 1, pp. 403, 569.
19 *Ibid.*, 569, 581; Dawes, "The Battle of Shiloh," in *Massachusetts Military Papers*, VII, 146–47.

which poured from the hill. He seemed indifferent to the hot fire, but very anxious to take those guns." [20] The opportunity Hardee awaited came not as a result of Shoup's artillery fire, but from Thomas C. Hindman. After breaking the Union position on the third ridge, Hindman turned his brigade obliquely to the left, bringing his men to an enfilading position on Sherman's left. Hindman unlimbered his artillery, and its fire soon made Sherman's position untenable. About this time enemy fire struck Hindman's mount. The horse fell, severely injuring Hindman and depriving the Confederacy of his services during the remainder of the battle.

As Sherman's left collapsed, Hardee unleashed his waiting troops on the right, and Sherman's defense line buckled. Hardee followed this attack with a pursuit led by Wharton's and Morgan's cavalry.[21]

The Confederates re-enacted this scene all along the front. The Federals fell back from position to position, each time coming closer and closer to the bank of the river. By noon all four of the Confederate corps had been committed. Although Hardee's corps was seriously reduced by losses, the other corps continued the attack. Federal stragglers poured into Pittsburg by the thousands, lining the banks with disorganized, panicked men. Union generals estimated their numbers at between four thousand and ten thousand.

Early in the afternoon the battlefront stabilized. The heaviest fighting occurred in the right center, where mingled Confederate commands opposed a stubborn Union defense at a place known as the Hornet's Nest. Numerous Confederate brigades broke on this strong defensive position. The Union general, B. M. Prentiss, refused to yield ground, although Federal divisions on his flanks retired. At 2:30 P.M. General Johnston was struck and mortally wounded while attempting to reduce this position. The effect of Johnston's death upon the Confederate attack is disputable. Certainly it sapped much of the vigor from the Confederates. Hardee emphasized the significance of the event: "In my opinion . . . but for this calamity, we would have achieved before sunset a triumph signal not only in the annals of this war, but memorable in future history." [22]

Soon after Johnston's death, General Beauregard, the new commander-in-chief, detailed Hardee to gather a force and help the other units dislodge Prentiss. Hardee assembled elements of Anderson's and

20 Duke, *Reminiscences*, 84.
21 *Ibid.; Official Records*, X, Pt. 2, p. 461.
22 *Official Records*, X, Pt. 1, p. 569.

Gibson's brigades and attacked.[23] Elements of four Confederate corps swarmed about Prentiss, striking him in the front and on both flanks. One of Beauregard's staff officers, who went to Hardee to learn how matters progressed, reported, "I found his command charging the enemy—the General with his men, cheering them on. Nothing could exceed his coolness and gallantry. He was always in the thickest of the fight. His answer, to my question if he wished anything, was, 'Tell the General we are getting along very well but they are putting it to us very severely.' Not once did he ask for assistance." [24]

At one point Hardee found the First Missouri Regiment "lying down and hugging the ground." Up ahead were the guns of the Washington Artillery which had just been captured by the enemy. To one Missourian, it seemed that "we were about to be annihilated." Hardee rode along the front of the regiment and reassured the men. Then he ordered up the Louisiana "Crescent Regiment" and directed the two commands to retake the captured guns. "General Hardee took his place in front of the Regiment, ordered the charge and led it in person. He was the bravest man I ever saw in my four years experience in the war. . . . We followed him with a yell at the charge bayonets and drove back the enemy from the guns and restored them to the grateful Louisianians. . . ." [25]

Late in the afternoon Prentiss' resistance ended, and he surrendered his command of over two thousand men. Hardee, Bragg, Polk, and Breckinridge met in the center of his position. A major of the Twenty-fifth Alabama stepped up to the group and presented Hardee with a captured stand of colors.[26] The rejoicing but tired Confederates now turned to the remaining Federal lines. Hardee quickly dispatched a regiment to the rear with Federal prisoners and then directed Woods's brigade to form for the final assaults.

The victory seemed won. Most of the Union army was dispersed and driven against the banks of the river. Union officers were everywhere "coaxing, praying, exhorting" their men to fight.[27] The Con-

23 Pierre Gustave Toutant Beauregard, "The Shiloh Campaign," in *North American Review*, CXLII (February, 1886), 171.
24 Roman, *Military Operations of General Beauregard*, I, 525.
25 Joseph Boyce Reminiscences, 1862 (Howard-Tilton Memorial Library, Tulane University). This would be the last charge Hardee would lead in person until the battle of Bentonville.
26 *Official Records*, X, Pt. 1, p. 544.
27 Mildred Throne (ed.), *The Civil War Diary of Cyrus F. Boyd, Fifteenth Iowa Infantry, 1861–1863* (Iowa City, 1953), 32; Leander Stillwell, *The Story of a Common Soldier of Army Life in the Civil War 1861–1865* (2nd ed., Erie, Kans., 1920), 49.

federate commands moved up for the next contest in three lines and "in high feather." [28] The enemy lined up on the bluffs a few hundred yards to receive the attack. At this moment staff officers from General Beauregard appeared and ordered the attack to be broken off.

Beauregard based his decision upon the disorganized condition of his army. Most of the men were exhausted, and many units existed in name only. Many of them had ceased fighting and gone to the rear through fear, fatigue, curiosity over the captured Federals, or eagerness to seize some of the spoils in the enemy camps. Enemy gunboats had opened on the Confederates, the fire of which did little damage but, according to Hardee, "was perfectly appalling to our men." [29] Furthermore, only a few minutes of daylight remained. Most of the Confederate corps commanders were surprised at the order, however. General Polk thought it cost the Confederates the battle. Hardee never denounced Beauregard's order, but stated in his official report that the "advance lines were within a few hundred yards of Pittsburg, where the enemy were huddled in confusion, when the order to withdraw was received." [30] The correctness of Beauregard's decision can be and has been debated with substantial arguments buttressing both sides. Perhaps the most important fact is that Beauregard was not and had not been in the front lines when he ordered the cessation of the attack and could not have known the true situation.

General Hardee passed the night of April 6 on the right of the Confederate line with Colonel Martin's Second Confederate and Colonel Wheeler's Nineteenth Alabama regiments. During the night Colonel Nathan Bedford Forrest awoke the general and reported that heavy enemy reinforcements were arriving by water at Pittsburg. Hardee directed him to locate General Beauregard and give him the information. Forrest returned at 2 A.M., not having found Beauregard. Hardee ordered him "to return to his regiment, keep up a vigilant, strong picket line, and report all hostile movements." [31] Several observers, and Beauregard himself, criticized Hardee for failing to take action on Forrest's information.[32] Regarding this point one must keep in mind the state of the Confederate army at 2 A.M. that night. Furthermore, Forrest reported information known by many Confederates. One soldier wrote that he "could hear and count the arrivals and de-

28 Pickett, *Hardee*, 11.
29 Hardee to Mrs. Shover, April 9, 1862, in Shover Letters.
30 *Official Records*, X, Pt. 1, pp. 406–407, 569.
31 *Ibid.*, 534; Thomas Jordan, *The Campaigns of Lieut.-Gen. N. B. Forrest* (New York, 1868), 136–37.
32 Roman, *Military Operations of General Beauregard*, I, 307.

partures of the Yankee boats during the night & from their number knew that they were either withdrawing or reinforcing heavily." [33] During the night a new Federal army appeared on the field—three fresh divisions from Buell's army and Lew Wallace's division from Crump Landing.

In contrast with the cheery Sunday morning, Monday brought rain. Early in the morning after the men had completed "a capital breakfast of bacon and coffee," Hardee deployed Wheeler's regiment to the front of the Confederate right. Then with an assortment of troops from J. R. Chalmers' brigade, J. M. Withers' division, and his own corps, Hardee moved up to support what he believed to be General Breckinridge's command. A sudden enemy thrust surprised Hardee's men at this point and one of his regiments, the Second Texas, broke to the rear.[34] Hardee regrouped his linsey-woolsey force and again advanced along the Bark Road toward the bluffs.

Near the river Hardee encountered a Federal force. His men charged the Union position, the enemy retreated, and Hardee captured five pieces of artillery. A Confederate regimental commander gave this version of the encounter: "From here, under the eye and orders of Major-General Hardee, who inspired every confidence, twice . . . we drove back the legions of the enemy . . . the enemy disappearing under the river bank each time . . . and we falling back under cover of the hill. They making their appearance at three different points, we rallied upon them. I think they concluded we had 5,000 instead of 1,100 men and gave up taking the Bark road, they not knowing it was the same troops charging on them each time. . . ." [35]

The Louisiana Crescent Regiment and one of Cleburne's regiments soon joined Hardee's forces, enabling him to hold his position against a Union brigade and two regiments throughout the morning. While Hardee conducted the defense of the Bark Road the battle raged savagely on the left in the vicinity of Shiloh Church. Here a much heavier enemy force pressed the Confederates back steadily until about noon, "when, as if by mutual consent, both sides desisted from the struggle." About 1 P.M., when the heavy enemy attacks slackened,

33 G. K. Miller to Celestine Miller, April 15, 1862, in Miller Papers.
34 *Official Records*, X, Pt. 1, p. 556. Hardee did not forget this rout and spoke of it during the summer of 1862. His remarks occasioned charges by a Texas congressman, Louis T. Wigfall, but Hardee's position was substantiated by staff officers who had been present at the time the stampede occurred.
35 *Official Records*, X, Pt. 1, pp. 622–23.

General Beauregard decided to retire. Hardee deployed his forces to either side of the Bark Road to cover the withdrawal.[36]

The battle of Shiloh mutilated the western army of the Confederacy. It deprived the South of slightly over ten thousand men killed, wounded, and missing. Johnston, Gladden, and a host of lesser officers would never fight again. Tennessee, with its teeming reservoir of manpower, was virtually lost; the fall of Corinth would only be a matter of time; and the Memphis and Charleston Railroad, the trunk line of the Confederacy, remained imperiled. Strategically and tactically, Shiloh must be regarded as a Union victory. Although the battle temporarily crippled Grant's army, supplied many of the Confederates with new firearms, and revealed the merits and demerits of many western commanders, the object of the Confederates—the destruction of Grant's army—was not realized.

The tactics of the Confederates evoked complimentary comments even from their enemy. The attack, in particular, was well executed. Johnston's men drove the Federals from seven consecutive positions, and the element of surprise seemed complete. Yet the Confederates had to halt and re-form continuously, allowing the Union forces to retire and prepare for the next attack. The final attacks on April 6 were delivered in piecemeal fashion, primarily because of the thousands who straggled to the rear. Although the initial battle formation allowed Hardee's more experienced troops to deliver the first shocking blow, it negated close control by division and corps commanders. Soon after the impact of the first attack Hardee lost operational control of his men, as the supporting corps became intermingled with his men. Moreover, the second line, anxious to enter the fight, fired into the first line during the assault phase. The Confederates committed all of their reserves early, and with the conglomerate battle line that resulted, commanders had no local reserves upon which to call. This formation, itself, surrendered larger unit integrity and mobility, sacrificing their initial crushing power. "Before the battle of the first day had been half fought the entire army was disjointed." [37]

In light of the recent organization of the army and the type of men who filled its ranks, this was fatal. The army had "not yet [been] molded into a consistent whole." The general officers lacked the time

---

36 W. I. Hodgson to P. Anderson, April 9, 1862, in Confederate States of America Archives, 1861–65 (Duke University Library); *Official Records*, X, Pt. 1, pp. 619, 623.
37 Polk, *Leonidas Polk*, II, 105.

to acquaint themselves with their commands. The army sorely needed arms, equipment, transportation, competent junior officers, and discipline. To emphasize their inexperience one Confederate brigade commander declared: "I had never seen a man fire a musket. . . . We were all tyros—all, the rawest and greenest recruits—generals, colonels, captains, soldiers." [38] The deaths they saw on all sides and their own exhaustion and deprivation weakened the will of these men and consequently placed an undue burden upon the experienced officers. Leaders such as Hardee, Bragg, Polk, and Johnston had to remain exposed on the front line doing the work of brigade and regimental commanders.

Shiloh bequeathed General Hardee a shattered corps. His casualty lists were staggering. Hardee's corps and Cleburne's brigade lost the highest percentage of men of any corps or brigade in Johnston's army.[39] Hardee spoke of the battle in the following terms:

We gained a great victory at a great sacrifice of life but owing to the arrival of Buell it has not been so productive of results as might have been desired. . . . Our loss has been heavy. . . . Being in advance my forces suffered most. I am not so much impressed as many respecting the invincibility of our volunteers & of their determination to be free—they are good for the dash, but fail in tenacity. I don't think we can yet regard ourselves as soldiers—our men are not sufficiently impressed with a sense of honor that it is better to die by far than to run—we fail also in company officers, they want skill and instruction and lamentably neglected their duty.[40]

Hardee's individual performance during the battle restored much of the prestige that he had lost in Kentucky and Tennessee. A large degree of the credit for the success of the initial attack must be given to him and his corps. His action following the attack, however, would do credit to a brigade or division commander, not to a corps commander. In fact, he had no corps after midmorning on April 6. His command thenceforward consisted of assorted units that he grouped together temporarily for limited objectives. At Shiloh he proved his worth as a fighter but not as a corps commander.

Many of the official reports and contemporary accounts of the battle applauded Hardee for his bravery and exemplary bearing. He repeatedly exposed himself to enemy fire and personally led numerous charges. "I had my beautiful black shot in the shoulder and two balls passed through my coat, one wounding me slightly (very) in the

38 W. P. Johnston, *Johnston*, 565.   39 *Official Records*, X, Pt. 1, p. 395.
40 Hardee to Mrs. Shover, April 9, 1862, in Shover Letters.

arm. . . . Providence has mysteriously preserved me for another time or a different fate." [41]

The wounding of Hardee's mount, Black Auster, triggered the imagination of one citizen who joined in the rush to commemorate the Confederate heroes. Although Confederate commanders often had poems written in their honor, this is the only poem known to have been dedicated to Hardee.[42]

> General Hardee at the Battle of Shiloh
>
> . . . . . .
>
> Charging thro' slippery pools of blood,
> And over heaps of slain
>
> . . . . . .
>
> Amidst the carnage and the crash,
> Black Auster fearless stood,
> Receiving on that field of fame,
> His baptism of blood.
> A mingled sacrificial stream
> Fell trickling to the ground,
> From gallant Auster's bleeding side,
> From Hardee's sacred wound
>
> Bring laurels for the Hero's brow,
> Of never-fading sheen,
> And twine in Auster's sable mane,
> Garlands as fresh and green—
>
> For fame, their blended names has given
> To immortality
>
> . . . . . .

The retreat to Corinth progressed slowly throughout the night of April 7. Although the enemy did not pursue, the Confederates were apprehensive. As the retreating column neared Monterey, horsemen galloped along the line shouting that the Yankee cavalry had broken through the rear guard. Wagon-drivers unhitched their mules, dumped provisions and wounded men upon the ground, and fled. Not until night did the officers quiet the panic-stricken men. The retirement continued, but irreplaceable items had been left behind. Rain began to fall early during the night. Many of the men abandoned the gummy

41 *Ibid.*; Roy, "Odds and Ends."
42 Clipping from the Chattanooga *Rebel*, n.d., in I. Solomon Scrapbook, 1861–62 (Duke University Library). Black Auster recovered, however, and carried his master on the battlefields of Perryville and Murfreesboro. Roy, "Odds and Ends."

roads and took to the woods, following a course that paralleled the regular route. But everywhere, the Confederates "travelled in a quagmire of excoriating mud." [43] General Bragg rode into Corinth at 2 P.M. on April 8. He reported to Beauregard by letter, because he found himself "utterly unable" to come to headquarters. "I left General Hardee behind in command, with working parties on the road; but the men are exhausted, dispirited, and work with no zeal." [44]

General Hardee remained with the working parties throughout the afternoon and into the night. The men labored, retrieving the abandoned guns and pushing the wagonloads of wounded through the mud. At last more teams and wagons arrived, and the work eased. Soon Corinth came into view.

43 Noblitt, "Forty-Fourth Tennessee Infantry," in *Military Annals of Tennessee*, 531; L. G. Marshall, "Jackson's Battery—Carnes' Battery—Marshall's Battery," *ibid.*, 810.
44 *Official Records*, X, Pt. 2, p. 339.

VIII

"Banners to the Breeze"

THE SOLID counterthrust delivered by the Confederates at Shiloh
had staggered the main Union army in the West. But while Grant's
army prepared for the next test of strength, other forces in the West
threw a flurry of damaging body blows that left the Confederates
breathless. Island No. 10 fell; Huntsville fell; Decatur fell; New Orleans fell. The Confederates could not effect any combination that
would halt this series of disasters. Concentration had exacted its price.

To stabilize the front Beauregard urged an even greater concentration at Corinth. Davis complied, and thousands of fresh troops arrived
from the western Confederate states, but because of poor sanitation,
Corinth soon became the graveyard for many. Hardee remarked,
"Our army diminished 13,000 in less than 3 weeks in effective men &
during this time we [received] some accession to our force from
Mississippi and Alabama." [1]

Although Hardee fared better than most, he spent several weeks
"indisposed," partly because of his injured arm—the only wound he
received during the war. It was a minor wound, and Hardee dismissed
it as a "slight scratch." To boost his morale Mrs. Shover supplied him
with food and delicacies, and the women of Bowling Green, Nashville, and Murfreesboro visited his camp and doubtless saw to it that
he did not suffer from malnutrition or want of diversion. [2]

Hardee devoted most of his efforts in the days after Shiloh to
reorganization and training. He raised John S. Marmaduke to Hindman's brigade command and set about consolidating the broken Arkansas regiments, which were cut off from their normal supply of

---

1 Hardee to Mrs. Shover, June 1, 1862, in Shover Letters.
2 Hardee to Mrs. Shover, May 7, 14, 1862, *ibid.*

recruits. Hardee held constant inspections and expended a great deal of effort training his grand division of eight thousand.

At Corinth appeared the nucleus of Hardee's staff, which at times contained as many as twenty members. The indispensable figure was Thomas Benton Roy. Roy had been a law student in Virginia when the war opened, and he had enlisted in the Seventeenth Virginia Regiment. Soon he was transferred to Colonel Thomas Jordan's office on Beauregard's staff, as a clerk. He came west from Virginia with Jordan and Beauregard in early 1862 and remained on Beauregard's staff until Hardee appointed him, upon Jordan's recommendation, as his assistant adjutant general. Hardee made a lasting impression on the twenty-three-old Roy. Roy had heard that "Bragg and Hardee, and other old Army officers, would not mind ordering out a brace of us, on any little short coming, and having us shot, 'for the encouragement of the others.'" Hardee seemed to live up to his advance billing. "I had never seen him before, and his presence, and bearing, and the very sound of his voice, seemed to me expression of a dynamic power, that could, if it were, lift a man out of his boots, or take the roof off of a house." To Roy's surprise, however, Hardee "received and treated me with the utmost kindness."

A few days after Roy joined Hardee's staff, they made a night ride together. Although most of the staff kept silent in the presence of the General, Roy talked to him, and "a chance reference to an essay of Macaulay's that had impressed each of us alike, launched us on an animated literary discussion, which lasted throughout the night." Starting then, he wrote, "Genl. Hardee and I soon became, and ever remained, as fast friends, and as good comrades, as if we had been of similar age and rank." The proud and popular Virginian was a man of manifold interests, of charm, and of sincerity. Devoted to his commander, he brought needed efficiency to his office and later as chief of staff would set the tone for the rest of his staff. Hardee never had a better or closer friend, and after the death of Willie, Roy became in effect his son.[3]

Another officer who joined Hardee's staff in 1862 was William Douglas Pickett. Older than Roy, this Alabamian had experience as a civil engineer and had served in the Mexican War. As assistant inspector general Pickett would remain with Hardee throughout the

3 Thomas Benton Roy Military Service Record, Record Group 109; hereinafter cited as Roy Military Service Record. Roy, "Odds and Ends."

war. Samuel L. Black brought Hardee more combat experience than either Pickett or Roy. Black had been a lieutenant colonel in one of Hardee's Arkansas regiments. When the regiments were reorganized, he lost his position, but Hardee knew his capabilities and placed him on the staff. As an inspector general Black proved to be "one of the most energetic & efficient officers in the army." [4] Actually, he replaced a staff officer, St. John R. Liddell, whose leadership abilities were so pronounced that Hardee gave him brigade command under Cleburne. Other staff officers who would serve Hardee throughout most of the war were Surgeon D. W. Yandell, Lieutenants D. H. Poole and D. G. White, and Captain Thomas "Sid" Hardee, Hardee's nephew.

The reorganization period at Corinth ended when Halleck arrived at Pittsburg Landing from St. Louis. Organizing his army into three sections, Halleck began his approach march. Most commentators regard Halleck's attack on Corinth as the height of slow—senselessly slow—maneuvering; others consider it a classic example of methodical investment. Halleck took a month to cover the distance between Pittsburg Landing and Corinth, but at the end of the month the Confederates abandoned their vital railroad center, despairing of attacking the superior Union forces in their entrenchments. Halleck gained this great "bloodless victory" by moving deliberately, covering a great lateral distance rather than by marching the army in compact bodies on a narrow front. He kept advanced units out as a perpetual reconnaissance in force. This method was well adapted to the ever-present threat of a Confederate attack, and was dictated by the net of terrible roads, by the terrain, and by the miserable weather. Beauregard appreciated Halleck's methods. "I fear he is advancing with gradual approaches." [5] Beauregard would have much preferred a rapid advance and assault by his opponent. Hardee agreed with Beauregard. "Our position is very strong and if [Halleck] attacks our entrenchments we shall certainly whip him." He believed that Halleck would instead attack by a series of turning movements or attempt to demoralize the Confederates with a prolonged bombardment.[6] The Confederates arranged their defenses carefully on a commanding ridge in

4 Hardee to S. Cooper, October 26, 1862, in Letters Received, Adjutant General's Office.
5 *Official Records*, X, Pt. 2, p. 528.
6 Hardee to Mrs. Shover, May 7, 1862, in Shover Letters.

front of the town. Polk commanded the left sector, Bragg the center, and Hardee the right. Breckinridge remained in reserve, and the cavalry to the front contested Halleck's advance.

Halleck closed on Farmington during the first week in May. His advance under John Pope pushed out aggressively from the main body and was soon beyond supporting distance. Beauregard decided to strike and chose Earl Van Dorn's newly arrived Army of the West for the mission. The attack on Pope failed, however, as Van Dorn found the avenues of approach impossible. Halleck quickly sensed the danger and sent strong support to Pope. Never again would the Confederates have a chance to crush a fraction of Halleck's army.

Beauregard wanted to attack again, and he sought his generals' advice. All except Hardee agreed. He wrote, "I thought as we did not attack him when he first commenced to fortify that we ought to wait until he took up a second position, which he will be compelled to do as he cannot reach us even with his heaviest guns where he is. I do not believe, also, that our men will be able to march up and attack entrenchments; none but well disciplined and instructed troops can be relied on to do this. I hope I am mistaken but I fear I am right." [7]

Regardless of Hardee's misgivings Beauregard decided to go ahead with the attack. Again he assigned Van Dorn to strike the Union left flank. Hardee would be in close support. Originally scheduled for the morning of May 21, the attack was delayed until May 22, then delayed again until finally Van Dorn reported that he was calling it off. Hardee, who accompanied Van Dorn's maneuvering column, attributed the situation to the failure to reconnoiter the route properly and to the inevitable tangles of lengthy approach marches. [8]

After the second abortive attack, Hardee formally proposed immediate evacuation in a lengthy memorandum. [9] After deliberation Beauregard admitted the logic of Hardee's argument, and swallowing the political and military consequences, he ordered the evacuation to be carried out on May 29.

That night the Confederates slipped out of Corinth unopposed. Hardee led his men across the Tuscumbia River and then moved off toward Rienzi and Booneville. Bushrod Johnson with two regiments acted as Hardee's rear guard. He beat back several halfhearted attacks

7 Hardee to Mrs. Shover, May 19, 1862, *ibid.*
8 *Official Records*, X, Pt. 2, pp. 537–38; Liddell's Record; Hardee to Mrs. Shover, May [n.d.], 1862, in Shover Letters.
9 William Joseph Hardee, Military Situation Summary, May 25, 1862, in possession of Stanley F. Horn, Nashville, Tenn.

by the pursuing enemy and burned the Tuscumbia railroad bridge. Fortunately he waited until all of the trains that were to use the bridge had crossed, thus avoiding the disaster that befell six trains on the other side of Corinth.

Halleck entered Corinth just after the Confederates withdrew. He sent Pope in pursuit, and Pope found the Confederates drawn up for battle at Baldwyn. Both sides declined the battle, and Beauregard retired to Tupelo on June 7.

While Halleck consolidated his territorial gains, the Confederates consolidated their army. Beauregard took a leave of absence for his health, giving the War Department an excuse to replace him, and he was superseded by Braxton Bragg. Bragg greeted his dispirited army with these welcome words: "A few more days of needed reorganization and I shall give your banners to the breeze—shall lead you to emulate the soldiers of the Confederacy in the East." [10]

Bragg knew his army well and was aware of the task before him. He particularly lamented the lack of capable officers. He felt that he had only "one suitable major-general"—Hardee; the ranks of the brigadiers were filled with "dead weight." [11] He began the reorganization by assigning Polk as second in command and by giving Hardee direct command of the Army of the Mississippi. Although Bragg's intentions were never explicitly stated, this shift of senior officers seems to have been designed to give Hardee immediate supervision of the training of the army.

Hardee assumed command at Tupelo on July 1. He established a rigorous routine for the 31,000 men. Drilling, on the company, regiment, brigade, and division levels, occupied the troops every day. Hardee rotated among the units, inspecting and drilling them himself. He held examinations to determine officers' qualifications and instituted a system of reviews. William P. Johnston inspected the army for Davis while Hardee was in command. He found a "great emphasis on drill"; "discipline seemed excellent." Morale had been restored as a result of reconditioning of the army and because of the healthy campsite. The soldiers agreed with Johnston about Tupelo; it "was a pleasant relief from the horrors of camp life at Corinth." [12]

While Hardee prepared the army for action, Bragg considered how

10 *Official Records*, XVII, Pt. 2, p. 626.
11 *Ibid.*, 647–48.
12 William J. Rogers Diary, 1862–63, July, 1862, in Roy Watterson Black Collection, 1814–1939 (Southern Historical Collection); Pickett, *Hardee*, 13–14; *Official Records*, X, Pt. 1, pp. 780–83.

the army could be employed most effectively. He had planned to attack Halleck at Corinth, but he abandoned this idea when he learned that Halleck had sent Buell with a large force to capture Chattanooga. Edmund Kirby Smith, defending Chattanooga, lacked the means to prevent its seizure, and he implored Bragg to aid him.

With Morgan and Forrest slowing Buell's advance, Bragg believed that he could reach Chattanooga before Buell. If he succeeded, not only would that critical city be safeguarded but a host of offensive opportunities might unfold. To occupy Halleck's army and to protect Mississippi Bragg left Van Dorn and Sterling Price behind. If his Tennessee venture went well, they would advance north also to follow up the enemy retreat.

Bragg instructed Hardee to move the army to Chattanooga with all possible haste, and then he went ahead to confer with Kirby Smith. Hardee started the wagons and artillery overland on July 21. The troops went by rail to Mobile and then by steamer to Montgomery. At Montgomery they boarded troop trains again and rode to Chattanooga. A staff officer who helped work out the details for the movement for Hardee left this impression of his commander: "I have, and always had, the highest of opinion of General W. J. Hardee. He was a thorough soldier, well trained in all things relating to army organization, discipline and drill, . . . energetic, exact in the performance of his duties, and knowing how to get the best work out of his subordinates. He exposed his person in battle with nonchalance, without bravado, winning the utmost confidence of his troops; he was direct and plain in speech and manner; he seemed not to prefer himself to command, but few could better have commanded an army." [13]

The leading elements of the army entered Chattanooga on July 27. Within ten days the four divisions had arrived, and Bragg assumed operational control. He divided his army into two wings, totaling about twenty-eight thousand men. Polk's wing consisted of the divisions of Cheatham and Jones Withers; Hardee's wing contained Simon Bolivar Buckner's and Patton Anderson's divisions.

General Bragg's plan of campaign entailed a joint movement by his own and Kirby Smith's forces toward Kentucky. Kirby Smith would move directly from East Tennessee on Lexington, Kentucky, bypassing the enemy at Cumberland Gap. This invasion would clear Bragg's right flank, threaten Buell's communications, and serve as a shield and

13 *Official Records*, XVI, Pt. 2, 731; Rogers Diary, July 25–August 2, 1862; Claiborne Letters and Reminiscences.

screen for Bragg. Assured that the enemy would not be able to concentrate against him while advancing, Bragg first intended to feint at Nashville. Then he would march as quickly as possible to Glasgow, Kentucky. At Glasgow Bragg planned to await developments. From there he could cut Buell's line of communications, strike Buell's flank, or proceed north to join Kirby Smith.

General Bragg had to delay his march into Tennessee until the slow-moving artillery and wagons came up. By August 16 he began throwing elements of his command across the Tennessee River, and on August 28 his two wings started over Walden's Ridge. Buell was superior to Bragg in numbers, but his forces were scattered along the railroad lines from Nashville to Stevenson, Alabama, and from Decatur, Alabama, to Bridgeport, Alabama. The Union army also had sizable garrisons at Cumberland Gap and at McMinnville, Tennessee. Buell first attempted a concentration at Altamont, Tennessee, but when the Confederates entered Sequatchie Valley, he decided to abandon the movement because it now offered the enemy the opportunity of defeating him before the concentration could be completed. Instead, he ordered his troops to unite at Murfreesboro.

From Pikeville in Sequatchie Valley the Confederates made a night march over a large arm of the Cumberland Mountains. Once across the mountains Bragg brushed by McMinnville, threatening it with Hardee's wing, and then went on to Sparta. At Sparta Bragg turned northwest toward Carthage. This change of direction could be interpreted by Buell either as an advance on Nashville or as an attempt to cross the Cumberland River for operations in Kentucky. Thus far the Confederate advance had consumed a fortnight, and results had already been produced. Most of the Union troops in southwestern Tennessee had been drained out of the area into the north-central part of the state. The rapid movement had neutralized Buell's superior numbers, which were now being drawn back to Nashville or started out on roads heading north, to protect the Bowling Green line of communications. Already this line had proved to be vulnerable to the far-reaching raids of Morgan and Forrest, which destroyed bridges and communication facilities between Nashville and points north.

Bragg crossed the Cumberland on September 9 and 10 at Carthage with Hardee's wing. Polk crossed the river farther east. Once across the river Hardee headed directly for Glasgow for a junction with Polk. He moved his wing in an extended formation, with Buckner's and Anderson's divisions sometimes ten miles apart. Bragg introduced a novel device on the march to maintain the health, morale, and marching speed of his army. As the supply wagons became empty, they were distributed among the divisions to carry the sick and weary.

Hardee reached Glasgow on September 12. While he waited for Polk to come up, Hardee sent secret agents into Bowling Green, screening his presence with Wheeler's cavalry. Bragg intended to wait at Glasgow until Buell committed himself, but an "indiscreet" action by one of Polk's subordinates upset his plans. General James Chalmers had been sent forward toward Munfordville to obtain information, but he went beyond his instructions and recklessly attacked the entrenched garrison. He met with a bloody repulse.

When Bragg learned of Chalmers' defeat, he ordered a general advance upon the town. A witness recorded that when Hardee received the order, he shouted, "My God! What does Bragg mean: We can cross the river here with one corps, advance the other direct on M. [Munfordville] and thus force a surrender with the least loss. . . . Mount and follow me to Army Hd Qrs." [14] After he conferred with Bragg, the order was changed. As Hardee was well acquainted with the town's defenses, he advised Bragg to have Polk invest it from the north, where its defenses were weakest. While Polk maneuvered north of Green River, Hardee would close in from the south. Colonel John T. Wilder, the Union commander, did not hesitate long, once he learned of the overwhelming Confederate numbers and the rows of six- and twelve-pounders trained on his works. On September 16 he unconditionally surrendered the town and its garrison of four thousand men.[15]

The capture of Munfordville caused Buell to leave Bowling Green and head north at once. Bragg moved quickly and blocked Buell at Horse Cave. There the Confederates awaited Buell's attack. Joe Wheeler commented, "The entire army was in the best of spirits. I met and talked with Generals Hardee, Polk, Cheatham, and Buckner; all were enthusiastic over our success, and our good luck in getting Buell where he would be compelled to fight us to such a disadvantage." [16]

14 J. M. Kinnard to T. M. Owen, August 13, 1910, in Owen Collection.
15 *Official Records*, XVI, Pt. 2, pp. 833, 837.
16 Joseph Wheeler, "Bragg's Invasion of Kentucky," in *Battles and Leaders*, III, 10; B. Bragg to wife, September 18, 1862, in Braxton Bragg Letters, 1861–63 (Library of Congress).

Buell, however, had no intention of attacking Bragg's army. He halted his army and waited. Two days passed, and Bragg became uneasy. He assembled a council of war and informed his officers that only two days' rations remained. He also read them dispatches from Kirby Smith urging concentration because of the sizable Cumberland Gap garrison that threatened his rear. In light of these factors Hardee and the others advised Bragg to abandon the Horse Cave position and move north.[17]

As the Confederates marched toward Bardstown, Hardee guarded the rear. His responsibilities required him to work very closely with the cavalry that Bragg assigned him. During this march a close association between Hardee and Wheeler developed. Hardee, with his long years of cavalry experience and with his knowledge of Wheeler as a promising West Point cadet, made good use of his young lieutenant. He demanded that Wheeler submit frequent and detailed reports, and Wheeler responded with a vengeance. Indeed, the weary-eyed T. B. Roy complained that these reports "obtained during the day . . . would begin to come in, and were continued, with the briefest intervals, during the night; so that, while the average officer or soldier could rely upon some substantial rest and sleep, between 10 P.M., and 3 A.M., Hardee could not hope for as much as an hour, nor his Adjt Genl for any at all." Hardee left a great deal to Wheeler's discretion, and his cavalry commander justified his confidence. The picketing, intelligence, and combat missions of his command won the admiration of the army and proved to be a worthy example of what could be accomplished when cavalry co-operated closely with the main infantry body. The long association with Hardee had its effect on Wheeler. In 1893 he said that "if he, that day, should receive a dispatch ending up with—'by command of Lt Genl Hardee' ordering him to jump off a roof, he would instantly jump, if only from mere force of habit." [18]

Bragg had been greatly discouraged by the failure of the Kentuckians to turn out in support of the Confederacy. After his army arrived in Bardstown, he turned over immediate command to the senior officer, Polk, and departed for Lexington. In a month Kirby Smith had been able to recruit only about a brigade. He commented,

17 Liddell's Record; Claiborne Letters and Reminiscences; *Official Records,* XVI, Pt. 1, p. 1090.
18 Roy, "Odds and Ends."

"Their hearts are evidently with us but their blue-grass and fat-grass are against us." [19] Bragg believed that the inauguration of Governor Richard Hawes might help to accomplish politically what he had been unable to do militarily. Because of Bragg's deep interest in politics and his political experience, his action is understandable. Considered from the military aspect, however, it was injudicious at best. He deprived his army of his leadership when it faced the superior numbers of the enemy. The Bardstown "rest stop" and the inauguration of Hawes gave Buell the initiative he had badly needed since the opening of the campaign. With his forces scattered over the face of north-central Kentucky and with the main body of these forces leaderless, Bragg invited disaster.

While the Confederates rested at Bardstown and tried to erect a new state government, Buell moved up the railroad toward Louisville unmolested. In Louisville he combined his forces with the thousands of green volunteers sent across the Ohio by the alarmed Midwestern states. By the first of October Buell had organized his forces. Then he began his advance upon the dispersed Confederates. On October 2 this threat became evident to the Confederates at Bardstown. Polk had just been ordered to advance upon Louisville by way of Elizabethtown. This Union advance in force changed matters completely. Polk wrote Bragg that the Union army was moving forward in three columns. "If an opportunity presents itself I will strike." Otherwise, "will fall back on Harrodsburg and Danville . . . [to join] General E. K. Smith, and Stevenson. . . . It seems to me we are too much scattered." [20] Bragg had also learned of the advance, but as he was out of touch with the immediate situation, he believed the enemy to be marching east directly against Frankfort, giving Polk an ideal opportunity to strike the exposed southern flank. Therefore, he ordered Polk to attack. Polk's information, however, led him to believe that instead of moving in force on Frankfort the enemy was heading straight for Bardstown. Wheeler soon confirmed these apprehensions.[21] Polk therefore submitted Bragg's order to a council of war. Buckner was absent at Danville setting up a camp to train the new Kentucky troops, but Hardee, Anderson, Cheatham, and S. A. M. Wood all supported Polk in his decision to fall back toward Harrods-

19 *Official Records,* XVI, Pt. 2, pp. 845, 876.
20 *Ibid.,* 898.
21 J. M. Kinnard to T. M. Owen, August 13, 1910, in Owen Collection.

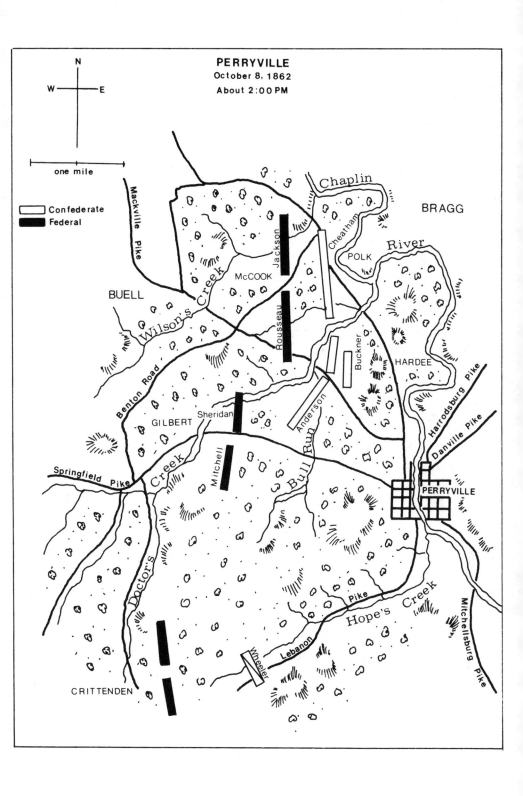

PERRYVILLE
October 8, 1862
About 2:00 PM

N
W — E
S

one mile

Confederate
Federal

Mackville Pike

BUELL

Wilson's Creek

McCOOK

Jackson

Rousseau

Chaplin River

BRAGG

Cheatham

POLK

Buckner

HARDEE

Benton Road

GILBERT

Sheridan

Creek

Mitchell

Anderson

Bull Run

Springfield Pike

Doctor's Creek

PERRYVILLE

Harrodsburg Pike

Danville Pike

Pike

Hope's Creek

Mitchellsburg Pike

Wheeler

Lebanon

CRITTENDEN

burg to unite with Bragg rather than advance against the superior force confronting them.[22]

The Union advance had also alarmed Kirby Smith. When Bragg ordered him to Frankfort, he protested and urged Bragg to concentrate all of his forces for a battle against Buell's united command. Buckner joined Kirby Smith in this appeal, but Bragg insisted that "he could crush Buell with his own command alone and that he should carry out his intention of inaugurating Gov. Hawes at Frankfort." [23] Bragg did make some concessions. He told Polk to concentrate at Harrodsburg and sent the brigades of Cleburne and Preston Smith and one of Carter L. Stevenson's brigades to that point.

Thus on October 4 Kirby Smith's force awaited the Union attack in Frankfort, while Polk retreated slowly toward Harrodsburg, with his command divided into two columns to expedite the movement. He took the direct route through Springfield, and Hardee took the route from Bardstown to Glenville to Mackville to Kenton, a "most execrable" dirt road damaged by recent rains.[24] When Polk learned of Hardee's difficulties with the terrain, he allowed him to leave his assigned road and join him on the Springfield road. The Confederate column passed through Springfield and headed for Harrodsburg via Perryville, where on October 6, Hardee reported to Bragg and Polk that the enemy was pressing him. Polk ordered Hardee to halt there and to force the enemy to reveal his strength. To aid Hardee he sent back Patton Anderson's division and Cleburne's brigade.[25]

On October 7 Buell's advanced units encountered Hardee's cavalry near Perryville, and presently the famous fight for the water supply began. Hardee's men held the springs of water in the fork of the Chaplin River. Buell's men had experienced an "almost total want of water for nearly thirty-six hours, and when they learned that water was nearby, they could hardly be restrained." [26] Daniel McCook's brigade of Phil Sheridan's division determined to capture the water supply, and throughout October 7 small detachments fought. "Both

22 *Official Records,* XVI, Pt. 1, pp. 1099–1101; Pt. 2, p. 897.
23 Kirby Smith to J. S. Johnston, October 31, 1866, Edmund Kirby Smith Account of the Kentucky Campaign, in Kirby Smith Papers.
24 *Official Records,* XVI, Pt. 2, p. 905.
25 Stoddard Johnston Diary (1862–63), October 6, 1862, in Braxton Bragg Papers, 1861–65 (Western Reserve Historical Society, Cleveland, Ohio); Polk to Bragg, October 6, 1862, in Polk Papers.
26 *Official Records,* XVI, Pt. 2, p. 612.

sides seemed willing to die rather than leave the creek so scarce was the water." [27] Hardee, however, held back his main force, waiting until his opponents revealed their true strength. When he learned that heavy infantry was advancing in support of the detachments at the water holes, Hardee notified Bragg.

Until he received Hardee's dispatch, Bragg had intended for the Army of the Mississippi to move on toward Lawrenceburg to unite with Kirby Smith. News from Kirby Smith that the enemy had crossed the Kentucky River had confirmed his belief that the main Union body was operating in that vicinity. He issued a confidential circular that ordered Cheatham and Withers, of Polk's wing, to concentrate with Kirby Smith at Versailles near Lawrenceburg. Hardee would come on to Versailles as soon as he could. But when Bragg received Hardee's dispatch about the enemy's heavy force, he changed his plans and ordered Cheatham's division to support Hardee, who was to engage the enemy. Withers would go on as planned, to rendezvous with Kirby Smith at Versailles.[28]

After sending his dispatch to Bragg, Hardee expected to fight at Perryville. He rode over the terrain with his staff and St. John Liddell, searching for a good position for the line of battle and for artillery emplacements. He asked Liddell's opinion as to the position, and Liddell "unhesitatingly answered that we could hardly have a better one, and that our possession of the water in Choplin [sic] Fork was a decided advantage." After reconnoitering the terrain, the group stopped at the Widow Padlock's home in Perryville. While Liddell and the staff labored over terrain sketches, Hardee engaged the widow and her daughters in conversation. Liddell recorded the scene: "The gallant General was now quite at home, bandying compliments, particularly with the widow, who not to be beaten, expressed her sincere sympathy with the general, that one so advanced in years should be engaged in the dangers and troubles of war. 'Why Madam' exclaimed the General, . . . touched to the quick, 'How old do you take me to be?' 'Well sir, I am 72 and I think you about a year younger.' " [29] Hardee, supported by Liddell, fired a last shot as he left the house, but the victory remained with the widow. The staff had evidently not

27 Kean Reminiscences.
28 Johnston Diary, October 7, 1862; Army of the Mississippi Confidential Circular, October 7, 1862, in Polk Papers; *Official Records*, XVI, Pt. 1, pp. 1091–92, 1096.
29 Liddell's Record.

been as absorbed as they seemed for the incident continued to come up in later months to plague Hardee.

That night Hardee received simultaneously Bragg's confidential circular and the order directing Cheatham to come to his assistance. Since the times of dispatch were not recorded on the messages, Hardee supposed that the order to remain at Perryville and engage the enemy with Cheatham's support had been written later. Both orders disappointed and alarmed Hardee. He saw that Bragg was separating his forces and decided that he must appeal to his commander to effect a junction before one of the two parts of the army was overwhelmed by Buell. He returned to his tent and wrote out an unusual letter:

Permit me, from the friendly relations so long existing between us, to write you plainly. Do not scatter your forces. There is one rule in our profession which should never be forgotten; it is to throw the masses of your troops on the fractions of the enemy. The movement last proposed will divide your army and each may be defeated, where as by keeping them united success is certain. If it be your policy to strike the enemy at Versailles, take your whole force with you and make the blow effective; if, on the contrary, you should decide to strike the army in front of me, first let that be done with a force which will make success certain. Strike with your whole strength first to the right then to the left. I could not sleep quietly to-night without giving expression to these views. What ever you decide to do will meet my hearty co-operation.

If you wish my opinion, it is that in view of the position of your depots you ought to strike this force first.[30]

Before Hardee dispatched this letter to Bragg, he called in Anderson and Wood and read it to them. What Wood thought is not known, but Anderson "fully concurred." The letter did not cause Bragg to change his troop dispositions, but it did cause him to come to Perryville rather than to go to Lawrenceburg, as he had intended.[31]

Later in the evening Hardee sent for Wheeler to go over the plans for the next day. After Wheeler had been briefed on the position of the line of battle, he was ordered to oppose the advancing elements of the enemy until they reached Chaplin's Fork. He would retire behind the infantry when pressed back to the creek. Hardee next ordered Liddell to take his brigade out to the vicinity of Doctor's Fork, a tributary of Chaplin Creek. When Wheeler retreated, Liddell must contest the enemy's advance as long as possible, to allow the main line of battle to be formed. As the evening wore on, Cheatham appeared

---

30 *Official Records*, XVI, Pt. 1, p. 1099.
31 *Ibid.*, 1100; Johnston Diary, October 7, 1862.

with his division, and Hardee placed him on the main line. After these dispositions had been made, General Polk rode up from Harrodsburg to Perryville and assumed command of the entire force.[32]

At the time Polk arrived, skirmishing was already under way. After his meeting with Hardee, Wheeler had led his cavalry beyond Doctor's Fork and ambushed the advancing Federals. The federal infantry recovered quickly and threw out skirmishers, and fighting continued through the night. Wheeler found himself pressed back to Chaplin's Fork, so according to plan, he retired behind Liddell's line. Liddell continued the fight into the morning hours.

Polk came to Perryville armed with an order from Bragg stating that he had "better . . . give the enemy battle immediately"; he was to "rout him, and then move to our support at Versailles." At 6 A.M. Polk wrote Bragg that picket firing had begun. "Understanding it to be your wish to give them battle," he continued, "we shall do so vigorously." The term "vigorously" is open to different interpretations. Polk interpreted it to mean the "defensive-offensive"—that is, to await the attack of the superior enemy and to counterattack when a favorable opportunity presented itself. This mode of battle had been decided upon by Polk and his general officers at a daybreak council of war.[33]

The Confederates formed their line of battle on the steep eastern side of Chaplin's Fork, well to the rear of Liddell's position. By 8 A.M. Liddell was under heavy pressure from the enemy skirmish lines. At 11 A.M. Polk ordered him back to the main line. The increasing Federal pressure toward the Confederate right caused Polk to alter the line of battle by sending Cheatham's division to the right. The Confederate line now was made up of Cheatham on the right, Buckner in the center, and Patton Anderson on the left. Wheeler's cavalry had been moved to the left to protect the direct approaches to Perryville and to interdict the battlefield.

Much had occurred between 6 A.M. and 11 A.M. General Bragg had reached Perryville at 9:30 A.M. He was surprised to learn that the battle had not opened in earnest. Polk told him that Liddell was under heavy attack and that the enemy were to their front in large force. Bragg then ordered Polk to have the troops attack at once. News from Wheeler indicated the approach of another heavy enemy body to the

32 Wheeler, "Bragg's Invasion of Kentucky," in *Battles and Leaders*, III, 15; *Official Records*, XVI, Pt. 1, pp. 1092, 1157–58.
33 *Official Records*, XVI, Pt. 1, pp. 1096, 1101, 1110.

southwest of Perryville and confirmed Bragg in his decision to strike immediately. After he issued his order, a delay ensued, and according to Bragg, Hardee rode up to him and voiced his fear that Polk would not attack. Bragg then rode up to the main line and saw to it that the army moved forward.[34]

Immediately in the path of the Confederate attack was the corps of Hardee's old West Point subordinate, Alexander McCook. McCook had posted his two divisions under James E. Jackson and Rousseau on the opposite side of Chaplin's Fork. The corps of Charles C. Gilbert was near at hand, with Sheridan's division advanced to a position on McCook's right. The main body of the Union army under Thomas was farther to the right, approaching Perryville. Because of the unusual atmospheric conditions that prevailed that day, Thomas never heard the noise of the battle and was informed that the fighting had begun only after it was too late to take effective action.[35]

The Confederates opened the battle with Cheatham's attack against Jackson's division. Once Cheatham became engaged, Hardee's two divisions attacked. Buckner's division moved forward shortly after 12:30 P.M. Hardee, who spent most of the afternoon with Buckner's division, directed Bushrod Johnson to assault the right of McCook's corps at the point where the Mackville road crossed Doctor's Fork. Cleburne was to follow as a supporting force. The enemy was well positioned behind rail and stone fences and had the added advantage of enfilade fire from Sheridan's division of Gilbert's corps. Before Johnson assaulted, he oriented himself on a barn at the right of McCook's line. This barn, subsequently known as the "burnt barn," had just been set afire by shells from the Confederate artillery, and the wind took the smoke streaming down McCook's entire line, obscuring it from view. Johnson moved down into the valley and started up the opposite side. His men advanced from rail fence to stone fence to rail fence to stone fence. The enemy fire took a heavy toll, and the brigade buckled. To Johnson's left Adams' brigade of Anderson's division had been repulsed by the left of Sheridan's line and the right of McCook's. Hardee took two of Johnson's regiments and ordered them with Adams to renew the attack. Meanwhile, Cleburne had moved up behind Johnson. Taking advantage of the stone walls that Johnson had captured, Cleburne went to Johnson's left, executed a wheeling movement to the right, and attacked across Johnson's front to the right

34 Liddell's Record; *Official Records*, XVI, Pt. 1, pp. 1087, 1092–93, 1101, 1110.
35 *Official Records*, XVI, Pt. 1, pp. 50–51, 186.

flank of McCook's corps. McCook's flank brigade fired their volley at Cleburne's skirmishers. Before they could reload for another volley, Cleburne's line of battle was upon them. McCook's right crumbled and rushed to the rear. Cleburne pursued, assisted by Wood's brigade on his right. Cleburne soon halted to re-form, and when he renewed the pursuit, he struck George Webster's brigade which had been waiting in reserve. He did not advance farther.[36]

Hardee had been fortunate in his attack. Buckner and Anderson had Sheridan's division and the right of Rousseau's division to contend with. Sheridan and Rousseau were both on high ground. Between their position was a depressed area where Doctor's Fork split off from Chaplin Creek and headed west. The Union commanders failed to defend this gap, thus exposing both Sheridan's flank and Rousseau's flank. Anderson with one brigade kept Sheridan occupied to the front while Adams and two of Johnson's regiments kept his left flank threatened. This prevented Sheridan from detaching forces to assist Rousseau. Cleburne nicely utilized the gap between Sheridan and Rousseau when he attacked. Instead of continuing down Doctor's Fork, Cleburne changed direction to the right, which enabled him to catch Rousseau in the flank. Rousseau could not concentrate against Cleburne's enveloping force because of the brigades of Wood and John C. Brown, which were attacking him from the front.

Cheatham on the right had been even more successful than Hardee. His attack struck the raw troops of Jackson's division and pulverized them, killing Jackson and one of his brigade commanders and scores of their troops. Union troops being pushed up from the rear found McCook's corps "badly cut up and retreating (they then haven [sic] fallen back nearly 1 mile) and were being hotly pressed by the enemy." [37] To halt the rout McCook threw in the brigades of Webster, Michael Goodling, and John C. Starkweather. The first two stopped Cleburne and Wood. The latter checked Cheatham.

At sunset fighting continued on the right. Cheatham, now supported by Liddell's brigade, which was sent over by Hardee, fought on against the remnants of McCook's corps. The important engagement at sunset, however, occurred on the extreme left. Anderson had barely managed to hold his own against Sheridan's numbers in the afternoon. As night approached, he found himself heavily outnum-

---

36 *Ibid.,* 1079–80, 1111, 1121, 1125, 1129, 1131; LII, Pt. 1, pp. 51–52; Claiborne Letters and Reminiscences; Liddell's Record.
37 *Official Records,* XVI, Pt. 1, pp. 1079–80.

bered and forced to retreat. Colonel William Carlin of R. B. Mitchell's division had come up from the rear to Sheridan's support. Together with the troops from Sheridan's right he attacked Anderson and drove him steadily back toward Perryville. Behind Carlin were about twenty thousand men of Crittenden's corps. Crittenden had been held back so far by the remarkable Wheeler. Wheeler had attacked the leading elements of this corps as it approached Perryville earlier in the day, and his attack had created the impression with Crittenden that he confronted a much heavier force than a mere cavalry brigade.[38]

Nevertheless, the furiousness of Carlin's attack and the news of large bodies of Union troops approaching Perryville led Bragg to call a council of war. When his generals learned of the situation on the left, they agreed with him that Perryville should be abandoned and a junction formed with Kirby Smith. Late at night, therefore, the Confederates began pulling back their lines.[39]

The Confederate withdrawal came as a welcome surprise to McCook, who had had three generals and about a thousand men killed. Early that night he had seen Confederate campfires to his front, his left, and his right. In their hands he had been forced to leave several of his artillery pieces and all of his personal baggage.[40] McCook had suffered about three fourths of the 3,299 Union casualties. As he was opposed by two corps to his one, it is a wonder that he did not lose more. Indeed, with all the green troops he commanded, it is a wonder that his corps maintained its ground at all.

The Confederates did not buy their victory cheaply. Perryville cost them 3,145 men, including Cleburne and Brown wounded and S. A. M. Wood severely wounded. Hardee's corps, with two divisions on the field, had lost more heavily than Polk's. On the asset side of the Confederate ledger were the guns captured from McCook and thousands of small arms and pieces of equipment gathered up off the battlefield. Bragg, Hardee, and other veterans of Shiloh referred to Perryville as the severest struggle they had witnessed. Hardee told one of Bragg's

---

38 Kenneth Powers Williams, *Lincoln Finds a General*, 4 vols. (New York, 1949–56), IV, 132–33.
39 *Official Records*, XVI, Pt. 1, p. 1093; Claiborne Letters and Reminiscences; David Urquhart, "Bragg's Advance and Retreat," in *Battles and Leaders*, III, 603.
40 McCook appealed to his good friend Hardee to recover his clothing for him, laughingly stating that the only Confederate general who could wear it was Humphrey Marshall, who weighed three hundred pounds. Hardee investigated the matter but learned that unfortunately Bragg had already disposed of McCook's effects.

staff officers after the battle "that it was 'Nip & Tuck' & he once thought 'Nip' had it." [41] Hardee reserved this comment and would use it once again to describe a battle.

At Perryville sixteen thousand men under Bragg struck the advance elements of Buell's army. The Federals had about thirty-six thousand men on the field, but they were widely dispersed, giving Bragg the opportunity to throw his masses against fractions. If at any time during the battle the forces of either Thomas or Crittenden had come up and launched an attack on the weak Confederate left, they might have achieved a complete victory. Bragg's attack against the main force of the enemy with only a part of his command is probably open to as much criticism as Buell's tactics, if not more. Bragg ran a terrible risk. The chances for success were negligible; the chances of failure were great. Considered tactically, Perryville stands as a victory for the Confederates. Their offense succeeded in routing the Union left, and they withdrew from the field in good order when they learned that their own left was endangered. Strategically considered, Bragg failed to halt Buell's advance or to crush one of his columns. Inasmuch as Buell succeeded in pushing the Confederates aside at Perryville and was not deterred from his objective of driving them from Kentucky, the over-all victory should go to his force.

Hardee's role at Perryville was equal to, if not better than, his performance at Shiloh. He spotted the gap in the center of the Union line and threw Cleburne into it, breaking McCook's right and containing Sheridan. Hardee is responsible for placing the Confederates in their positions the night before the battle and for designing the plan of action for Wheeler and Liddell. The temporary stand by these two brigades enticed forward the advance elements of McCook's corps and ensured that the main line could be formed leisurely. Hardee has been censured by Bragg for his part in the dawn council of war that decided to adopt the "defensive-offensive" rather than a direct attack, but everything hinges about Bragg's order to Polk. Polk thought Bragg's order to be "simply suggestive and advisory"; "clearly not preemptory." The text of Bragg's letter supports this understanding: "You had better move with Cheatham's division to his [Hardee's] support and give the enemy battle immediately. . . ." [42] It does not say "attack immediately." Hardee and Polk certainly prepared to "give the enemy battle," but prudence told them that they should not

41 Johnston Diary, October 8, 1862.
42 *Official Records*, XVI, Pt. 1, pp. 1092–93, 1096, 1102.

attack the enemy at once but should await his attack and then turn on him when the opportunity came. Hardee and Polk were learning that to use one's discretion when under the command of Braxton Bragg was often a hazardous course.

Daylight on October 9 found the Confederates on the road to Harrodsburg. After uniting with Kirby Smith's army at Harrodsburg, Bragg stationed these troops in a line of battle and led Kirby Smith to believe that here he intended to fight. Late in the day Bragg disappointed Kirby Smith and his enthusiastic troops by ordering a retirement to Bryantsville (Camp Dick Robinson). Bragg and his officers had decided upon this course after learning that Buell was advancing toward Danville, threatening their left flank and threatening to cut them off from their supply dump at Camp Dick Robinson.[43]

The Confederate army occupied a strong defensive position at Camp Dick Robinson on October 11. Buell declined to make the frontal attack that the Confederates wanted and swung around again to the left. To leave Bryantsville was to abandon Kentucky, but after painful deliberation the Confederates reached their decision and withdrew. When the Kentucky campaign had been concluded, the Confederates piled up excuses for the course they took. They had quite a few plausible ones: they had been outnumbered; Kentucky had failed to rally to the Confederate cause; if they had given battle, they might have jeopardized the great quantities of stores collected during the campaign; had they fought, they would have fought far from their base of communications, whereas the enemy would have fought close to his; there had been disturbing rumors from the south that Van Dorn's auxiliary forces had been defeated at Corinth. Most of all it seems that the generals had feared a defeat in their isolated position. If defeated, they could well have lost their army and all of the precious supplies on a forced retreat back to Tennessee.

The decision to abandon Kentucky had been reached in a council of war. The results of this council shocked the army, particularly the Kentuckians. One Kentucky staff officer, Thomas Claiborne, had lost face when the army turned back. He took advantage of his close relation with Hardee and his fellow Kentuckian Buckner to ask them why the decision had been made. Hardee answered that they lacked the manpower to fight Buell and that "the condition of the army

---

43 Johnston Diary, October 10, 1862; Kirby Smith Account of the Kentucky Campaign; *Official Records*, XVI, Pt. 1, p. 1093.

required" a retreat. Claiborne still could not believe that the generals
had advised such a course of action. Buckner finally told Claiborne
reluctantly, "We advised in a council today," that the army "has lost
confidence in Bragg, all are agreed on retreat." Caliborne then pressed
further, asking if Bragg could not be replaced. Buckner replied, "Ah,
we have no power to supercede him & he would not resign." [44] St.
John Liddell also approached Hardee on the subject and arrived at a
slightly different conclusion. He began his conversation with deroga-
tory remarks about Bragg giving up Kentucky. Hardee jokingly said,
"You speak very plainly—I am half inclined to arrest you." The
brigade commander would not be turned aside and continued to question the decision. Hardee then told him that "when all the facts were
known, Genl Polk would be credited for saving Bragg's Army in causing its timely withdrawal from Kentucky. This remark proved to me
what I suspected, that Bragg was not well supported by his Generals,
on whom he had every reason to rely. —I afterwards heard, that he
wished to concentrate his wings to give general Battle, but unfortunately gave way to the pressure of his council Officers, which with his
own apprehensions, too quickly turned the balance." [45] Bragg, however, in his acid discussion of the campaign never made such a charge.
Furthermore, it is known that except for Kirby Smith and Humphrey
Marshall, all of the officers in the council favored leaving Kentucky.[46]

In a letter to Jefferson Davis' aide, Colonel William P. Johnston,
Hardee revealed his opinion of Bragg's handling of the campaign.

Unfortunately for Bragg he has given his enemies just grounds for attacking him. Grave, unpardonable errors were committed; errors which
any man of good practical sense without military education or experience
ought not to have committed. If his instructions and orders had been carried out, the Army would have been destroyed. He ordered Polk, then
encamped with his Army at Bardstown, to occupy Elizabethtown and to
invest Louisville. At another time, while the enemy was moving heavy
columns on us at Bardstown, but threatening a feint on our right flank
towards Frankfort, he ordered Polk with the greater part of his force to
move through Taylorsville and attack Buell in flank & rear. At Perryville
he reversed the military rule of attacking fractions of the enemy with the
mass of his forces and deliberately attacked Buell's Army with a fraction
of his own. . . . To relieve Bragg is easy enough, to provide a competent

44 Claiborne Letters and Reminiscences.
45 Liddell's Record.
46 *Official Records*, XVI, Pt. 1, p. 1093; Johnston Diary, October 12, 1862; Kirby
    Smith Account of the Kentucky Campaign.

successor is a more difficult matter. Bragg has proved a failure, it is true, but . . . have we any body who will do better. I confess this has been a strong reason in restraining me from speaking out boldly in reference to the failure in Kentucky.[47]

With their faith shaken in their commander, the disappointed Confederates left Bryantsville on October 13 for Lancaster. There the army split into two columns. Kirby Smith's column headed for Cumberland Gap and Knoxville by way of Big Hill. The Army of the Mississippi moved by way of Crab Orchard through Mount Vernon and London toward Cumberland Gap. Buell pursued as far as Crab Orchard and then turned off toward Nashville. He had found the country over which he passed "a desert," and to further discourage him, the Confederates had resorted to a favorite tactic—Morgan was unleashed against his rear.

Finally, after great effort, the Confederates succeeded in moving their trains across the mountains. By October 19 the van of the column under Hardee reached Cumberland Gap. From there Hardee proceeded to Morristown, Tennessee, where he received orders directing him to middle Tennessee. The Kentucky campaign was over.

47 Hardee to W. P. Johnston, November 19, 1862, in Johnston Papers.

IX

Bullets and Bottles of Brandy

"IT HAS been determined, as a measure of the first importance, that a combined movement should be made at this time into Middle Tennessee." [1] This directive, which came from the War Department on November 1, had been anticipated by Bragg. Shortly after the battle of Perryville he had ordered Breckinridge with a division into middle Tennessee to secure that area. Then when the Army of the Mississippi neared Knoxville, Bragg told Polk to begin preparations for shifting the army to Murfreesboro. Bragg left the army in Knoxville and proceeded to Richmond for a conference with Seddon and Davis. Four days later, on October 28, Polk issued the order for the movement. The army began leaving the next day. They traveled to Chattanooga by rail, changed trains there, and proceeded as far as Estill Springs. From there they marched to Shelbyville.[2]

General Hardee followed his command to middle Tennessee. He had spent a few days in Chattanooga recuperating from a short illness and enjoying the company of his friend Ella Newsome. Mrs. Newsome was a lady who devoted her time and efforts to the Confederate hospitals and won a place in many letters and journals of wounded soldiers. It was a pleasant period of convalescence for the general, who was not seriously ill. Horseback excursions up Lookout Mountain, parties, and other enjoyable pursuits made the little railroad junction and trading center hard to leave. When Hardee arrived in Estill Springs, he reported back to his friend: "I have a small house, known in Georgia and Florida as 'two pens and a passage,' which furnishes me a room for an office and a room for a chamber. Dr. Yandell and

---

1 *Official Records*, XX, Pt. 2, p. 384.
2 Liddell's Record; *Official Records*, XVI, Pt. 2, p. 976; Johnston Diary, October 10, 24, 1862.

Major Roy sleep in the same room with me. The other members of my staff are encamped in the immediate vicinity." [3]

Hardee went to Estill Springs without knowing "precisely where my command was." When he discovered Buckner and his division there, he decided to set up headquarters. Anderson and his division were about two miles back toward Chattanooga at Allisonia. Hardee went to visit Bragg at Shelbyville soon after he arrived, and the latter briefed him on the situation in middle Tennessee. Buell had been replaced by William S. Rosecrans, and Rosecrans had concentrated about eighty thousand troops around Nashville. To annoy Rosecrans and to prevent a sudden attack from Nashville, Bragg strengthened his cavalry. Forrest roamed below and to the west of the Cumberland, and Morgan operated north of the river. Bragg intended to deploy his forty thousand infantrymen near Murfreesboro and to await opportunities for offensive action. [4]

Before moving the army to Murfreesboro Bragg divided it into two army corps under Lieutenant Generals Polk and Hardee. [5] Polk commanded the divisions of Cheatham, Withers, and Breckinridge; Hardee had Buckner and Patton Anderson. Later in November Bragg broke up the division of the wounded Anderson and divided it between Polk and Hardee. He then transferred Breckinridge to Hardee. Completing the Napoleonic concept of a corps, Bragg finally added a brigade of cavalry to each, designating Wheeler to work with Hardee and John A. Wharton to work with Polk. When he had finished consolidating the armies of Kentucky and Mississippi, Bragg labeled the whole the Army of Tennessee.

Of course, the creation of corps meant promotions. Two of Hardee's colonels were promoted to brigadier general—Lucius E. Polk and Roger W. Hanson. Hardee assigned the Kentuckian Hanson to command a Kentucky brigade under Breckinridge and placed Lucius Polk under Buckner. Buckner, however, did not remain long as a division commander. Mobile needed someone to coordinate its de-

---

3 Hardee to Ella K. Newsome, November 15, 1862, in Jacob Fraise Richard, *The Florence Nightingale of the Southern Army* (New York, 1914), 67; Richard Barksdale Harwell, *Kate: The Journal of a Confederate Nurse* (Baton Rouge, 1959), 76–77.

4 *Official Records*, XX, Pt. 2, pp. 213, 421–22; Richard, *The Florence Nightingale*, 67.

5 Hardee had been promoted to lieutenant general on October 11. He would rank from October 10. This made him junior to Longstreet, Kirby Smith, and Polk, and senior to Holmes, Jackson, and Pemberton.

fenses, and Hardee recommended Buckner.[6] When Buckner left, Cleburne was promoted to major general and given his division. This promotion surprised many. Both S. A. M. Wood and Bushrod Johnson were senior to Cleburne and had given capable performances during the past six months. Cleburne's performance, however, had been outstanding. In Kentucky he had won acclaim for his action at the battle of Richmond under Kirby Smith and for his fine work at Perryville. This record, in addition to Hardee's efforts, secured him the promotion. When President Davis visited the army in December, he brought Cleburne's commission with him and made it known that he had yielded finally to Hardee's requests.[7]

Davis found the army in Murfreesboro in good spirits. A dazzled reporter who accompanied him dramatized a grand review of the army, held in the president's honor.

And here is General Hardee, whose excellent Text Book of tactics was the bane of our youthful military education, but whose volumes, nevertheless, have acted the Drill Master for both armies in this war. General Hardee, whom the ladies all adore! I know two fair ones myself who are dying about him. He always was a gallant and graceful gentleman in the parlor as well as on the field. But he has been disappointed in love, says my little bird, for all that. . . . The little simpleton! She might have had a General and a hero for a husband. Hardee who is a philosopher as well as a hero, recovered like a man and has been in love a dozen times since.[8]

The "philosopher" found the essential feminine company at Wartrace and Murfreesboro, in the persons of Miss Rowe Webster, the Ready sisters, and others. John Morgan also frequented the Ready household. The courtship of Morgan and Mattie Ready, which had taken place between raids, culminated in a colorful wedding in mid-December. Hardee rode twenty miles on horseback from his station at Eagleville to witness the marriage of one of his favorite belles. Bishop Polk performed the ceremony, with Bragg, Hardee, Cheatham, Breckinridge, and many others in attendance. Morgan presented his friend with a beautiful thoroughbred.[9] He felt indebted for Hardee's help in securing him his promotion to brigadier general, but Hardee

---

6 Liddell's Record; *Official Records,* XX, Pt. 2, p. 449.
7 Liddell's Record; Hardee to Cooper, October 28, 1862, in Letters Received, Adjutant General's Office.
8 Clipping from unidentified newspaper, dated December 17, 1862, in Solomon Scrapbook, 1861–62.
9 Pickett, *Hardee,* 49; Richard, *The Florence Nightingale,* 69, 71; Urquhart, "Bragg's Advance and Retreat," in *Battles and Leaders,* III, 605n.

had actually gone beyond this. When Davis came to Murfreesboro, Hardee had urged him to make Morgan a major general, but Davis had declined saying, "I do not wish to give my boys all of their sugar plums at once." [10] As Christmas approached Willie Hardee, who was in school in Marietta, Georgia, came to Murfreesboro to spend his vacation with his father. To further soften a Christmas in camp, old army friends with Rosecrans took advantage of the numerous flags of truce, "and almost always some kind message . . . was sent thereby to General Hardee, usually accompanied by a bottle of brandy." [11]

After Christmas bullets came in place of the bottles of brandy. Rosecrans had spent the late fall bringing up troops, training and equipping his command, and opening the Louisville and Nashville Railroad. By December 26, he was ready to advance. On that day three columns headed south from Nashville. Crittenden moved out by the Murfreesboro Pike; Thomas moved toward Murfreesboro by way of the Wilson Pike; and McCook advanced toward Hardee's position at Triune. He would attack Hardee there, and his subsequent movements would depend on his opponent. If Hardee retreated toward Murfreesboro, McCook would follow with his entire force; otherwise, he would divide his force, sending part in pursuit and part toward Murfreesboro.

Hardee had left his base at Estill Springs late in November. Bragg had ordered him with his corps to Eagleville, a little town on the Nashville and Shelbyville pike about ten miles south of Triune and fifteen miles southeast of Murfreesboro. Hardee put his main force at Eagleville and pushed forward Wood's brigade to Triune. When Wood reported McCook's approach, Hardee strengthened his force by sending up Cleburne with two other brigades and Adams' brigade from Breckinridge, but Bragg, upon hearing the news, ordered Hardee to come to Murfreesboro. Hardee then withdrew from Triune, leaving Wood and some cavalry to skirmish with the enemy.[12] McCook moved close to Triune and was surprised on the morning

10 Duke, *Reminiscences*, 317.
11 Richard, *The Florence Nightingale*, 69; Kirby Smith to B. A. Putnam, December 28, 1862, in Kirby Smith Papers; Urquhart, "Bragg's Advance and Retreat," in *Battles and Leaders*, III, 605n.
12 *Official Records*, XX, Pt. 1, pp. 843, 896; Hardee's Murfreesboro Report, in William Joseph Hardee Papers, 1863–71 (Duke University Library).
    Generally, Hardee's battle reports are superior pieces of work, characterized by clarity and helpful detail. This report is his longest and his finest. The tone, like his personality, is precise and candid. Criticism is meted out where he felt that it was deserved. The unique feature of Hardee's model reports is the careful terrain analysis that he always includes.

of November 27 to find that the Confederates had disappeared into the fog. He did not know in what direction Hardee had retired, so he followed cautiously.

When Hardee arrived at Murfreesboro, he joined Polk and Bragg at Bragg's headquarters to go over plans for the proposed engagement. Bragg had chosen for the field of battle a section of ground about two miles northwest of Murfreesboro. Stone's River was the important terrain feature. It roughly bisected the area from north to south, and the Nashville and Chattanooga Railroad and the Nashville Pike bisected it from east to west. Open fields and thick cedar brakes covered the area. Although the river would polarize the Confederate position, it did not offer an obstacle to either the defenders or the attackers, since at this season it could be waded easily. Bragg placed Polk's corps to the left of the Nashville Pike and Hardee to the right. Stone's River made a bend at this point and thus separated the two corps. For his reserve Bragg ordered up the division of John P. McCown and the brigade of John K. Jackson from Bridgeport. Hardee occupied his assigned position on Sunday morning, December 28. He placed Breckinridge on the front line, with Cleburne about a thousand yards in the rear. Bragg had given him Jackson's brigade, and this he held as a reserve.[13]

December 29 passed without a battle. Crittenden advanced within sight of the Confederates but halted while Thomas moved up on his right. McCook had not yet reached the battlefield, but his approach from Triune worried Bragg. To strengthen his line in the direction of McCook's approach, Bragg decided to commit his reserve. He placed McCown's division on Polk's left.

When McCook came up on December 30, Rosecrans placed him on the right of Thomas. Now Rosecrans had Crittenden on the left facing Hardee, Thomas in the center facing Polk, and McCook on the right facing McCown. Rosecrans planned to attack the next morning making the main effort with Crittenden's corps.

Bragg also planned to attack the next morning. Wither's division of Polk's corps would strike Thomas, and then the other divisions would join in from left to right. With the arrival of McCook, Bragg changed his plan, shifting Cleburne to the left with McCown and ordering Hardee to take command of both divisions. Breckinridge would remain on the right to protect that flank and to act as the army

---

13 Urquhart, "Bragg's Advance and Retreat," in *Battles and Leaders*, III, 605; Hardee's Murfreesboro Report; *Official Records*, XX, Pt. 1, pp. 673, 838, 917–18, 944; Pt. 2, p. 464.

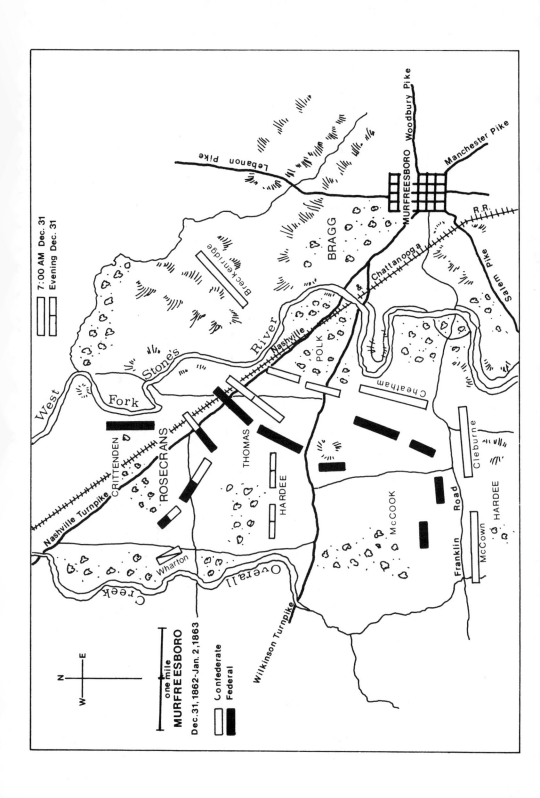

MURFREESBORO
Dec. 31, 1862–Jan. 2, 1863

Confederate
Federal

one mile

N
E
W
S

7:00 AM Dec. 31
Evening Dec. 31

MURFREESBORO
Woodbury Pike
Manchester Pike
Lebanon Pike
R.R.
Salem Pike
Nashville & Chattanooga

BRAGG
Breckenridge
POLK
Cheatham
Cleburne
HARDEE
McCown
McCOOK
Franklin Road
Wilkinson Turnpike
Overall
HARDEE
THOMAS
ROSECRANS
CRITTENDEN
Nashville Turnpike
Wharton
Creek
West Fork
Stone's River
Nashville

reserve. To further increase Hardee's assault force, Bragg sent over Wharton's cavalry brigade.

When Hardee received his orders, he rode to the left ahead of Cleburne. There he found McCown's division drawn up in two lines, with the brigades of Matthew Ector and James E. Rains in front and Evander McNair's brigade in the rear. McCown's right and Cheatham's left met at the Franklin road. Hardee examined McCown's position and was dissatisfied with the placement of Rains's brigade. He ordered McCown to place McNair on the front line and to shift Rains's position.[14]

Cleburne marched through the evening, and his last brigade arrived after midnight. As the troops came up, Hardee put them on a line about five hundred yards in the rear of McCown. They were told that they would attack at dawn. To maintain the element of surprise Hardee's men did not build campfires, although the night turned off "intensely cold and the men were nearly frozen." To their front they could see the glow of the enemy's fires.

From the light of McCook's campfires it appeared that Hardee's flanking force would have to advance against the right center of McCook's line, but actually McCook had had fires built far out to his right to conceal his true position. Hardee's position could not have been more favorable, for his corps was aligned beyond McCook's flank. With the exception of one or possibly two brigades, McCook's corps was to the north of the Franklin road, and all seven of Hardee's brigades were south of it. Hardee met with McCown and Cleburne just before dawn and gave them the plan of attack that Bragg intended to employ. Each of his seven brigades would advance obliquely to the right. If Hardee succeeded in catching McCook's right flank, this maneuver would roll up the Union line.

Dawn brought a cold, frosty morning. Hardee had his commissary men out early, distributing "good drinks" of whisky to the shivering troops. Just as Hardee prepared to advance, he noticed something wrong with McCown's line. He went up and had McCown move McNair forward to link with Ector's brigade. Once this had been attended to, Hardee ordered the attack. "It was not yet clear day." [15]

14 Hardee's Murfreesboro Report; *Official Records*, XX, Pt. 1, pp. 917-19.
15 *Official Records*, XX, Pt. 1, p. 919; Cheatham's Murfreesboro Report, in Benjamin Franklin Cheatham Collection, 1846-84, in possession of Mrs. Telfair Hodgson, Sewanee, Tenn.; Liddell's Record; Ted R. Worley (ed.), *The War Memoirs of Captain John W. Lavender, C. S. A.* (Pine Bluff, Ark., 1956), 38; Roy to J. M. McCown, February 20, 1863, in William Joseph Hardee Letterbook, 1862-76 (Alabama State Department of Archives and History).

McCown's troops stepped off smartly just after 6 A.M. They struck the brigade of Augustus Willich in a matter of minutes. Willich's men were preparing breakfast when they heard the pickets' warning fire. They formed quickly into line but were not ready to meet the attack. McCown overran Willich and continued. In their haste Ector's men pursued Willich westward, forgetting about their wheeling movement to the right. McNair and Rains turned to the right but encountered a fire from their own right flank. Evidently Cheatham's division had not attacked and wheeled with them. Trying to keep their line intact with Ector but buffeted by the firing from the right, McCown's division drifted to the left. Now Cleburne's division moved up.

Hardee moved forward with Cleburne and saw to it that Cleburne executed his wheel to the right. Presently Cleburne's men encountered enemy rifle fire. This surprised them and their leaders, for they believed they were still behind McCown's line. It turned out that they had moved into the space between McCown and Cheatham. A sharp half-hour fight occurred at the Franklin road. McCook's men fought from behind rail fences and large limestone boulders. The brigades of Liddell, Johnson, and Polk charged and drove the enemy's first line back to their second line. They re-formed and charged again. This time the Confederates sent both lines reeling back. The Union division of R. W. Johnson collapsed. Cleburne's men pressed their advantage but were soon hit by enfilade fire from the right, as McCown had been. A gap existed between the right of Cleburne and the left of Cheatham, and Thomas had infantry and artillery in this open space. Hardee now called up his only reserve, Wood's brigade, and sent it into the gap.

McCook's corps fell back nearly a mile and a half before a rallying point was found. In their close pursuit Hardee's men became fatigued, and the lines tended to become fragmented and disorganized. Cleburne's men found the enemy's second line at the Wilkinson Pike. Here the enemy resisted stubbornly, and the Confederates paid heavily before they dislodged their opponents. Finally the brigades of Liddell, Polk, and Wood broke up the enemy position with a determined assault. The enemy retreated north, leaving behind two hospitals and an ammunition train. Brigadier General Joshua Sill had been killed.

At this point Hardee regained control of McCown's division. He ordered Rain's brigade back to the right to attack an enemy battery; McNair and Ector continued toward the Nashville Pike. In response to repeated calls from his commander McCown tardily started moving all of his division to the right. In doing this he inadvertently cut off Liddell's brigade, which had stopped to refill ammunition pouches at the captured ordnance train. When Liddell advanced again, he found himself on the extreme left of Hardee's line. McCown's division now bore the brunt of the fight. Rains's brigade ran into stubborn opposition and was routed, and Rains himself was killed. The invigorated enemy next turned on the brigades of Ector and McNair. These brigades were also giving ground when Liddell came up from the left and the rest of Cleburne's brigades came up from the right. The united force turned against McCown's pursuers and drove them back in turn. Some of the most costly fighting of the day took place here.

Hardee had now worked his way behind the Union center. Union reinforcements were brought up to meet Hardee's front, and these troops, together with those of Thomas on Hardee's right front, poured a devastating fire into the Confederate flank. Hardee sent a message to Bragg telling him that Cheatham had not kept up with his men and had left his right exposed; he asked for reinforcements. This was the critical moment in the attack, and no reinforcements came. Hardee later said: "We had lost nearly a third of the commands engaged. If, at the moment when the enemy were driven from the thick woods north of the Wilkinson turnpike, a fresh division could have replaced Cleburne's exhausted troops and followed up the victory, the rout of Rosecrans' army would have been complete."

After defeating the enemy north of the Wilkinson Pike, Hardee halted and regrouped his command. This took time, for Cleburne's and McCown's troops had become greatly disorganized and many regiments had been decimated. Rosecrans took advantage of this lull in the attack and formed a new line of defense south of the Nashville Pike. Into this line he put the reorganized divisions of R. W. Johnson and Jefferson C. Davis. He also added three brigades from Crittenden's corps. Behind these troops was chaos. Trains, stragglers, wounded, and reserves mixed together in a confused mass that would have been easy prey for any organized division. When his corps had been re-formed, Hardee led them forward to break the backbone of Rosecrans' army. Cleburne, now joined by Preston Smith's brigade of Cheatham's division, gained an initial success, but then the enemy counterattacked. Artillery fire from the right ripped into Hardee's line, and an ugly rumor spread through the ranks that they had been flanked. This was more than the men could stand. The enemy overran

Cleburne's line, and the Confederates retreated. Hardee and Cleburne succeeded in re-forming them about five hundred yards to the rear.

When Hardee's infantry attacked, his cavalry, under Wharton, had attacked simultaneously from the extreme left and had routed the cavalry opposition. At the Wilkinson Pike Wharton encountered the fleeing enemy infantry and captured over a thousand men and some artillery. He proceeded to the Nashville Pike, fighting enemy cavalry and infantry on the way. Finally he drove the enemy over Overall's Creek and soon found himself astride the enemy's line of communication. Here he gathered above five hundred more prisoners and either captured or destroyed several hundred wagons.

The attack of Hardee's corps had succeeded largely because of the assistance rendered by Polk, whose divisions under Cheatham and Withers had kept Thomas fighting for his life, even though they had been unable to gain much ground. Polk appears to have failed in his attacks because he lacked the needed number of troops and because Cheatham had failed to open his attack with McCown and then wheel to the right. As a result, Polk spent a long day delivering repeated costly and fruitless frontal attacks.

The Confederate right under Breckinridge remained inactive during the morning of December 31. Had these reserves been used at the critical moment on the hinge of the Union line between Cheatham and McCown, or later to reinforce Hardee beyond the Wilkinson Pike, there probably would have been a Confederate victory. Instead, Breckinridge stayed glued to his position. Apparently, however, there was no call for his services until late in the morning. When finally contacted, Breckinridge replied that the enemy was advancing upon him. These reports proved inaccurate, and Breckinridge at last sent help about noon. Bragg sent Breckinridge's brigades, not to the left, but to aid Polk. These brigades attacked once they had crossed the river and met the same fate as Polk's men. Late in the afternoon, after the fighting on the left had subsided, Hardee went to Breckinridge's division to supervise its employment. He quickly saw that further attacks over the open ground against the enemy would be futile and "reckless."

Thus the first day's fighting ended, with Polk's line in about the same position as when the attack began. Hardee's line rested several hundred yards south of the Nashville Pike. Cleburne connected with Cheatham's line, then came McCown, and then Liddell on the far left. "Our bivouac fires were lighted at night within 500 yards of the railroad embankment." During the night Hardee's line remained relatively quiet except for sporadic skirmishing.

On January 1, neither army attempted to change its position; neither ventured to attack in force. During the night Bragg unleashed Wheeler and Wharton again, and once again the cavalry got to the rear of the enemy and destroyed a wagon train.

Rosecrans decided to await Bragg's attack on January 2. The attack came as expected, but it came from one of Hardee's divisions, which Hardee had not expected. When the attack occurred, Hardee was making a reconnaissance with St. John Liddell in front of his position. The two generals turned when they heard the firing. "We listened attentively and finally heard the shouting of the Federals at the successful repulse. My hopes, I freely confess, sunk within me." Without consulting Hardee, Breckinridge's commander, Bragg had ordered Breckinridge to attack a hill to his front. Breckinridge drove the enemy from the hill, pursued, and then fell victim of a vicious counterattack from three fresh Union brigades, supported by fifty-eight pieces of artillery. Breckinridge fell back in confusion, with a shattered division.

Breckinridge's repulse destroyed all of Bragg's hopes for success. Fearing a renewed attack on his broken right, Bragg ordered Hardee to fall back from his advanced position. Hardee made a night march and reoccupied the line from which he had launched his attack.[16]

The following morning Bragg called his two corps commanders to his headquarters and told them that the captured papers of McCook, combined with reports from Wheeler, showed that Rosecrans had more men than Bragg had thought and that he was receiving heavy reinforcements. Bragg thought they should retreat; Hardee and Polk agreed.[17]

At Murfreesboro the Confederates had lost 10,266 of 35,000 men. The Union army had thrown about 45,000 men into the battle and lost about 12,000. Hardee had suffered heavy losses. Breckinridge and Cleburne lost about 2,000 men each. McCown lost about 1,000, and Wharton lost about 500. For their efforts Hardee's men captured twenty guns, several thousand prisoners, and a great quantity of

16 *Official Records*, XX, Pt. 1, pp. 297–98, 320, and *passim;* Hardee's Murfreesboro Report; Liddell's Record; Roy to McCown, February 20, 1863, in Hardee Letterbook (Alabama).
17 Irving A. Buck, *Cleburne and His Command* (New York, 1908), 80–81; Hardee's Murfreesboro Report.

valuable small arms. As Bushrod Johnson put it, "My men also armed themselves very generally with long-ranged guns, by exchange."

The attack on December 31 represents probably Hardee's best effort as a battle leader. His opening attack had been savage and its weight far out of proportion to its numbers. He drove superior forces back about three miles and engaged at one time or another during that drive four enemy divisions and parts of two others. His attack opened at the time expected, and his men generally followed the tactical plan assigned to them. The long periods of drill had paid handsome dividends. Cleburne's troops executed their wheeling movement with precision. As the battle progressed, the troops had to make frequent adjustments to the right by flanking movements. These they seem to have accomplished skillfully. The entire corps had attacked obliquely to the right as planned, but the line had become too extended. This tactical mistake came from McCown's lack of control over his division, which, it should be remembered, had not been trained by Hardee, nor had its leader ever been under his command. Regardless of their propensity to wander, McCown's men and particularly those of Cleburne had done the best that could have been expected from them in the assault. In advancing toward the Nashville Pike they had fought four or five pitched battles. After sustaining heavy losses, brigades like those of Polk and Wood and Rains had re-formed and attacked again and again. The exhausted condition of the seven brigades and the preponderance of force brought against them at the Nashville Pike finally halted them.

Hardee had no superior as a corps commander on December 31. He should be credited particularly for keeping constant pressure on the enemy line—pressure that never allowed his opponents to regroup satisfactorily until late in the afternoon. As soon as one part of his line slowed or wavered, Hardee called in another portion of his line. When McCown swung too far to the left in the morning, Cleburne's oblique movement brought him into the widening gap between McCown's right and Cheatham's left. When Cleburne's brigades became weakened and the attack threatened to stall after the fight at the Wilkinson Pike, Hardee pulled in McCown from the left and had him keep up the pressure. Next to controlling McCown, employing the artillery gave Hardee the most trouble during the battle. Time and time again the Union artillery slowed and threatened to halt the attack, so Hardee spent a great deal of his time placing his batteries in position to knock out the enemy batteries and to give supporting fire to the infantry. It was difficult to keep pace with the fast-moving infantry, and it was difficult to match the excellent guns of the enemy and the expert way they were handled. In Hardee's summary of the battle, he largely credited the Union artillery with the failure of the Confederate attack. He felt that when infantry fought infantry the Confederates could best them, but "in every form of contest in which mechanical instruments, requiring skill and heavy machinery to make them, can be used, the Federals are our superiors. . . . Long-ranged cannon and improved projectiles" contributed greatly to Confederate losses and final defeat.[18]

Bragg started his army south to the Elk River on January 4, 1863. There he expected to take up a defense line against the advancing Rosecrans. Rosecrans, however, did not have the reinforcements he needed and contented himself with remaining at Murfreesboro. The reinforcements that Bragg thought he had received proved to be phantoms in the minds of imaginative cavalry scouts. By January 7 Bragg felt more confident and moved his army north to the line of the Duck River. To hold this line he placed Polk on the left at Shelbyville and Hardee on the right at Tullahoma. With the exception of some shifts in dispositions in late April the armies of Rosecrans and Bragg retained their relative positions until the opening of the June campaign.

Once the threat of enemy attack had subsided, internal discord appeared in the high command of the Army of Tennessee. The condition grew worse during the spring, erupted violently at Chickamauga, and ended only with the replacement of Bragg by Johnston in December of 1863.

The seeds of discontent had been sown as early as the Kentucky campaign. By October 25 one observer had reported, "I cannot express the dissatisfaction that prevails in the army." [19] This came sharply to Bragg's attention on January 10, 1863. An article in the Chattanooga *Rebel* had censured Bragg for the defeat at Murfreesboro and had claimed that he no longer held the confidence of his army. The retirement from Murfreesboro had been "against the advice of his general officers." Troubled, Bragg called in his staff and read the article to them. He stated that if its allegations were true, he would

18 Thomas L. Livermore, *Numbers and Losses in the Civil War in America, 1861–65* (Boston, 1901), 97; *Official Records*, XX, Pt. 1, pp. 197, 201, 215, 674–75, 779; Hardee's Murfreesboro Report.
19 G. A. Henry to L. T. Wigfall, October 25, 1862, in Wigfall Family Papers, 1858–1909 (Library of Congress).

retire. The staff held a meeting and concluded that "under existing circumstances the general interest required that Gen. Bragg should ask to be relieved." Bragg then prepared a circular to be sent to his corps commanders inquiring about the retreat from Murfreesboro and the state of the feeling in the army. When his staff learned of the circular, they urged Bragg not to send it. They succeeded in having him omit "those portions asking for an expression of opinion as to the confidence of the Army. The letter, however, was still broad, & tended to open up controversy." [20]

Bragg sent the letter to his corps commanders, asking them to submit written proof that they had supported his decision to retreat from Murfreesboro. He felt compelled to call upon them because "it becomes necessary for me to save my fair name, if I cannot stop the deluge of abuse, which will destroy my usefulness and demoralize this army." Then he appended this critical statement: "I shall retire without regret if I find I have lost the good opinion of my generals upon whom I have ever relied as upon a foundation of rock." [21] Polk and his division commander Cheatham returned the reply that Bragg expected, stating that they had urged the retreat from Murfreesboro, but Hardee's reply stunned Bragg. Hardee stated that he had agreed with the decision to retire, but added that after consulting with his subordinates, "I feel that frankness compels me to say that the general officers, whose judgment you have invoked, are unanimous in the opinion that a change in the command of this army is necessary. In this opinion I concur." [22] Breckinridge reinforced Hardee, stating that he and all four of his brigadiers thought that Bragg had lost the confidence of his men. Cleburne sent a similar statement.[23] When Polk learned of the nature of Hardee's reply, he wrote Bragg asking precisely what he wanted for an answer. Bragg knew that Polk and Cheatham would pursue the matter at least as far as Hardee and his division commanders. He wrote back to Polk, "It was never intended by me that this should go farther than the parties to whom it was addressed. . . . The paragraph related to my supersedure [*sic*] was only an expression of the feeling with which I should receive your re-

---

20   Johnston Diary, January 10–11, 1863.
21   Bragg to Cheatham, January 11, 1863, in Cheatham Collection: *Official Records*, XX, Pt. 1, p. 684.
22   Hardee to Bragg, January 12, 1863, in Polk Papers.
23   J. C. Breckinridge to Bragg, January 12, 1863 (certified copy by T. B. Roy), in Louisiana Historical Association Collection (Howard-Tilton Memorial Library, Tulane University); *Official Records*, XX, Pt. 1, p. 684.

plies should they prove I had been misled in my construction of your opinions and advice." [24] Thus prevented from answering Bragg as he wanted, Polk wrote Davis, asking that Bragg be relieved and that Joseph E. Johnston replace him.[25]

The situation had now passed beyond Bragg's control. He wrote to his friend Benjamin Ewell that his subordinates were trying to place the responsibility of the Murfreesboro failure on his shoulders:

In this movement, I regret to say, are men who have possessed my confidence, and who are indebted to me for all in life. But such is human gratitude. Should this movement go so far as to impair the confidence of my army, or seriously embarrass me in the control of these general officers, the cause must suffer irreparable loss, and it would be better for me to retire, at least for a time, though I must say there is no man here to command an army. The one who aspires to it is a good drill master, but no more, except that he is gallant. He has no ability to organize and supply an army, and no confidence in himself when approached by an enemy.[26]

Bragg's reference to Hardee is obviously unfair and reveals the extent to which he had been hurt. Hardee and Bragg seem to have worked well together in Mississippi, and Bragg had entrusted him with great responsibilities, but friction developed during the Kentucky campaign, according to Liddell and Thomas Claiborne. In all fairness, Hardee carried out his assignments fully and co-operatively through the battle of Murfreesboro. In submitting his answer to Bragg's letter, Hardee qualified his remarks by saying that he entertained the "highest regards for your purity of motive, energy and personal character." With his high sense of duty Hardee felt compelled to speak frankly about the relationship of Bragg to his army. Hardee may have thought he was doing best for the army when he opened the gates of controversy, but he only weakened the army's command structure and created an unforgiving enemy. That he wanted a change in the supreme command is certain, but that he deliberately set out to undermine Bragg's position is to be doubted, because of his actions in the past and because of his refusal to accept the command of the army when it was later offered him. Bragg's accusations rest only upon the flimsy rationalization that he had prepared to shield his own feelings.

Bragg did not feel that the "confidence of my army" had been impaired; but nearly everyone else did. President Davis wrote Bragg's

24 *Official Records*, XX, Pt. 1, p. 701.
25 *Ibid.*, 698; XXIII, Pt. 2, pp. 632–33.   26 *Ibid.*, LII, Pt. 2, p. 407.

departmental commander, Johnston, that the situation "manifests . . . a condition of things which seems to me to require your presence." [27] Johnston visited the army late in January and found a want of confidence among the senior officers. In spite of this he advised that Bragg should not be relieved but that if Davis decided to relieve him, "no one in this army or engaged in this investigation ought to be his successor." [28] Davis, who had been willing to have Bragg relieved, now had his hands tied effectively. There the matter rested until the middle of March.

Johnston's support of Bragg, however, "did not restore harmony between the corps commanders and their commanding general. Seldom did either of them visit headquarters except officially." Soon an acrimonious dispute broke out between Polk and Bragg over the Kentucky campaign. Hardee could not avoid the controversy and soon found himself accused by Bragg of "sustaining Polk in his disobedience" at Bardstown and at Perryville. Hardee refused to answer Bragg's accusations, believing that to reopen the discussion of the Kentucky campaign might lead to Polk's court-martial and certainly would add fuel to the discontent that already prevailed. Privately, he wrote Polk that he intended to ignore the matter, but "if you choose to rip up the Kentucky campaign you can tear Bragg to tatters." Following the Kentucky dispute, Bragg wrote that it would "not be possible for the cordial official confidence to exist" between him and his corps commanders. "I have been much to blame for dividing too much responsibilities of my command with juniors, senior to me in years, however. This is all corrected. They know I am now their 'commanding general,' as I told them. . . ." [29] Thus matters stood through the spring.

While the relations between their leaders deteriorated, the strength, training, and welfare of the soldiers improved. Hardee's corps increased in size from 13,000 to 16,500 between January 17 and June 10, 1863. By February 21 a staff officer could write, "The army is well provided for, in food, clothing & equipment, and is now larger and better than when the battle of Murfreesboro was fought." [30]

27 *Ibid.*, XXIII, Pt. 2, p. 613.
28 J. E. Johnston to Davis, February 3, 1863, in Joseph Eggleston Johnston Papers, 1855–84 (Duke University Library).
29 Urquhart, "Bragg's Advance," in *Battles and Leaders*, III, 608–609; *Official Records*, XVI, Pt. 1, pp. 1098, 1101; XIII, Pt. 2, p. 653.
30 W. D. Gale to wife, February 21, 1863, in Gale Family Letters and Papers, 1825–92 (microfilm copy, Joint Universities Library, Nashville, Tenn.).

Hardee closely supervised the training of his corps during the spring. Discipline tended to be stern, and corporal punishment and the shooting of deserters were not uncommon. Foraging and the expropriation of farmers' fences and fancies were sharply dealt with. One new member of the corps remarked in a letter home, "The fact of being in Hardee's corps is sufficient proof that we have to 'Toe the mark.' " [31]

As always in his corps, the men drilled every day possible. Hardee saw to it that drill competitions were held between brigades and between divisions, and periodically he challenged Polk to a drill contest. The men practiced maneuvers hour after hour and became proficient at loading and firing while marching. To check on their progress Hardee held frequent inspections. Indeed, it has been maintained that probably he alone among the Confederate corps commanders "inspected the arms and accoutrements of every soldier of his corps." [32]

One of the outstanding features of Hardee's corps was the emphasis on reviews. The reviews not only improved the drill of the corps as a unit but had other results as well. For Hardee, a review was not a review without a gallery, and he always went to great lengths to provide one. His reviews became an institution, and delighted Southern ladies came frequently from as far as northern Alabama to attend them. Eager young staff officers rode off into the countryside and brought back "loads" of guests. At one April review, for instance, five hundred women turned out to cheer the men. Hardee did not intend for the women to be mere window dressing. In the middle of the review he would call forward men in his command who had behaved meritoriously, introduce them to the ladies, and have an account of their services read aloud. After the reviews Hardee would have entertainment provided for his visitors; tournaments, horse races, banquets, parties, dances, and serenades. [33]

Hardee's guest list contained male as well as female visitors. One observant guest, Lieutenant Colonel James A. L. Fremantle of the Coldstream Guards, attended a review of Liddell's brigade at Bell

31 J. W. Ward to father, March 28, 1863, in J. W. Ward Letters, 1862–63 (Emory University Library); Rogers Diary, March–April, 1863; Bell Irvin Wiley (ed.), *Fourteen Hundred and 91 Days in the Confederate Army, A Journal Kept by W. W. Heartsill* . . . (Jackson, Tenn., 1953), 130.
32 Buck, *Cleburne*, 103; Roy to Breckinridge, February 18, 1863, in Hardee Letterbook (Alabama); Roy, "Odds and Ends."
33 I. A. Buck to sister, March 22, 1863, in Buck Papers; Coleman Diary, February 9, 19, 1863; Taylor Beatty Diary, April 10, 1863.

Buckle with Hardee. He reported, "Each regiment carried a 'battle flag,' blue, with a white border [Cleburne's Division], on which were inscribed the names 'Belmont,' 'Shiloh,' 'Perryville,' 'Richmond,' 'Kentucky,' and 'Murfreesboro.' They drilled tolerably well, and an advance in line was remarkably good; but General Liddell had invented several dodges of his own, for which he was reproved by General Hardee. . . . The soldiers afterwards wanted General Hardee to say something, but he declined. I imagine that the discipline in this army is the strictest in the Confederacy, and that the men are much better marchers than those I saw in Mississippi." [34]

Soldiers throughout the United States and the Confederacy shared with Hardee's men the hours spent in drills and staging reviews. Since the drill was essential to maneuvers on the battlefield, a soldier had to be at least acquainted with these exercises to be of value in formal fighting, and Hardee's *Tactics* was the standard text.

The technical and colorless wording of the manual gave great difficulty to volunteer officers, who virtually had to memorize it. Wrote one, "Hardee for a month or more was a book of impenetrable mysteries. The words conveyed no ideas to my mind, and the movements described were utterly beyond my comprehension; but now the whole thing comes almost without study." [35] Thousand shared the attitude of this volunteer. The Union general Jacob D. Cox remarked that Hardee's *Tactics* "had been the authoritative guide of our army drill, and by that means his name had been made very familiar to every officer and man among us." [36]

"Every officer and man" meant foreigners as well. Because of the large number of German regiments in the Union army, publishers brought out editions of the manual with commands in English and explanations in German.[37] Nearly all the state governments, North and South, provided manuals for their men. North Carolina, for instance, ordered five thousand copies of Hardee's *Tactics*.[38] Sales of the work skyrocketed. This, of course, was of interest and of financial importance to Hardee. From the time of the manual's publication in

---

34 Walker Lord (ed.), *The Fremantle Diary* . . . (Boston, 1954), 123–24.
35 Ford (ed.), *Memoirs of a Volunteer*, 40.
36 Cox, *Military Reminiscences*, II, 525.
37 William Joseph Hardee, *Schuetzen und leichte Infanterie Taklik: enthaltend die Schule des Soldaten und der Compagnie, das Bajonet Exercitium und Instruction mit dem Degen* (New York, 1863).
38 North Carolina *Executive and Legislative Document No. 7, Extra Sessions, 1863–1864* (Raleigh, 1864), 58.

1855 to the outbreak of the war he had received his payments from Lippincott and Grambo in Philadelphia, but the war cut him off from his publisher and from his payments. Since Lippincott and Grambo had failed to have the manual copyrighted, editions were put out by a number of publishers in both North and South.[39]

Soon after the war began, Hardee entered into an agreement with a Southern publisher, S. H. Goetzel of Mobile. Hardee had revised the manual during his stay at Fort Morgan, and Goetzel had secured the copyright, guaranteeing Hardee twenty cents per copy sold. To ensure that the edition received the proper reception, Goetzel and Hardee sent one of the first copies to President Davis, hoping that the Confederate government would place a large order and that they would get the contract. To their surprise the Confederate House of Representatives postponed indefinitely a resolution sponsored by the Committee of Military Affairs to purchase ten thousand copies.[40] To add to their discouragement, other editions began to pour from the presses.[41] To combat this, Hardee published a notice that Goetzel's edition "is the only COMPLETE, CORRECT AND REVISED EDITION, and THIS EDITION ONLY contains the IMPROVEMENTS AND CHANGES which I have recently made." [42] Goetzel wrote to Secretary of War George W. Randolph urging that the War Department respect their copyright and not purchase copies of other editions.[43] Nothing, however, prevented eager publishers from continuing to bring out their own editions of Hardee's *Tactics*. Finally Hardee and Goetzel brought suit against one of these publishers and a Mobile bookdealer. Judge William G. Jones condemned the copyright, however, ruling that "the technical ground of former publication, which made the work *publici juris* to the people of the United States, was against Hardee's complaint." [44]

After losing their copyright Hardee and Goetzel tried legislative

39 Hardee, *Memorial to the Congress of the Confederate States.* For additional information on Hardee's copyright difficulties, see Thomas Conn Bryan, "General William J. Hardee and Confederate Publication Rights," in *Journal of Southern History,* XII (May, 1946), 263–74.
40 *Journal of the Congress of the Confederate States of America, 1861–1865,* 7 vols. (published as *Senate Documents,* 58th Cong., 2nd Sess., Doc. 234), I, 193.
41 Hardee, *Memorial to the Congress of the Confederate States.*
42 Hardee to L. P. Walker, June 18, 1861, in Letters Received, Office of the Secretary of War.
43 S. H. Goetzel to G. W. Randolph, October 20, 1862, *ibid.*
44 Bryan, "Hardee and Confederate Publications Rights," *loc. cit.,* 268.

means. On August 20, 1861, Thomas R. R. Cobb presented a petition prepared by the two plaintiffs to the Confederate House of Representatives. The memorial called for a special copyright, which would override the decision of Jones and give them the sole legal rights to the manual. After being read, the memorial was sent to the Committee on Patents. The issue next appeared before the Confederate Congress in December, 1863. An Alabama congressman, Edward S. Dargan, again presented Hardee's and Goetzel's memorial and introduced a measure to grant the special copyright. After being read the first and second times the bill was referred to the Committee on Patents. On December 30, 1863, the bill came up for consideration. It provided:

1. That W. J. Hardee, of Georgia, and S. H. Goetzel, of Alabama, or either of them, are hereby empowered and authorized to enter and secure a copyright for the work entitled 'Hardee's Rifle and Infantry Tactics,' for their joint benefit, in the form and manner now required by existing laws for the securing of copyrights in any district court of the Confederate States of America, and the copyright so entered and secured shall be valid and binding in all respects in all the courts of the Confederate States.
2. That said copyright shall take effect only from the day or the record thereof in the district court, and shall continue in force fourteen years from the approval of this act.

The House defeated this bill, 36 to 24. If enacted, it would have damaged the interests of many publishers in the Confederacy who had either already brought out editions or had them in the process of being printed. To save the bill and to protect the interests of the other publishers, an amendment was introduced stipulating that "this act shall not be so construed as to have a retroactive operation, so as to prevent the sale of tactics heretofore printed." In this form the bill passed, 41 to 17. The Senate after offering another amendment that the House would not accept, passed the bill. Davis signed the act into law on February 16, 1864.[45] The returns realized by Hardee after he secured the copyright are not known. As the heavy publication of the manual came in the first year of the war, it is doubtful that he received substantial royalties.

In April, 1863, however, Hardee worried more about a reported enemy advance than about royalties. News of an enemy division moving toward the railroad line between Manchester and McMinnville reached Tullahoma. The enemy also was reported advancing upon

45 *Journal of the Confederate Congress,* I, 373; III, 571, 576–77, 719, 734; VI, 554, 851.

Beech Grove through Hoover's Gap. Bragg ordered Hardee to transfer his corps to Wartrace in order to drive the enemy back through
the gap and to protect the railroad. With the arrival of Hardee's corps
the threat evaporated, and Hardee set up his headquarters at Beech
Grove, a little village near Wartrace.[46]

At Beech Grove Hardee lived in the home of Mrs. Mary Irwin. For
the first time in the war Hardee kept part of his family with him for
an extended period, as Anna and Sallie remained with him during the
spring. They had beaux by the dozen, and a full program of entertainment provided by their father. Hardee carefully selected young
officers to escort his daughters. One such officer was a young Captain
Coleman. Coleman's diary had earlier been filled with entries that
manifested depression and a preoccupation with death, but one day in
May he came to Beech Grove and met the Hardee girls. His spirits
soared for the first time in months. The following day the captain reappeared and took one of the girls to church. Following church he
stayed for lunch and met the general. Since this was the first social
contact Coleman had had with this commanding officer, he carefully
recorded his impression. "He is very agreeable and pleasant—a finished polished gentleman—possessing the gentlest feelings, with the
stern manliness of the soldier. My short intercourse with him increased my already high opinion of him. He seems to be a tender &
affectionate father. May his life be long spared to his country and
family." [47]

Colonel Fremantle also visited Hardee at Beech Grove. He was impressed by the general—"a fine, soldierlike man, broad-shouldered
and tall. He looks rather like a French officer." (No comment would
have pleased Hardee more.) Coming in contact with Hardee's staff
and some of his brigadiers, Fremantle learned a few Hardee anecdotes.
Before he left Beech Grove, he knew about the Widow Padlock and
several other incidents that Hardee wished had been forgotten.

Hardee . . . has the character of being a great admirer of the fair sex.
During the Kentucky campaign, . . . he was in the habit of availing himself
of the privilege of his rank and years, and insisted upon kissing the wives
and daughters of all the Kentucky farmers. And although he is supposed
to have converted many of the ladies to the Southern cause, yet in many
instances their male relatives remained either neutral or undecided. On

46 *Official Records*, XXIII, Pt. 1, p. 277; XXIII, Pt. 2, p. 760; circular, April 20,
    1863, in Army of Tennessee, Orders and Circulars of Lieutenant General
    William J. Hardee's Corps, 1863–65.
47 Coleman Diary, May 23–24, 1863; Lord (ed.), *Fremantle Diary*, 111–12.

one occasion General Hardee had conferred the "accolade" upon a very pretty Kentuckian to their mutual satisfaction, when, to his intense disgust, the proprietor produced two very ugly old females, saying, "Now, then, General, if you must kiss any you must kiss them all round," which the discomfited general was forced to do, to the amusement of his officers.[48]

Hardee had to keep alert to prevent his corps from forgetting military responsibilities in the pleasant surroundings of Beech Grove, and he adopted the habit of riding out to his generals' headquarters. When he arrived at Breckinridge's, for instance, he would talk over the military situation with him and would leave behind a set of detailed questions designed to instruct as well as to stimulate. The questions might be, what action will you take if Cleburne is attacked at Liberty Gap? How many roads are there leading to Brown's position? In what condition are they? Have you provided infantry security to augment the cavalry patrols? What about lateral roads entering your position? How long would it take to have a certain artillery battery mounted and ready to move? [49]

In May, Rosecrans began to make plans for an offensive. He knew that Bragg awaited him in fortifications at Tullahoma, with heavy bodies at Shelbyville and Wartrace. To circumvent Bragg's advanced corps Rosecrans planned to make a great sweeping movement around Hardee on the Confederate right. Once past Hardee he would move on to the Elk River and attempt to break Bragg's communications with Chattanooga.

Hardee knew the weakness of the extended line he held and informed Bragg that "an enterprising enemy could force a passage through Liberty Gap and cut my command in two. . . ." He further advised Bragg that if he wanted to hold Hoover's Gap, he ought to send a larger force than the brigade he had ordered Hardee to place there. He felt that the army was far too dispersed, as had been the case in Kentucky. Hardee, backed by the opinions of his engineers, also disagreed with the selection of Tullahoma as the backbone of the Army of Tennessee's defenses. Bragg, however, did not heed Hardee's objections and strongly fortified Tullahoma.[50]

The enemy advance came on June 24. Rosecrans feinted toward Polk's position at Shelbyville and then threw the weight of his army against Hardee. Hardee's brigades defending Hoover's Gap were

---

48 Lord (ed.), *Fremantle Diary*, 111–12.
49 *Official Records*, XXIII, Pt. 2, pp. 830–31.
50 *Ibid.*, 617–18, 760, 862.

quickly overwhelmed, and Hardee had to order Cleburne's and Stewart's divisions back to Wartrace. Bragg felt that he could not effect a concentration of both of his corps at Wartrace, so he ordered Polk and Hardee to fall back on Tullahoma.[51]

On June 30 Rosecrans approached Tullahoma in heavy force. The Confederates deliberated and then decided to abandon the town. If they had remained, Rosecrans could have pinned their army with his main force and still have had sufficient force to have sent a strong flanking element behind them to sever their lines of communication. The Confederates therefore withdrew on June 30 and retired south of the Elk River.

The Army of Tennessee faced about at Cowan, Tennessee, and took up a defensive position. Rosecrans soon confronted them, and Polk and Hardee, secretly sending messages back and forth about Bragg's bad health and his inability to take the field, again counseled retreat.[52] While Wheeler protected the rear of the column, the Army of Tennessee crossed the Cumberland Mountains on July 3 by way of Sewanee, Tennessee. The army marched on to Chattanooga, and there, on July 15, Hardee received orders from the War Department directing him to join Johnston in Mississippi.

51 For a detailed account of Hardee's activities during the June, 1863, campaign, see Hughes, "Hardee, C. S. A."
52 Hardee to L. Polk, July 1, 1863, in Hardee Military Service Record.

X

"Come to Your Colours"

THE SURRENDER of Vicksburg had drastically altered the military situation in Mississippi, eliminating 30,000 Confederates at one stroke. Joseph E. Johnston, left with only 23,000 men to confront Grant's army of over 60,000 men, quickly fell back to Morton, Mississippi. The War Department had no troops to spare but at least provided him with experienced leadership by sending Hardee, a general requested repeatedly by the citizens of Mississippi.[1]

Hardee arrived at Morton on July 19 and wrote back to his friend Polk:

I found Genl. Johnston at this place, with an army according to his own confession, much reduced in numbers by desertion and somewhat demoralized. My experience has fully confirmed his statement. He has now a little over 18,000 effective infantry. I would not like to say what I thought of the organization, discipline, and general efficiency of his command. I fear I will not be able to do as much good as you anticipated. I *know* I wish I were back at Chattanooga with my corps. I don't think Johnston knows exactly what to do with me. He seemed glad to see me, but my status is not determined.[2]

Johnston considered splitting his four divisions into two corps, giving Hardee command of one and keeping the other himself. He also thought of making Hardee his second in command. The issue had not been resolved when Johnston learned that Sherman had withdrawn from Jackson back to Vicksburg. Since this probably meant a

1 B. T. Kavanaugh to Davis, August 13, 1863, in Owen Collection.
2 Hardee wrote: "I think I may venture to say to you in the confidence of friendship that Johnston is wanting in all those particulars in which you feared he was deficient, and in addition has a very *inefficient staff*." Hardee to Polk, July 27, 1863, in Polk Papers.

lull in operations, Johnston decided to go to Mobile and investigate its defenses. He left Hardee in command of the Confederates in Mississippi.[3]

During the two weeks that Hardee held command, the enemy remained relatively quiet. Hardee's official activities during this period consisted of repelling enemy raids on the Mobile and Ohio Railroad and keeping his four divisions in condition and position for future operations. He ordered his cavalry commander "to take energetic steps" to round up the deserters "with which the country is swarming." To protect his men from the temptation to desert, Hardee canceled all furloughs for his command. Perhaps the most important service Hardee rendered was to gather intelligence for the War Department. He sent out numerous agents and could report on July 30 that Grant had moved his army from Vicksburg. Its destination remained unknown, but evidence pointed to either Mobile or Tennessee. Hardee could report with certainty that Grant's army had not yet passed down the Mississippi beyond the mouth of the Red River.[4]

Johnston's return in early August left Hardee with no real duties to perform. He wrote in disgust to a friend, "I have been idle and worthless." [5] He and his staff all missed the corps back in Chattanooga. Roy wrote, "He is not at all pleased with Mississippi and give[s] a gloomy account of every thing." [6] Finally on August 19 Hardee received his assignment, but from the War Department, not from Johnston. He would take command of the paroled Mississippi and Louisiana prisoners of the Vicksburg garrison, who had been ordered to reassemble. The War Department allowed Hardee to select the assembly area, later extending his command to include the paroled troops from Arkansas, Texas, and Missouri.[7]

Hardee faced an enormous if not an insoluble problem in collecting and holding together all the paroled prisoners until they could be exchanged and could properly take their place in the army once again. Following the surrender General John C. Pemberton had failed to

3 Joseph Eggleston Johnston, *Narrative of Military Operations* (New York, 1874), 228.
4 General Orders No. 2, July 25, 1863, in Army of Tennessee, Orders and Circulars; *Official Records*, XXIV, Pt. 3, p. 1037; XXXI, Pt. 3, p. 829; LII, Pt. 2, pp. 513–14.
5 Hardee to Rowe Webster, August 5, 1863, in Miscellaneous Manuscript Collection, 1861–65 (Tennessee Historical Society, Nashville, Tenn.).
6 I. A. Buck to sister, August 5, 1863, in Buck Papers.
7 *Official Records*, Ser. II, Vol. VI, 219; S. Cooper to Hardee, September 2, 1863, in Letters Received, Adjutant General's Office.

keep his army intact, and the garrisons of Vicksburg and Port Hudson had scattered to the winds. He had granted his soldiers a general furlough (after many had already left on their own). One of the few soldiers who stayed behind said that the "soldiers that arè with us are the worst whipped men I ever saw, and all the Citizens of Miss come out plainly and say that it isn't worth while to fight any longer, there is a great many of our soldiers Running away I Dont think that it will be a great while before we will all be at home." [8] Many of the Southerners in the Mississippi Valley had become completely disillusioned with the Confederacy. They felt that the government had failed to protect them, and they asked themselves why they should encourage men to return to the army to fight and perhaps be killed in distant states. Even areas under Confederate control showed symptoms of this feeling, and the local commanders feared that a peace movement would soon become a serious reality.

On August 27, 1863, General Hardee assumed command of the paroled Confederates that had been assembled at Demopolis, Alabama. Feeling that the situation justified emotional phrasing, he issued this greeting to his new command:

In anticipation that you will soon be exchanged, the work of reorganization must proceed with energy. . . . Soldiers, look to your country! The earth ravaged, property carried away or disappearing in flames and ashes, the people murdered, the negroes arrayed against the whites, cruel indignities inflicted upon women and children. Destruction marks the path of our invaders. Their motto is 'Woe to the conquered.' He who falters in this hour of his country's peril is a wretch who would compound for the mere boon of life robbed of all that makes life tolerable.

Fellow soldiers! There is but one path to follow; it leads to the camp. Come to your colours and stand beside your comrades. . . .[9]

The new command looked imposing on paper, comprising as it did the divisions of John S. Bowen, Martin L. Smith, John H. Forney, and Carter L. Stevenson. In actuality the command consisted of about a thousand Alabamians under Stevenson and a badly eroded Missouri brigade, which had virtually no hope of refilling its ranks. Rather than at Demopolis, where the Alabama troops were assembling, Hardee decided to establish his headquarters at Enterprise, Mississippi. Allow-

8 W. J. Brigham to J. Brigham, July 31, 1863, in John Trotwood Moore Confederate Collection, 1861–65 (Tennessee State Library and Archives, Nashville, Tenn.).

9 *Official Records*, Ser. II, Vol. VI, 232–33.

ing Stevenson to remain at Demopolis, Hardee ordered the paroled
prisoners from the other states to assemble at Enterprise.[10]

The coming of September found the Vicksburg troops dragging
into Enterprise in disheartening numbers. As they arrived, Hardee saw
that they returned to their proper units and that they received the
necessary equipment. When the notification of exchange came in,
Hardee informed the commander of the unit concerned and ordered
him to rearm his command. From the testimony of one Missouri
brigadier it is evident that Hardee had an ample supply of good arms
on hand. By September 19 the Missouri brigade had been "fully supplied with most excellent new Enfield rifles." To revitalize both the
armed and the unarmed units Hardee instituted a training program.

Hardee's real problem, however, was not the training of these
skeleton units; it was to get the men to return to the army in the first
place. Hardee put notices in the papers and kept a small army of men
out, arresting those who had not returned. Once soldiers managed to
get across the Mississippi, his system was not very efficient. Even if
they wanted to rejoin the army, these troops had a difficult time. Since
several of the Arkansas and Missouri regiments had been ordered west
of the Mississippi immediately after the surrender, numbers of men
were left on the east bank, unable to rejoin their proper parent units.
Hardee sought and finally received authority to consolidate these men
into the Trans-Mississippi units that remained on the east side of the
Mississippi. Soon the decimated division of John Bowen reappeared as
a tiny but determined brigade of 1,300 men under Brigadier General
Francis M. Cockrell. The Port Hudson garrison unfortunately had
lost nearly all of its officers at the surrender, when the Union authorities decided not to parole them. Without these officers Hardee
never succeeded in reassembling the units.[11]

When Johnston went to Atlanta in September, Hardee again found
himself in command. He traveled about the department, inspecting
units and making organizational changes.

10 *Ibid.*, Savannah *Daily Morning News*, September 5, 1863; Johnston, *Narrative of Military Operations*, 254–55.
11 *Official Records*, XXIV, Pt. 3, pp. 1051–52, XXX, Pt. 4, p. 669, XXXI, Pt. 1, p. 704, LII, Pt. 2, pp. 521–22, 540, Ser. II, Vol. VI, 299; S. Cooper to Hardee, October 9, 1863, in Hardee Mililtary Service Record; Hardee to Cooper, September 17, October 3, 1863, in Hardee Letterbook (Alabama); Field Return of William J. Hardee's Command, October 18, 1863, in Confederate States of America Archives, 1861–65 (Duke University Library).

While Hardee was attending a review of Stevenson's troops at Demopolis in September, he met Mary Foreman Lewis. This slim, sophisticated brunette blasted Felicia Shover, Ella Newsome, and all the others from his mind. Unable to repress his joy and excitement, Hardee wrote to Regina Harrison and chided her in his customary mock-serious tone for rebuffing his advances and those of a friend: "With respect to one of them, at least, you have lost your chances. Since his disappointment, he has determined to concentrate his forces and attack in another quarter. See what you have lost! If a forced reconnaissance which he intends to make on Thursday next near Demopolis shall prove successful he intends to bring on a serious engagement immediately." [12]

Although Hardee seemed to be succeeding with Miss Lewis, his work with the Vicksburg garrison did not progress so favorably: "I have used every effort to reassemble the command, but so far with but discouraging results. I find a general disposition among the paroled prisoners, in which they are sustained by public sentiment, not to report until exchanged, and am convinced they can only be brought in by compulsory means. A speedy exchange would materially aid my efforts." [13]

Shortly after Hardee sent this report to Adjutant General Cooper, President Davis came to Demopolis to learn firsthand about conditions in Mississippi. He met with Hardee on October 18 and 20, and these talks resulted in Hardee's transfer back to Chattanooga to replace Leonidas Polk on October 27. [14]

During his three-month interlude in Mississippi Hardee had accomplished little of lasting military value. Johnston had used him as a substitute commander, and he seems to have performed these duties in a capable manner. With the exception of improvements brought about by inspection and reorganization, however, an officer of far less ability and experience could have done as much. His excellence as a trainer and an organizer produced results with the Vicksburg prisoners, but these results were insignificant when compared with what might have been expected from his applied effort as a corps com-

---

12 Hardee to Regina Harrison, October 11, 1863, in Stephen Dill Lee Papers, 1784–1929 (Southern Historical Collection); John Witherspoon DuBose, "Chronicles of the Canebrake," in *Alabama Historical Quarterly*, IX (Winter, 1947), 543.
13 *Official Records*, LII, Pt. 2, pp. 543–44.
14 Johnston, *Narrative of Military Operations*, 261; Davis to Bragg, October 23, 1863, in Rowland (ed.), *Jefferson Davis*, VI, 62.

mander with the Army of Tennessee. Hardee did succeed in gathering over five thousand of the prisoners and in having them equipped and trained. These accomplishments would serve as valuable groundwork for Polk when he came to Mississippi to take Hardee's position. The conclusion is inescapable, however, that the Confederacy wasted the talents of one of its finest combat leaders at a time when his army needed him badly. At Chickamauga in September, the Army had fought the greatest battle it would ever fight, and it had had to do so without its best corps commander.[15]

Bragg, caught in the frightful controversies that wrecked the command of his army, had solicited Hardee's services as early as October 1. When Davis came to Enterprise, he probably intended to have Hardee transferred, and when Hardee asked him if he might return to the army, this settled the issue. In sending Hardee back, Davis hoped that he would be able to help Bragg in "checking . . . discontents" and in his other problems.[16] Davis intended to hold a conference with Hardee in Atlanta about his new assignment, but could not get there in time. Instead he wrote this short note: "The information from the army at Chattanooga painfully impresses me with the fact that there is a want there of that harmony, among the highest officers, which is essential to success. I rely greatly upon you for the restoration of a proper feeling, and know that you will realize the comparative insignificance of personal considerations when weighed against the duty of imparting to the Army all the efficiency of which it is capable." [17]

En route to his new assignment Hardee encountered a reporter of the Atlanta *Appeal* who recorded this impression: "Hardee is . . . plain, unassuming, domestic . . . takes things coolly until aroused, and then becomes a perfect lion. There is not a warmer or more genial nature in the army. The humblest private may approach him . . . and be assured of a ready ear. . . . He has a frank, open face, fine blue eyes, and is just gray haired enough and bearded enough to make one voluntarily venerate his many years of usefulness and experience." [18]

15 Colonel Archer Anderson, who was intimate with the higher echelon of the Army of Tennessee, thought that Hardee's absence at Chickamauga was a "serious misfortune." "The army lost in this crisis of its history, the most brilliant corps commander, the war produced on our side, after . . . Jackson and Longstreet." J. Johnston to Roy, December 10, 1881, in the W. J. Hardee Collection, in possession of Hardee Chambliss, Jr., Fairfax, Va.
16 *Official Records*, LII, Pt. 2, pp. 534, 554; W. M. Polk to wife, October 29, 1863, in Gale-Polk Papers, 1815–81 (Southern Historical Collection).
17 Davis to Hardee, October 30, 1863, in Rowland (ed.), *Jefferson Davis*, VI, 72.
18 Wheeling (W. Va.) *Daily Register*, November 25, 1863.

From Atlanta Hardee traveled at once to Chattanooga, accompanied by Howell Cobb. The two men arrived on October 31. A week later Cobb could report to Davis that feeling between Bragg and most of the discontented officers had subsided, although Buckner and James Longstreet still displayed open hostility for their commander. Cobb hoped that the Buckner situation might be remedied by an undisclosed change to be attempted by General Hardee: "Genl Hardee . . . was well received by all, and you may calculate upon the happiest effects from his presence there. He was laboring earnestly (and I think successfully) to bring about cordiality & confidence, where there had been the greatest need for it." [19]

Hardee had stepped into a hotbed of discontent. Since the battle at Chickamauga the senior officers of the Army of Tennessee had been alienated from their commander. As Bragg dispensed responsibility for the failure to follow up the victory, his army declined in effectiveness, and the ill feelings of the corps commanders permeated the whole army. "I do not know a single contented General in this army," said Bragg's chief of staff, "a very sad fact in the presence of the enemy." Out of two wing commanders and four corps commanders present at Chickamauga, only W. H. T. Walker and the wounded Hood remained in Bragg's favor. Longstreet remained with the army but displayed open hostility. All of the others had gone by early November. Polk had escaped a court-martial only by Davis' refusal to accommodate Bragg. He had been sent to Mississippi in exchange for Hardee. Buckner took an extended leave of absence and never returned. D. H. Hill was relieved of command. Among the division commanders Cheatham had asked to be relieved, Hindman had been relieved under charges, Forrest had left, and so had Bragg's chief of staff, W. W. Mackall. Thus on Hardee's arrival there had been almost a complete turnover in the high command of the army. Most of these officers had been very popular with their troops, and when they left, a cry went up from the ranks. W. W. Mackall, who knew Bragg better than most and who remained loyal until he felt he was compromising himself, admitted Bragg's patriotism. Bragg's "whole soul is in it," but "he is as much influenced by his enemies as by friends— and does not know how to control the one or preserve the other." He "is as blind as a bat to the circumstances surrounding him." [20]

19 H. Cobb to Davis, November 6, 1863, in Jefferson Davis Letters, 1808–89 (Emory University Library).
20 Mackall to wife, September 29, October 10, 1863, in Mackall Papers.

The fact that Davis kept Bragg in command in the face of this formidable resistance represents one of his greatest errors in judgment. Certainly Bragg excelled as a disciplinarian; certainly he had demonstrated aggressiveness in his battles and campaigns; certainly he had shown willingness to sacrifice anything for his country. Yet Braxton Bragg had cost the Confederacy drums of blood and had not yet produced a clear-cut victory. His ruthless standards had brought him personal enemies and enemies for the administration. He had also displayed a curious lack of confidence at critical moments.

For Hardee to return voluntarily to the army to serve under this man can perhaps only be explained by his patriotism, by his loyalty to Davis, by his love for his corps, and by the frustrations of his Mississippi interlude. It had been Hardee that brought the controversy into the open in the winter of 1862–63, and the ill feeling bred in those days could not be forgotten by either party. That he worked positively to assist Bragg at this time is a tribute to the man. He did it at a personal sacrifice.

The town that Hardee came to help Bragg capture had evaded the Confederates since the victory at Chickamauga. Thomas and the remnants of Rosecrans' army were besieged, his army at times near starvation. With characteristic energy Thomas strengthened his defenses to the point that Bragg dared not assault. Chattanooga was of critical importance to the Union, and Thomas knew it.

Chattanooga was of great importance to the Confederacy as well. Its loss had cut off the Georgia iron mills from their normal supply of ore. Instead of giving the Confederates an excellent sally port into Tennessee, Chattanooga now gave the enemy a window into Georgia.

Once the issue of the Mississippi River had been settled, Grant took energetic steps to assist Thomas. Joseph Hooker had been sent with two corps from the Army of the Potomac to offset Longstreet's transfer from Virginia. Hooker had arrived in Bridgeport, Alabama, as October opened and waited only for the opening of communications with Thomas to bring his troops to Chattanooga. Sherman had started to Thomas' relief in late September. Crossing the state of Tennessee he had been delayed by S. D. Lee's cavalry, but in early November he neared Bridgeport. "Danger was thickening fast around Bragg which he seemed singularly indifferent to." [21] In late October at Brown's Ferry, Thomas ousted Longstreet's men from Lookout Valley by a

21 Liddell's Record.

cleverly conceived and wonderfully executed night maneuver. Longstreet's counterattack at Wauhatchie failed, and the road to Chattanooga stood open for Hooker and Sherman.[22]

Just after Hardee arrived in Chattanooga, he went with Longstreet
and Breckinridge to the "point" of Lookout Mountain for a reconnaissance. About two feet from the toes of his boots the rock on which
he stood plunged a hundred feet to a gently sloping bench of land.
On this bench or plateau was the Craven farm and a winding road
leading into Chattanooga. Below the Craven farm the mountain sloped
rather sharply for a thousand feet. High river bluffs kept Hardee from
seeing what became of it. Just below these bluffs was Moccasin Bend,
where the Tennessee River smashes into the face of Lookout and then
recoils north. To his left was Lookout Valley, the sprawling play-
ground of Lookout Creek. Beyond the valley rose Raccoon Mountain,
Lookout's smaller and gentler sister. North of Raccoon and divided
from it by the fleeing Tennessee was Walden's Ridge, which Hardee
had crossed only a year before. To the front and in the foreground
was Chattanooga. No longer a small trading center, it now resembled
a big city with its avenues of white tents and its countless log buildings. To the right front was Orchard Knob, a slight rise of ground
at present used by the Confederates as an outpost. To the immediate
right was Chattanooga Creek, which twisted its way through Chattanooga Valley. Across Chattanooga Valley the foothills of the
Cumberlands began, eventually blending in the distance with the
big North Carolina mountains. The first of these foothills, a long
ridge immediately east of Chattanooga, attracted Hardee's attention.
Missionary Ridge began to the north at the Tennessee River and ran
about eight miles south to Rossville, Georgia. Two gaps broke its
otherwise closed front, the first a short distance south of the river
and the second near Rossville. Upon closer examination one could
see that its face was scarred with countless gullies and ravines. The
spine of the ridge was narrow and its western side sharp and uninvit-
ing. Three miles from Chattanooga, it completely imprisoned the
town to the east.

The Confederates and Federals had grudingly divided up this ter-
rain. By November 3, the Federals had Raccoon Mountain, Lookout
Valley, Chattanooga, and all the land to the north and west. The
Confederates had Lookout Mountain, Chattanooga Valley, Orchard

22 For more complete information on the battles around Chattanooga, see
    Thomas Robson Hay, "The Battle of Chattanooga," in *Georgia Historical
    Quarterly*, VIII (June, 1924), 121–41, and Horn, *Army of Tennessee, passim.*

Knob, Missionary Ridge, and all the land to the south and east. The Federals held most of the river, but the Confederates on Lookout Mountain and on the northern end of Missionary Ridge denied them its free use.

The three generals had come to Lookout to determine whether they could attack the enemy in his newly won position in Lookout Valley. After deliberation they decided that an attack would be impractical. They had only one inadequate road over which they could move troops across the face of Lookout, and this road was exposed to the enemy batteries on Moccasin Bend. The Confederate position offered few advantages, they decided. It extended about fifteen miles from the north end of Missionary Ridge to Lookout Mountain. It would be very difficult to defend such a long line with the limited number of Confederate troops available. As for besieging Chattanooga, Longstreet declared with brutal frankness, "We were trying to starve the enemy out by investing him on the only side from which he could not have gathered supplies." [23]

Later in the week the three corps commanders held a conference with Bragg to discuss strategic combinations. Longstreet suggested a plan that he maintained gained a hearing only because of Hardee's support. Longstreet advocated a rapid attack upon East Tennessee to crush Burnside's force. Bragg hesitated to endorse the plan because of the threat of Sherman's approach to Chattanooga, ". . . but he and others were of opinion that the army sent to East Tennessee could whip Burnside, and, if need be, return before Sherman could reach Chattanooga. It was agreed, also, that the movement in East Tennessee would compel Grant to send re-enforcements to that quarter." Bragg told Longstreet that he could lead the column and take Hood's and McLaws' divisions. He promised to send additional men to give Longstreet a force of fifteen thousand men.[24]

The departure of Longstreet left Bragg with about thirty-seven thousand men, divided into two corps under Hardee and Breckinridge. Hardee, with the divisions of Cheatham, Cleburne, Stevenson, and Walker, held a line running from Missionary Ridge to and including Lookout Mountain. Cleburne remained on the ridge, Walker guarded the ground from the ridge to Chattanooga Creek, Cheatham held the bench on the face of Lookout Mountain, and Stevenson defended Lookout itself.

During the early weeks of November the Confederates seem to

23 *Official Records*, XXXI, Pt. 1, p. 218.
24 *Ibid.*, 455, 474, Pt. 3, pp. 634–35; LII, Pt. 2, p. 560.

have anticipated an attack on their left (Hardee's position). Hardee
made frequent reconnaissances with Bragg and with his division
commanders over his line. Everyone appeared to agree that the position at the mountain would be "extremely difficult" to defend. Any
line of battle established on or near the Craven farm would be en-
filaded by the enemy artillery on Moccasin Bend. Furthermore, Lookout itself extended over seventy miles down into Alabama. The
Confederates chose to defend the northern eighteen miles of it from
Lookout Point to Johnson's Crook. This extensive area was covered
mainly by cavalry and a few infantry pickets. Because of the numerous passes across Lookout Mountain and the mountain's great
length, Bragg and Hardee knew that it probably could not be successfully defended against a superior enemy. They therefore shielded
their weakness by frequent forced reconnaissances near Trenton and
Johnson's Crook. For the portions of his line at Chattanooga, Hardee
set to work at once to erect breastworks. Since his men at Lookout
could not work in the daytime because of the enemy batteries, Hardee
had them work at night. Thus in the first three weeks of November
the men labored to complete a line capable of defense. Hardee repeatedly urged his generals to hurry.[25]

To increase the efficiency of his army, Bragg, the organizer, had
made almost a wholesale reorganization of his army on November 12.
The division commands remained about the same with the exception
that Bragg assigned W. H. T. Walker to Hardee, but among the brigades and regiments not less than eighteen exchanges took place.
Bragg designed most of these changes to disperse the Tennesseans,
whom he had distrusted from the outset. A year earlier he had written
his wife, who suggested that he not allow the Tennesseans to be
brigaded, "Your advice . . . is fully adopted in my order of today,
organizing my command. All Tennesseans are scattered among better
men in small squads, so that we can hold them in observation. I
never realized the full correctness of your appreciation of them until
now." [26] The Tennesseans had been concentrated in the divisions of
Cheatham and Stewart had only one Tennessee brigade apiece.[27]

The third week in November found Hardee pressing the construc-

25 *Ibid.*, XXXI, Pt. 2, pp. 685–86, 717–18.
26 Bragg to wife, March 30, 1862, in Bragg Papers.
27 James Iredell Hall, "Notes on the Civil War," in James Iredell Hall Papers,
    1861–65 (Southern Historical Collection); *Official Records*, XXXI, Pt. 3,
    pp. 685–86.

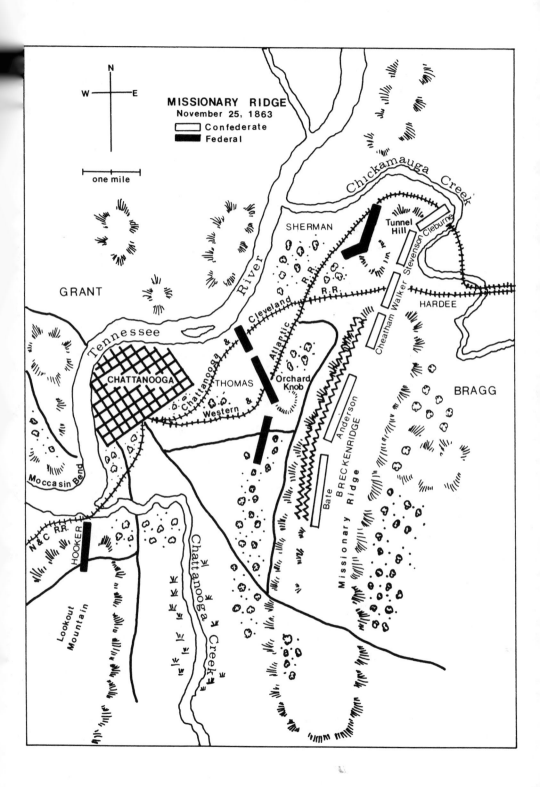

MISSIONARY RIDGE
November 25, 1863
☐ Confederate
■ Federal

one mile

N
W — E
S

GRANT

Tennessee River

Chickamauga Creek

SHERMAN

Tunnel Hill

Stevenson
Cleburne
Walker
Cheatham
HARDEE

Cleveland R.R.

Atlantic R.R.

CHATTANOOGA

THOMAS

Chattanooga &

Western &

Orchard Knob

Anderson

BRECKENRIDGE

Bate

BRAGG

Missionary Ridge

Moccasin Bend

N & C R.R.

HOOKER

Lookout Mountain

Chattanooga Creek

tion of his line "with vigor, by day and night." The arrival of the advance elements of Sherman's army in Lookout Valley had caused Hardee to become apprehensive. Bragg too evinced alarm by calling on Johnston for reinforcements. He had powerful reinforcements at hand under Longstreet but decided to allow Longstreet to continue his campaign against Burnside. Reports strengthened his conviction that Grant would quickly detach troops to assist Burnside. When Bragg heard of enemy forces moving up the Tennessee, he further weakened his army by ordering the divsions of Buckner and Cleburne to Loudon, Tennessee. These divisions would ensure that he would not be cut off from Longstreet and would also assure Longstreet of quick and sizeable reinforcements if he needed them.[28]

Knowing both Bragg and Longstreet, Hardee suggested that a liaison officer be sent to Longstreet to explain the situation around Chattanooga and to co-ordinate the movements of the two Confederate armies. The sending of two more divisions to East Tennessee alarmed him as much as the arrival of Sherman. He therefore advised Bragg, "If Burnside is strongly fortified and cannot be captured without a siege, my conviction is that he ought to retire without delay." Consequently, on the day that he received Hardee's message, Bragg wrote Longstreet that nearly eleven thousand troops were on their way to his support, ". . . but if practicable to end your work with Burnside promptly and effectively, it should be done now." [29]

Grant could not have asked for better co-operation from his opponent. As soon as Sherman arrived, Grant sent him along the north side of the Tennessee to the mouth of north Chickamauga Creek, where pontoons had been collected. Sherman would cross the river at that point and attack the north end of Missionary Ridge. Hooker would move up from Lookout Valley, drive the Confederates from the mountain, and then cross Chattanooga Creek and head for Rossville, Georgia. From Rossville he could strike Bragg's left flank and rear. Thomas would move out from Chattanooga to Orchard Knob. The signal for his attack on the Confederate center would be the appearance of Hooker advancing north on Missionary Ridge.

The three-day battle for Chattanooga opened on November 23. To the amazement of the Confederates Thomas took his army out of

28 *Official Records*, XXXI, Pt. 2, p. 667.
29 *Ibid.*, Pt. 3, pp. 736–38; Johnston Diary, November 12, 1863.

Chattanooga for the first time since Chickamauga and placed them in a line of battle. Then he moved forward swiftly and literally smothered the Confederate outpost at Orchard Knob. Thomas' massive reconnaissance amounted to a "surprise in open daylight." The appearance of Thomas and the reports of Sherman moving up the Tennessee caused Bragg to change his defenses. Now he believed that his right rather than his left would be attacked. He therefore ordered Hardee to the right with the nearest division at hand, which proved to be Walker's. Hardee turned over the command of the left to an astonished Stevenson and took one of his brigades to fill the hole in Chattanooga Valley left by the removal of Walker. Another brigade from Cheatham was also thrown into the valley defenses. Bragg also halted Cleburne's division at Chickamauga Station as it boarded trains for East Tennessee. Buckner had already left. Cleburne would now act as the army reserve. That night Sherman began crossing the Tennessee River; by morning he had eight thousand men on Bragg's right flank, with more to come.[30]

November 24 brought a race for position on the Confederate right. Sherman spent the morning transferring his troops across the river and establishing connection with Thomas' forces. To be sure, he had gained the northern end of Missionary Ridge, pushing aside negligible opposition, but he found that the heights he had captured were not connected with the main part of the ridge. He possessed only a detached hill.[31]

The Confederates, focusing their attention on Thomas, seemed unaware of Sherman's presence until the afternoon. To lengthen Hardee's position on the right, Bragg sent up Cleburne from reserve. His presence not only would give more lateral occupation of the ridge but would give security to the railroad bridge across the Chickamauga just behind the right. Major D. H. Poole showed Cleburne the position Hardee wanted him to occupy. He had Cleburne place Lowrey, Polk, and Smith on a line extending from Tunnel Hill to Walker's right, a distance of about a mile. Tunnel Hill, which thus became the Confederate right, was an elevated portion of Missionary Ridge.

About 2 P.M. the Confederates became alerted to Sherman's presence. Cleburne was informed that five enemy divisions had crossed or were crossing the Tennessee. He must hold his position and protect

30 *Official Records*, XXXI, Pt. 2, pp. 671, 674, 719; Johnston Diary, November 23, 1863.
31 *Official Records*, XXXI, Pt. 2, p. 573.

the railroad bridge "at all hazards." This meant, of course, that Cleburne should change his front. First he sent Smith's brigade out to try to take the detached hill near the Tennessee. Smith found Sherman's advance already on the hill and could not occupy it. He fell back across the small valley and threw up defensive works on the main ridge. Cleburne left Lowrey and Polk on the main line south of the railroad tunnel and put Liddell's (Govan's) brigade out on a spur of the main ridge that branched off to the rear into the Tennessee Valley. This widened the face of Cleburne's defenses to the north. After Cleburne had made these dispositions, Hardee came up. He and Cleburne rode over the ground together and examined the terrain and the troop dispositions. Hardee agreed with Cleburne's placement of troops generally and ordered him to destroy a bridge across Chickamauga Creek directly behind Cleburne's right flank.[32]

As they made their tour of the north end of the ridge, the two heard the familiar noise of battle from the direction of Lookout Mountain. The fog that enveloped the lower slopes prevented them from learning the nature or result of the fight, but slowly reports of defeat drifted in. Hooker had attacked in force and had driven Stevenson's men from position to position. The brigades of Jackson, Walthall, and Moore could never stabilize their line and were thrown off the mountain.

When Bragg learned of the disaster, he ordered Stevenson to abandon the mountain and Cheatham to abandon the valley. Both divisions retired to the main ridge when they found the opportunity. When Cleburne learned of the defeat at Lookout, he believed that the army would withdraw from Missionary Ridge at once. He therefore sent most of his artillery and wagons across Chickamauga Creek. About 9 P.M. he sent a message to Hardee by Irving Buck, asking if Bragg had decided after all to hold the ridge.[33]

Buck found Hardee deep in conference with Bragg and Breckinridge. The three generals deliberated over whether the army should retire or not. Hardee urged an immediate withdrawal over Chickamauga Creek. Breckinridge argued that "if they couldn't fight here with such advantage of position, they couldn't fight anywhere." Bragg agreed with Breckinridge, saying also that he did not believe that sufficient time remained to withdraw the army safely. When

32 *Ibid.*, pp. 346–47; Buck, *Cleburne*, 165; Hay, "Battle of Chattanooga," *loc. cit.*, 128.
33 Buck, *Cleburne*, 166; *Official Records*, XXXI, Pt. 2, p. 747.

he saw that Bragg and Breckinridge had determined to remain on Missionary Ridge, Hardee stated that if they expected him to hold his position on the right he must be reinforced. As a result Bragg ordered the divisions of Cheatham and Stevenson, which had been ordered to take station behind Breckinridge, over to Hardee. Hardee sent word back to Cleburne through Buck, "Tell Cleburne we are to fight; that his division will be heavily attacked, and they must do their very best." When the dispatch arrived, Cleburne ordered his artillery and trains back across the creek. That night a hunter's moon lit the landscape, and the Confederates on the right could see the campfires of the enemy to their front and right, and far off to their left on Lookout, "twinkling sparks . . . showed picket skirmishing still going on." [34]

In the early hours of November 25 General Grant reviewed the situation of his army. Sherman had arrived in his assigned position and would be ready to launch his attack against the Confederate right. Thomas stood ready in the center, awaiting the signal to attack. Hooker had cleared Lookout Mountain and had linked up with Thomas' right. With his line intact from Lookout to the Tennessee River, Grant would wait for Hooker to fall on Bragg's left near Rossville while Sherman fell on Bragg's right. Thomas could relieve the pressure from or follow up victory by either of these flank attacks.

After he left the conference at Bragg's headquarters, Hardee rode out to Cleburne's position. If they must fight for the ridge, Hardee determined that his men would have the best possible defense line. He and Cleburne again looked over the ground, and Hardee ordered him to make some major shifts in his dispositions. Hardee brought up two regiments of Polk's brigade and placed them on a hill which controlled the vital East Tennessee and Georgia Railroad bridge and the Confederate line of retreat. Two of Lowrey's regiments were also brought up and placed on a piece of the ridge that jutted out to the east. These changes forced Smith's brigade to alter its line. Hardee placed Smith's left at Tunnel Hill and extended his line north until it linked with Govan. The movement of all of these troops from the western defenses to the north weakened that line. It left an interval

34 Liddell's Record; Buck, *Cleburne*, 166–67; K. Falconer to Cheatham, November 24, 1863, in Cheatham Collection; Johnston Diary, November 24, 1863; *Official Records*, XXXI, Pt. 2, pp. 78, 747.

of nearly a mile between Smith's left and Walker's right, filled only with the two remaining regiments of Lowrey's brigade.[35]

The support that Bragg had promised Hardee began moving toward the Confederate right early in the morning. Hardee brought Stevenson's division to the gap between Cleburne and Walker. Brown's brigade went into position on the north side of the tunnel and Cumming's brigade to the south. Cheatham's division took its place on Walker's left flank. By midmorning these troops had arrived, and all set to work feverishly to prepare their defenses on the military crest of the ridge. Hardee ordered Cleburne to take charge of the defense of the ridge to the north of the railroad tunnel while he managed affairs to the south.[36]

Until 10:30 A.M. only heavy skirmishing occurred. Sherman's troops had lapped around the west face of the ridge and had begun to press Cleburne and Stevenson. After several attacks were repulsed, the enemy secured a lodgment in some abandoned farm buildings, and their sharpshooters kept the Confederates down behind their log and earth defenses. To clear the farm buildings Hardee ordered a charge by a regiment of Stevenson's men and the charge succeeded in driving the enemy from their position. Although their attempts to carry the Confederate line had been frustrated, Sherman's men still held ground uncomfortably close to Hardee's line. The accuracy and volume of their rifle fire incapacitated important batteries, and finally infantry had to work the exposed guns. To strengthen the artillery emplacements near the tunnel, Govan's brigade was called up from the rear. George Maney's Tennessee Brigade and Cumming's Georgia Brigade were ordered over from Walker's division to support Cleburne.[37]

With Sherman encountering determined resistance, Grant directed Thomas to make a secondary attack against Bragg's center. Thomas would try to take the works at the bottom of the ridge and Grant hoped that this would draw off some of the troops confronting Sherman. Hooker had not yet appeared, having been delayed unexpectedly by crossing Chattanooga Creek and by the capricious roads of Chattanooga Valley.

---

35 Buck, *Cleburne*, 165–66; *Official Records*, XXXI, Pt. 2, pp. 726, 747–49.
36 *Official Records*, XXXI, Pt. 2, pp. 726, 735.
37 *Ibid.*, pp. 735, 749; Buck, *Cleburne*, 170–71; Coleman Diary, November 25, 1863.

In the center of his line Bragg had placed Breckinridge's corps in two rows of works. At the base of the ridge Bragg had a heavy concentration of men in rifle pits and trenches, with another line along the top of the ridge. Thus he had achieved defense in depth. In doing so he had further weakened the impact of his inferior numbers and had placed his first-line men in a position where they faced possible death from the enemy in front and possible death from comrades in arms behind them. Both of Bragg's lines could deliver destructive fire as long as the enemy was over three hundred yards away, but once the attackers got beneath the umbrella of fire, the rear line could fire only at the risk of hitting their own men.[38]

At 3:30 P.M. Thomas started forward. He received heavy and deadly fire as he approached the Confederate first line. When the Union troops got closer, the Confederates fired a final volley and fled to the rear. The Union soldiers could not remain in their exposed position, so without orders they began the pursuit. "Our line at the top of the Ridge could not fire upon the enemy without killing their own men who were either in advance of the enemy or mixed up with them." The Confederate line at the top of the ridge held momentarily and then collapsed. The initial breakthrough came at Patton Anderson's position. Once on the crest of the ridge the Union troops fanned out to the left and right. On the extreme left of the Confederate line Hooker had come up at last and scattered a brigade Breckinridge had sent to that flank. General William B. Bate's division succeeded in holding back the enemy long enough for Breckinridge's corps to make its escape. With the exception of Bate's division the remainder of the Confederate left had become a disorganized, terrified mob. As one soldier said, "I turned with a heavy heart but a mighty nimble foot and followed the men who were ahead of me." Bragg could not understand the collapse of his line: "A panic which I had never before witnessed seemed to have seized upon officers and men, and each appeared to be struggling for his personal safety, regardless of his duty and his character. . . . No satisfactory excuse can possibly be given for the shameful conduct of our troops. . . ."[39]

An entirely different battle had been fought on the Confederate

---

38 Hall, "Notes"; *Official Records*, XXXI, Pt. 2, p. 740; James Patton Anderson Autobiography, 1864 (Southern Historical Collection).
39 *Official Records*, XXXI, Pt. 2, pp. 132, 665–66; Hall, "Notes"; Pickett, *Hardee*, 21; Augustus Kean Memoirs, in Cabarrus Family Notes, 1799–1932 (Southern Historical Collection).

right that afternoon. The enemy continued to attack Smith's position in increasing numbers. Maney's brigade arrived to relieve Smith's troops but had to wait in the rear, for these Texans "declined to be relieved, saying that it was the first time they had ever had a chance to fight the Yankees from behind breastworks and that they were rather enjoying it." [40] Sometime after 2 P.M. another Federal brigade moved up to try its chances against the Confederate line. When the men had advanced as far as they could, they took whatever cover they could find and hung on to their position. Cleburne and Stevenson failed to dislodge them with artillery because the pieces could not be depressed sufficiently. They tried rolling large stones down on the attackers, but this had no effect. The enemy could and did fire at Hardee's men. Casualties mounted from the "continuous sheet of hissing, flying lead." Hardee determined to dislodge the enemy. First he attempted to move cannon into position to deliver a flanking fire, but the cannoneers could not find a position from which they could hit the enemy. Next he tried to maneuver a brigade into a position to deliver enfilade rifle fire. This also failed. Now Hardee turned to Stevenson's brigades, which had come up, and selected regiments from Cumming's brigade to charge. Rushing out through a small opening in the breastworks, the Georgians took three charges to dislodge the enemy. In the third charge two of Maney's regiments joined in the frontal assault while the Roger Q. Mills regiment of Smith's brigade attacked from the left. The attack cost Cleburne the services of brigade commander Smith and regimental commander Mills, but the enemy abandoned the position and fell back in confusion, leaving colors and many prisoners behind.[41]

As Thomas' attack on the Confederate center developed, Bragg called on Hardee for support. Hardee sent Brown's brigade. Then the continued heavy firing to his left made him fear for the safety of Cheatham's flank. He left Cleburne and went to the left, ordering Cleburne to send over all of his "available" men. Maney's and Cumming's brigades prepared to leave, but meanwhile Hardee sent back "appalling news." [42] When he arrived on the left of his corps, Hardee had found Cheatham facing to the south rather than to the west. The Union breakthrough had menaced Cheatham's flank and Cheat-

---

40 Hall, "Notes."
41 *Official Records*, XXXI, Pt. 2, pp. 735–37, 750; Buck, *Cleburne*, 171–72.
42 *Official Records*, XXXI, Pt. 2, pp. 726, 752–53; Hay, "The Battle of Chattanooga," *loc. cit.*, 129.

ham had responded at once, throwing back Walthall's brigade across the top of the ridge. He first tried to restore the shattered main line with a counterattack by Jackson's and Moore's brigades, but after hard fighting they were sharply repulsed. The enemy now advanced north on Walthall's position. Although he gave up some ground, Walthall supported by Brown managed to hold his line. Hardee approved the action Cheatham had taken and remained at this critical point.[43] He sent back orders for Cleburne to take command of his, Walker's, and Stevenson's divisions. His corps would withdraw across Chickamauga Creek as soon after darkness as possible.[44]

After night fell, Hardee began pulling out his units, starting on the left. Cheatham withdrew, then Walker, then Stevenson. Cleburne waited until last. It took a sharp attack by Lowrey's brigade to free the divisions from contact with the enemy. Then, behind cover of a strong skirmish line, he retired his brigades. By 9 P.M. the rear of Cleburne's division had crossed Chickamauga Creek, burning the bridge behind them.[45] At Chickamauga Station the soldiers found "everything in confusion—stragglers innumerable hunting their commands. Cleburne's division alone seems to maintain any order. Ah the bitter humiliation of this disastrous day." [46] Fortunately for the Confederates, Bate's division and Hardee's corps slowed enemy pursuit, and enemy columns lost their way over the strange roads. The dark night effectually ended any pursuit by Grant's entire army. Sheridan, however, kept on after the Confederates. He compelled the Confederate rear guard to destroy the bridge over Chickamauga Creek prematurely, and thus he captured several hundred stranded troops.[47]

The battles around Chattanooga came close to destroying the morale of the Army of Tennessee. Desertion, panic, and disillusionment infected its ranks on the dreary march to Dalton. Men tried to forget; one hoped "that I may be spared such scenes in future, for a time

---

43 E. C. Walthall to Cheatham, March 17, 1876, and Cheatham to Walthall, March 28, 1876, in Cheatham Papers; Pickett, *Hardee*, 21; *Official Records*, XXXI, Pt. 2, p. 526; Edward Turner Sykes, *Walthall's Brigade* (Vol. I of *Mississippi Historical Society Publications*, Centenary Series, ed. Dunbar Rowland, Oxford, Miss., 1916), 541.
44 *Official Records*, XXXI, Pt. 2, pp. 752–53.
45 *Ibid.*; Buck, *Cleburne*, 173; Pickett, *Hardee*, 21.
46 Coleman Diary, November 25, 1863.
47 *Official Records*, XXXI, Pt. 2, pp. 35, 132.

my spirits were below zero." [48] The retreating army left behind 6,667 men, in addition to a heavy number of stragglers en route to Dalton. Out of this number only about 2,500 had been killed or wounded. The rest had been captured. They also left behind forty cannon, several stand of colors, and the reputations of at least two generals—Bragg and Breckinridge.[49]

Several of the Confederate commanders, however, had either made their reputations or added luster to distinguished careers. States Rights Gist, who had commanded Walker's division in the battle, raised himself greatly in the esteem of the army, as did Cumming, Walthall, and Lucius Polk. William B. Bate had been known as a competent brigadier previously; now senior officers looked upon him as a good prospect for the permanent command of a division. General Bragg chose to ignore his old enemy Cheatham in his report, but the army knew that Cheatham had conducted himself well. Cleburne stood out above all the others. Missionary Ridge was his battle, as far as the Confederates were concerned. He followed his good work with the fine rear-guard action at Ringgold two days later, and for this success he received the thanks of the Confederate Congress.

In his report General Bragg particularly commended Hardee. He maintained that Hardee had preserved the Confederate right by his timely intervention with Cheatham's division when the center crumbled. He also credited Hardee for a great deal of the success in repulsing Sherman. He concluded his remarks by saying, "Lieutenant-General Hardee, as usual, is entitled to my warmest thanks and high commendation for his gallant and judicious conduct during the whole of the trying scenes through which we passed." [50] In a letter to his friend the Reverend John W. Beckwith, Hardee admitted that he had "received more credit than I deserve." [51] He knew that the credit for throwing up a defense across the ridge after the breakthrough belonged to Cheatham and Walthall. He also knew that the credit for the handling of the troops on the right belonged to Cleburne. Neither of these specific incidents should have been claimed for him as they were, but he did merit notice for the behavior of his corps

48 J. T. Haley to Mr. and Mrs. Faw, December 17, 1863, in John Trotwood Moore Collection.
49 Livermore, *Numbers and Losses*, 107.
50 *Official Records*, XXXI, Pt. 2, 666.
51 Hardee to J. W. Beckwith, December 10, 1863, in Beckwith Papers.

as a whole. He had general supervision over Cleburne, Walker (Gist), Stevenson, and Cheatham during the battle. These four divisions had soundly defeated Sherman, and they had held the right—that portion of Bragg's line that protected the only escape route. Although Hardee had advised against a stand at Missionary Ridge, he had co-operated energetically and cordially with Bragg. His deployment on the right had been sound, and he had provided Cleburne with the needed reserves that enabled him to thrust back the only serious lodgment the enemy made. His dispatch of Brown's brigade to Cheatham's relief had aided materially in stabilizing the critical line across the top of the ridge. Hardee's withdrawal had been executed with care and skill. His troops had retired safely.

On November 26 the army encamped at Ringgold, Georgia. Cleburne remained behind as the rear guard and beat off a heavy attack by Hooker.[52] As the army neared Dalton, stragglers returned, and with them came St. John Liddell who had been on a leave of absence. He was appalled: "Hardee and Bragg came along and stopped a while to talk with me. The latter was so much depressed, that I had not an unkind word at hand to reproach him for such unmitigated follies as he had gone into at Mission Ridge. He had been simply infatuated. As to Hardee—a soldier by education and nature, he was hardened to disasters, bore all with his usual cheerful philosophy and calling me aside said, 'I want to tell you a secret. I am engaged to be married to a most estimable young lady.' I looked incredulous—'I am in earnest—good by' and went away." [53]

52 For an account of Cleburne's action at Ringgold, see Hughes, "Hardee, C.S.A.," 292 ff.
53 Liddell's Record.

XI

"Let the Past
Take Care of Itself"

"I DESIRE to say, in assuming command, that there is no cause for discouragement. The overwhelming numbers of the enemy forced us back from Missionary Ridge, but the army is still intact and in good heart. Our losses were small and will be rapidly replaced. The country is looking to you with painful interest. I feel that it can rely upon you. Only the weak and the timid need to be cheered by constant success. The veterans of Shiloh, Perryville, Murfreesboro and Chickamauga require no such stimulus to sustain their courage and resolution. Let the past take care of itself; we can and must secure the future." [1] Thus General Hardee addressed his new command, the Army of Tennessee. Braxton Bragg, overwhelmed by the extent of the Missionary Ridge disaster, had requested that a court of inquiry be appointed and that he be relieved of command. The War Department complied with Bragg's latter request, directing him to turn over the command to Hardee, the second ranking officer in the army. Hardee assumed command on December 2, 1863.[2]

The greatest problem confronting Hardee was rebuilding the wreckage that was the Army of Tennessee, but a more immediate problem was preserving the army so that it could be rebuilt. If Federal pressure continued, the army might be scattered about in the mountains of North Georgia, or it might melt away as it retreated farther south. As a shield against Grant's pursuit, Hardee stationed

---

1 William Joseph Hardee Circular, December 2, 1863, in Tennessee Miscellaneous Manuscript Collection.
2 *Official Records,* XXXI, Pt. 2, p. 682, Pt. 3, pp. 764–65.

Cleburne's division at Tunnel Hill. He deployed cavalry in the enemy's front, placed Wheeler between Dalton and Cleveland to observe and to cover his right, and ordered five hundred cavalry at Lafayette to guard his left.[3]

Once his security had been arranged, Hardee set to work to strengthen the position at Dalton, constructing defense works along Rocky Face Ridge and in Crow's Valley. He repaired and built military roads around Dalton and sent out numerous scouting parties and intelligence agents.[4]

Grant soon pulled his advance units back from Ringgold. He dispersed his army, sending units to other areas and a large column into East Tennessee. By employing his army to consolidate his gains in Chattanooga and in East Tennessee, Grant gave Hardee a respite and an opportunity to take the initiative.

Hardee, however, refused to attempt any offensive action against Grant's dispersing army because of the Army of Tennessee's battered condition. To remain inactive would allow Grant to consolidate his gains and would work even more harm to the morale of the Army of Tennessee, so Hardee recommended to Cooper that his army be immediately reinforced. He did not advocate bleeding the emaciated garrisons at Mobile, Savannah, or Charleston, but suggested that competent officers of high rank be sent throughout the South searching for available military units, which Hardee believed existed in numbers sufficient to strengthen his army adequately. "Every available man should be put into the field, our forces concentrated, and be prepared for the offensive. Tennessee and Kentucky should be the theater of operations. Their redemption will secure us supplies, relieve us from the danger now threatened, and insure us an early possession of the great objectives for which we are contending." Otherwise, "in our present condition it is necessary to avoid a general action; and should the enemy uniting his scattered columns, advance, a retrograde movement becomes inevitable." [5] Thus for the three weeks that Hardee held the command, the army remained on the defensive in Dalton. The only aggressive action Hardee took was to send out Wheeler

3 Hardee, "Cleburne," *loc. cit.*, 156; *Official Records*, LII, Pt. 2, p. 573.
4 *Official Records*, XXXI, Pt. 3, p. 803; Hardee to Beckwith, December 10, 1863, in Beckwith Papers.
5 *Official Records*, LII, Pt. 2, pp. 575–76.

on an ill-fated raid against Grant's East Tennessee lines of communication on December 27.

By December 8 the Army of Tennessee had already begun to revive. Hardee kept an eye cocked toward Chattanooga, thankful for every day that Grant allowed him. Colonel Joseph C. Ives, sent by Davis to investigate the army's condition, reported that Hardee "considers that his force, if not attacked for two or three days, will be in good fighting order. During the past twenty-four hours 1000 more men returned to the army from the rear." From December 2 to December 26 Hardee's numbers went from 30,127 to 36,017 effectives. This increase resulted from the return of stragglers, from the return of men on duty in Alabama gathering conscripts, and from the nearly three hundred men sent up daily by Gideon J. Pillow's conscript bureau. As Hardee worked feverishly to build up his army, Joseph Johnston threatened to undo his efforts, asking that Quarles's and Baldwin's brigades be returned to Mobile. Hardee, commonly the epitome of military propriety, went outside prescribed official channels and appealed to the War Department to keep these brigades with the Army of Tennessee. He pointed out that two infantry brigades and two thirds of his cavalry still remained with Longstreet and that Quarles's and Baldwin's brigades were "indispensable" to him. The War Department supported Hardee, and he kept his brigades; he also won a well-deserved rebuke from the angered Johnston.[6]

The Army of Tennessee needed additional manpower badly. It also needed supplies to replace the many items lost in the Missionary Ridge rout. To obtain clothing Hardee sent many of his Georgia and Alabama troops to their homes, where local authorities helped provide for them. Governor Brown of Georgia even dispatched an agent to Europe to purchase blankets. For most of its supplies, however, the army depended upon the Georgia railroads. Initially, this dependence proved a curse rather than a blessing, because discord among the numerous railroad companies created a series of logistical bottlenecks. Hardee thereupon drew upon the bountiful supply of political generals available in the Army of Tennessee and brought forth the influential and diplomatic Henry R. Jackson of Georgia. Jackson went to confer with the railroad officials and soon produced "happy

6 *Ibid.*, pp. 573–74, XXXI, Pt. 3, pp. 412, 781–82, 809, 870–71, Ser. IV, Vol. II, 1064; Cooper to Hardee, December 7, 1863, in Letters Received, Adjutant General's Office.

results." Rations became "full and uniform," adequate forage was ensured, and the army soon possessed supplies to sustain it through January. Although the soldiers remained inadequately clothed, their
stomachs could be satisfied with a good supply of flour and meal.
Hardee enriched this diet with apples, vegetables, and sorghum, but
the meat problem remained acute throughout December. Hardee appealed to his departmental commander, Johnston, saying that "unless
supplies can be obtained from Mississippi, this army will be without
meat in two months," and that "without meat it will be impossible to
hold this army together." As an expedient, Hardee utilized Wheeler
as a provisioning agent in East Tennessee. The cavalry commander
brought back quantities of bacon and grain to help the army through
the crisis.[7]

To restore the morale of the Army demanded more than adequate
food, clothing, and shelter. Soldiers returned home from the army
depressed "because the army was so low spirited and demoralized, and
said they had lost all hope of ever gaining their independence." Like
the problems of supply and manpower the morale problem was not
solved until the spring, but Hardee initiated steps leading to a solution.
He first set up a lenient furlough policy, granting leaves for the
thirtieth man of each company. He promised a bonus forty-day
furlough for men who brought back a recruit for the army. Alarmed
at the tendency toward leniency in the military courts, Hardee urged
his judge advocates "to restore adequate punishment" for offenses.
The system of stopping pay had been abused, and he moved to correct this. As always, he emphasized military pomp and ceremony.
"General Hardee . . . was alive to the good policy of amusing and
occupying the minds of the troops by a system of drills, parades and
reviews." Army morale slowly began to respond to these measures.[8]

The organization of the army also needed attention, and while
Hardee was in command, it received it. Hardee replaced the forty
guns lost at Missionary Ridge and organized the artillery more effectively, placing three batteries of four guns in battalions. He assigned a battalion to each division, keeping four batteries back as an

---

7 *Official Records*, XXXI, Pt. 3, p. 781, XXXII, Pt. 2, p. 622; J. E. Brown to
   Hardee, December 16, 1863; in Aaron Wilbur Letters, 1863–65 (Emory University Library); Hardee to J. Ives, December 23, 1863, in William P. Palmer
   Collection, Western Reserve Historical Society, Cleveland, Ohio.
8 *Official Records*, XXXI, Pt. 3, pp. 475, 855, 869–70; Pickett, *Hardee*, 23–24.

army reserve. Five batteries were stripped of horses and guns and shipped to Atlanta to man its defenses.[9]

As commander of the Army of Tennessee Hardee had little opportunity to demonstrate qualities of high command, but even when this fact is taken into account, it must be acknowledged that he failed to display any marked strategic aptitude. His situation reports to Davis and Cooper are standard summaries proposing obvious solutions. If attacked at Dalton, he would have withdrawn deep into Georgia; he did not contemplate offensive action without heavy reinforcements. Hardee did accomplish much toward rebuilding the army, for he saw it through one of its darkest periods and provided the basis for many of Johnston's organizational successes in the spring. He gave promise of being an adequate army commander. Although he lacked the strategic ability and daring of Bragg, he could bring to the army greater combat proficiency than did Bragg, and greater hope of harmonious relations with subordinates. And although he was inferior to Johnston as a strategist and as an inspiring leader, he could give greater prospect of co-operation with his superiors. Trying to evaluate Hardee as a permanent commander of the army, however, leads one off into history in the subjunctive, for Hardee refused to accept the position.

At the time of his appointment Hardee had wired back conditional acceptance: "I fully appreciate the compliment paid to me by the President in this expression of his confidence, but feeling my inability to serve the country successfully in this new sphere of duty, I respectfully decline the command if designed to be permanent. In doing so permit me to add that I am desirous to serve the cause and the country, and will co-operate cordially with any officer the President may select." [10]

The disappointed and perhaps startled Davis knew that the logical appointee now was Johnston, but he first approached Lee on the subject. Reluctance underlined every word in Lee's reply. "I can see no good that will result. . . . I also fear that I would not receive

9 Army of Tennessee, General Orders No. 218, in Henry C. Semple Papers, 1847–78 (Southern Historical Collection); *Official Records*, XXXI, Pt. 3, pp. 790, 821; B. J. Semmes to wife, December 13, 1863, in Jorantha Jordan and Benedict Joseph Semmes Papers, 1848–65 (Southern Historical Collection); Hardee to Ives, December 23, 1863, in Palmer Collection.
10 *Official Records*, XXXI, Pt. 3, pp. 764–875.

cordial cooperation. . . ." Davis reached his decision by December 16, notifying Hardee that Johnston had been appointed.[11]

Many people in the South wanted Joe Johnston to have the command. Polk, who knew the Army of Tennessee as well as anyone, stated that this was the "general desire on the part of the army and the country." In a letter to Johnston, W. W. Mackall contended, "Almost every one expects you to take the command and consider H. a *locum tenens*." If Hardee had been ambitious for high command—and certainly up to this point he had always been professionally ambitious—he would have taken Davis' offer, regardless of what others wanted.[12]

The reasons why Hardee declined the permanent command of the Army of Tennessee are complex and lead deep into his character. Subsequently, his friends often attributed his decision to his excessive modesty and to his friendship for Johnston. His enemies and critics have usually said that he lacked the necessary self-confidence. General Liddell, after leaving Hardee at Dalton, visited Johnston in Meridian, Mississippi, where the two talked of Hardee as a possible commander. Johnston said, ". . . Hardee liked the show of War, but disliked its labors and responsibilities." This is an unusual statement, coming from a man who became one of Hardee's closest friends and was a warm admirer; but there is irony in it. Throughout Hardee's career one senses this conflict and dispels one's thought, saying, "No, it can't be true." But Johnston's statement cannot be discounted: it gives new meaning to many incidents in Hardee's life. That Hardee loved the color, the ceremony, the glamor, and the "fight" of war has been already demonstrated a number of times. That he disliked the labor of war seems an unfair charge. That he disliked the responsibilities of war cannot be documented with precise incidents, but the statement rings true as an impression of the whole man and his military career. Liddell followed up Johnston's comment with this observation: "I thought there was truthfulness in this remark—as Hardee was not self-confident—seemed to shun the weight of responsibility —and I believe was not intended by nature to be a great leader.—This he had the penetration to see, and the modesty to decline, when the Comd was offered to him, Hardee was an able second to any leader." [13]

11 *Ibid.,* 792, LII, Pt. 2, p. 576.
12 *Official Records,* XXXI, Pt. 3, pp. 796–97; Mackall to J. Johnston, December 9, 1863, in Mackall Papers.
13 Liddell's Record.

Members of Hardee's family have commented that he declined the command because of his friendship for Johnston and because "customary military courtesy [dictated] that [the command] should be first offered to General Johnston as the ranking officer." [14] Hardee himself stated, "I do not wish to be obstinate, nor am I disinclined to bear my full share of the responsibilities of the present crisis, but I feel I can be more useful as a Corps Commander than [as] the Commander of the army." [15]

When Hardee's previous career is considered, his statement appears to be completely logical. To believe that modesty kept Hardee from the command would impugn his confirmed good sense and his deep patriotism, unless "modesty" is taken in the sense that Liddell intended—that is, that Hardee was aware of his limitations, and that this self-knowledge kept inordinate ambitions under control. It is also questionable that Hardee was the close friend of Johnston at this time. Apparently, the only time that Hardee and Johnston could have known each other on an intimate basis was in Mississippi in the summer of 1863. Their careers had not meshed until that time, and it seems more reasonable to believe that the "great friendship" was fused in the furnace of the Atlanta campaign. Eminently a practical man, Hardee knew the advantages of Johnston as commander: First, he had a high regard for Johnston's military ability. Second, Hardee was a firm believer in military protocol, and Johnston was his senior and therefore entitled to the command. Third, he knew that Johnston was better known throughout the South and could command far more influential support than he could. Fourth, Johnston would come to the army clean of the failures of the past, with which Hardee knew that unfortunately he had too often been associated.

Hardee saw that the Army of Tennessee needed inspiration and confidence, which Johnston could provide better than he.

As for self-confidence, the term needs clarification. Without it Hardee could have never risen to the command position he held. Without it he could never have proven durable as a regimental, brigade, division, or corps commander. His presence seemed to exude confidence to his subordinates on or off the battlefield. Yet, if by a lack of self-confidence one means that Hardee did not feel able

14 C. S. H. Hardee, "Reminiscences"; author's interview with Mrs. Howard Bowen, August 5, 1957.
15 Hardee to Beckwith, December 10, 1863, in Beckwith Papers.

to fulfill the role of an army commander, the term is appropriate. Hardee seems to have felt that he possessed the capabilities of a good corps commander (capabilities rare enough in themselves), but he doubted that he would meet with success in a higher position. The position had already been the bane of the able Albert Sidney Johnston, Beauregard, and Bragg. It is difficult to believe that Hardee distrusted his ability to control the numbers of an army in battle, or on a march. He surely believed that he could see to their supply, morale, and discipline. Perhaps he doubted his ability to make the necessary combinations that would result in victory. Perhaps, he doubted as Lee did, that he would receive the "cordial cooperation" of the individualists and political generals. Perhaps he doubted that he could rally the support of the public as much as could the politically prominent Bragg, the well-connected Johnston, or the electrifying Beauregard. Perhaps, as he stated at the conclusion of the war, he knew in 1861 that victory was impossible and that he could never meet the demands of his superiors or of his country for success. All in all, he seems to have found himself in the position of corps commander, and he wanted no other at the time.

Another factor in Hardee's declining the command, slight in itself but worthy of consideration in light of Johnston's statement, is contained in a letter written in December from army commander Hardee to John W. Beckwith, Bishop of Georgia and Confederate chaplain. ". . . How to get away from this army is the question. If retained in command I don't see how it is possible." "It" was Hardee's forthcoming marriage to Mary Foreman Lewis. "My engagement . . . seems to be no longer a secret. I hope I shall have it in my power soon to call on you for assistance. Miss M. said in one of her first letters, that I must remember you were her Favorite Minister; and I need not assure you that you are also mine. . . . Haven't I won a prize in Miss Mary. She writes me such charming letters, so loving, & so affectionate, and expressed in such chaste & elegant language. For her sake I wish I were fifteen years younger." [16]

Mary Lewis was the same young lady that Hardee had met in Demopolis in September, 1863. He had seen her as often as possible in the interim, and the decision to be married had come swiftly. She was described as almost beautiful. All commented on her heavy black

16 *Ibid.*

hair, done up in a chignon, on her "large, soft, brown eyes," and on her thinness, which kept her from being a real beauty and foretold the disease that would kill her. Refined in appearance, Mary Lewis matched her physical attributes with wit, charm, and an exceptional education. She had an active interest in the fine arts and was known as an avid reader. A confirmed idealist, she also appeared to be a hero-worshiper. "She could never have married a man who could not be put on a pedestal." She found her hero when she was twenty-six.[17]

Mary Lewis had been brought up and had received her early education in North Carolina, where her family was prominent. Her father, Richard H. Lewis, had come to Marengo County, Alabama, in the 1830's from Edgecombe County, North Carolina. He lived a rather lonely life in the newly opened country, carving out two large plantations, "Bleak House" and the "Hermitage," and accumulating a modest fortune. His wife, Mary E. Foreman, presently joined her husband in Alabama, and there Mary was born. Both mother and child returned to North Carolina when the mother became ill. Mary Foreman Lewis died in 1840, and R. H. Lewis spent the remainder of his life shuttling back and forth between North Carolina and Alabama. His daughter Mary spent most of her early years in North Carolina with her uncle, Kenelm H. Lewis. When her father died in 1857, Kenelm Lewis, his "dearest brother & nearest friend," became the guardian of Mary and her brother Ivey. In the late 1850's Mary went abroad to study in Germany and France, meeting Ivey and his bride, Kate Rhodes, who were in France on their honeymoon. The three toured Europe extensively and collected paintings, which they brought back to "Bleak House," now Ivey's plantation home in Alabama. For a while they entertained the idea of opening a private art gallery in Selma. Mary continued to live with Ivey and Kate until the outbreak of the war.

Richard Lewis' children wanted for nothing. They spent a good part of every summer at various springs in Virginia and traveled extensively. Mary had become an heiress, inheriting the "Hermitage," and Ivey received "Bleak House." Luckily, Richard Lewis' over-

17 DuBose, "Chronicles of the Canebrake," *loc. cit.,* 543; Mrs. Allen C. Jones to T. R. Hay, March 22, 1942, in possession of T. R. Hay, Locust Valley, N. Y.; author's interview with Mrs. Howard Bowen, August 5, 1957; H. Wigfall to T. Wigfall, April 19, 1864, in Wigfall Family Papers.

seers stayed on with the children until both had gained experience in managing a plantation. At the outbreak of the war Ivey enlisted in the Cavalry of the Canebrake. He soon joined the Jeff Davis Legion and rose quickly to become major of that famous cavalry unit. Mary, not to be outdone, made perhaps the "handsomest Company flag sent to the Army from Alabama" for the infantry company of the Canebrake Legion. Mary seems to have spent most of the war years close to her plantation or in Mobile.[18]

General Johnston's arrival in Dalton on December 26 enabled Hardee to complete the arrangements for the wedding. He secured the services of the Reverend Mr. Beckwith and asked Cleburne to be his best man, the latter taking his first leave of absence since entering the Confederate Army. Mary had meanwhile gone to Mobile to buy her trousseau. When she was returning, her steamer struck an object in the river and capsized. She found herself trapped inside the cabin and was saved by a member of the ship's crew, who swam into the cabin and hoisted her out through the skylight. Mary had to spend several hours on the riverbank, warming herself by a fire, while she waited for the next boat. To repay her rescuer she gave him a gold watch and chain, which she had intended to give Hardee as a wedding present.[19]

Despite the steamboat disaster and the question of who would command a Confederate army, the wedding came off as scheduled. The night of January 13 was appropriate to Dickens' dark novel *Bleak House.* Pouring rain brought on the mud for which the canebrake country was noted, and servants labored back and forth from the carriages to the house, lifting ladies over the mud. "Bleak House" itself was decorated elegantly, and champagne flowed. Hardee and the officers accompanying him were in full uniform. Hardee's and Cleburne's staff members who came along were dazzled by the Mobile and canebrake belles. The setting was so overpowering that two of

18 DuBose, "Chronicles of the Canebrake," *loc. cit.*, 533–35, 543; R. H. Lewis to K. H. Lewis, March 5, 1847, January 1, 1853, and June 14, 1855, in Lewis Family Papers, 1801–1900 (Southern Historical Collection); author's interview with Mrs. Howard Bowen, August 5, 1957; receipt signed by Mary F. Lewis, March 1, 1862, in Mount Prospect Papers, 1799–1888 (Southern Historical Collection); Mrs. Allen C. Jones to T. R. Hay, May 4, 1942, in possession of T. R. Hay.

19 Buck, *Cleburne,* 210; I. A. Buck to Lucie Buck, January 3, 1864, in Buck Papers; DuBose, "Chronicles of the Canebrake," *loc. cit.*, 543–44.

Mary's close friends became engaged that night, as did Patrick Ronayne Cleburne.[20]

Hardee and his bride left on a wedding trip to Mobile, accompanied by many members of the wedding party. After about a week there they traveled across the South to Savannah and may have made a side trip down into Florida to see some of Hardee's old friends. At least, the Union commander in Florida thought so and reported that Hardee was in Lake City with a large force at his disposal. The Hardees remained in Savannah until about February 1, Hardee requesting that his leave be extended for five days.[21]

The newlyweds returned to Dalton in early February, accompanied by Hardee's daughters. They set up their home in a house with the "least possible amount of furniture." Hardee said they were camping out.

Mary Hardee enjoyed her first taste of army life. Officers paid frequent calls and showered attention on her. Irving A. Buck, who accompanied Cleburne to breakfast at the Hardees, wrote "I think [Hardee] has shown his usual good sense in his selection of a wife, she appears to be an exceedingly sweet lady. His daughters are very superior girls." The talented and romantic General Alexander W. Reynolds has been captivated. To excuse himself from one of Mary Hardee's invitations, he had replied:

> I yet hope though *now* declining
> I may have, some other time
> An invitation to your dining
> When I can pledge to thee & thine.[22]

For the spring reviews of Hardee's corps the general often appeared without his staff close on his heels. Roy, Pickett, White, Poole, and the others now watched the reviews on horses not to the

20 DuBose, "Chronicles of the Canebrake," *loc. cit.*, 544; Mrs. Allen C. Jones to T. R. Hay, March 22, 1942; Hardee to Beckwith, January 19, 1864, in Beckwith Papers.
21 Mrs. L. Polk to daughter, January, 1864, in Polk Papers; G. W. Brent to Hardee, January 25, 1864, in Army of Tennessee, Orders and Telegrams Sent, 1862, 1864, Record Group 109; *Operations on the Atlantic Coast 1861–1865, Virginia, 1862, 1864, Vicksburg* (Vol. IX of Military Historical Society of Massachusetts, *Papers*, Boston, 1912), 243.
22 Hardee to Mrs. Mary Erwin, February 10, 1864, in Tennessee Miscellaneous Manuscripts; I. A. Buck to Lucie Buck, February 9, 1864, in Buck Papers; Alexander Welch Reynolds' Poem, March 21, 1864, in Manuscript Division (Library of Congress).

left and rear of the general, but flanking Mary Hardee, who attended most of the reviews on horseback. The general would not allow her to watch the sham battles for fear that her horse would become frightened from the gunfire, but she had her way in another matter. She insisted that Hardee accept the offer of a painter who appeared in Dalton, and consequently he sat for the only painting he had made during the war.[23]

While Hardee was posing, Johnston's army grew in strength. Although he lost two brigades to other departments, Johnston increased the size of the army to forty-three thousand men, and the morale of the Army of Tennessee and its physical condition improved as the spring progressed. Johnston "infused a portion of his active spirit into his subordinate officers, and the consequence was that [they] were better clothed, and better provided for, in every way" than they had been for a year.[24]

The improving morale could be clearly seen in the re-enlistment program. Mass re-enlistments for the duration of the war began in Bate's Tennessee brigade, and the spirit of Bate's men quickly spread to the brigades of Strahl and Vaughan, and then to others. The Confederate high command was reassured by the result, even though the Alabama and Georgia troops seemed to hang back.[25]

Part of the Tennesseans' enthusiasm stemmed from the fact that at long last they had been grouped together in one division under their idol, Cheatham. In December they had been "very downhearted" when Bragg had parceled out the state troops to separate commands, and "constantly cherish[ed] the hope that soon we shall be again under *Mass Frank*." [26] Johnston next grouped the Georgians together under W. H. T. Walker, the trans-Mississippi troops under Cleburne, and other state brigades into state divisions.

23 Susan P. Lee, *Memoirs of William Nelson Pendleton, D. D.* (Philadelphia, 1893), 317; author's interview with Mrs. Howard Bowen, August 5, 1957; Mackall to wife, April 30, 1864, in Mackall Papers.
    The painter also approached Hood and Johnston, but neglected the chief of staff, W. W. Mackall. Downcast, Mackall remarked, "He has not asked me yet—perhaps he don't want handsome faces."
24 James L. Cooper Reminiscences, 1866 (microfilm copy in Joint Universities Library, Nashville, Tenn.).
25 *Official Records*, XXXII, Pt. 2, pp. 571–79; R. D. Jamison to wife, January 20, 1864, in Gale Family Letters and Papers, 1825–92 (microfilm copies in Joint Universities Library, Nashville, Tenn.).
26 J. R. Buist to C. T. Quintard, December 29, 1863, in Charles Todd Quintard Papers, 1857–99 (Duke University Library).

Johnston also sought to divide the Army of Tennessee into three corps. To do this he needed two lieutenant generals, and he asked the War Department if they could be sent from another department. Probably because of the influence of Bragg, and also because of the scarcity of competent lieutenant generals, the War Department did not allow the division, although it complied partially by sending John Bell Hood to Johnston in February, 1864.

Hood brought with him one of the most distinguished records of performance in the Confederate army. Known as a fighter, he inspired confidence and enthusiasm in any unit he commanded. Perhaps the War Department thought he could infuse the Army of Tennessee with the aggressive spirit that it needed.

When Hood arrived, he appeared dissatisfied with the personnel of his corps, as he believed that he had inherited all of the "untried" troops of the army.[27] His notion was obviously unfounded. Most of his troops and all of his senior officers had long combat records, but the best troops did seem to be grouped in Hardee's corps. The fact that Johnston had transferred Breckinridge's division (now commanded by William B. Bate) to Hardee in return for Stevenson's division added substance to Hood's belief.

Since the beginning of the war Bragg had shifted divisions frequently and thus had prevented the development of unity and cohesiveness within the corps. At Dalton, Hardee's corps solidified. It now contained the divisions of Bate, Cheatham, Cleburne, and Walker, totaling fourteen brigades (about nineteen thousand men); it would remain essentially unchanged until the end of the war.

Hardee now set to work to mold his men into a cohesive, effective fighting team. Constant rifle practice, drill, and inspections filled the average soldier's day. Hardee seems to have became a believer in the efficacy of sham battles as a training device. One distraught ordnance officer in Atlanta thought the officers of the Army of Tennessee had given up serious warfare for play-war: "The Army of Tennessee seems to be standing perfectly still with no prospect of a movement. . . . They are now amusing themselves with sham fights and the call is now constantly for blank [cartridges]." [28] This officer would have been even more disturbed had he witnessed another

27 *Official Records*, XXXII, Pt. 3, p. 607.
28 L. R. Ray to R. Thompson, March 23, 1864, in Lavender R. Ray Letters and Diary, 1861–65, edited by his daughter Ruby Felder Ray (typed manuscript in Georgia State Department of Archives and History).

kind of sham battle. On snowy days—and there were many that winter—elements of Hardee's corps waged snowball battles of massive proportions among themselves. The most memorable fight occurred between Cheatham's Tennesseans and Walker's Georgians, with ammunition from magazines of snowballs. Officers on horseback led several thousand men in realistic charges, flags flying. Once Cheatham had overpowered Walker, the Tennessee brigades turned to fighting among themselves.[29]

The stories of these mock engagements illustrate both the growing sense of division loyalty and the growing rivalry between units. Rivalry developed between the corps of Hood and Hardee also. An artillery officer fresh from Lee's army commented. "There is a spirit of rivalry between the two corps . . . which cannot fail of a beneficial effect. Division drills and reviews have been all the order of the day since I have been here. I have heard the opinions expressed several times by officers from the Va. army and who ought to be competent judges that this army is much better drilled than the other. I have no fears whatever for its fighting." [30]

Steady training routine resulted in a marked improvement in Hardee's corps. Hardee stayed close to his men, giving up quarters in Dalton.[31] He closely supervised the work of his division commanders, as he always had. He and his staff labored diligently to secure proper equipment for the men, and by April they had accumulated a surplus of arms and such equipment as knapsacks, canteens, and tents. They managed to solve one of the chronic Confederate

29 Alfred J. Vaughan. *Personal Record of the Thirteenth Regiment, Tennessee Infantry* (Memphis, 1897), 89–95; Artillery Journal, March 22, 1864, Cheatham Collection; Jones Diary, March 22, 1864.
30 H. Wigfall to mother, March 21, 1864, in Wigfall Family Papers.
31 "A marked feature in Hardee's camp life, especially while in winter quarters at Tullahoma & Dalton, was the social relations between himself & his subordinate officers. Scarcely a day but one or more of his Div., Brig., Regtl. & frequently Company officers, were gathered around his mess table in a social intercourse which was an agreeable variety to the monotony of camp life. The conversation on these occasions generally related to army matters, & valuable suggestions were given & received by commander and subordinates. This social intercourse gave Hardee an opportunity to form estimates of the character & capacities of his officers, which the restrictions of official intercourse do not afford. Knowledge which was of value in recommending promotions, & which in part accounted for the fact often remarked upon in the army that 'Hardee always had the best officers.' This social relation also fostered very strong personal attachments of his officers for Hardee, independent of their respect for & confidence in him as a commander." Roy, "Odds and Ends."

ordnance problems, for out of 16,000 rifles on hand in the corps, Hardee's men had 11,500 rifles of .57 and .58 caliber. Perhaps the most encouraging note of all was that out of 22,012 men present in Hardee's camps, 17,471 had enlisted for the war. Hardee would carry into the Atlanta campaign the largest, best trained, and most uniformly armed corps in the Confederate army.[32]

Hardee's division commanders also provided an element of strength for future campaigning. Cleburne had already proven his capacity and had shown that he would co-operate closely with Hardee. His division, composed principally of Arkansas and Texas troops, had been with Hardee since the beginning of the war, and both generals fully understood its capabilities. "Where this division defended, no odds broke its lines; where it attacked, no numbers resisted its onslaught, save only once [Franklin]—there is the grave of Cleburne and his heroic division." [33]

Cheatham's corps represented in everyone's mind Polk's corps, for Cheatham's division had been the heart of that corps until Polk left the army for Mississippi. Cheatham's record had been impressive until the battle of Missionary Ridge. Now with the Tennessee troops reunited, this division could prove to be the equal of Cleburne's.

W. H. T. Walker and Hardee had known each other forever, it seemed, although their relationship was not as close as that of Hardee and the other division commanders. The careers of Walker and Hardee in the old army had been remarkably parallel. Walker knew the business of war thoroughly and at Dalton brought his division around with startling rapidity. A former commandant of West Point, he could drill and discipline and had shown combat ability at Chickamauga The brave and impetuous Georgian would need little supervision in the coming campaigns, and Hardee could not have wished for surer hands to which to entrust one of his divisions.

The fourth division commander could prove to be the weak link in Hardee's command. When Hardee learned that Breckinridge would not command the division, he requested that John C. Brown be promoted to major general for the task.[34] The War Department decided to wait and allow Brown to develop further, however, and therefore

---

32 Mackall to wife, April 27, 1864, in Mackall Papers; *Official Records*, XXXII, Pt. 3, pp. 789, 801, XXXVIII, Pt. 4, p. 782.
33 Hardee, "Cleburne," *loc. cit.*, 161.
34 Hardee to Cooper, March 4, 1864, in George E. Maney Papers, 1863–1932 (Southern Historical Collection).

Bate, who brought the division to Hardee, came to be acknowledged as its commander. Bate was a popular leader of the same cut as Frank Cheatham, and his brigade had been the first in the army to enlist for the duration of the war. As a brigade commander he had proven that he was competent and could exercise initiative, and his record at Missionary Ridge demonstrated that he could stand up under adverse conditions. But Bate had never handled a division. Whether he could meet Hardee's standards as a division commander remained to be seen.

While the second largest army in the Confederacy remained passive at Dalton, columns from Grant's army moved east and west, fighting against Longstreet in East Tennessee and against Roddy and Forrest in middle and West Tennessee. In the first month of winter Grant concentrated on "cleaning up" and sealing up East Tennessee. In January his eyes turned west. Sherman was sent west with a force to conduct a raid into the heart of Mississippi. If successful, this raid would derange or perhaps destroy vital Confederate supply areas and, if the railroads were severed, would isolate Mobile.

On February 3 Sherman moved east from Vicksburg toward Meridian with about twenty-five thousand men. In conjunction with Sherman a column of seven thousand cavalry under General Sooy Smith started south toward Meridian from Memphis, while Thomas threatened Dalton, to prevent any forces from there being detached. To oppose Sherman's advance General Polk had about nine thousand infantry and ten thousand cavalry. Sherman moved steadily forward, driving the Confederate cavalry before him. Polk drew his infantry back from Meridian and placed it at Demopolis. As Sherman continued his advance deeper into Mississippi, Davis became alarmed. He wired Johnston about the situation and informed him of the possible consequences if Sherman was not stopped. "What can you do toward striking at him while in motion, and before he establishes a new base?" On February 15 Davis wired Johnston again, suggesting that infantry be detached from the Army of Tennessee to support Polk. Johnston replied that the time factor would prevent any detachments from his army from reaching the scene early enough to influence the course of events. Time was running out for the Confederates.

On February 14 Sherman entered Meridian, and presently he could report, "Meridian, with its depots, store-houses, arsenal, hospitals, offices, hotels and cantonments no longer exists." Davis receiving no satisfaction from Johnston, issued a peremptory order for

Hardee's corps to be sent to Polk "with all possible dispatch." Davis followed this message with a wire to Hardee on February 18, cautioning him not to carry transportation with him, as wagons would encumber him. The place where Hardee was to join Polk was not specified, as this would depend upon Sherman's movements. ". . . I hope you will be able to beat him before he reaches the Gulf or devastates the districts from which our supplies are to be drawn." Hardee replied immediately, stating that without his transportation he would be "tied to the railroad." Davis then told him to proceed anyway and to pick up his wagons at Polk's end of the line.[35]

Hardee began putting his corps aboard trains on February 18, and on February 19 he arrived in Montgomery in advance of his leading division. That night he wired Polk at Demopolis, inquiring where he should take his troops and where he would find transportation. The next day, February 20, Hardee wrote Davis that Mobile did not appear threatened, as Davis had feared it was. Hardee thought instead that Sherman intended to destroy as much of the Mobile and Ohio Railroad as he could and then return to Jackson. "If it is not your intention to make the campaign in Mississippi, I question the propriety of sending my troops to Demopolis, thereby opening up Georgia to the enemy. I think the enemy will next attempt to isolate Mobile by breaking the Mobile and Montgomery Railroad." At this point in his note to Davis, Hardee received orders from Polk, ordering him to Demopolis. As yet Polk had been unable to determine which direction Sherman would take, but anticipated an advance into the rich Alabama and Tombigbee valleys. Hardee then continued his letter to Davis, stating that he would at once put his troops in motion for Demopolis but that he disagreed with Polk on the probability of Sherman's advancing farther eastward.[36]

To move Hardee's troops from Montgomery to Demopolis required that steamers be sent up from Mobile. The movement of troops proceeded slowly. In answer to Hardee's dispatch of February 20, Davis sent word back the next day that "it is all important to crush the enemy in Mississippi, with the least delay." Polk, now fortified with Hardee's numbers, made plans to attack Sherman. He wrote to his cavalry commander, Stephen D. Lee, to keep up the attack against

35 *Official Records*, XXXII, Pt. 1, p. 176, LII, Pt. 2, pp. 619–25; J. Johnston to Davis, February 16, 1864, in Army of Tennessee, Orders and Telegrams Sent; Artillery Journal, February 18, and 19, 1864, Cheatham Collection.
36 *Official Records*, XXXII, Pt. 2, pp. 780–81. LII, Pt. 2, pp. 625–26.

Sooy Smith, saying that he would start William W. Loring's and Samuel G. French's divisions from Demopolis on the morning of February 23. Two important events frustrated the plans of Davis and Polk. On February 20 Sherman had decided to end his campaign and began drawing back toward Jackson. On February 21 General Thomas advanced two divisions of infantry directly against Johnston at Dalton with other divisions coming up in support. When this news reached Davis on February 23, he ordered that all of Hardee's infantry that had not passed farther west than Montgomery be sent back at once to Johnston's army. Hardee's men quickly began to retrace their steps. Thus ended Hardee's Mississippi campaign of 1864.[37]

Thomas had been ordered, as his part of Sherman's campaign, to make a diversion against Johnston. Thomas as usual did his part thoroughly and gave his opponent quite a fright. His leading divisions pushed on beyond Ringgold to within three and a half miles of Dalton. On February 24 and February 25 skirmishing occurred to the north and west of Dalton in Crow's Valley, in Mill Creek Gap, and along Rocky Face Ridge. This dress rehearsal for May, 1864, ended on February 25 when Thomas ordered his troops to return to Chattanooga. As the last Union troops were leaving on February 26, Cleburne's troops, just off the trains from Atlanta, launched a successful attack at Dug Creek Gap. Although the run to Demopolis had proven to be nothing more than a frustrating exercise in moving an infantry corps from one theater to another, the stand at Dalton gave the men of Johnston's army something to cheer about for the first time since Chickamauga. One observer thought that most people—including most of Johnston's men—had believed that he would retreat. His firmness was a pleasant surprise, "the effect of which was magical, inspiring [his soldiers] with an enthusiasm and confidence." [38]

In March, 1864, the complexion of affairs changed abruptly with the appointment of Sherman to the command of the Military Division

---

37 Davis to Hardee, February 21, 1864, in Rowland (ed.), *Jefferson Davis*, VI, 183; *Official Records*, XXXII, Pt. 2, p. 793, LII, Pt. 2, p. 628.
38 *Official Records*, XXXII, Pt. 1, p. 10, Pt. 2, pp. 458–59, 466, 470.
     The containment and localization of Sherman's offensive seemed to some observers to have been the result of the threat of Hardee's reinforcements coming up to support Polk. Actually, Polk's cavalry under Lee and Forrest administered a sharp defeat to Smith's cavalry force, preventing its junction with Sherman's infantry column. This, not Hardee's cross-country trek, was the decisive event in the Meridian campaign. T. Mackall to Mrs. W. W. Mackall, February 27, 1864, in Mackall Papers.

of the Mississippi. This new Union commander would have at his disposal the armies of the Cumberland, the Ohio, and the Tennessee. Sherman spent the month of March and most of April familiarizing himself with his new command, sifting and shifting his commanders, and trying to run Forrest to ground in Tennessee. In April he received his orders from Grant regarding the great spring offensive. Grant in conjunction with Butler would attack Lee, Banks would move against Mobile, Sigel would become aggressive in the pocket that was now West Virginia, and Sherman would tackle Johnston's army. Grant wanted him to ". . . break [Johnston's army] and to get into the interior of the enemy's country as far as you can, inflicting all the damage you can get against their war resources." [39] Later in April Sherman began regrouping his army for the attack on Johnston. The attack was to begin on May 5, coinciding with Union movements in the other theaters.

The Army of Tennessee stood ready. During the last few weeks Johnston had begun bringing up cavalry units he had left deep in Georgia to rest, recruit, and refit. On April 18 he ended all furloughs. The Confederates looked mighty fat and sassy.

39 *Official Records*, XXXII Pt. 3, pp. 313, 614-15.

XII

Spades Are Trumps

GENERAL JOHNSTON announced to the army on May 1 that the time had come for the ladies to be leaving, and Mrs. Hardee left with the others, boarding the train for La Grange, Georgia.[1] Meanwhile, the military situation changed significantly, for sifted scout reports pointed conclusively to an imminent enemy offensive. It now became evident that Sherman was drawing strength from troop concentrations in Tennessee and Mississippi. Johnston reacted quickly, calling up his scattered reserves in Georgia and requesting help from Polk in Mississippi and Dabney Maury in Mobile. By May 4 outpost duty had again become hazardous; the Atlanta Campaign began the next day.

The Union army opened the campaign with approximately 100,000 effective troops, divided into the Army of the Tennessee under James B. McPherson, the Army of the Ohio under John M. Schofield, and the massive Army of the Cumberland under George H. Thomas.[2] The last army comprised over half of Sherman's numbers and would be used as a sturdy base about which Schofield and McPherson would maneuver. During the first week of May Thomas occupied Ringgold, Schofield moved into Cleveland, and McPherson entered Rossville. Sherman intended first to take Tunnell Hill with Thomas' force and then to threaten Johnston with Thomas from the west and Schofield from the north. Meanwhile, McPherson would move south along Rocky Face Ridge, cut through Snake Creek Gap, and place himself astride the Confederates' line of communications and directly in their rear.[3]

1 Mackall to wife, May 3, 1864, in Mackall Papers; Hardee to Mary Hardee, June 4, 1864, in Hardee Letters (Alabama).
2 *Official Records*, XVIII, Pt. 1, pp. 62–63; William Tecumseh Sherman, "The Grand Strategy of the Last Year of the War," in *Battles and Leaders*, IV, 252.
3 *Official Records*, XXXVIII, Pt. 4, pp. 25, 38.

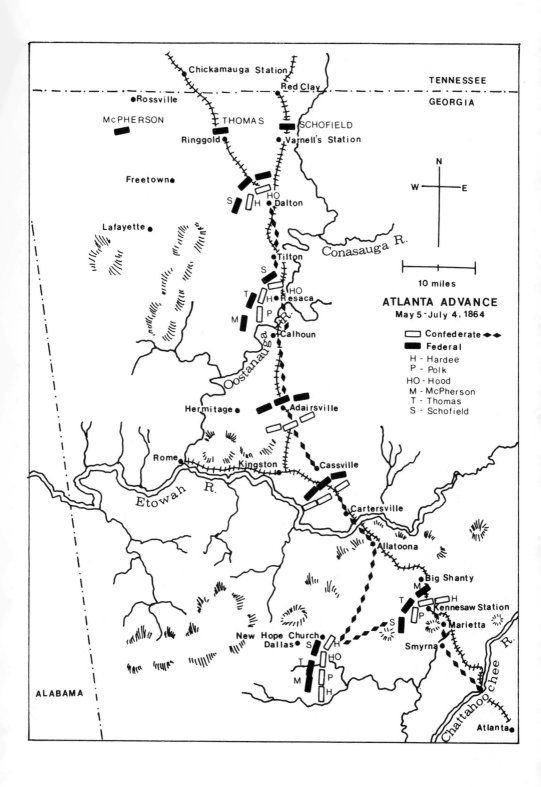

Chickamauga Station
Red Clay
TENNESSEE
GEORGIA
Rossville
McPHERSON
THOMAS
SCHOFIELD
Ringgold
Varnell's Station
Freetown
N
W   E
S
S H
HO
Dalton
Lafayette
Conasauga R.
10 miles
Tilton
S
T
HO
H Resaca
ATLANTA ADVANCE
May 5 - July 4, 1864
M
P
Calhoun
Confederate
Federal
H - Hardee
P - Polk
HO - Hood
M - McPherson
T - Thomas
S - Schofield
Oostanaula R.
Hermitage
Adairsville
Rome
Kingston
Cassville
Etowah   R.
Cartersville
Allatoona
Big Shanty
M
T   H
Kennesaw Station
P
S
Marietta
New Hope Church
Dallas   S
H
T
HO
Smyrna
M
P
H
Chattahoochee R.
ALABAMA
Atlanta

The Confederates initially opposed Sherman with some 43,000—two infantry corps of about 20,000 each, and some 2,500 cavalry. To supplement this inadequate force Johnston would receive about 20,000 men from Polk's department and from reserves in Georgia and Mobile.[4]

The topography of the Dalton area seemed to favor the defenders. Rocky Face Ridge would have been a respectable obstacle in height and length, but it began too far south and ran in the wrong direction. Advances from Ringgold and Cleveland would strike its right flank, not its front. The Confederates were well aware of this and positioned themselves to protect the gaps in Rocky Face and the relatively open country directly north of Dalton. The key problem for the Confederates was to determine the enemy's direction and strength. For this purpose A. P. Stewart was ordered to hold Mill Creek Gap with his division until he had forced the enemy to deploy. Hood controlled the forces on Rocky Face, and Hardee had his headquarters at Alt's Mill, north of Dalton, watching the approach from that direction. Hardee's troops were stationed from the crest of Rocky Face across Crow's Valley to the Cleveland road.[5]

Skirmishing began between infantry pickets on May 7 and steadily increased in intensity. The following day Thomas moved on Rocky Face, applying pressure on the ridge as far south as Dug Gap. Dug Gap had been left virtually unguarded, the force there consisting of only a small Arkansas cavalry regiment. Hardee heard musketry from this position and requested permission to send two of Cleburne's brigades to the scene. Hardee and Cleburne rode out in advance and, when they reached the crest of the ridge, found Dug Gap under attack by a division of Union troops. To assist Reynolds' Arkansas cavalry until the infantry came up, Hardee ordered up Grigsby's Kentucky cavalry. The Federal division under Geary was making progress against this cavalry, and the situation was tense. Soon the head of Granbury's brigade, Cleburne's division, appeared. In their eagerness the men in Granbury's advanced regiments seized the mounts left at the base of the ridge by the cavalry and rode dashingly up the ridge.

---

4 *Ibid.*, Pt. 3, p. 676.
5 *Ibid.*, Pt. 4, pp. 672–73; Artillery Journal, May 7, 1864, in Cheatham Collection; William Joseph Hardee, "Memoranda of the Operations of My Corps, while Under the Command of Genl J. E. Johnston, in the 'Dalton & Atlanta' and the 'North Carolina' Campaigns," in William Joseph Hardee Papers, 1863–71 (Henry E. Huntington Library).

A young Texan arrived at the crest first, galloped up to Hardee and Cleburne, threw himself off his horse, and asked, "Where am I most needed?" Comic relief conquered military grimness, and the two generals and their staffs were reduced to laughter. Hardee saw that the boy was posted; Granbury and Lowrey came up in time; and Geary's attack was repulsed.[6]

This encounter at Dug Gap, together with observations of other commanders along Rocky Face, indicated that a large portion of the Union army was moving south through the valley in front of the ridge. How far they had gone or were to go was not known. The Confederates, however, felt more concern for the pressure on Hood along the north portion of the ridge and for Schofield's movements directly north of Dalton. Hardee, who had the responsibility for the northern approach, returned from Dug Gap to Alt's Mill and called up two brigades from Cleburne to support Cheatham, who was posted in Crow's Valley.[7]

Actually the Confederates fell bait to a vigorous secondary attack by Schofield, which covered McPherson's turning movement. On May 9 Hardee faced Schofield on a line running from Rocky Face to the Cleveland road. The two forces skirmished throughout the day. Hardee's skirmish lines were driven from their advanced positions back to his line, but the main line easily resisted Schofield's secondary attacks.[8] The critical action during that day did not occur here but south of Dalton. McPherson, Hooker, and most of Thomas' army moved south toward unguarded Snake Creek Gap.

Events moved swiftly in the following days, and precious time elapsed before the Confederates realized Sherman's intent. As McPherson's troops appeared on the eastern side of Rocky Face, Johnston shifted two of Cleburne's brigades and some of Hood's troops toward threatened Resaca. Yet, through indecision on the part of all, these troops never reached Resaca nor returned to Rocky Face. Polk, who had appeared with fourteen thousand men instead of the division re-

---

6 Thomas Benton Roy, "Lieut. General William Joseph Hardee," manuscript in Hardee Collection (in possession of Hardee Chambliss, Jr., Fairfax, Va.); *Official Records*, XXXVIII, Pt. 3, pp. 614, 720; Joseph Eggleston Johnston, "Opposing Sherman's Advance to Atlanta," in *Battles and Leaders*, IV, 263; W. C. P. Breckinridge, "The Opening of the Atlanta Campaign," in *Battles and Leaders*, IV, 279.
7 Roy to P. R. Cleburne, May 8, 1864, in Army of Tennessee, Records of Major General Patrick R. Cleburne's Division, 1862–64, Record Group 109.
8 *Official Records*, XXXVIII, Pt. 2, p. 510, Pt. 4, pp. 97–99, 681.

quested of him, was directed to go to Resaca with the head of his column and take command.[9] Hardee misunderstood the situation as did many of the others. Schofield's well-executed diversion and his sudden retirement around Rocky Face on May 10 confused him. In a dispatch to Wheeler Hardee stated: "I am unable to decide what the Yanks are endeavoring to accomplish. The force in Crow's Valley, east of Rocky Face, is reported to be moving to our left. There seems to be no force threatening us except on Rocky Face, and that force has been unusually quiet today. All safe at Resaca. Hood and command will return this evening . . . I am only uneasy about our right, and won't be uneasy about that when Hood returns. Report promptly any movement of troops from Vernell's Station road. It is from that point I apprehend danger." [10]

On May 11 the real danger to the Confederate line of communications became clear. Hardee consulted scouting reports throughout the night and changed his mind about Union operations. Now he believed "that they are moving by their right toward the Oostenaula [River]." An hour after receiving this note from Hardee, Johnston ordered Wheeler to attack around the northern end of Rocky Face. This move against the enemy left would threaten Sherman's communications and above all would secure information. Wheeler's cavalry succeeded in discovering that the main Union strength had disappeared from its position opposite Rocky Face and in alarming the commander of the Union left. As the day advanced, McPherson emerged in organized strength in front of Resaca, and only caution kept him from capturing that key point. During the afternoon and evening of May 11 and throughout May 12 both armies rushed troops toward Resaca. Hardee accompanied Bate's and Cheatham's divisions; Walker had been sent earlier on May 12; and Cleburne was already in contact with the enemy flank in Sugar Valley. Most of Hood's troops at Mill Creek Gap broke contact with the enemy and marched to Resaca during the night of May 12. General W. W. Loring, commanding Polk's leading division, succeeded in holding McPherson back long enough for Hood and Hardee to get their corps into position.[11]

Johnston arranged his army in a rude semicircle extending from the

9 *Official Records*, XXXVIII, Pt. 4, p. 688.
10 *Ibid.*, 687.
11 *Ibid.*, Pt. 3, p. 722, Pt. 4, pp. 148, 692, 701–702; Artillery Journal, May 12, 1864, in Cheatham Collection; Mackall to W. H. T. Walker, in Records of Cleburne's Division.

Conasauga on the right to the Oostanaula River on the left. Polk filed into position on the left; Hardee held the center and Hood the right. Hood faced north, with Polk and Hardee facing west. Hardee distributed Bate, Cleburne, and Cheatham on his front from right to left. Walker's division acted independently south of the Oostanaula, watching the river crossings for a sudden turning movement by Sherman. Hardee drew Thomas for his opponent, whereas Hood faced Schofield and Polk faced McPherson.

The battle of Resaca opened the morning of May 13. Most of the first day passed in relative quiet, as both armies were preparing defenses and maneuvering for the best terrain. Despite the proximity of the two armies and some brisk skirmishing, Hood and Hardee both thought a general engagement unlikely the next day.[12]

Hood and Hardee were correct. No general engagement occurred at Resaca, but the following two days saw attacks and heavy skirmishing that caused the conflict to be dignified with the label, battle. Skirmishing began early in the morning of May 14 and continued throughout the day. In the afternoon Sherman made an attack on Hood's position and at 4:30 P.M. upon Hardee's.

To conduct the defense of his line Hardee placed his command post on an elevated piece of ground behind an inviting salient in his line. As usual, Hardee's command post proved to be in the thick of the fighting. A Tennessean recorded the scene: "The air is full of deadly missiles. . . . Lie down! thug, thug! General Hardee passes along the line. 'Steady, boys!' (The old General had on a white cravat; he had been married to a young wife not more than three weeks. 'Go back, General, go back, go back, go back!' is cried all along the line. He passes through that storm of bullets indifferent to their proximity (we were lying down, you know)." [13]

It would seem that such exposure was needless and foolish for an officer of such responsibilities, but it instilled confidence and substituted for a thousand Confederate bayonets. For Hardee it was simply in accordance with a tested rule of war, that "a command officer should be present at the point most severely attacked." His observance of this maxim "gave rise to a proverb in the army by which his own &

---

12 *Official Records*, XXXVIII, Pt. 3, pp. 615, 722, Pt. 4, pp. 698–99; Johnston, *Narrative of Military Operations*, 309; Mackall to wife, May 13, 1864, in Mackall Papers.

13 Samuel R. Watkins, *"Co. Aytch." Maury Grays, First Tennessee Regiment; or, a Side Show of the Big Show* (Nashville, 1882), 132.

other staff officers were guided when seeking him during an action. 'You had only to listen to see where the fire is hottest & go to it. You will be sure to find Hardee there.' " [14]

As the fighting progressed, bullets and shells whistled and exploded around the command post. Cleburne rode up to check on the state of affairs; then, smiling, he crouched low over his horse and galloped off, shouting, "General, I think my place is with my division." General J. J. Finley, commanding a Florida brigade under Hardee, rushed up and pleaded with Hardee to retire to a less exposed position. Hardee, however, remained until the enemy threat had been repulsed. Every horse and many men that were at corps headquarters were killed. Hardee lost both of Lewis' magnificent bay harness horses, and just as he prepared to mount a third horse, it was killed. Willie, who was serving with his father as a volunteer aide, also lost his mount.[15]

In spite of his efforts Hardee had not been able to keep Willie away from the army. Willie had been in school in Athens, Georgia, during the spring of 1864 until Terry's Texas Rangers passed through town. Willie was unable to resist, and enlisted. The colonel of the regiment, a friend of Hardee's, sent the sixteen-year-old back to school as soon as he learned of the enlistment, but the schoolmaster refused to receive Willie and packed him off to his father at Dalton. Thus Willie had been thrown into "the brier patch," and Hardee had acquired another problem. He wanted Willie back in school, yet was bursting with pride over his son's determination to enter the army; so he "compromised by telling him he should go thro' the coming campaign provided he would return to school at its close." [16]

During the night of May 14, Johnston decided to strengthen Hood's corps and attack the enemy right. Just as Hood launched his attack on May 15, however, a message came in from W. H. T. Walker stating that the enemy had forced a crossing of the Oostanaula. Johnston halted the attack and moved the Army of Tennessee at once across the Oostanaula.

Although the action of Hardee's corps was confined generally to

14 Roy, "Odds and Ends."
15 DuBose, "Chronicles of the Canebrake," *loc. cit.*, 539; Roy, "Hardee"; Roy, "Odds and Ends."
16 Hardee to Cooper, November 5, 1864, in District of South Carolina, Letters Sent, 1864, Record Group 109; J. K. P. Blackburn, "Reminiscences of the Terry Rangers," *Southwestern Historical Quarterly*, XXII (July, October, 1918), 170; Pickett, *Hardee*, 43.

repelling attacks and skirmishing, his men had behaved well at Resaca. It particularly pleased Hardee to witness Bate's initiation as a division commander, for Bate displayed command qualities under heavy pressure. Hardee's own performance had also been creditable. Although his comprehension of the enemy's intentions was deficient, particularly in the initial phase of operations, his quickness at Dug Gap had saved the army from serious difficulty, and his defensive action at Resaca had been confident and capable. The army's chief of staff, W. W. Mackall, who had never been enthusiastic about Hardee, admitted to his wife after Resaca, "Hardee has behaved handsomely and raised himself very much in my opinion." [17]

The armies broke contact at Resaca, and Sherman kept the initiative. Johnston attempted to check him at Adairsville and then at Cassville. Each time, however, something went awry, and the Confederates retired. The two armies did not fully make contact again until May 26, when they met at a road junction called New Hope Church, just east of Dallas.[18]

Sherman deployed Thomas in front of New Hope Church and McPherson on Thomas' right opposite Dallas, while Schofield extended the Union line to the left in hope of turning the Confederate flank. Johnston placed Hood opposite Thomas and Polk opposite McPherson. He split Hardee's corps, putting Cleburne on Hood's right and Walker in reserve. Hardee's two remaining divisions moved to Polk's left, Cheatham connecting with Polk, and Bate advancing on the Dallas and Atlanta road to within one and a half miles of Dallas. Hardee accompanied Bate and soon found himself under great pressure from McPherson. In the evening Bate was driven from his position on Ellisberry Ridge. This was a choice defensive position, and Hardee determined to retake it. That night Hardee called up Cheatham's division, ordering it to assault the ridge at dawn. Johnston allowed Hardee to strengthen himself even more by taking Walker's division and placing it on Bate's left.[19]

Hardee retook the ridge the next morning. Cheatham delivered repeated costly attacks while Walker by means of an envelopment

17 Mackall to wife, May 16, 1864, in Mackall Papers.
18 For a detailed account of Hardee's operations between May 15 and May 26, see Hughes, "Hardee, C.S.A."
19 *Official Records*, XXXVIII, Pt. 3, pp. 705–706; Artillery Journal, May 27, 1864, in Cheatham Collection.

forced McPherson to shift troops to his right. Heavy skirmishing continued along Hardee's line throughout the day. The gap between Hardee and Polk invited attack, for Cheatham had stretched his line beyond the sustaining point in an attempt to maintain the connection. To relieve Cheatham's situation Hardee recalled Govan's brigade from Cleburne. The line centered about Ellisberry Ridge evoked a high compliment from Hardee's old subordinate Oliver O. Howard. Howard called it "a grand military position . . . which it would do a West Pointer well to survey." [20] Cleburne had in the meantime been engaged in even more serious fighting than the rest of the corps. In the late afternoon his division and the right of Hood's corps repulsed a general assault by O. O. Howard's Fourth Corps. The ease with which Cleburne repulsed the Union attack in the battle known as Pickett's Mills stands as one of the finest performances of this excellent division commander. [21]

The fortunes of Hardee's corps were reversed the following day. During the afternoon Hardee sent Bate forward to develop McPherson's front row more clearly. Hardee believed that the enemy in his front might be weaker than generally supposed. However, Bate found McPherson behind a strong line of works. Eagerness exaggerated any reasonable hope for success. Bate charged but had to fall back with heavy casualties. Nonetheless, Bate's attack aided the Confederate cause because it came as the entire Federal army planned to slide to the left to outflank the Confederate right. Bate's attack, which some Union officers thought was made by three divisions, caused McPherson to pause and then to postpone the movement scheduled for that night. This change coincided nicely with an attack that Johnston proposed for Hood on May 29. Johnston explained his plans to the assembled corps commanders in the afternoon. Hood would withdraw from the line that night, and the rest of the army would readjust the line to fill the gap. Then Hood would move to the assault point and attack Sherman's left, and the other corps would join the attack in turn from right to left.

The climax of the week-long battle of New Hope Church came on the morning of May 29. Hardee stood beside Johnston awaiting the sound of Hood's guns. Presently a courier from Hood rode up and

20 Howard, *Autobiography*, I, 556; Cheatham Atlanta Campaign Journal, May 26, 1864, in Cheatham Collection; *Official Records*, XXXVIII, Pt. 4, p. 744.
21 Hay, "Atlanta Campaign," 25; Hardee, "Memoranda of Operations."

stated that Hood had discovered the enemy flank thrown back and
fortified. Believing it "inexpedient" to attack, he awaited orders.
Johnston felt that the propitious moment had passed and canceled the
attack. The long-frustrated Confederates were unable to conceal their
disappointment as they fell back on the defensive. Cleburne's division
was returned to Hardee, and with his reassembled corps Hardee ex-
erted continuous pressure on McPherson, delaying for days the general Union movement to the left.[22] During this period Hardee's line
extended over four miles, with large segments of the line held only by
skirmishers. Knowing the dangers of maintaining such a line and feeling that the close contact of the armies would be prolonged, Hardee
created a reserve from Cleburne's division. Except for the far left of
the army, where Bate's division and some cavalry skirmished continuously and repelled minor attacks along their long, tenuous line,
Hardee's front remained relatively quiet. The termination of the
battle of New Hope Church came on May 31. Unlike the situation at
Resaca, Hardee's corps had suffered the most; out of two thousand
Confederate killed and wounded, it lost over a thousand, most of
whom were in Bate's and Cleburne's divisions.[23]

On June 1 the Union army began sliding to the left toward the
Western and Atlantic Railroad and Allatoona. Bate and Walker thus
found themselves relieved completely of pressure, and the remainder
of Hardee's front was "almost without an enemy." Hood, however,
reported that the enemy was moving in heavy force against the extreme right of the army, which was held only by weak lines of
dismounted cavalry. To correct the inequality on his right, Johnston
ordered Hardee there with three of his divisions, Cheatham remaining
on the left. Cheatham rejoined Hardee on June 4, when he found that
the enemy had abandoned his front. No sooner had Cheatham taken
position than the Confederates began a general withdrawal to a new
line. "We had last night the hardest march I have known troops to encounter . . . through mud, & rain and darkness." Judging from the
tone of his letters, Hardee was somewhat out of sympathy with the
repeated withdrawals. Hood also seemed to favor the termination of
the retreat, although one staff officer commented that the army felt

22 *Official Records*, XXXVIII, Pt. 3, pp. 95, 706, 908, Pt. 4, p. 351; Hardee,
   "Memoranda of Operations"; Johnston, *Narrative of Military Operations*,
   334n.; W. D. Gale Journal, May 28, 1864, in Polk Papers.
23 *Official Records*, XXXVIII, Pt. 3, p. 687.

that Hood "talks about attack and not giving ground, publicly; and quietly urges retreat." [24]

The new Confederate line extended from north of Kennesaw Mountain to Gilgal Church, shielding Marietta and Kennesaw Station. Hardee held the right, Hood the center, and Polk the left. For the next week the front remained relatively quiet, while the Union army re-established contact. Hardee felt confident in this new position. ". . . I have no idea the enemy will come to attack us in our entrenchments. I wish we could fight, & while notwithstanding our losses, our army is still large & very effective." [25]

The focus of attention shifted from the main line to the skirmish line. It was on the skirmish lines that the armies suffered their principal losses. By the middle of June, 1864, Hardee thought that a brigade or even a division on the skirmish line was desirable—a concept unknown earlier in the war. The heavy skirmish line, "only less strong than the main one," could withstand attacks of up to three lines of battle without creating a sensation. In Hardee's corps the first duty of brigade and division leaders was to set out their skirmish lines. Hardee ordered his subordinates to see that these lines retreated only when confronted by formal lines of battle, never when opposed only by enemy skirmish lines.[26]

Together with the emphasis on skirmishers came the policy of entrenching, another foreign concept in the early part of the war. In the summer of 1864 troops of both armies threw up rude but effective earthworks whenever they halted. War became more grinding, choice of terrain more important, and open fields now benefited the defenders more than the attackers. The ponderous, precise battalion evolutions of Scott's and Hardee's manuals perished from the impact of trench warfare, of repeating rifles, of accurate, long-range artillery, and of strong skirmish lines. The concepts of the skirmisher and of light infantry so strongly emphasized by Hardee's manual, however, provided the means of adaptation.

During these days the "everlasting 'pop,' 'pop' " of the skirmishers

---

24 Hardee to wife, June 2, 5, 1864, in Hardee Letters (Alabama); Taylor Beatty Diary, Vol. III, June 4, 1864; *Official Records*, XXXVIII, Pt. 3, pp. 990–91, Pt. 4, pp. 408, 437; George Anderson Mercer Diary, June 5, 1864 (Southern Historical Collection).
25 Hardee to wife, June 7, 1864, in Hardee Letters (Alabama).
26 Hardee, "Memoranda of Operation"; *Official Records*, XXXVIII, Pt. 4, p. 751.

became the soldiers' "background-music." For Hardee himself the Atlanta campaign was "literally a life in the saddle." The constant fighting, entrenching, and marching severely punished the men physically. Even "veterans of *three years* Campaigning are daily giving away under it." To the exasperation of the motherly Roy, Hardee stayed on or near his front line exposing "himself greatly too much." Having to leave his bride in May had been difficult for Hardee, and he had never expected to be separated from her as long as he had been. Mary Hardee stayed in La Grange, Georgia, with Sallie and Anna. They were comfortably situated, although the cost of living deprived them of long-known luxuries. Mrs. Hardee busied herself caring for her family and making visits to the hospitals, a practice Hardee forced her to abandon because of her delicate health. Sallie also spent a great deal of her time nursing the wounded Confederates. Chaplain J. W. Beckwith commented that Sallie "is a charming person & is enthusiastic in her devotion to the Hospital. I have never seen a young girl devote herself so exclusively to this work." [27] Hardee tried and seems to have failed in his attempts to keep Sallie from the hospitals. Sallie would leave her post only to go to Florida to stay with Dena, allowing Bess to come to La Grange.[28]

Son Willie led a pleasant life with his father. Together with his friends, the Harrison cousins of Mississippi, and other yearling staff officers, he carried some prestige as an aide-de-camp, although he rendered only slight military contributions. Willie had come to care a great deal about Mary Hardee, and Hardee found him a "very affectionate son," but he wanted him back in school.[29]

Hardee lived in private homes during part of the first half of the Atlanta campaign, but generally he lived in tents. His clothes were carried in one carpetbag. Most of the diversion from his mighty military responsibilities came through his daily correspondence with his wife. His long, detailed letters are written with charm, as always, with marked affection, and with ever-increasing seriousness.

27 Roy to Beckwith, June 3, 1864, and Beckwith to wife, July 6, 1864, in Beckwith Papers; Hardee to wife, June 1, 13, 1864, in Hardee Letters (Alabama).
28 Anna Dummett chose to remain in northern Florida, near her aged and infirm mother, who refused to leave St. Augustine. The ties between the Hardees and Elizabeth Dummett, Hardee's sister, remained close ones. Hardee wrote her periodically and always spoke of her in the highest terms, and his daughters arranged their lives so that one of them could always be with her.
29 Hardee to wife, June 10, 1864, in Hardee Letters (Alabama).

The general, like his army, had turned to religion in 1864. The twin influences of General Polk and the new Mrs. Hardee had a great deal to do with his being confirmed in the Episcopal church. Both of his wives and all of his children had been members of the church, and he had attended services but had never been confirmed. After his confirmation Hardee strove to align his life with his ideals. "I am trying hard to lead a godly life. In time I hope to conquer the old Adam." [30] He frequently attended services held for the men at the front and occasionally had private services in his quarters, which his staff attended.

His staff, Roy, W. D. Pickett, S. H. Black, D. H. Poole, and the others remained as before, "active, entertaining & energetic." As the war progressed Roy had become indispensable. He handled the rest of the staff with tact, and together with the general created one of the tighest knit and most efficient staffs in the Confederate army. An air of exclusiveness pervaded this group of men, perhaps encouraged by Hardee's rigid maintenance of a small mess. As chief of staff Roy relieved Hardee of labor whenever possible, writing most of the official and many of the private letters for him. When Hardee found himself unable to write his customary letter to his wife, Roy found the time to do it for him. Hardee trusted Roy completely and treated him like a son. As far as can be determined, this diligent chief of staff never took a leave of absence and remained with his chief throughout the war. Roy "has been continuously on duty with me since . . . [Shiloh]. He has on all occasions & in every situation, whether in camp, in garrison, or in the battlefield performed his duties gallantly, zealously, intelligently, and to my entire satisfaction." [31]

The new defensive line to the north of Kennesaw Station Hardee felt to be "strong enough to resist any attack of the yankees," but he could not conceal his apprehension over Bate's isolated position on Pine Mountain, a mile in front of the main line of resistance. Although Bate's position was strong, it lacked flank support, and Thomas soon began to menace it by jamming the corps of Howard and Palmer into the interval between Pine Mountain and the Kennesaw defense line. Hardee consequently requested that Johnston investigate Bate's situation to determine if it should be held or abandoned. The two generals, accompanied by Polk, who wished to observe his own line from this vantage point, rode forward to Pine Mountain. Hardee, after examin-

---

30 Hardee to wife, June 5, 1864, *ibid.*
31 Hardee to Cooper, December 28, 1864, in Roy Military Service Record.

ing the ground to his satisfaction, came down from the exposed observation point and began talking to Colonel W. D. Gale, Polk's staff
officer and son-in-law. At this juncture the enemy, within easy range,
spotted the group on the hill and opened fire. Polk and Johnston
separated, and Johnston began moving toward Hardee and Gale; Polk
lingered, taking another look—his last look.[32]

Polk's death did not deprive the army of an excellent commander,
but of a competent senior officer of long experience and the man who,
more than any other, had given the Army of Tennessee its moral tone.
Hardee lost a friend whom he had come to admire more each year, and
a spiritual leader. The night after Polk's death Hardee had a poignant
experience. He received a religious pamphlet that Polk had intended
to give him, soaked with the blood of his esteemed friend.[33]

The Confederates abandoned Pine Mountain on June 15, the day
after Polk's death. The following day Hardee changed his line, bend-
ing it back perpendicular to the main line and placing it with Mud
Creek to the front. This high ground had a weak point where it was
linked with Polk's (now Loring's) corps. This salient was never successfully eliminated by the engineers, nor strongly defended. Consequently, the ever-watchful Howard, across Mud Creek, exploited
the opportunity, assaulted, and overran the defect in Hardee's
line.[34]

The night of June 18 Johnston's entire army withdrew to perhaps
its most formidable position. Massive Kennesaw Mountain anchored
the new line, which flanked off behind Noyes and Noonday creeks.
Loring held the center, Hood the right, and Hardee the left. Loring
possessed the chief terrain advantage, occupying Kennesaw Mountain

---

32 Hardee to wife, June 10, 1864, and S. Elliott to wife, June 14, 1864, in Hardee
    Letters (Alabama); W. D. Gale Journal, June 14, 1864, in Polk Papers
    (Southern Historical Collection); Mackall to wife, June 15, 1864, in Mackall
    Papers; J. E. Johnston to Rt. Rev. C. J. Quintard, October 9, 1885, in Joseph
    E. Johnston Letters (University of the South Archives, Sewanee, Tenn.)
33 Hardee to D. West, June 15, 1864, in Gale-Polk Papers.
       In a letter to his wife three days later Hardee speculated over his chances
    of being killed. His flippant tone was obviously forced. "I thought the death
    of our dear old friend Genl. Polk would cause you to feel uneasy about my
    safety. According to the doctrine of chances, I am in less danger now than
    before, there being but three Lieut. Genl's & one being killed the chances
    for the safety of the other are greatly increased." Hardee to wife, June 17,
    1864, in Hardee Letters (Alabama).
34 Howard, *Autobiography*, I, 565–66; Johnston, *Narrative of Military Op-
    erations*, 338.

itself. Hood defended the ground east of Loring to the bast of Brush Mountain. Hardee had a long line that extended from Kennesaw Mountain south across the Lost Mountain and Marietta road. The enemy followed Hardee closely when he retired, causing him some anxiety that he would not be able to establish his new line in time. He did succeed in forming his line but his "pickets [had] been driven in in some places inconveniently near to our main line."[35]

Sherman kept the pressure on Hardee's stretched line for the next two days. More important, Sherman threatened to sever the Powder Springs Road, one of the Army of Tennessee's main escape routes to the Chattahoochee River. Hardee left Johnston's headquarters before the latter had received this intelligence. "I don't know what he will do under the circumstances. I found Hood with him when I arrived & I left him there. . . . Hood, I think, is helping the General to do the strategy, and from what I can see is doing most of it. I only hope it may be well done. If we can only whip the fight I shall be satisfied." [36] Johnston decided to answer Sherman's turning movement by shifting Hood's corps to the left. When he arrived on this new front, Hood immediately attacked Sherman's right flank, incurring heavy losses but halting the enemy's movement toward the Chattahoochee.[37]

Thus far in the campaign Johnston had followed a singularly consistent plan. First he established a defensive line and tried to collect as high a payment as possible from Sherman when the latter moved up to invest the position. Then he would select another favorable position farther south, steal off to it silently in the night and begin the process all over. At Kennesaw Mountain Sherman besieged the position and paid his customary installments in flesh; but Johnston did not retire this time. After his flanking movement to the right had been thwarted by Hood, Sherman decided to force the Confederate center. Fortified with memories of Missionary Ridge and the knowledge of having the psychological element of surprise, Sherman methodically prepared for an attack against the right of Hardee's works. Thomas would be his instrument.

The Federals began to secure their assault position on June 22 by

35 Hardee to wife, June 19, 1864, in Hardee Letters (Alabama).
36 Hardee to wife, June 20, 1864, *ibid.*
37 Horn, *Army of Tennessee*, 334. Horn believes that Hood made the attack on his own responsibility. It seems more plausible that Johnston at least left the possibility of attack to Hood's discretion, for the movement certainly fitted nicely with the Confederate defense scheme.

driving Cheatham from a ridge in front of his main line. As this ridge provided Hardee with defensive depth and promised security against surprise, he had Cheatham try to retake it. Cheatham's attempt failed, and he was compelled to take up a main line farther back. The en-anxiety that he would not be able to establish his new line in time. gineers chose another line on Kennesaw Mountain, and Cheatham occupied it at night. The next morning he discovered defects that left parts of his assigned slope concealed from direct rifle fire. Then Sherman bludgeoned the Confederate defense with a prolonged bombardment (which probably cost him his advantage of surprise). Next, to deceive Johnston, he had McPherson attack the southwestern end of Kennesaw while Schofield threatened the Confederate left. Johnston, however, had a magnificent vantage point atop Kennesaw and could hardly be deceived. Sherman assaulted on June 27.

For forty minutes prior to Thomas' attack the Union artillery delivered preparatory fire. Then the Fourth, Fourteenth, and Twentieth corps under Howard, Palmer, and Hooker charged up the steep slopes in massed columns. The attack focused on Cheatham's and Cleburne's positions, particularly on a salient in Cheatham's line. Cheatham had carefully prohibited his batteries from answering the Union artillery during the prolonged bombardment, and they now waited, masked till the last moment, for the attacking infantry. Cheatham and Cleburne withheld their rifle fire until the enemy was sixty yards away. Then with a roar the Confederates opened fire and literally swept away the leading Federal forces. Thomas threw column after column into the attack only to see his division formations wither and crumble. Through determination and disregard of life the Union troops got up to the Confederate works but no farther. Many of the Northern soldiers saved themselves by lying down on the slope or hiding behind the bodies of comrades; "it was almost sure death to take your face out of the dust." While Cheatham and Cleburne fired directly on the enemy, Samuel G. French had his artillery fire across their front, cutting down rows of the assaulting forces. The battle of Kennesaw Mountain ended in the afternoon with both Federals and Confederates exhausted from the fighting and the excessive heat. Hardee lost 206 men; the enemy in his front lost about 3,000.[38]

The following days accentuated the nerve-racking warfare of the

38 *Official Records*, XXXVIII, Pt. 4, pp. 545, 693; Cheatham's Atlanta Campaign Journal, June 22, 27, 1864, and Artillery Journal, June 27, 1864, in Cheatham Papers.

previous week. The "dead angle" under Cheatham's salient offered the enemy protection from grazing fire. There they entrenched, just yards from Hardee's main line. Each day the Union soldiers worked closer to the Confederate works. Men grew tense. One lapse in attentiveness and an enemy force might be over the works and into the trenches. One nervous private could occasion the eruption of fire across a division front. ". . . It was only necessary to expose a hand to procure a furlough." [39]

By shifting McPherson's army to the Confederate left on July 2, Sherman broke the deadlock. The point of McPherson's advance was aimed directly down the Old Sandtown Road toward Atlanta. It also threatened the important crossings of the Chattahoochee as well as the railroad. Johnston had the unenviable choice of abandoning his communications and trying to either slip past or overwhelm the entrenched Thomas, or of abandoning the Kennesaw line. He chose the latter alternative, making a delicate and successful night withdrawal to a previously surveyed position seven miles south of Kennesaw Mountain at Smyrna Station. [40] Sherman closed in and again tried to turn the Confederate line that was heading for the roads that led to the river crossings. As a consequence Johnston on July 4 retreated to a strong bridgehead on the north bank of the Chattahoochee.

After exploratory probing Sherman satisfied himself as to the strength of Johnston's position and determined not to commit his army against it. Instead, he set about forcing the Confederates to evacuate it. McPherson, with Thomas in support, began demonstrations, and the cautious Confederates kept all three corps bottled up in the bridgehead in anticipation of a major attack. Meanwhile, Schofield eased off to the north and crossed the river at a point near Soap Creek, which was virtually unprotected. Thus flanked, Johnston withdrew from the bridgehead to the south bank of the Chattahoochee and on into Atlanta. [41]

General Hardee crossed the Chattahoochee with about fourteen thousand men, nearly five thousand less than he had had in early May. Johnston's army now numbered about fifty thousand, excluding the

39 *Official Records*, XXXVIII, Pt. 3, p. 716; Cheatham's Atlanta Campaign Journal, June 28, 1864, in Cheatham Papers.
40 *Official Records*, XXXVIII, Pt. 5, pp. 3, 860; Artillery Journal, July 4, 1864, in Cheatham Papers.
41 *Official Records*, XXXVIII, Pt. 5, p. 92; W. J. Hardee Confidential Memorandum, July 9, 1864, in Records of Cleburne's Division; Artillery Journal, July 6, 1864, in Cheatham Papers.

Georgia militia, which had just joined under Major General Gustavus W. Smith. His army had numbered about forty-five thousand men in May and had since received significant increases in cavalry and by the addition of Polk's corps.[42]

The tone of the army had been improved since May 5. Although often discouraged by the successive withdrawals, the army retained almost absolute faith in its commander and looked forward to the climactic battle for Atlanta. Hardee had gained a new peer in Alexander P. Stewart, who had risen by distinguished service to the command of Polk's corps. As yet unproven in battle as a corps commander, he had won the confidence of his troops and promised in the future to equal if not to excel Polk's performance. Stewart had once been a subordinate of Hardee's and had won his commendations. In the future they could be expected to work well together.

Thus far in the campaign Hardee's division commanders had proven worthy of the hopes vested in them. Cleburne had lived up to his past performances and was generally regarded as the outstanding division commander in the army. Cheatham had at last found himself, and his accomplishments had surpassed his performance under Polk's command. The War Department and the commander of the Army of Tennessee regarded this extremely popular Tennessean as potential material for a corps commander. The little-known and always underestimated Bate had progressively improved as a division commander. His division, however, still needed the sensitive operational response that Cleburne's possessed. Hardee had supervised this division closely throughout the campaign, but it had been so perfected that now he would have more time to spend with the other divisions. Walker, despite his explosive temperament, could inspire his Georgians to their best efforts and had the confidence and ability to operate independently with his division. Like Cleburne, he needed but little supervision, although unlike Cleburne, he seldom voluntarily asked for his corps commander's advice. Yet these able officers lacked political connections and had little besides military credentials to boost them to higher command. By either engaging in controversial issues or lacking finesse in dealing with those in authority, both Cleburne and Walker had damaged their chances for higher rank.

Sherman's army spent the period from July 9 to July 19 crossing

42 *Official Records*, XXXVIII, Pt. 3, pp. 676, 679.

the Chattahoochee and moving down upon Atlanta, and the Confederates, encamped behind Peachtree Creek and in Atlanta, prepared once again for the arrival of the enemy. Elaborate works in depth north of the city had been started as early as the summer of 1863 by General Jeremy F. Gilmer, and fields of fire had been cleared in front of them up to the maximum effective range of the Confederate cannon.[43]

The chief event of this fortnight, however, was not connected with the development of this defense system. It was the removal of Joseph Johnston from command of the Army of Tennessee by Jefferson Davis. The steps leading to Johnston's dismissal and the expediency or justice of that act do not properly fit into the discussion of Hardee's Civil War career except as the controversy touched him. He was a close friend of both Johnston and Davis, and he regarded them, and was regarded by them, highly. He seems to have deplored their mutual antagonism and did not involve himself personally. Perhaps it is sufficient to state that Johnston had not satisfied the expectations of Davis, who was under great public and political pressure to have something done in Georgia. Davis could not see hope for a reversal of fortune with Johnston in command. Removing him was a drastic measure to take with the climax of the Atlantic campaign at hand. Davis knew this; but he believed the situation called for drastic measures.

The choice of the new commander of the Army of Tennessee perplexed Davis. The field of choice was limited. Davis felt that Bragg and Beauregard had eliminated themselves by past performance and by the prejudice against them in influential and powerful quarters. Longstreet, Kirby Smith, and others were not familiar with the situation in Georgia or with the army. With the press of circumstances a general from the army should be chosen to replace Johnston. There were only two logical choices: Hardee and Hood. Hood promised aggressive and probably competent army leadership if chosen. Hardee promised competent but not necessarily aggressive leadership if chosen. As Secretary of War Seddon stated, Hardee "seemed a natural appointment," but he had damaged his cause with the President and the cabinet by his refusal to assume permanent command of the Army of Tennessee in December, 1863. "Whatever might be his

43 *Ibid.*, XXXI, Pt. 3, p. 575.

estimate of Genl. Hardee's qualifications, the President thought such distrust of himself must render his selection hazardous and unwise." [44] Before he relieved Johnston, Davis sought advice from Lee concerning the future commander of the army, particularly inquiring about Lee's opinion of Hood. Lee replied, distressed that such a course was deemed necessary. As for Hood, he "is a good commander, very industrious on the battlefield, careless off, and I have had no opportunity of judging his action when the whole responsibility rested upon him. I have a high opinion of his gallantry, earnestness and zeal. General Hardee has more experience in managing an army." For purposes of evaluating Hardee, much hinges on the interpretation of Lee's closing remark. Douglas Southall Freeman believes that a tone of caution pervades the letter, which Lee concluded by giving a "quiet recommendation" of Hardee if Davis insisted on this drastic course. [45]

The key recommendation turned out to be not that of Lee but that of Braxton Bragg, who in all fairness should have been the better judge of the matter. Bragg's letters and telegrams to Davis leave no doubt as to whom he preferred—Hood. Bragg had been in Atlanta since July 13 reviewing the military situation. All of his reports were damaging to Johnston and played a prominent role in Johnston's removal. Bragg found "but little encouraging" in the affairs of the Army of Tennessee. He thought that Johnston would continue to decline to initiate a general engagement with Sherman. He intimated that an immediate change of commanders was necessary but believed that Hardee, the second in command, "generally favored the retiring policy" of Johnston. Hardee, furthermore, did not possess "the confidence of the army to the extent of the chief." "If any change is made Lieutenant-General Hood would give unlimited satisfaction. . . ." In a later letter Bragg referred to the possibility of Hardee's appointment: ". . . it would perpetuate the past and present policy which he has advised and now sustains. Any change will be attended with some objections. This one could produce no good." Hood himself helped push Hardee aside by remarking that he, Hood, had "so often urged that we should force the enemy to give us battle as to almost be re-

44 J. A. Seddon to L. T. Wigfall, February 10, 1879, quoted in Rowland (ed.), *Jefferson Davis*, VIII, 351; *Official Records*, XXXVIII, Pt. 5, p. 988.
45 *Official Records*, LII, Pt. 2, p. 692; H. Wigfall to mother, July 31, 1864, in Wigfall Family Papers; Douglas Southall Freeman, *R. E. Lee*, 4 vols. (New York, 1934–35), III, 462.

garded as reckless by the officers high in rank in this army, since their views have been so directly opposite." [46] Hood's statement appears to be purposely misleading. Although Hardee probably never urged offensive movements by the Army of Tennessee, he never opposed giving battle to Sherman's army. He probably differed with Hood on the feasibility of attacking Sherman's superior numbers without advantages of circumstance. He certainly supported the attack plans at Resaca, Cassville, and New Hope Church. Bragg's opinions of Hardee seem, as so often, to be based on questionable information. How Bragg could speak authoritatively about Johnston's policy and Hardee's full support of that policy, without even consulting the commander or making a fair attempt to survey the opinion and condition of the army, is mystifying. Hardee's private letters lead one to doubt Bragg's assumption that Hardee was in full accord with Johnston's handling of the campaign, and they may even refute it.

Given the basic demand of the President and the Confederacy for aggressive leadership, Hood and Hardee were better choices than Johnston; and Hood was a better choice than Hardee. In its desperation the Confederacy wanted a miracle; Hardee probably would have fought for Atlanta whether Johnston would have or not, but Hardee did not think in terms of military miracles and almost surely could not have produced one. Hood believed that military miracles were brought about by assuming and sustaining the offense. Whether Hardee's views were practical and Hood's impractical is not the essential question. Only Hood saw real hope for turning the tide of the war. The Confederacy wanted a gambler and a visionary. They could not win without one. In light of the performance expected, Hood appears to have been the better choice.

After receiving Johnston's telegram of July 16 stating that circumstances dictated that he must continue his defensive policy, Davis relieved him from command on July 17.

The next morning the three corps commanders of the Army of Tennessee came to Johnston's headquarters to plead with him not to give up the command of the army until the battle for Atlanta had been fought. Johnston refused them, saying, "Gentlemen, I am a soldier. A soldier's first duty is to obey—I turn over the command of the army tonight." The three juniors then went further. They dis-

---

46 *Official Records*, XXXVIII, Pt. 5, pp. 878, 880, XXXIX, Pt. 2, pp. 712–14, LII, Pt. 2, p. 707.

patched a joint telegram to Davis requesting that he postpone the change of commanders "until the fate of Atlanta shall be decided." Davis replied immediately, "The order has been executed, and I cannot suspend it without making the case worse than it was before the order was issued." Hood took command of the army that evening.[47]

47 J. P. Young to T. R. Hay, March 26, 1921, quoted in Hay, "Atlanta Campaign"; *Official Records*, LII, Pt. 2, pp. 708–709; Davis to J. B. Hood, Hardee, and A. P. Stewart, July 18, 1864, in Hood Papers.
    For an intelligent study of the controversy over the removal of Johnston and the appointment of Hood, see Thomas Robson Hay, "The Davis-Hood-Johnston Controversy of 1864," in *Mississippi Valley Historical Review*, XI (June, 1924), 54–84.

XIII

Scapegoat

THE LATE summer of 1864 was a bitter time for the Confederates. The fighting was heavy; the military results were disheartening; and the debate over responsibility was acrimonious. For Hardee it proved to be the most difficult period of his military career.

On July 18, prospects had seemed fairly promising. Although Sherman had crossed the Chattahoochee, he had a lengthy and exposed line of communications and a difficult river at his back. To their backs the Confederates had the massive Atlanta defenses, alternate lines of communications, and the people of Georgia. They had a leader who was known for aggressiveness and daring. The time had come to strike back in force.

Once across the Chattahoochee, Sherman moved quickly to invest Atlanta. Thomas, with the bulk of the Union force, moved toward Peachtree Creek from the north. Schofield headed for Decatur to establish a strong position on the railroad while McPherson destroyed the railroad around Decatur and then advanced west toward Atlanta. By late afternoon on July 19 Thomas reached Peachtree Creek. That night and throughout the following day his troops crossed the creek. At 1 P.M. on July 20 Howard had established his position and felt secure enough to send out a division toward Atlanta. This division, Newton's, went forward and seized a ridge that ran parallel to the creek and the Union front. No sooner had Newton seized this ridge and begun to fortify than the Confederates launched a heavy attack.[1]

While Sherman had been closing in on Atlanta, Hood prepared his army to give battle. Hood moved his troops out toward Peachtree Creek about four miles from Atlanta. He established the line of battle roughly parallel to and west of the creek. Hardee held the center, with

1 *Official Records*, XXXVIII, Pt. 1, pp. 297, 306, 156, Pt. 5, pp. 179–95, 202–203.

Stewart on his left and Cheatham (now commanding Hood's corps) on his right.[2] Hood placed the division of Georgia militia under Gustavus W. Smith farther to the right, between Atlanta and Decatur. On the morning of July 20 Hood called together Smith, Cheatham, Stewart, and Hardee and explained the plan of battle. Hardee would open the attack at 1 P.M., searching out the left and rear of the enemy that had crossed the creek. When he reached the desired position, Hardee would turn his command left and attack down the Union line. As Hardee pressed the enemy back, Stewart's corps would advance against the enemy in echelon of brigades from right to left. Hood hoped that this attack would either throw the enemy back across the creek or drive him down its south edge. The crossing of Peachtree Creek was made contingent upon the success of the initial attack. While Stewart and Hardee conducted the attack, Cheatham would maintain his position on the right, facing Schofield and McPherson.

Developments during the morning made it necessary for Hood to change his disposition, shifting Cheatham farther to the right to protect the approach to Atlanta from Decatur. To compensate for this, Hardee and Stewart would each have to extend half of a division front to the right. Hood maintained that he carefully instructed Hardee to leave a staff officer at the point at which his left would be located. This would ensure that Stewart closed up properly with Hardee's left.[3]

As soon as he received his orders, Hardee sent staff officers to examine the ground to his front. His officers returned about noon, reporting that the ground benefited the defenders. Much of the terrain around Peachtree Creek was thickly covered with trees; swamps and close underbrush covered most of the rest of the ground. Observation and control would be difficult. Shortly before noon Hardee put his corps in line of battle with Bate on the right, Walker in the center, and Maney on the left; Cleburne he held in reserve.

---

2 Hood had appointed Cheatham with reluctance. "I have no major-general in that corps whom I deem suitable for the position, and it was Hardee's opinion that Cheatham was the best man at my disposal, my corps commanders concurring also." To fill Cheatham's place as division commander Hardee chose George Maney, a brigadier of long experience and a man who held the esteem of the Tennessee troops. *Official Records*, XXXVIII, Pt. 5, p. 892.

3 John B. Hood, *Advance and Retreat* (New Orleans, 1880), 166; *Official Records*, XXXVIII, Pt. 3, pp. 630, 871; Samuel G. French, *Two Wars, an Autobiography* (Nashville, Tenn., 1901), 218-19.

Not until nearly 1 P.M. did Hardee begin shifting his troops to the right to close the gap between his corps and Cheatham's.[4] As he started to shift to the right, Hardee designated his staff officer Samuel H. Black to wait at the point where his left flank would be. Black went to his station and showed one of Stewart's staff where Hardee's left would rest. Then to his surprise, Hardee's left brigade moved farther and farther to the right and finally out of sight. Black then acted on his own initiative and ordered the brigade to stop. The brigade commander refused, because his division commander had sent orders for him to continue moving. Black then rode up to Hardee and asked what had happened. Hardee replied that Hood had ordered him to maintain the connection with Cheatham and that Cheatham had continued to move farther to the right. Later Black wrote, " I know that General Hardee expressed his impatience at the delay, and his annoyance at the repeated movements to the right." [5] Each change of position to the right cost the Confederates time and allowed the Union troops to strengthen their defenses. At 2:30 P.M. Hardee notified Stewart that he was ready to attack, but by the time the lines were straightened and the units advanced, it was 3:15 P.M. Hardee complained to Hood fifteen minutes later, "The movement to the right has caused great delay; and I fear some disorder." [6] Thus the battle of Peachtree Creek opened two and a half hours later than Hood had intended.

Alexander P. Stewart lead his troops forward in his first battle as a corps commander. Some overeager units in his command had attacked as early as 2:30 P.M., because someone took Hardee's notice that he was *ready* to attack as meaning that he had attacked. As 3 P.M. approached, Stewart ordered Loring to halt his movement to the right and to fill the interval between his division and Hardee's corps with skirmishers. Loring then attacked, thinking that Maney's division on his right had already advanced. His men moved forward across generally open ground. They soon struck the enemy works and captured them, but finally the enemy to Loring's front and to his right drove his men back. He had been premature. When he assaulted the Union position, Maney's division, which he should have followed, was labor-

4 *Official Records*, XXXVIII, Pt. 3, p. 871.
5 S. L. Black to Roy, May 31, 1880, quoted in Thomas Benton Roy, "General Hardee and the Military Operations Around Atlanta," in *Southern Historical Society Papers*, VIII (August and September, 1880), 347–48.
6 Hardee to Hood, July 20, 1864, in Charles Colcock Jones Papers, 1763–1893 (Duke University Library).

ing through the dense woods. Thus as Loring retired, Maney was just moving up to the attack. On Stewart's left Samuel G. French did not engage the enemy except with skirmishers.[7]

The battle progressed differently on the right of Hood's attacking line. General Hardee's right division, under Bate, advanced at about 3:15 P.M. and encountered no opposition. Walker advanced as soon as Bate had moved forward far enough to create the proper echelon interval. The right brigade of Walker's division also found no enemy to their front and continued. The left and center of Walker's division found more opposition than they could handle. Maney, coming up on Walker's left, also ran into trouble. The division of John Newton took the brunt of Walker's and Maney's attacks. Newton remarked that his opponents "charged with a rapidity and an absence of confusion I have never seen equalled." From his fortified position on the ridge parallel to Peachtree Creek, Newton, assisted by elements of the Twentieth Corps, repulsed Walker. Walker retired with a badly damaged division. The Confederates, according to Howard, had been "cut down like grass." Walker left his brigade commander Clement H. Stevens dead on the field. Maney also met with a repulse but not with as many casualties as did Walker.

General Bate stumbled on through the underbrush, trying to locate the enemy left flank that he was to attack. Because of the curved formation of Thomas' line Bate never found any enemy flank to his front. Hardee sent Colonel W. D. Pickett to learn what had happened. About 6 P.M. Pickett caught up with Bate, who had now turned his division to the north and was advancing slowly toward the enemy left flank, impeded by the heavy undergrowth. Pickett reported to Hardee, "I fear he will not be able to strike the enemy flank much before dark." With Bate now moving to the assault position, Hardee sent Walker's division to the right to assist him. For the frontal assault Hardee brought up Cleburne. He would be joined by Maney. Before Cleburne ordered his division to attack, he rode forward with Hardee to examine the ground immediately to the front. Presently an enemy shell struck uncomfortably close. Since Hardee believed that a Confederate battery stood between them and the enemy, he continued the reconnaissance, but when a second shell came screaming past, Cleburne and Hardee realized that they were at "point blank" range from

7 *Official Records*, XXXVIII, Pt. 3, pp. 871, 876–77, 880, 902, 925, 938.

an enemy battery. The group rode off the field but not before a third shell had struck and killed a member of Cleburne's escort.

After his close brush with death Hardee ordered Cleburne to begin the attack. As Cleburne briefed members of his staff, a courier rode up from Hood. He announced that McPherson was advancing from Decatur directly on Atlanta and already occupied a position near the Confederate exterior defense line. Hood felt that he must have another division if McPherson was to be halted, and he therefore called on Hardee for one of his. Since Hood had urged "all haste," Hardee decided to send Cleburne, whose division was at hand and had not suffered damage in the fighting. His countermanding order reached Cleburne as he prepared to assault. "Five minutes more would have been too late, and would have found this command heavily engaged." With Cleburne's attacking force removed, Hardee called off the frontal attack. He saw that only minutes of daylight remained and that Bate would not reach the attack position on the flank until dark. He therefore determined to cancel the flank attack as well.[8]

The failure of the Confederate attack at Peachtree Creek proved costly to Hardee personally. In his official report and in his memoirs General Hood attributed the defeat directly to Hardee, who failed to carry out Hood's orders, and his statement gained widespread credence. Colonel Roy in his defense of Hardee's operations under Hood demolished some points in Hood's argument, such as that Hardee failed to station a staff officer at the designated point on his left and that Hardee attempted to undermine confidence in the outcome of the attack by cautioning Cleburne about the breastworks against which he must charge.

Although Roy successfully defended his chief on these points, he is unconvincing in regard to Hood's two major charges. The contention that Hardee deranged the timing of the attack cannot be disputed. He did delay the attack for over two hours. Much depends upon the perspective from which Hardee's decision to continue the shift to the right is viewed. As events turned out, no enemy force attacked the joint between Hardee's and Cheatham's corps. If Hardee had not continued shifting to the right and had left a gap between the

---

8 *Ibid.*, Pt. 1, pp. 290, 297, Pt. 3, pp. 698–99, Pt. 5, p. 897; Mercer Diary, July 20, 1864; Roy, "General Hardee," *loc. cit.*, 349, and D. G. White to Roy, April 6, 1880, quoted therein, p. 382; Buck, *Cleburne*, 269–70; Roy to D. C. Govan, March 8, 1880, in Govan Papers.

two corps, and if an enemy attack had then come through this opening, he would have been open to even greater criticism. Facing this
conflict in orders and without a superior to whom he could immediately appeal (for Hood was not at the front), Hardee chose the more
cautious course. With Cheatham "nearly two miles to my right instead of a division length," Hardee determined to close the gap and
then attack. He felt the undefended interval constituted a hazard that
was more important than opening the attack at the announced time.
The cautious course, however, is often not the proper course for an
army engaged in making an important general attack. Each moment
that the Confederates delayed allowed more of Thomas' men to cross
Peachtree Creek and allowed the enemy works to be strengthened.
In the past Hardee had often exercised his discretion in combat and
then appealed to his commander. This time his action seriously embarrassed his commander's plans. As an experienced soldier Hardee
knew that his primary responsibility was to open the attack at as near
the designated time as possible. Since his action delayed the attack,
resulted in a major and unexpected troop movement, and produced
confusion, Hardee should be held sharply responsible for his independent decision. But to charge him with failing to carry out orders
is unrealistic. He had two conflicting orders, and as he stated, he
could not have carried out both.

Hood also claims that "Hardee failed to push the attack, as ordered,
and thus the enemy, remaining in possession of his works on Stewart's
right, compelled Stewart by an enfilade fire to abandon the position
he had carried." This criticism had large circulation. The Augusta
Constitutionalist, for instance, picked up the argument and published
its version, which claimed that Hardee's action caused the Confederate effort to make a "partial success out of what would have been a
complete victory." Some of Stewart's men claimed that Hardee's
corps did not engage the enemy but only skirmished. Hardee took
four divisions into the battle; only two engaged the enemy. In this
light it does seem that Hardee did not fully commit his forces. The
fact remains that Walker's division suffered heavy casualties and that
Maney's division lost more men in this battle than it had lost thus far
in the entire campaign. Bate's division never met the enemy, having
found no enemy in its front and having made a circuitous march to
reach the enemy rear and flank. And Cleburne's division, Hardee's reserve, had been dispatched to assist Cheatham, in response to Hood's
own request, at the time when Hardee had ordered it to attack. Thus

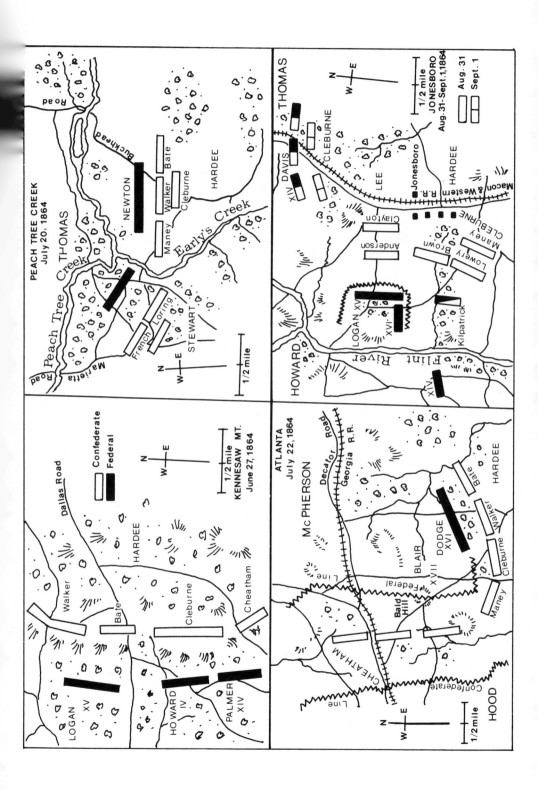

PEACH TREE CREEK
July 20, 1864

THOMAS

Peach Tree Creek

Marietta Road

French
Loring
STEWART

Buckhead Road

NEWTON

Maney
Walker
Cleburne
HARDEE

Bate

Early's Creek

N
W—E
S

1/2 mile

KENNESAW MT.
June 27, 1864

Dallas Road

Walker
HARDEE
Bate
Cleburne
Cheatham

LOGAN
XV

HOWARD
IV

PALMER
XIV

☐ Confederate
■ Federal

N
W—E
S

1/2 mile

JONESBORO
Aug. 31–Sept. 1, 1864

THOMAS

N
W—E
S

DAVIS
XIV
CLEBURNE

HOWARD

LOGAN XV
XVI

Flint River

Anderson
Clayton

Lowery
Brown
Maney
CLEBURNE

LEE

Jonesboro

Macon & Western R.R.

HARDEE

Kilpatrick

XIV

1/2 mile

☐ Aug. 31
☐ Sept. 1

ATLANTA
July 22, 1864

McPHERSON

Decatur Road

Georgia R.R.

Federal Line

BLAIR
XVII

DODGE
XVI

Bald Hill

CHEATHAM

Bate
Walker
HARDEE
Cleburne
Maney

Confederate Line

HOOD

N
W—E
S

1/2 mile

it seems that an accusation that Hardee failed to push the attack is unfair. General Johnston later talked to "officers of high character" about Hardee's activities at Peachtree Creek. The accounts sometimes conflicted, "but none censur[ed] Hardee." [9]

Generally considered, however, Peachtree Creek does stand as one of Hardee's poorest performances. Meticulous regard for details rather than concentration on essentials characterized the action. Hardee's judgment concerning the shifting of troops to the right was poor. He failed to make a personal reconnaissance initially. The attack was delivered piecemeal, and subordinate units were not closely controlled. Contact between Bate's and Walker's divisions appears to have been lost, and the attack of Maney followed that of Walker at too long an interval, permitting the enemy to defeat first one and then the other. Perhaps Cleburne should have been committed earlier. In any event, to have allowed Bate's division to thrash about ineffectually on the enemy flank represents a serious error on Hardee's part, for he should have had this important force of maneuver under tight control.

On the following day, July 21, 1864, Sherman consolidated his position in front of Atlanta, and McPherson closed up on the left, exerting continuous pressure on the part of Hood's line held by Cleburne. The excessive heat and the accurate Union artillery fire made Cleburne's stand an ordeal. He considered it "the bitterest fight of his life." He succeeded in his mission, however, and held back the heavy enemy forces opposing him, inflicting a particularly sharp repulse to Frank Blair's Seventeenth Corps. Meanwhile, Hood had withdrawn the rest of his men from their advanced line on the night of July 20. They occupied a new line closer to Atlanta and on higher ground. Throughout July 21 the Confederates worked hard on their entrenchments. Sherman did the same. He did not think that Hood would repeat his attack, yet he cautioned his subordinates, ". . . it is well to be prudent." [10]

It was well for Sherman to be prudent, for Hood did intend to try again. He planned to attack the Union left rear, and Hardee would again be the attacking force, supported by Wheeler's cavalry. Once Hardee had driven in the enemy left, Cheatham would then open his attack. G. W. Smith and Stewart would follow Cheatham's attack.

9 *Official Records*, XXXVIII, Pt. 3, pp. 630–31, 698–99; J. E. Johnston to L. T. Wigfall, February 28, 1865, in Wigfall Family Papers; C. Gallaway to W. M. Polk, February 15, 1865, in Polk Papers; Grand Summary of Casualties in Cheatham's Division, during the First Campaign of 1864, to include July 22nd, in Cheatham Papers.
10 Hardee, "Cleburne," *loc. cit.*, 158; *Official Records*, XXXVIII, Pt. 5, p. 212.

The order that Hood gave to Hardee is of importance because in his report and in his memoirs Hood again states that Hardee failed to carry out his commands. Hood maintained that he directed Hardee "to *completely* turn" McPherson's left. He was to "march entirely around and to the rear of McPherson's left flank, even if he was forced to go to or beyond Decatur." Hardee would march not on the direct road to Decatur, for that was occupied by McPherson, but out the McDonough road to Cobb's Mill, and thence to the enemy rear. Hardee and his supporters, including Joseph E. Johnston, held that this was the original plan, but that Hood changed his orders and decided to strike McPherson in the flank. Colonel Roy went to great length to build up circumstantial support for this argument. In amassing detail, Colonel Roy suppressed one piece of evidence that seems conclusive. Cheatham had stated, "My distinct recollection is that Genl Hood was very decided that Genl Hardee should move to the rear of Genl McPherson's flank by the way of Decatur; but on account of the lateness of the hour, the distance to be travelled, and the condition of the troops, he finally consented that Genl Hardee should have discretion to make the assault on the flank and rear of McPherson." [11]

This evidence supports Hardee's contention that there was another meeting with Hood on the night of July 21, and it also supports his contention that Hood changed his order. It does not exactly fit with Roy's and Hardee's accounts, because it states that Hardee was not ordered to attack McPherson's left and rear but that he *could* do so. Cheatham's statement also refutes Hood's claim that he ordered Hardee "to *completely* turn" McPherson.

After Hood issued his initial order, Hardee directed Cleburne at 7:30 P.M. to break contact with the enemy and pull back into the inner defenses. Cleburne, however, encountered great difficulty in breaking contact. Thus at 11 P.M. Hardee ordered him to leave his skirmishers out and fall in behind Walker's division at 1 A.M. Not until nearly 3 A.M. did the last of the corps leave Atlanta. [12]

The ensuing approach march proved arduous. Hardee's troops,

11 Hood, *Advance and Retreat*, 177; Johnston to Wigfall, February 28, 1865, in Wigfall Family Papers; Roy, "General Hardee," *loc. cit.*, 354; Cheatham to Roy, n.d., quoted in Roy to Cheatham, October 15, 1881, in Cheatham Papers.
12 Roy to Cleburne, July 21, 1864, in Records of Cleburne's Division; Roy, "General Hardee," *loc. cit.*, 358; Artillery Journal, July 22, 1864, in Cheatham Papers.

worn out by the fighting on July 20 and the incessant, hot entrenching and Cleburne's fighting on July 21, moved slowly. Many had missed sleep during the previous night. The column wound its way over the McDonough road to Cobb's Mill, six miles southeast of Atlanta. Then Hardee turned his men northeast to the "Widow Parker's" place, about three miles from Decatur. The "single, narrow" road over which the men marched delayed the column even more.

To the annoyance of everyone, Wheeler's cavalry kept churning down the road, brushing the infantry off to the sides. When Hardee reached the Widow Parker's, he decided that he was in McPherson's rear and turned his corps northwest toward the enemy. Just before dawn, while they were still miles from their objective, Hardee called his division commanders and Wheeler together. At the time the generals met, the troops had not yet come up. Everyone displayed "regret and annoyance" over the slowness of the march. Hardee briefed his lieutenants on the situation as he knew it, telling them particularly about a long, deep pond that lay across their path. The meeting broke up, and the generals headed back to their commands. Wheeler stated that "when I left General Hardee to prepare for the attack, we knew we were in rear of General McPherson's line, at least in rear of his left. . . ." [13]

Hardee deployed his corps on the road from Cobb's Mill to Decatur as they came up. Not until 12:30 P.M. was the arrangement of the line of battle completed. Hardee formed his corps with Cleburne on the left on the McDonough Road, then Walker, Bate, and Maney to the right. The divisions would be in double lines. Unit commanders carefully warned their men not to stop the attack either for spoils or for prisoners. As the troops prepared to attack, Wheeler sent word to Hardee that a sizable Union cavalry force had been spotted to their right, apparently headed south on a raid. Hardee replied that he could not afford to lose Wheeler's men at this juncture. "We must attack, as we arranged, with all our force." Wheeler's part in the attack would be to drive the enemy cavalry from Decatur and occupy it, covering Hardee's exposed right and interdicting the area of combat.[14]

---

13 Pickett, *Hardee*, 31; Buck, *Cleburne*, 273–74; John Witherspoon DuBose, *General Joseph Wheeler and the Army of Tennessee* (New York, 1912), 371; Roy, "General Hardee," *loc. cit.*, 358; Artillery Journal, July 22, 1864, in Cheatham Papers; Roy, "General Hardee," *loc. cit.*, 365.
14 Pickett, *Hardee*, 31–32; *Official Records*, XXXVIII, Pt. 3, pp. 352–53, 739–41.

While Hardee prepared his line of battle, important things had transpired at the enemy position. Union skirmishers had found that Hardee's men had abandoned their positions. McPherson, on Sherman's order, sent out a division to make a reconnaissance in force. Before McPherson moved forward with the Army of the Tennessee and occupied a new position, Sherman sent two divisions of Grenville M. Dodge's Sixteenth Corps to McPherson to be emplaced on the extreme left and rear of the new position. Dodge moved up with his two divisions behind Blair's Seventeenth Corps, which was on McPherson's left. He quickly saw that McPherson would not move forward to occupy the new position before night, so he ordered his men to entrench as usual and await the advance of McPherson. In actuality Dodge had formed a new Federal line, refusing the left of the army and protecting the rear of McPherson. This was one of the most fortunate moves made by the Union armies in the war.[15]

About noon Dodge heard firing. He became suspicious and ordered his Second Division to change direction so that it would face southeast. Firing had actually begun about midmorning, when Blair's most advanced pickets had met some of Wheeler's cavalry. These pickets believed that the enemy had intended a raid on Blair's hospitals. Blair immediately sent an infantry regiment to deal with the cavalry. The Sixty-Eighth Ohio soon found more to deal with than cavalry.[16]

Hardee's approach march began about noon. At least one of his subordinates had started earlier, sending out skirmishers to capture the enemy trains. The entire corps set out in good order with orders to guide left on Govan's brigade, which was marching on the McDonough Road. Govan watched anxiously as the difficult terrain led the divisions to stray to the right, and finally the other brigades in his own divisions (Cleburne's) became disconnected also. Hardee wrote later, "I marched in line for two miles through a dense forest, where I could not see ten paces. Of course it was impossible to keep up an alignment." The country had never been cultivated. Thick oak forests, wired together with brier patches and swamps, impeded the advance. Brigade commander Mark Lowrey later reported that

15 Marginal notation by Colonel Willard Warner (Sherman staff officer), in John M. Palmer, *Personal Recollections of John M. Palmer* (Cincinnati, 1901), 450; *Official Records*, XXXVIII, Pt. 3, pp. 21–22, 269–370, 872.
16 Society of the Army of the Tennessee, *Report of the Proceedings*, 45 vols. (Cincinnati, 1866–1922), XVI, 484; *Official Records*, XXXVIII, Pt. 3, p. 369.

"the advance line soon seemed to have had much difficulty in keeping the proper direction, soon moved by the right flank, then forward, then by the right flank again, then forward, then by the left flank. The difficulty of following the movements in such dense woods can scarcely be imagined." The combination of the heat, the soldiers' loss of sleep, and the tortuous terrain cut holes like cannister shot in the Confederate ranks.[17]

Bate and Walker soon struck the large pond about which they had been warned. To skirt this obstacle required a great deal of time. A regiment of Walker's division then came on a giant brier patch. One of Walker's staff suggested that it be by-passed even though the line would be deranged. Walker, however, decided to ask Hardee. He rode up and before he could explain.

... General Hardee turned roughly and rudely upon him and said loudly in the presence of staff officers and orderlies: "No, Sir! This movement has been delayed too long already. Go and obey my orders!" . . . [Walker's] fierce flare at his commander was not to be repressed. . . . As we rode, [Walker] said in tones in which rage and self-control contended, "Major, did you hear that?" I replied: "Yes, General Hardee forgot himself." He answered: "I shall make him remember this insult. If I survive this battle, he shall answer me for it." . . . [Hardee quickly dispatched a staff officer to Walker and gave his regrets for] his hasty and discourteous language and would come in person to apologize, but that his presence was required elsewhere, and that he would do so at the first opportunity. I said, "Now that makes it all right." But being still in great wrath, he said: "No, it does not. He must answer for this." [18]

Maney's division struck the same large pond, and Hardee decided that instead of maneuvering Maney around the obstacle, he would shift him to the extreme left. It was nearly 5 P.M. before Maney formed in rear of Cleburne's division.

Although there had been clashes between the Union pickets and the advancing Confederates, no serious conflict occurred before Hardee's masses fell upon Blair's and Dodge's positions. When Hardee struck the Union line, his left division under Cleburne appeared to the front and to the rear of McPherson's left flank. While part of Cleburne's command engaged Blair's men, the larger segment charged

17 *Official Records*, XXXVIII, Pt. 3, p. 737; D. C. Govan to W. W. Belknap, December 15, 1878, and Mark P. Lowrey's Report of the Operations Around Atlanta, in *Veteran*, II (January, 1882), 8; Roy, "General Hardee," *loc. cit.*, 360.
18 Joseph B. Cumming, "Walker Memorial Speech," 8, in Joseph B. Cumming War Recollection, 1861–65 (typed copy in Southern Historical Collection).

through the gap separating Dodge and Blair. Cleburne's attack succeeded in driving Blair's left division back toward the bald hill,
where they received support and took a strong position. Walker then
came up and attacked Dodge's position. Walker made a series of
charges over open ground. Dodge's artillery and rifle fire ripped wide
holes in his ranks. The impetuous Walker was killed as he rode to
the front to urge his men on, and brigade commander Gist was
wounded. The division became disorganized and was becoming scattered. Bate attacked next, but the enemy had time to prepare to
meet him. Dodge gave some ground but managed to hold off Bate
also, assisted by elements from the Thirteenth and the Fifteenth corps.
Maney's division now came up behind Cleburne and joined in the
attack. Together with Cleburne and units from Walker's division
they drove the enemy back to his defenses on Bald Hill and delivered
repeated attacks upon this position, taking a heavy toll. "Even before
we had begun the advance many of our men were shot down, and
as we approached nearer their works their fire became still more
deadly. As I looked down the line I could see men dropping by the
scores." According to a Union brigadier on Bald Hill, the enemy
came "advancing up to our breast-works on the crest of the hill,
planted their flags side by side with ours, and fought hand-to-hand
until it grew so dark that nothing could be seen but the flash of the
guns. . . ." ". . . The sword, the bayonet, and even the fist, were effectually used, and the enemy repulsed with a slaughter I never before witnessed." Maney's and Cleburne's men succeeded in capturing
part of the enemy second line, but could not hold it. They needed
fresh supporting troops, but none were to be had.[19]

When Hood saw Hardee's men engaging the left of Blair's line, he
ordered Cheatham forward. Cheatham made a vigorous attack that
finally punctured the Union line, but it seems to have come after
Cleburne's drive had lost its initiative. Thus Blair's men fought their
defenses in reverse and their opponents one at a time.

Hardee succeeded in completely turning the enemy left. He assailed Dodge on the left, center, front, and rear. He assailed Blair in
a like manner. He opposed, in all, elements of four Union corps. He
captured about 1,500 prisoners, eight guns, and at least fifteen colors.
His men killed army commander McPherson. For this success Hardee
paid a great price. He lost 3,299 killed, wounded, and missing. Of this

19 Hall, "Notes"; *Official Records*, XXXVIII, Pt. 3, p. 547.

number Cleburne lost about 1,500. Hardee lost about 60 field officers, 30 of whom belonged to Cleburne. This exceptionally high loss in officers was capped by the death of the capable Walker.[20]

Hood evaluated Hardee's efforts in the following terms: ". . . the failure in the battle of the 22nd is to be attributed to the effect of the 'timid defensive' policy upon this officer, who, although a brave and gallant soldier, neglected to obey orders, and swing away, totally independent of the main body of the Army." "It had rested in his power to rout McPherson's Army by simply moving a little farther to the right, and attacking in rear and flank instead of assaulting an intrenched flank." The enemy treated Hardee with more charity. Oliver Otis Howard called Hardee's approach a "Jacksonian march." Jacob D. Cox felt that Hardee's action, "viewed as a piece of military maneuvering, will excite more admiration among students of the art the more it is examined." Nearly all of the Union commanders believed that Hardee launched attacks "determined and fierce enough to relieve him from all blame in that matter." [21]

That Hardee attacked with all the vigor of which his corps was capable is evident. That Hardee failed to turn the enemy left is not supported by any evidence. All of the corps with the exception of one brigade attacked to the left of Blair's flank. When the fact is considered that Dodge's presence was totally unexpected and that even this corps was flanked on its left, there is little question about the matter. The charge that Hardee failed to obey orders and fall upon the rear of the enemy has been sufficiently exploded by Colonel Roy's long article. Cheatham's evidence also shows that Hardee acted in good faith and properly followed his directions. A. P. Stewart held that if Hardee had gone farther to the right, as Hood had said he should, it is "probable [that] he would have lost his corps." [22]

Considered tactically, there are several points that merit comment. The approach march from the Atlanta–Decatur road to the enemy line contributed greatly to the failure of the attack. Hardee selected

20 Artillery Journal, July 22, 1864, in Cheatham Papers; *Official Records,* XXXVIII, Pt. 5, pp. 900, 903; Pickett, *Hardee,* 33; Hall, "Notes"; Roy, "General Hardee," *loc. cit.,* 367.
21 Hood, *Advance and Retreat,* 180, 183; Oliver Otis Howard, "The Struggle for Atlanta," in *Battles and Leaders,* IV, 315–16; Jacob Dolson Cox, *Atlanta,* (New York, 1882), 176; Grenville Mellen Dodge, *The Battle of Atlanta and Other Campaigns, Addresses, Etc.* (Council Bluffs, Iowa, 1910), 41.
22 Alexander Peter Stewart, "The Army of Tennessee, a Sketch," in *Military Annals of Tennessee,* 101.

his deployment point much too far from the enemy lines. In view of the very difficult terrain it seems that Hardee should have moved his command much closer in column formation before deploying. To cover the miles separating him and the enemy in such a wide and cumbersome formation invited confusion and resulted in a disjointed attack. If the four divisions had attacked Dodge and Blair suddenly and simultaneously, the result would probably have been much different. The error of allowing skirmishers to precede the main body at a considerable distance to capture enemy wagon trains is inexcusable, assuming that Hardee's men intended to maintain completely the element of surprise.[23] The attack caught Sherman and McPherson off guard, but it would have been more effective if the units immediately facing Hardee had been surprised, as at Shiloh.[24]

Hardee's use of reserves is also open to question. For the attacks he deployed all four of his divisions abreast, in double lines. If he had held back one division, he could have exploited the opportunities developed in the attack and could have rushed assistance to critical points. As it was, Maney became his reserve but spent most of the afternoon fighting his way through the woods laterally from the extreme right to the extreme left.

The night following the battle of Atlanta, Hardee pulled back his most advanced units, some of which still held parts of the main Union line. He remained on Sherman's left flank throughout the next day. His men spent the day gathering up the numerous small arms and pieces of equipment found in the captured enemy first line, while their commander worried about a possible Federal attack against his right flank near Decatur.[25] On July 24, 1864, Hood ordered Hardee back to a new and safer line. The same day Hardee decided to break up W. H. T. Walker's division, because his other three divisions had been decimated by the late series of engagements and needed strengthening. Walker's division had lost its commander, two of its brigade commanders, and a number of its senior officers. Walker's Georgians therefore were distributed: Mercer's brigade

23 The evidence suggests that brigade commander Govan did this on his own initiative and without Hardee's knowledge.
24 Palmer, *Personal Recollections*, 451.
25 *Official Records*, XXXVIII, Pt. 5, p. 905; Wirt Armistead Cate (ed.) *Two Soldiers. The Campaign Diaries of Thomas J. Key, C. S. A. December 7, 1863–May 17, 1865 and Robert J. Campbell, U.S.A. January 1, 1864–July 21, 1864* (Chapel Hill, 1938), 98.

went to Cleburne, Gist's to Cheatham, and Stevens' to Bate.[26] Cheatham had returned to command his division because of the arrival of Stephen Dill Lee, who had done good service in Mississippi as a cavalry leader and had been promoted to lieutenant general. He would permanently command Hood's corps.

Sherman assumed the offensive again on July 28, resorting to his old tactic of creeping around the Confederate flank. He now chose to turn Hood's left. Hood determined to meet this turning movement by sending most of Stewart's and Lee's corps out on Lick Skillet Road. Shortly after midday Lee and Stewart began to attack, and a major engagement soon developed. Later in the afternoon a series of couriers came to Hardee's line from Hood's headquarters. In answer to summons Hardee went to Hood's headquarters, where he received the order "to proceed to the field, and, if necessary, to assume command of the troops engaged." Hardee, accompanied by Roy, rode over to the battle, but the engagement was ending as he arrived, and he did not assume command.[27] The battle of Ezra Church, as it was later called, did great damage to Lee's and Stewart's corps. Although the Confederates attacked desperately, they failed to drive the enemy. Hood, as at Peachtree Creek and Atlanta, could not understand why. Were the men losing their spirit?

For a month no major engagement occurred, but Sherman continued to press the Confederate left. As the pressure mounted and as the Confederate line grew more tenuous, Hood had to call Hardee over from the right. Near East Point Hardee experienced incessant heavy skirmishing. Casualties mounted from these furious little battles. As Sherman kept bringing up more strength and kept sliding to his left, Hardee's position became dangerous. "It is easy for [the enemy] to outflank me and I am apprehensive he may do it at any time. I sent word to Hood several days ago that if he wished me to protect East Point, I must have another Division. My line is very thin, much thinner than that held by anyone else, & it is impossible to extend any further." [28]

26 Special Field Orders No. 56, July 24, 1864, in Army of Tennessee, Special Field Orders and Special Orders, 1864–65, Record Group 109; *Official Records*, XXXVIII, Pt. 5, p. 907.
27 Roy, "General Hardee," *loc. cit.*, 370; Hood to Hardee, July 28, 1864, Hood Field Dispatch Book, in John Bell Hood Papers, 1862–74, Record Group 109; *Official Records*, XXXVIII, Pt. 3, p. 699.
28 Hardee to wife, August 13, 1864, in Hardee Letters (Alabama).

Hardee felt less fear for the safety of his family. Mary Hardee stayed at the Wesleyan Female College in Macon, where she had friends like the Johnstons and did not want for proper food or lodging. After much urging Mary finally secured Hardee's permission to visit Atlanta. She came up during the second week in August and periodically thereafter. When the Confederacy took over the college for a hospital in August, Mary had to move her residence. This time Hardee did not intervene to find her a place. Instead he thought "it best to let you take care of yourself for once." [29]

Although Hardee worried about Sherman's movements toward East Point, Sherman was not free from worry himself. The continuous fighting had depleted his army. Moreover, by October more than half of his army would be entitled to discharge. He therefore resolved to reach a decision quickly. He would raise the siege and swing the bulk of his army wide around Hood's left, breaking the railroad between Jonesboro and Atlanta. Leaving sufficient force behind to guard the crossings of the Chattahoochee, Sherman struck out on August 26, 1864. He disengaged all of his army except for a few brigades on the extreme right.

Lee's and Stewart's troops soon found themselves without an enemy to the front. Everyone wondered where Sherman had gone. What were his intentions? "The prevailing impression, " reported Hood's chief of staff, "is that they are falling back across the Chattahoochee River." As a precautionary measure Hood strengthened Hardee's position at East Point and sent two brigades to Jonesboro. "General Hardee is at East Point, with instructions from these [Hood's] headquarters to use his own discretion in the dispositions of troops in that quarter." [30]

Events developed with great rapidity on August 30. Hardee believed the enemy to be swinging south, so he established his headquarters at Rough and Ready and decided to move troops there. Hood, however, did not believe that the enemy posed an immediate threat and told Hardee so. "Genl Hood does not think the necessity will arise to send any more troops to Jonesboro today. . . . Genl Lee is instructed to move Patton Anderson's Division near the R Road to assist you if need be." To confirm his suspicions Hardee had sent

29 Hardee to wife, August 6–22, 1864, *ibid.*
30 *Official Records*, XXXVIII, Pt. 3, pp. 693–94, Pt. 5, pp. 609, 698; Hood to Hardee, August 28, 1864, in Hood Field Dispatch Book.

Colonel Pickett out on a scouting mission. Pickett found unmistaka-
ble signs of an enemy movement to the south toward Jonesboro and
also toward Rough and Ready. Hardee relayed this information to
Hood, who sent back a dispatch at once, telling Hardee "to take
whatever measures you may think necessary to prevent the enemy
from gaining Jonesboro or Rough and Ready this afternoon, so that
[Hood] may make other dispositions tonight. He does not think they
will attack Jonesboro today." At 3:20 P.M. Hood ordered Hardee
to have his men in readiness to march. At 6 P.M. Hood sent another
dispatch: Cavalry units reported that the enemy might break the
railroad at night between Jonesboro and Rough and Ready. "Please
prevent it if possible." Hood sent another courier ten minutes later,
directing Hardee to move to Jonesboro with his corps that night;
Lee's corps would accompany him.

In the four days since he had pulled out of the Atlanta trenches,
Sherman had maneuvered his army in separate columns south and
then turned east toward the Macon Railroad. On August 30 Schofield
neared Rough and Ready, while Howard with the Army of the Tennessee approached Jonesboro. Thomas, with the Army of the Cumberland, kept between the two wings. Howard's scanty water supply
led him to continue to the Flint River a mile from Jonesboro. John
Logan's Fifteenth Corps and Judson Kilpatrick's cavalry reached
and crossed the Flint at the close of the day, but the Confederate
brigades in Jonesboro kept them from capturing the town or cutting
the railroad. That night Logan entrenched within sight of the town.
Howard moved up the Sixteenth Corps in support of Logan. The
"saucy position" pleased Howard. From here he could reach the
railroad at Jonesboro with artillery and even with rifle fire.[31]

While Howard took up his position commanding Jonesboro and
Atlanta's remaining railroad communications, Hood met with Hardee
and Lee. Hood knew that he faced a desperate situation. If Sherman
gained control of the Macon Railroad, Atlanta could not be held
much longer. He decided to send Hardee and Lee with their corps
to attack the enemy menacing Jonesboro. Believing that only
three corps constituted the enemy force, Hood ordered Hardee to
take command of his two corps and drive the enemy back across the
Flint. Hood stated that he told Hardee emphatically that the retention

---

31 Hood to Hardee, August 30, 1864, in Hood Field Dispatch Book; Pickett,
Hardee, 33–34; *Official Records*, XXXVIII, Pt. 3, pp. 44–45; Howard,
Autobiography, II, 32–36.

of Atlanta depended upon his success: "Tell your officers and men
it is imperative to drive the enemy into and across the Flint." The
meeting broke up late in the night, and Hardee boarded a train
for Jonesboro, arriving before dawn of August 31. To his surprise
he did not find any of his corps in the town.[32]

Hardee had left Cleburne in charge of the corps when he went to
meet with Hood and Lee and had ordered Cleburne to move through
Rough and Ready and on to Jonesboro as quickly as possible. That
evening the entire corps was in motion, the rear guard disengaging
from the East Point trenches by 11:30 P.M.

Cleburne led the advanced elements through Rough and Ready in
the early evening. The march was difficult because he lacked both
guides and proper maps. As the column advanced toward Jonesboro,
the enemy appeared in force blocking the line of march. Cleburne
decided to detour around them, and this caused great delay. Finally,
after marching all night the head of the weary column appeared in
Jonesboro about 9 A.M.

Hardee met the troops at the railroad and began forming them for
battle. As Lee's troops came up they were positioned on the right
of Hardee's corps facing west. While the troops prepared for battle,
Hardee issued his orders to Cleburne and Lee. Cleburne would open
the battle on the left. Lee would attack when he saw that Cleburne
had become "hotly engaged." [33]

By 1:30 P.M. the last brigades of Lee's corps arrived. At 2 P.M.
Hardee wrote to Hood, "Lee's Brigades have come up & I have
ordered the advance." At the same time Hood sent Hardee the encouraging news that the cavalry had encountered strong opposition
at Mount Gilead. "This sent to you to show that enemy have not
all his troops in your front." [34]

Thus with about twenty-three thousand troops Hardee prepared
to attack about fourteen thousand entrenched Federals under the
command of his old friend Oliver O. Howard. Howard held his
"saucy position" in a saucy manner. Probably unaware of the fact
that Hardee had moved two corps into Jonesboro, Howard believed

32 Henry Champlin Lay Diary, August 31, 1864, in Henry Champlin Lay Papers,
    1844–1908 (Southern Historical Collection); Hood, *Advance and Retreat*,
    205; *Official Records*, XXXVIII, Pt. 5, p. 1002.
33 *Official Records*, XXXVIII, Pt. 3, pp. 726–27, 764, 772, 777, Pt. 5, p. 1006;
    Pickett, *Hardee*, 34; Lay Diary, September 7, 1864.
34 Lay Diary, August 31, 1864; Hood to Hardee, August 31, 1864, in Hood Field
    Dispatch Book.

that Logan's Fifteenth Corps and Kilpatrick's cavalry would be a sufficient force on the east side of the river. He would keep the bulk of the Sixteenth and the Seventeenth corps masked on the west side of the river. During the morning of August 31 Howard decided to probe the Confederate defenses. He ordered a reconnaissance in force for that afternoon and sent over a division of the Sixteenth Corps and a brigade of the Seventeenth to give Logan the necessary support. Fifteen minutes before Logan's soldiers were to leave their trenches, the Confederates appeared, marching straight toward them.[35]

About 3 P.M. Cleburne opened his attack on the enemy right. His first line, composed of his own division commanded by Mark Lowrey and Bate's division commanded by John C. Brown, marched forward and then began obliquing to the right. The two divisions became separated, and Maney's division moved up from reserve to fill the gap. Brown made his assault on the enemy line and met with a repulse. Maney hesitated when he saw Brown fall back and only made a piecemeal attack. On Maney's left Lowrey moved to the attack against the enemy main line. As he crossed the open ground, Lowrey met a heavy fire from the front and a disconcerting fire from the left flank from Kilpatrick's artillery and cavalry armed with "sixteen shooters," as the dismayed Confederates called them. To silence this annoying fire Lowrey's men began turning to their left instead of to the right. They succeeded in forcing Kilpatrick from his line, and then, against orders, Hiram Granbury led his men in pursuit over the Flint. Brigade after brigade followed. Howard reacted by sending two divisions of the Fourteenth Corps to guard that flank. Before a serious engagement west of the Flint could begin, Lowrey regained control of his division and moved it back to the east side of the river. Then Lowrey linked his command once again with that of Maney and prepared to attack the enemy main line.[36]

By the time Lowrey returned with his division, Hardee had sent Colonel Roy over to Lee's side of the field to learn about his condition and to determine whether Lee could renew the attack. Lee replied emphatically that he could not. Indeed, he had a demoralized corps on his hands and a new enemy force coming up on his

35 *Official Records*, XXXVIII, Pt. 2, pp. 856, 860, Pt. 3, pp. 45, 391; Howard, *Autobiography*, II, 38–39.
36 *Official Records*, XXXVIII, Pt. 2, p. 860, Pt. 3, pp. 700–701, 708, 726–27; Cooper Reminiscences, 1866.

right to attack him. Earlier in the afternoon Lee had waited until he
thought he heard the firing of Cleburne's troops. Then at 2:20 P.M.
he attacked. Patton Anderson commanded the first line and Henry
Clayton the second. Anderson led part of his troops to within pistol
range of the enemy line, but they could not advance farther and
suffered heavy casualties. The reserve line came up slowly and in
insufficient numbers. As brigade commander Henry R. Jackson
advanced to assist Anderson, he found one brigade "huddled together
in the abandoned skirmish line of the enemy." This brigade and
another "could not be prevailed upon to advance beyond this line."
Jackson went ahead with his men up to the enemy line, where his
brigade "lost with fearful rapidity more than one third of its numbers." Lee commented on the attack by his corps as "not made by
the troops with that spirit and inflexible determination that would
insure success." The attack was a feeble one and a failure.

Learning that Lee had been repulsed and that the enemy was advancing on his flank, Hardee decided to send a division from Cleburne's corps to assist him. He ordered the general attack to cease
and had his men take up defensive positions. "I now consider this a
fortunate circumstance, for success against such odds could at best
only have been partial and bloody, while defeat would have been
almost inevitable destruction to the army." [37]

While Hardee and Howard had been fighting at Jonesboro, the
remainder of the Union army had continued the advance and had
broken the railroad at numerous points between Rough and Ready
and Jonesboro. Sherman ordered Schofield and Thomas to move
toward Jonesboro. "I must interpose our whole army between Atlanta
and the enemy now in Jonesborough." He would get Hardee first,
then Atlanta.[38]

Hood had a different plan. Now that Sherman was concentrating
against Hardee, Hood decided to bring Lee's corps back to Atlanta.
At 6 P.M. (before Hood could have known the results of the battle
of Jonesboro) he directed Hardee to send Lee back at 2 A.M. and to
use the remainder of his force to safeguard Macon. Feeling that Atlanta might be attacked the next day, Hood also asked Hardee to
send back Reynold's brigade and another from his own corps if

37 H. R. Jackson to Cheatham, December 10, 1864, in Cheatham Papers;
Official Records, XXXVIII, Pt. 3, pp. 700–702, 764.
38 *Official Records*, XXXVIII, Pt. 5, pp. 726–27, 732.

he could. It is quite evident that Hood did not believe that Hardee confronted anything like the bulk of Sherman's army. Before he learned of the order to remove Lee, Hardee had wired Davis the results of the battle and stated, "I can hold this place unless the enemy cross the Flint River below me. My aim will be to keep my command between the enemy and Macon." [39]

The departure of Lee, however, left Hardee in an awkward and difficult situation. His position had little to recommend it defensively. Generally, Hardee's troops held a long line in single rank parallel to the Macon railroad. The terrain offered no advantage, and the Federals did not allow him sufficient time to fortify it properly. Retreat would endanger the rest of the army in Atlanta and would be hazardous, considering the great number of wagons that had been sent to Jonesboro for safekeeping. Hardee, however, decided to hold his position and set to work at once to readjust his line. Lowrey took his division and occupied the works abandoned by Lee. Maney moved up and took over the lines that Lowrey had left.

To Hardee's relief the enemy did not attack in force the following morning. This allowed the Confederates some time to build up their defenses, although they were harassed by Howard's sharpshooters and artillery. Howard kept up the pressure by this means and by limited attacks throughout the morning and the early afternoon. Sherman planned for the main attack to be delivered by Thomas against Hardee's right. Thomas, however, moved ponderously and did not appear on the field until late in the afternoon. Indeed, the Fourth Corps lost its way maneuvering to attack Hardee's rear and did not arrive in time for the battle. The Fourteenth Corps of Jefferson C. Davis, however, did come up late in the afternoon. Until the time of Davis' attack the Confederates had met the Union attempts against their line successfully.

At 4 P.M. Davis attacked a salient on the right of Hardee's line held by Govan's brigade. Govan repulsed the first attack. Davis regrouped and sent his three divisions forward along the railroad tracks. Hardee rushed all of his reserves to the spot, but this time Davis broke through Govan's line, taking Govan and over six hundred of his men as prisoners. Hardee and Cleburne managed to restore the line through fierce

39 Hood to Hardee, August 31, 1864, in Hood Field Dispatch Book; *Official Records*, XXXVIII, Pt. 3, p. 701, Pt. 5, p. 1007; Hardee to Davis, August 31, 1864, in Davis Letters (Tulane).

counterattacks by the brigades of Lewis, Vaughan, and Granbury. When day ended the fighting, Hardee still held his line. He had fought off more than five Union corps.[40]

Soon after dark Hardee received discouraging news. The enemy had cut the Decatur road some four miles behind his position. This and the massive force opposing him made a longer stay at Jonesboro foolhardy. After he had determined to retire, Hardee received a wire from President Davis stating that reinforcements made up of Georgia militia and factory workers were on their way. Davis urged Hardee to defeat "the detachment" opposing him and then to march to Hood's relief. The promise of reinforcement, however, meant little at this time. Hardee began withdrawing his troops from the front lines shortly after midnight and set them in motion for Lovejoy's Station. As soon as Sherman learned of Hardee's retirement, he ordered Thomas to pursue "with vigor."

Hardee's men marched through the night and reached Lovejoy's Station early on the morning of September 2. They immediately threw up breastworks. Soon after 10 A.M. the enemy arrived and began skirmishing. This time the Confederates fought behind good defensive works, and their line had natural advantages. The strength of this new line surprised the attackers. "Strange to say, [they] were as well constructed and as strong as if these Confederates had a week to prepare them." About 4 P.M. Thomas attacked with the Fourth Corps, supported by elements from Howard's Army of the Tennessee. This time Hardee's men withstood the assaults easily and repulsed the Fourth Corps, inflicting "considerable loss." [41]

The firing at Lovejoy's Station was heard by Hood's troops retreating from Atlanta. Hood wrote Hardee to hold on; he was sending Stewart and Lee to his support. On the morning of September 3, 1864, Stewart arrived at Hardee's position and replaced Hardee's worn-out troops.

Two days after the fight at Lovejoy's Station Hood wrote to Bragg, "I can with justice blame no one with this failure [the fall of Atlanta]." When his official report was published, however, Hood had a different tale to tell, a version he enlarged upon in his memoirs. In essence Hood stated that Hardee's failure at Jonesboro caused

40 *Official Records*, XXXVIII, Pt. 1, p. 513, Pt. 3, pp. 46, 166, 696, 728–29, 742, 745; Roy, "General Hardee," *loc cit.*, 373–75.
41 *Official Records*, XXXVIII, Pt. 1, p. 166, Pt. 3, pp. 696, 736, 906, Pt. 5, pp. 746, 1011.

the fall of Atlanta. In his official report, written in February, 1865, Hood obviously attempted to cover up for his own mistakes, and the result is more an attack on Hardee than an account of the operations around Atlanta. It is filled with errors and half-truths, and it credits Hood with knowing things that he could not possibly have known at the time. Generally, Hood's incriminating remarks hinge about the failure of Hardee to push the attack at Jonesboro. "The vigor of the attack may be in some sort imagined when only 1400 men killed and wounded out of the two corps engaged." Hood's opinions gained wide circulation, and soon important political figures, including Clement C. Clay, voiced the opinion that Hood could have held Atlanta if it had not been for Hardee.[42]

Hood's report damaged Hardee, but it also brought wrath from several quarters down on his own head. Joseph E. Johnston, for instance, determined to press charges against Hood. Hardee immediately filed his own report, which is unique in the series of reports he submitted during the war. He frankly designed it "as an answer to the misrepresentations contained in General Hood's report." He asked Secretary of War Breckinridge to publish the report for the "truth of history" and for "my own reputation." [43]

The mass of the evidence shows that Hood was doubtful at least of Sherman's intent for three days after he swung his army southeast of Atlanta. When Hood did learn that Jonesboro was threatened, he divided his army and sent two corps to confront what he believed to be a fraction of the enemy force. When he decided to move, the enemy was already in the vicinity of Jonesboro and was threatening or holding nearly every point between that place and Rough and Ready. Hood lost Atlanta when Sherman placed himself astride his lines of communications. Moving Hardee to Jonesboro would not have prevented this. If Hood thought that Jonesboro was to be the critical point, why did he not go himself with all of the troops he could spare from the Atlanta defenses? He lost perhaps his only opportunity for victory when he failed to strike Sherman in the flank as he moved around East Point. As for the battle of Jonesboro Hood is correct when he criticized Hardee for not vigorously attacking the enemy. Hardee admitted this himself. It is not "surprising that troops who had for two months been hurled against breast-

---

42 *Ibid.*, Pt. 2, p. 730, Pt. 3, p. 633; Mary Boykin Chesnut, *A Diary from Dixie*, ed. Ben Ames Williams (Cambridge, 1949), 513.
43 *Official Records*, XXXVIII, Pt. 3, p. 697.

works only to be repulsed or to gain dear-bought and fruitless victories, should now have moved against the enemy's works with reluctance and distrust." Hardee took his men into the battle "under the most unfavorable conditions, after a 15 hour march, completely worn out, . . . and knowingly attacked a superior force, under most disadvantageous circumstances." Yet at Atlanta on July 22 Hardee's men had gone into battle under even worse physical handicaps. At Jonesboro the morale of the troops seems to have been at its lowest point. Patton Anderson and a few others carried out their assignments with energy, but they were exceptions.[44]

Hardee failed as an army commander at Jonesboro. His tactical plan resembled the one that Bragg employed at Murfreesboro, but here the Confederates did not attack on the extreme right of the enemy and roll up the enemy flank, nor did they wheel to the right as they should have. Bad timing characterized the attack generally. Hardee's plan called for a wide frontal assault on the concave Union line, but a lack of co-ordination between the two wings led Lee to attack prematurely. The poor timing should be attributed directly to Hardee, for a dispatch from him to Lee shows that Hardee had not kept abreast of the situation on the right. Lee's attack was generally timid and proved costly to troops like Anderson's who made a determined effort to reach the Union line. Cleburne's attack also lacked vigor, and the maneuvering of his corps was unbelievably bad. His division became separated early in the attack and did not swing to the right as ordered. Lowrey's division on the left went off on a tangent across the Flint River and failed to give the other divisions the support they needed. Cleburne's divisions also failed to make the sustained attack of which they had so often been capable. A great deal of the disorder in Cleburne's corps can be explained by the fact that none of the division commanders had had more than six weeks' experience in his position. Furthermore, the battle of Jonesboro was the first battle in which Cleburne had commanded a corps. Many of these factors, including faulty leadership on the part of his junior officers and the deterioration of morale, were beyond Hardee's control at the time. Nevertheless, Hardee should be held

44 *Ibid.*, 633; C. Irvine Walker, "Sketch of the Career of the 10th and 19th South Carolina Regiments in the Service of the Southern Confederacy during the War with the United States, 1861–1865," typed copy in C. Irvine Walker Collection, 1861–65 (Southern Historical Collection).

responsible for the generally poor performance of the two corps entrusted to his direction.

On the other hand, the battles of September 1, 1864, at Jonesboro and September 2, at Lovejoy's Station did credit to Hardee and his command. Now his corps fought alone against a much heavier Union force. Although they were outnumbered and their defensive works were poor, they succeeded in holding their position and inflicting serious loss upon the enemy. Hardee handled his divisions well and seems to have gotten the maximum performance out of his men. His retreat from Jonesboro to Lovejoy's Station was conducted with skill. A malfunction here could have cost him his corps.

Following the battle of Lovejoy's Station, Hardee and Hood both realized the seriousness of the situation. With Atlanta lost and with the army generally demoralized, Hood called on President Davis for immediate reinforcement. Hardee backed up Hood's appeal with a letter of his own to the President. "Unless this army is speedily and heavily re-enforced Georgia and Alabama will be overrun. I see no other means to avert this calamity. Never in my opinion was our liberty in such danger. What can you do for us?" The appeals to Davis resulted in little, for as Davis replied to Hardee, "no other resources remain." [45]

Sherman broke off his pursuit of Hood's army during the first week in September and returned to Atlanta. Hood quickly sent Hardee with his corps back to Jonesboro, where he remained until September 19, when he took up a new position between Fairburn and Palmetto. While his army remained on this line, Hood prepared for an offensive north across the Chattahoochee. The thought of resuming the offensive invigorated many in the army, but when the time came, the army was to advance without its senior corps commander, Hardee.

From the moment Hood had assumed command of the Army of Tennessee, strained relations had existed between him and Hardee. Matters grew worse during August and finally became impossible in September. Hardee had opposed the promotion of Hood to supreme command: "It is well known that I felt unwilling to serve under General Hood . . . , because I believed him, though a tried and gallant officer, to be unequal in both experience and natural ability to so

---

45 *Official Records*, XXXVIII, Pt. 5, pp. 1016, 1018, 1021.

important a command." Hardee had grown attached to Johnston during the early Atlanta campaign, and although he did not fully agree with Johnston's strategy, he believed him to be much better qualified for the position than his successor. Another factor in the matter was that Hood was Hardee's junior in rank and years, and therefore Hood's appointment could be and was interpreted as a lack of confidence in Hardee. This was a serious matter to a professional soldier, and Longstreet probably echoed Hardee's feeling when he stated, "I thought it unwise to choose a junior for an assignment to command over his senior officers, and *prejudical* to the *esprit de corps* of any army, except under the most eminent services. . . ." [46]

Soon after the battle of Atlanta Hardee had set about to secure his release from the Army of Tennessee. Taking advantage of Bragg's presence in Atlanta, Hardee asked him if he might be transferred to his command. Bragg agreed with Hardee and wrote to Davis, "There does not exist that cordiality and mutual confidence and support necessary." He suggested that Hardee be exchanged for Richard Taylor. "With Taylor in Hardee's place this army would be invincible."

The exchange would have pleased Hardee, for he wrote his wife: "It would suit us exactly to get command of the Dept. of Miss.; we could be together, and I should have a suitable command." Davis, however, would not permit the exchange of Hardee and Taylor. "In both cases it would be at the sacrifice of knowledge of country and troops." [47] In another letter to his wife Hardee revealed that he considered resigning from the service if he did not receive his transfer. He cautioned Mary Hardee to consider the matter carefully, "for on your decision I shall act. It is a grave step to take in time of war and in the face of the enemy, but if you think it is right . . . I am prepared to do it. I can be perfectly happy at the Hermitage but whether you can is another matter, but this ought hardly to be considered in deciding what I ought to do in matters where my personal honor & feelings are involved. A woman's instincts are some times of more value than a man's reason and judgment." [48] Leaving such a decision up to her showed that he had already resigned in spirit.

46 R. M. Gray Reminiscences, 1862–67 (typed copy in Southern Historical Collection); James Longstreet, *From Manassas to Appomattox: Memoirs of the Civil War in America* (Philadelphia, 1896), 467.
47 *Official Records*, XXXIX, Pt. 2, p. 760, LII, Pt. 2, pp. 713–14; Hardee to wife, n.d., in Hardee Letters (Alabama).
48 Hardee to wife, August 2, 1864, in Hardee Letters (Alabama).

Three days later Hardee's determination had weakened. "I am not entirely satisfied that I would be doing right just now to resign. There is always a reflection on an officer who resigns in the immediate presence of the enemy, and more particularly when that enemy is invading his own country and his own State. I want to do what is best regardless of passion, prejudice or my own personal feelings."

Bragg's application for his release having failed, Hardee wrote directly to the President asking for a transfer. In closing he said: "I rely upon your kindness to relieve me from an unpleasant position." Hardee received his reply on August 5: "I regret that your position is felt to be unpleasant. You need no assurance that no wound was intended. Your letters when Commander-in-chief, created the belief that the course adopted would be satisfactory to you. The country needs every effort of all her sons. You can most aid our cause in your present position. Other motives will not be necessary to you." At the same time Davis wrote to Hood, who had also been seeking Hardee's transfer, that "General Hardee's minute knowledge of the country, and his extensive acquaintance with the officers and men of the command, must render his large professional knowledge and experience peculiarly valuable in such a campaign as I hope is before you."

As soon as he could have Davis' reply deciphered, Hardee fired back this message: "No letter of mine while Commander-in-chief was intended to convey the impression that the appointment of a junior to command me would be satisfactory. The justice or propriety of that appointment I do not propose to question. I only ask to be relieved from a position which is personally humiliating. This I think due to an old soldier who has faithfully endeavored to perform his duty and who is still willing to make any sacrifice for the cause except his self-respect. I respectfully renew my request to be relieved. Genl. Hood approves my application."

Davis immediately wired back: "Your telegram of yesterday received with regret and disappointment. . . . I now ask is this a time to weigh professional or personal pride against the needs of the country—or for an old soldier to withdraw the support he can give the public defense from the place where it is most wanted? Let your patriotic instincts answer, rejecting all other advices." [49]

49 Hardee to wife, August 5, 1864, Hardee to Davis, August 3, 6, 1864 (copies), and Davis to Hardee, August 4, 7, 1864 (copies), *ibid.*; Davis to Hood, August 5, 1864, in Hood Papers.

This answer officially closed the matter temporarily, but after the battle of Jonesboro the Hardee-Hood animosity flared up brightly. This time it seems that Hood took the initiative. He applied to Bragg on September 8 to have Hardee exchanged with Taylor. Then on September 13 he appealed to Davis: "In the battle of July 20 we failed on account of General Hardee. Our success on July 22 was not what it should have been, owing to this officer. Our failure on August 31 I am now convinced was greatly owing to him. Please confer with Lieutenant-Generals Stewart and S. D. Lee as to operations around Atlanta. It is of the utmost importance that Hardee should be relieved at once. He commands the best troops in this army." [50]

Hood had become convinced that Hardee, "if not consenting to a frustration of my plans, was at least willing I should not achieve signal success." He claims in his memoirs that Stewart, Lee, and G. W. Smith agreed with this interpretation. Stewart did hold that the differences between Hood and Hardee impaired the latter's services at Peachtree Creek, but did not go farther in his remarks. G. W. Smith stated that Hardee was responsible for discord in the army during the late summer, but did not charge Hardee with failing to carry out his assignments. S. D. Lee left no mention of the subject in his writings. Hardee himself held, "that . . . I failed to accomplish all that General Hood thinks might have been accomplished, is a matter of regret. That I committed errors is very possible, but that I failed in any instance to carry out in good faith his orders I utterly deny; nor during our official connection did General Hood ever evince a belief that I had in any respect failed in the execution of such parts of his military plans as were intrusted to me. On the contrary, by frequent and exclusive consultation of my opinions, by the selection of my corps for important operations, and by assigning me on several occasions to the command of two-thirds of his army, he gave every proof of implicit confidence in me." [51]

The question of whether Hardee gave his commander his full support and gave it cordially is virtually impossible to determine conclusively. It was obvious to most of the higher ranking and well-informed men in the army that strained relations existed between Hardee and Hood, but whether this carried over into the actual conduct

---

50 *Official Records*, XXXIX, Pt. 2, p. 832.
51 Hood, *Advance and Retreat*, 250, 251; Stewart, "The Army of Tennessee," in *Military Annals of Tennessee*, 99–100; *Official Records*, XXXVIII, Pt. 3, pp. 697–98.

of operations is another matter. Certainly at Atlanta neither Hardee nor the Army of Tennessee seemed as effective as in the past. Too many factors enter into an explanation—lack of morale, difficulties of trench warfare, and others—to enable one to isolate a single cause. Until firmer evidence is uncovered to support Hood's accusations, Hardee should not be condemned for improper spirit. In the past he had had strained relations with his commanders and had continued, like the professional soldier that he was, to carry out his orders as best he could. Hood could scarcely blame the entire army for the defeats around Atlanta. What could be more obvious than to assign responsibility to his senior corps commander, who had conducted the critical movements during these operations and who had openly opposed his selection as commander in chief? As an aggressive optimist Hood could hardly admit to himself or to others that perhaps his army lacked the capability to carry out its assignment or that he himself was deficient. To maintain his confidence and that of his army he had to find a single, simple explanation for the disaster.

On September 17 Hood again applied to Davis for Hardee's release, suggesting that Cheatham (who with others later became his scapegoats in the Tennessee campaign) replace him. In view of the sad state of the Army of Tennessee, the critical strategic situation in the West, and the conflict between Hardee and Hood, Davis felt compelled to visit the army. He arrived on September 25 and held a series of conferences with his generals. He also visited Hardee's command and reviewed the troops informally, at which time he was received unenthusiastically. As they rode back from the review, Hardee took the opportunity to tell Davis what he had "long wanted him to know."

I reviewed Hood's military course from Dalton to the present time. I commenced by saying that there were two facts connected with Hood's promotion to the command of the Army, which were particularly mortifying to me. First: that Bragg had been sent to this Army, and not withstanding my long association with it had never said a word to me on the subject of the campaign. 2nd that Hood had been placed in command because he was regarded as, par excellence, the fighting man, whereas in fact if Johnston had followed his advice, the army would have crossed the Chattahoochee two or three weeks before it did. I then went on and gave him time and place when Hood had not only recommended, but urged Johnston to retreat. I told him also that Johnston had given him three opportunities to attack the enemy in flank, at Resaca, New Hope Church and Kennesaw. I gave him a full account of his conduct till he assumed command. I told him how open and frank my course had been since that time, and that I challenged Hood to show wherein I had failed to cooperate with him. I then contrasted my conduct with his in relation to the Jonesboro fights and characterized Hood's as unjust, ungenerous and unmanly. Finally I told him that things had reached a point when it was necessary for him to relieve either Hood or myself, that I did not ask him to relieve Hood, but insisted on his relieving me. I told him that if he wished to know what the Army wished, I would tell him that it wanted a change of commanders. He then discussed the matter, but did not say what he would do. I told him Johnston had a wonderful hold on the affections of the Army, that the men were devoted to him. He discussed Johnston and satisfied me that he would not send him back. He then spoke of Beauregard and I told him frankly that Beauregard would be very acceptable to this Army.[52]

Davis left for Montgomery on September 27. The next day he wired Hood to issue orders for Hardee's release. ". . . I can say with certainty that General Hardee was not relieved because of any depreciation of his capacity, his zeal, or fidelity," ". . . My objections to complying with his wish were entirely complimentary to him. My assent to his persistent request to be relieved was finally given because of irreconcilable differences between himself and the officer commanding-in-chief." [53]

On September 28, 1864, Hood issued the order relieving Hardee from command. He would proceed at once to Charleston and assume command of the Department of South Carolina, Georgia, and Florida. Davis had assigned him to this particular command because of his "great experience" and "in my estimation . . . great merit." Furthermore, "the possibility of obtaining reinforcement from citizens of the country was reasonably thought to be increased by the assignment of Genl. Hardee, a distinguished Georgian, to the command of the department." [54]

The evening before he left for Charleston Hardee "was flattered . . . with the most touching ovation that has been given any officer. The whole corps quitted quarters & besieged his encampment in a forest of pines. Scarcely enough men were left for guards. Officers and

---

52 Memorandum signed by Hardee, September 27, 1864, in Davis Papers (Tulane).
53 *Official Records*, XXXIX, Pt. 2, pp. 879–80; Davis to J. Seddon, September 28, 1864, Davis to Hood, September 28, 1864, in Rowland (ed.), *Jefferson Davis*, VI, 344–45; Davis to Roy, February 29, 1880, quoted in Roy, "General Hardee," *loc. cit.*, 377.
54 Davis to S. Jones, February 19, 1884, in Rowland (ed.), *Jefferson Davis*, IX, 276.

men were moved to tears at parting with the noble old hero. . . ." "Amid cheers for 'Old Reliable,' . . . the crowd rushed towards their loved commander, and thousands . . . from Arkansas, Alabama, Mississippi, Tennessee and Texas had the melancholy pleasure of taking by the hand and saying farewell to the war-worn veteran who led them on so many bloody fields." They had lost "the pride of our corps." [55]

55 G. A. Williams to Lucie Buck, October 3, 1864, in Buck Papers; unidentified newspaper clipping, September 12, 1864, in Hardee Family Papers, in possession of Mrs. Howard Bowen, Birmingham, Ala.; L. P. Yandell to Roy, June 12, 1880, and D. G. White to Roy, April 6, 1880, quoted in Roy, "General Hardee," *loc. cit.*, 381–82; C. H. Olmstead to wife, September 28, 1864, in Olmstead Papers; Taylor Beatty Diary, September 28, 1864; Cooper Reminiscences.

XIV

Reliance on a Scapegoat

On October 5, 1864, Jefferson Davis made a speech in Augusta, Georgia, designed to mollify if not to inspire his countrymen. Behind him on the platform sat Howell Cobb, Beauregard, and Hardee. In his speech Davis complimented the three, paying tribute to the latter as a mainstay of the Army of Tennessee, one of the South's heroes of long standing, and Georgia's "own and true Hardee." After his speech Davis conferred with Beauregard and Hardee about the proposed operations of Hood's army. During the train trip with Davis to Augusta, General Hardee had acquainted himself with Hood's plan for throwing the Army of Tennessee across Sherman's communications. Hardee had misgivings about Hood's proposed campaign, but stated fairly, "I cannot say that the plan will succeed, but think it the best which can be done, if that does not succeed no other will." [1]

After leaving Augusta, Hardee went to Charleston, accompanied by his indispensables, Roy and Pickett. Mary Hardee and at least one of the girls also went with him. The general established his family in Summerville, twenty miles from Charleston, to protect them from yellow fever, which was killing up to twenty people a day in Charleston.[2] On October 5, 1864, the Charleston *Mercury* extended a warm

---

1 Rowland (ed.), *Jefferson Davis*, VI, 356, IX, 276, VIII, 416; Charleston *Daily Courier*, October 15, 1865; Davis to S. Jones, February 19, 1884, in Davis Papers (Tulane).

   Hardee also took advantage of the trip to visit Johnston in Macon. He spent most of the time bringing his former commander up to date on the recent affairs of the Army of Tennessee.

2 Hardee to Cooper, November 8, 1864, in Department of South Carolina, Georgia, and Florida, Letters Sent, 1863–64, Record Group 109. Black and Poole would also follow at a later date.

and flattering welcome to Hardee, and that same day he officially assumed command of his department.[3]

At the time Hardee arrived, Charlestonians were still digging their city out of the rubble left by the great summer bombardment. The city and harbor were the most heavily fortified in the Confederacy and had been defended successfully since 1861. Moreover, in light of the effective network of complementary forts such as Sumter and Moultrie, the city was in no real danger from sea attack. The attitude of the inhabitants has been expressed by Henry Timrod, "Thus girth without and garrisoned at home,/Day patient followed day." [4]

Charleston and Savannah constituted the seaports of note in the vast expanse of the Department of South Carolina, Georgia, and Florida. The possession of Florida did not seem to concern particularly either the Union or the Confederacy; except for extensive cattle herds there it could claim little strategic importance. Georgia and South Carolina, however, were in many respects the "heartland" of the Confederacy and must be defended at all hazards. There were between twenty and twenty-five thousand Federals in the area, and there were Federal beach-heads in all three of the states. Poised on the northwestern fringe of Hardee's department were the armies of the Cumberland, the Ohio, and the Tennessee, with which he was familiar. To defend his department Hardee had 12,446 effectives, most of whom were clustered around Charleston and Savannah. These could be supplemented, of course, by an unpredictable number of state troops and armed civilians. To command his scattered forces Hardee had only a few generals, and these few had led either undistinguished or controversial careers. Major General Sam Jones had commanded troops in the fringe areas of East Tennessee and West Virginia, showing some ability in administration but weaknesses in co-operation and combat experience. Hardee had worked with him in 1862 and knew his limitations. Major General Lafayette McLaws had had ample combat experience in Longstreet's corps, but "his record as a divisional commander had not been one of uniform promptness and of average success." This professional soldier had come to the department when he had been relieved of command at Knoxville. William

3 Charleston *Mercury*, October 5, 1864; General Orders No. 75, October 5, 1864, Department of South Carolina, Georgia, and Florida, General Orders, Circulars, and Special Field Orders, 1864–65, Record Group 109.
4 Henry Timrod, "Charleston," *Southern Poets*, ed. Edward Winfield Parks (New York, 1936), 117–18.

B. Taliaferro, James H. Trapier, and the others offered little promise of distinguished service. These were the men with whom Hardee would work.[5]

Hardee's departmental problems lend themselves to cataloguing rather than to summarizing. Paramount as ever was manpower. With all but essential troops already stripped from the department, and with some of these also gone, Hardee had to scrape together adequate forces to defend the major seaports and to maintain at least a semblance of military power in remote areas. He seriously needed a mobile reserve but never obtained it. One of the expedients by which he attempted to solve the manpower question was to induce foreigners among the Union prisoners to enlist. He also departed from an established policy by opening communications with the commander of the Union forces along the coast concerning the exchange of prisoners. He secured the removal of Confederate prisoners from Morris Island, where they had been placed under Confederate fire in retaliation for exposure of Union prisoners to Union fire in Charleston. Later Hardee succeeded in having these prisoners exchanged. Hardee did not work for the exchange solely to increase his manpower. Union prisoners were being dumped in his department without proper means for subsistence and often without notice; "there are already in the Department more prisoners than I can properly guard." Hardee's own men suffered from a lack of clothing and blankets. Many were barefooted. As for rations, one irate brigadier complained to Roy that "rats [are now] a substitute for *Longhorn*." [6]

Throughout the fall of 1864 Hardee was immersed in administrative detail. He spent his time locating and training artillerists, building wharves, placing obstructions in the approaches to Charleston harbor, strengthening the forts, and making frequent inspections. He distributed working parties to collect unused and endangered railroad iron to be used in replacing damaged or worn rails on vital lines. Some iron was turned over to navy rolling mills. Hardee requested permission to form a torpedo-boat corps, whose mission would be

---

5 *Official Records*, XXXV, Pt. 2, p. 643; Douglas Southall Freeman, *Lee's Lieutenants: A Study in Command*, 3 vols. (New York, 1942-44), I, 435.

6 Hardee to Cooper, October 6, 10, 1864, in Telegrams Received, Adjutant General's Office; *Official Records*, VII, pp. 981-82, XXV, Pt. 2, pp. 327, 640, XLVII, Pt. 2, pp. 412-13; Hardee to Cooper, October 6, 1864, Department of South Carolina, Georgia, Florida, Letters Sent; W. H. Kennedy to Roy, October 25, 1864, in Charleston Harbor Papers, 1861-65 (Emory University Library).

similar to that of the Revolutionary galleys on which his grandfather had served, harassing the enemy along the coast.[7]

Hardee had to consider the department to the north in his plans for allocating men and resources. The fall of 1864 was a critical period for the defenders of Wilmington, and in response to their urgent calls Hardee sent one of the few regiments left for the Charleston garrison. To create a new outlet for blockade-runners in the event Wilmington fell, the War Department urged Hardee to investigate the possibilities of Savannah, as Charleston was the only port in his command "through which any blockade running is being done." [8] Hardee aided the port collectors, helped regulate the use of the railroads, secured necessities for the navy, and recruited Irishmen to fill the depleted Irish regiments of the Army of Tennessee. Departmental duties, he feared, might become routine; but they did not. Sherman saw to that.

While Hardee adjusted to the problems and personnel of his command, Hood and Sherman maneuvered across northern Georgia. Hood declined a general engagement and moved off into Alabama. Sherman reacted by sending about one third of his men under the able Thomas to oppose Hood, and four corps were grouped around Atlanta. Sherman placed the Fourteenth and Twentieth corps under Henry W. Slocum and the Fifteenth and Seventeenth under Oliver O. Howard. These two infantry wings plus Judson Kilpatrick's cavalry number about sixty-five thousand effectives.

On November 16, 1864, this force, led by Sherman himself, departed from Atlanta and disappeared into central Georgia. Sherman had decided to "strike out for Savannah," destroying as he went the military resources and morale of the Confederate heartland. With a base at Savannah, he felt confident that a new vista of military possibilities would be opened. Sherman's objective was unknown to the Confederate commanders, and they spent the following month ineffectually opposing his advance. In desperation the Confederate War Department combined the inactive forces in Augusta with

7 Department of South Carolina, Georgia, Florida, Letters Sent (October 5, 1864–November 15, 1864); J. Chesnut, Jr., to Hardee, October 19, 1864, in James Chesnut Letterbook, 1864–65 (Emory University Library); J. M. Fairbanks to G. R. Fairbanks, October 27, 1864, in Fairbanks Letters; *Official Records of the Union and Confederate Navies in the War of the Rebellion*, 31 vols. (Washington, 1894–1919), Ser. I, Vol. XVI, 460; hereinafter cited as *Naval Records*.
8 *Official Records*, XXV, Pt. 2, p. 638, XLII, Pt. 3, pp. 1157, 1177, 1181, 1183; Hardee to Cooper, October 29, 1864, in Telegrams Received, Adjutant General's Office.

Hardee's troops in front of Sherman.[9] Bragg was given command of both forces and ordered to halt Sherman. Bragg accepted the task, but declared "that no practicable combination of my available men can avert disaster." [10] With Bragg in command of the theater, Hardee's activities and responsibilities were confined to the Savannah area. At Savannah Hardee would act independently until he came under Beauregard's control in December.

Panic gripped the area around Savannah during the closing days of November. The city, like Charleston, had successfully withstood attack throughout the war. Its coastal defenses were the work of the Confederate Department of Engineers and contained an enormous amount of firepower from three mutually supporting defense lines. The entrance to the Savannah River was impassable because of the obstructions and the network of guns.[11] But now, places that had not seen a blue uniform since 1860 (and would not see another until after the surrender) were reported occupied. Rumors had Sherman's columns crossing every stream and menacing every town in southeastern Georgia. It was trying for Hardee to sift information under such circumstances. Even Wheeler, a reliable source of information in the first three and a half years of the war, seemed unable to penetrate the heavy curtain of foragers that surrounded Sherman's army. Behind these "bummers" ranged cavalry patrols that insulated the main columns and deceived the defenders as to the actual strength behind the screen. The general direction of Sherman's advance, however, could not be concealed for long.

Anticipating an attack on Savannah, Hardee set to work to prepare the city's defenses. As early as November 20 Hardee had transferred guns from the coastal fortifications to the western side of the city. He now ordered all able-bodied men in the city to report for duty. All soldiers on furlough and assignments, together with convalescents, were organized into battalions under Major General Lafayette Mc-Laws. A few units from the north, including the veteran Tenth North

9 For a full account of Hardee's attempt to resist Sherman's advance from Atlanta to the vicinity of Savannah, see Hughes, "Hardee, C.S.A.," 456–63.
10 *Official Records*, XLIV, 877; Hardee to Beauregard, November 21, 1864, in Confederate States of America Archives (Duke University Library); Jones, *Siege of Savannah*, 96.
11 Jones, *Siege of Savannah*, 98; *Official Records*, XLIV, 13; Madeleine Vinton Dahlgren, *Memoir of John A. Dahlgren, Rear-Admiral United States Navy* (Boston, 1882), 488–89.

Carolina, arrived and were put to work on the trenches. Hardee arranged with his navy commander, W. W. Hunter, to use the gunboat *Macon* to patrol the Savannah River. He assigned Wheeler the task of destroying everything the enemy could use between the Ocmulgee River and the city. As soon as all the roads leading to Savannah had been obstructed, Hardee released Wheeler from his position in front of Sherman and ordered him to operate on the enemy's flanks and rear. Wheeler would not now be confined in the narrow, marshy terrain around Savannah, but Hardee had relinquished the buffer between Sherman's army and his own.[12]

Amid the calamity reports pouring into Savannah came a particularly ominous one. A lonely Confederate sentinel on the bank of the Broad River sat eating sweet potatoes that he had just fried for his breakfast. The river that he guarded lay just above Savannah and led directly inland to the Savannah and Charleston Railroad, which constituted Hardee's line of communications with the rest of the Confederacy. As the sentinel peered into the heavy fog that hung over the river, several large enemy steamers suddenly loomed out of the haze, headed up the river. The astonished picket hurried off, leaving his breakfast untouched. The steamers brought the division of General John P. Hatch, part of John G. Foster's Union forces at Port Royal, South Carolina. Hatch disembarked about five thousand men at Boyd's Landing, just across the Georgia line in South Carolina, and advanced inland toward the railroad. Only one cavalry regiment was there to oppose them.[13]

Hardee responded to the threat by ordering General Sam Jones at Charleston to Grahamville and Pocotalago, both in South Carolina, with two Georgia infantry regiments.[14] After dispatching Jones to the threatened point, Hardee wrote to Secretary of War Seddon: "As railroad and telegraphic communications may soon be cut with Charleston I desire you to know that I have, including the local troops, less than 1,000 men of all arms. General [G. W.] Smith is expected

---

12 Savannah *Daily Morning News*, November 28, 29, 1864; Hardee to W. W. Hunter, November 27, 1864, in Savannah Squadron Papers, 1862–65 (Emory University Library); *Official Records*, XLIV, 906.

13 Dahlgren, *Memoir*, 479–80; *Official Records*, XLIV, 420; Charles Colcock Jones, Jr., *The Battle of Honey Hill* (Augusta, 1885), 11; Taylor, *Destruction and Reconstruction*, 262.

14 Hardee to S. Jones, November 29, 1864, in Sam Jones Papers, 1861–64, Record Group 109.

with 3,200 men, but has not arrived. If railroad communications is [*sic*] cut with Charleston, which is threatened by ten gun-boats and barges, of course no re-enforcements can be sent from Augusta." [15]

The fate of Savannah depended upon blocking Hatch's advance. Hardee wired G. W. Smith to take the first two trainloads of Georgia militia through Savannah to Grahamville, and to "drive the enemy back to their gun-boats." [16]

Gustavus W. Smith and his sleeping soldiers pulled into Savannah from Macon at 2 A.M., November 30, and Hardee's dispatch was delivered to Smith at the railroad depot. He left his men asleep and went directly to Hardee's headquarters. Awakening his commander, Smith told him. "If you can can satisfy me that it is absolutely necessary that my command shall go into South Carolina, I will endeavor to carry out your orders. If you do not satisfy me . . . I will be under the disagreeable necessity of withdrawing the State forces from your control." With the help of a map and a handful of dispatches, Hardee satisfied Smith that it was necessary. While Smith's troops were hurried into South Carolina, Hardee impatiently wired Jones asking why his troops had not left Charleston. Where were the troops from Augusta? [17]

At midmorning on November 30, Smith reported to Hardee that he had engaged the enemy at Honey Hill and that he needed reinforcements. The Charleston troops had not arrived. Later in the day Hardee anxiously opened another dispatch from Smith. It proved to be one of the most welcome reports that he received during the war. The enemy had been repulsed.[18]

As soon as he learned that reinforcements were nearing Grahamville, Hardee left the telegraph office and went to join Smith. He found the enemy "badly whipped" and allowed Smith to take his troops back to Savannah. The enemy advanced again on December 2 but retired without a battle. Leaving the defense of the railroad to Jones, Hardee returned to Savannah. He needed about three thousand troops

15 *Official Records*, XLIV, 905.
16 Roy to G. W. Smith, November 29, 1864, in Department of South Carolina, Georgia, Florida, Letters Sent.
17 Gustavus Woodson Smith, "The Georgia Militia During Sherman's March to the Sea," in *Battles and Leaders*, IV. 666–67; *Official Records*, XLIV, 415; Hardee to Jones, November 30, 1864, in Sam Jones Papers.
18 Jones, *Siege of Savannah*, 92; *Official Records*, XLIV, 929; Hardee to Jones, December 5, 1864, in Sam Jones Papers; Jones to Roy, January 11, 1865, in Confederate Miscellany (Emory University Library).

to keep the situation under control. Bragg sent word on December 3 that he was dispatching ten thousand men to Hardee's assistance. If he had indeed sent ten thousand men, Hardee could have forgotten about his exposed communications. The few thousand that Bragg did send were needed in the lines about Savannah while the area around Pocotalago and Grahamville remained in Jones's hands. Jones expressed dismay when he inspected his motley command of two Georgia regiments, some reserves, and several battalions from other units.[19]

Jones might be dismayed, but his situation could not be improved without more assistance from Augusta or Richmond. Hardee was more concerned about Sherman's sixty thousand troops already around Millen, Georgia, and the Augusta railroad than about Jones' problem.

To slow Sherman's advance Hardee sent McLaws with a brigade of Georgia militia and Baker's North Carolina troops to Station Number 4½ on the Georgia Central Railroad. McLaws found the position untenable and fell back, with Hardee's approval, to Station Number 1½, about four miles from the city.

From December 5 to December 7 Sherman drew closer to Savannah. The enemy who had crossed the Ogeechee River forced the abandonment of the outposts on the Augusta railroad. Hardee now brought the navy into play, ordering the *Macon* and a floating battery to protect the railroad bridge across the Savannah River.[20] In Hardee's rear at Grahamville trouble also developed as the enemy secured a lodgment near the railroad. Jones attempted to drive the enemy from their new positions but failed. Hardee urged Jones to encourage his men and to try to drive the enemy back. He needed a fighting commander at Grahamville as badly as he needed more troops.[21]

Beauregard in Charleston displayed alarm at the deterioration of the situation as revealed in Hardee's telegrams. He asked both Hardee and Jones to come up for a conference. Hardee replied that he and

19 *Official Records*, LIII, 35; Jones, *Siege of Savannah*, 55.
20 Jones, *Siege of Savannah*, 51–52; *Official Records*, XLIV, 938; *Naval Records*, Ser. I, Vol. XVI, 472; Roy to W. W. Hunter, December 7, 1864, in Savannah Squadron Papers.
21 To Jones's credit, he never allowed the enemy to approach any closer to the railroad. Although the enemy could and did shell the line, only one locomotive and one car were damaged during the next two and a half weeks, and the trains continued to run. Jones to Roy, January 11, 1865, in Confederate Miscellany; Jones, *Siege of Savannah*, 93–94; *Official Records*, XLIV, 420, 443–44, 934–35.

Jones could not come "without injury to the service" and suggested that Beauregard come to Savannah. Later on December 8, Hardee wired Beauregard stating, "I hope you will not fail to come here to-night. It is all important that I should confer with you." [22]

Before leaving Charleston for Savannah, Beauregard sent Hardee a wire that set forth the guiding principle for the defense of Savannah: "Having no army of relief to look to, and your forces being essential to the defense of Georgia and South Carolina, whenever you shall have to select between their safety and that of Savannah, sacrifice the latter, and form a junction with General Jones, holding the left bank of the Savannah and the railroad to this place as long as possible." [23]

While Hardee was waiting for Beauregard he received from Wheeler an intercepted enemy message disclosing Sherman's planned dispositions for the direct investment of Savannah. This relieved Hardee's worries about Sherman's swinging north to cut his communications with Charleston. Now certain of the enemy's objective and dispositions, Hardee immediately ordered all able-bodied men in Savannah to the trenches and began moving his troops to the main defense line located about two and a half miles from the city. He urged the people of the city to send him their spades, axes, and other tools. The mayor of Savannah strongly backed his request.[24]

Beauregard arrived early on December 9 and spent most of the day conferring with Hardee. Hardee informed him that the enemy was about six miles from his intermediary line, which protected the Charleston and Savannah Railroad and its bridge across the Savannah River. Sherman's army was advancing in separate columns down the Middle Ground Road, the River Road, and the Augusta railroad, with thirty-five to forty thousand men, the bulk of his army of sixty thousand. The main body of Hardee's ten thousand troops occupied the main works while General Hugh W. Mercer and Adjutant General Henry Wayne delayed Sherman. Hardee expected the enemy to strike the main line on December 9 or December 10. As for the north side of the Savannah River, Hardee did not place troops there, believing that the navy would deter the enemy. If the enemy did succeed in crossing the river, the boggy rice fields would prevent a rapid

22 Hardee to Jones, December 8, 1864, Roy to Jones, December 8, 1864, in Sam Jones Papers; Hardee to Beauregard, December 8, 1864, in Confederate Archives.
23 *Official Records*, XLIV, 940.
24 *Ibid.*, 410; Hardee to Beauregard, December 9, 1864, in Confederate Archives; Savannah *Daily Morning News*, December 8–9, 1864.

strike in force. Beauregard asked Hardee about his plans for evacuation. Hardee told him that none had been made, as he was relying on the gunboats in Savannah harbor to ferry his troops to South Carolina. Beauregard thereupon directed Hardee to begin at once the construction of pontoon bridges across the Savannah. After reiterating his order giving the safety of the army priority over that of the city and cautioning Hardee to look to his communications, Beauregard left the city to visit Jones at Pocotalago.[25]

The intermediate line of which Hardee spoke collapsed before Beauregard left the city. Old and infirm General Mercer, who had commanded one of Hardee's brigades at Atlanta, had no sooner occupied this line of detached works behind the Monteith Swamp than the enemy outflanked him and rushed toward the main defense line. The two armies had at last made contact.[26]

The armies of Sherman and Hardee confronted each other on a peninsula about thirteen miles wide, bordered on the north by the Savannah River and on the south by the Little Ogeechee River. Below the Little Ogeechee a series of interlacing creeks and swamps created a natural barrier. Hardee availed himself of the advantages of the terrain and constructed his line following a series of creeks from the Savannah to the Little Ogeechee. All approaches to Savannah from the west, and there were only five, must cross this line. After obstructing these approaches, Hardee cut the canals and rice dikes. Then he opened the sluices and flooded the fields, submerging the entire front of the Confederate line with from three to six feet of water.[27]

The advantage of terrain could only assist, not replace, the human barrier. Opposed to Sherman's sixty thousand troops were only ten thousand Confederates, divided into divisions under Smith, McLaws, and Ambrose R. Wright. Wright had replaced Mercer on December 10, when the siege proper opened. Wright's presence promised experienced, capable combat leadership. He also represented powerful political support. As President of the Georgia Senate, he had taken command of the Georgia state forces east of the Oconee

---

25 Alexander Robert Chisolm, "The Failure to Capture Hardee," in *Battles and Leaders*, IV, 680; Hardee to Beauregard, December 9, 1864, in Confederate Archives; *Official Records*, LIII, 381–82.
26 Mercer Diary, December 8, 1864.
27 *Official Records*, XLIV, 277; Berry G. Benson Manuscript, in Berry Greenwood Benson Papers, 1845–1922 (Southern Historical Collection); Jones, *Siege of Savannah*, 78.

River after the fall of Milledgeville. Wright held the left of Hardee's line at Savannah with a miscellaneous force of veterans, workers, clerks, militia, and locals. His line, mounting thirty-two guns, extended for seven miles from the Little Ogeechee to Shaw's Dam.

McLaws with Hardee's best troops, held the key center position. Among the four thousand tried troops holding his four miles of trenches from Shaw's Dam to the Georgia Central Railroad crossing was the famous Orphan Brigade from Kentucky. These men knew Hardee well, and he knew that they were reliable. As their spokesman, Johnny Green, put it, "We have seen a great deal of service with [Hardee] and the men all admire him." [28]

Gustavus W. Smith held the right. Smith and Hardee had been associated during the battles around Atlanta when Smith commanded a division of Georgia militia. Smith was known in the South as a one-time engineer, manufacturer, politician, wing commander, and assistant secretary of war. His military competence was suspect. His part of the line at Savannah consisted of two and a half miles of trenches stretching from the railroad crossing to the Savannah River. To hold this line he had about two thousand militia and twenty guns.[29]

Generally Hardee's defense line centered around a tandem of earth redoubts that commanded likely avenues of approach. One or more forts had been advanced to give enfilade fire down the line. As far as possible Hardee had these forts connected with rifle trenches, two or more in depth. At points where the five main causeways entered his defenses, Hardee placed twenty-four- and thirty-two-pound cannon that easily outmatched the light Union artillery. He had drawn this heavy ordnance from the wealth of guns protecting Savannah's seaward side.[30]

When both wings of Sherman's army closed in on Hardee's defenses, he withdrew the outposts defending the Savannah and Charleston Railroad bridge and had the bridge destroyed. By this action he cut off Savannah from her normal and most important means of communication. Hardee reported to Beauregard that the enemy was all along his front and that skirmishing had begun in earnest. And he had no reserve. Hardee tried to manufacture some corps reserves by hav-

---

28 A. D. Kirwan (ed.), *Johnny Green* (Lexington, 1956), 179.
29 Jones, *Siege of Savannah*, 86, 112–13; Ezra A. Carman, *General Hardee's Escape from Savannah* (Washington, 1893), 4.
30 *Official Records*, XLIV, 57; Jones, *Siege of Savannah*, 80–85; C. S. H. Hardee, "Reminiscences."

ing McLaws withdraw a Georgia regiment from his line, hoping to replace it with more artillery. Seeking a more realistic reserve, Hardee requested that a Georgia regiment serving with Sam Jones be sent to him. Beauregard, who had taken over supervision of Jones's command, tried to procure the troops for Hardee in South Carolina but could not take away Jones's troops at the moment, for he was planning an attack on Hatch, an attack that never materialized. The following day, December 11, Hardee again called on Beauregard for troops. "I have been obliged to extend my line. It is impossible to hold it without immediate reenforcement." Hardee did receive some help at this time by the acquisition of E. C. Anderson's detached cavalry regiment and by ordering S. W. Ferguson's cavalry into the trenches.[31]

On December 10 and December 11, the skirmishing continued, and minor attacks were repelled at Shaw's Dam, at Fort Hardeman, and at Williamson's. To strengthen his right flank at Fort Hardeman and to provide cover in the event of evacuation over the river, Hardee ordered back the *Macon* and the *Sampson* from their patrol duty. On their return down the winding Savannah, Federal batteries surprised them, disabled and captured the tender *Resolute* and forced the two larger ships back up the river. This action disquieted Hardee. It deprived him of the *Sampson,* which he had intended to station at the right flank of his line to deliver supporting fire, but more important, it meant that Sherman had challenged his control of the river and might send troops to the north bank of the Savannah. In anticipation of this movement, Hardee ordered Wheeler to move his cavalry from Sherman's rear to the South Carolina side of the Savannah. With his headquarters at Hardeeville, Wheeler was to prevent the enemy from crossing.[32]

By this time little doubt existed that Savannah would ultimately have to be evacuated, but immediate evacuation did not seem imperative. The nature of Sherman's previous campaigns indicated that he would employ the most economical and certain means of approach.

31 *Official Records*, XLIV, 951–52; Hardee to Beauregard, December 10, 11, 1864, in Confederate Archives; E. C. Anderson to Roy, December 26, 1864, in George W. and Edward C. Anderson Papers, 1784–1896 (Southern Historical Collection); S. W. Ferguson Reminiscences, in Heyward-Ferguson Papers and Books, 1806–1923 (Southern Historical Collection).

32 Frobel Notes on the Siege of Savannah, in C. C. Jones Papers; Jones, *Siege of Savannah,* 117–18; Hardee to Beauregard, December 12, 1864, in Confederate Archives; Carman, *Hardee's Escape,* 12–13; Hardee to W. W. Hunter, December 12, 1864, in Savannah Squadron Papers.

At Savannah this meant that he would open a line of communications with his naval forces lying off the coast and with Foster's infantry at Hiltonhead. An attack against Hardee's lines of breastworks, arranged in depth, seemed imprudent without an established base. Sherman felt little apprehension that his quarry could escape quickly. The city had been isolated from the Confederacy except for a tenuous route by water across the Savannah. General Henry Slocum had broken the Savannah and Charleston rail communications when he moved up against the right of Hardee's line. Slocum's presence on the banks of the Savannah River also halted traffic on the river. General Howard had penetrated south to Flemingo, breaking the Gulf Railroad at that point.

The immediate obstacle preventing Sherman from opening communication with the sea was Fort McAllister, an isolated bastion dominating the Great Ogeechee River. Sherman's men already felt the need for supplies. In the Union camps even hard crackers were selling for a dollar, when they could be found. Beyond Fort McAllister were the Union fleet and great quantities of supplies, and Sherman decided to take the fort at once.[33]

The 250-man garrison expected to be attacked, but the attack was expected to come from the river, which was controlled by the garrison's guns, on exposed barbette mounts. Sherman, however, ordered Hazen's division to attack from the rear, the land side of the fort. When Hazen did so on December 13, the defenders were quickly overcome. That evening the Union army opened communications with Dahlgren's naval forces. Sherman was jubilant. Disdaining his commander's "cockiness," one of his staff officers wrote that Sherman "says the city is his sure game and stretches out his arm and claws his bony fingers in the air to illustrate how he has his grip on it." [34]

With the fall of Fort McAllister and with heavy Union siege guns coming ashore, Hardee began to feel those bony fingers. He wrote Davis, emphasizing the seriousness of the situation. Foster's force under Hatch menaced his flimsy line of communication, and Sherman was now ready to strike. "Unless assured that force sufficient to keep open my communications can be sent me, I shall be compelled to evacuate Savannah." Davis replied that no troops could be sent be-

---

33 *Memoirs of William T. Sherman, by Himself,* 2 vols. (New York, 1891), II, 193; John C. Van Duzer Diary, December 13, 1864 (Duke University Library).
34 J. C. Gray, Jr., to J. C. Ropes, December 14, 1864, in John Chipman Gray and John Codman Ropes, *War Letters, 1862-1865* (New York, 1927), 42.

cause of the critical state of affairs in Virginia. Hardee also communicated his anxiety to Beauregard. "Our occupation of Savannah depends on your ability to hold the railroad. Whenever you are unable to hold the road I must evacuate. . . . Inform me instantly if Foster is reinforced by Sherman or otherwise. I feel uneasy about my communications." [35]

A new threat materialized north of the Savannah River. Elements of Slocum's corps on the south bank of the river jumped in small numbers from island to island in the middle of the river, searching for rice and for better flank protection. A regiment was soon on Argyle Island, and Wheeler, after repelling several sorties on the north bank, admitted reluctantly that a lodgment had been made. If this lodgment grew to brigade or division strength, Hardee's last lifeline could be cut. Hardee also had serious trouble at this main defense line. A mutiny had occurred in the Foreign Battalion that he himself had recruited with care. Fortunately, the mutiny exposed itself prematurely and was easily put down. Hardee dealt with the situation summarily, executing seven ringleaders on the spot and shipping the battalion immediately to Florence, South Carolina. In exasperation he urged that similar efforts to enlist foreign troops be prohibited.[36]

On December 16, Hardee called his generals together for a council of war. Most of the generals agreed that Savannah should be evacuated as soon as the pontoon bridge had been completed. General P. M. B. Young, fresh from the Army of Northern Virginia, was ordered by Hardee to collect rice flats along the Savannah to be used in the construction of the bridge. Young reminded Hardee that he had intended to attack the enemy lodged on the north side of the river the next morning. Hardee replied that the assault "was of no importance" compared with procuring the rice flats. With difficulty Young gathered the flats and also managed to deliver an effective attack.[37]

While the Confederates attacked the enemy fragments that had roamed across the river, the Federal commanders prepared for the assault of Hardee's main line. They constructed fascines, stringers, and ladders, all the while skirmishing constantly to develop the weak points in the Confederate line. Larger guns brought by boat from Hiltonhead and the presence of the navy assured additional artillery

35 *Official Records*, XLIV, 960; Davis to Hardee, December 17, 1864, in Rowland (ed.), *Jefferson Davis*, VI, 421.
36 Carman, *Hardee's Escape*, 13 ff.; Mercer Diary, December 15, 1864; Jones, *Siege of Savannah*, 138; *Official Records*, XLIV, 966, Ser. II, Vol. VII, 1268.
37 P. M. B. Young to C. C. Jones, n.d., in C. C. Jones Papers; *Official Records*, XLIV, 962–63; Carman, *Hardee's Escape*, 20.

support. Fully confident of success, Sherman demanded Hardee's surrender on December 17. He told Hardee that a supply base had been established and that he had guns large enough to reduce the city. ". . . I have for some days held and controlled every avenue by which the people and garrison of Savannah can be supplied. . . ." He would be willing to grant reasonable terms, but if he was forced to resort to assaults or a prolonged siege, he would "make little effort to restrain [his] army burning to avenge." [38]

Hardee waited before replying to Sherman. Beauregard arrived, and the two discussed plans for the evacuation and the subsequent disposition of the troops. On December 19 Hardee, in the frozen language that he could command so well, wrote to Sherman refusing to surrender. He stated that his two lines of defense still remained intact, that Sherman did not have any troops nearer than four miles to the city, and that in spite of Sherman's efforts, he still was in touch daily with Charleston. In reply to Sherman's threat Hardee answered, "I have hitherto conducted the military operations entrusted to my direction in strict accordance with the rules of civilized warfare, and I should deeply regret the adoption of any course by you that may force me to deviate from them in the future." [39]

December 19, 1864, should have been evacuation day for the Confederate forces. Everything, however, depended on the completion of the pontoon bridge, which had been delayed by fogs, ships running aground, and many other unpredictable factors. During the day the enemy attacked on A. R. Wright's front, but was repulsed.[40] On the north side of the river the enemy forces became aggressive as they grew in numbers. The Union regiments there attacked and drove back a Confederate cavalry brigade, establishing themselves at Izard's—much closer to the Confederate line of retreat. Hardee crossed the river to observe the fighting. The situation looked critical, and he wired General Taliaferro in Charleston to come to Hardeeville with what men he had. Hardee also sent Wheeler about seven hundred men and six guns, cautioning that "the road to Hardeeville must be kept open at all hazards." [41]

38 Jones, *Siege of Savannah*, 139–40.
39 *Ibid.*, 141–42; *Naval Records*, Ser. I, Vol. XVI, 484; *Official Records*, XLIV, 964–65.
40 A. R. Wright to Roy, January 20, 1865, in Confederate Archives Miscellany.
41 Jones, *Siege of Savannah*, 145; Hardee to Beauregard, December 19, 1864, in Confederate Archives; Carman, *Hardee's Escape*, 23–25; *Official Records*, XLIV, 967–69.

Until the moment the formal siege began, or perhaps even later, Hardee seems to have entertained the idea of evacuating Savannah by boat.[42] The limited number of craft, accentuated by the fact that Slocum had turned back the *Macon* and the *Sampson*, relegated this plan to the status of an alternate, and Hardee gave priority to the completion of the bridge. About thirty rice flats seventy to eighty feet long were fastened end to end and covered with timber ripped from the Savannah wharves.[43] To supplement the inadequate engineer companies, Georgia militia and Confederate sailors provided the necessary working parties. The bridge spanned the Savannah River in three sections. The first segment ran from the city to Hutchinson's Island, then across that island by causeway to the second bridge, which spanned the middle of the river to Pennyworth Island. A road across Pennyworth Island connected with the third span, which reached across the Black River to Screven's Ferry. On December 13, when Fort McAllister fell, Hardee had completed the bridge only as far as Hutchinson's Island. When the enemy appeared in increasing numbers on the north side of the river, Hardee decided to build a floating dock on the north side of Hutchinson's Island and to complete the crossing by ferry, but he discarded this plan when Sherman did not press his riverhead advantage on the north side of the Savannah. Throughout the period of construction the Confederate navy protected and concealed the pontoon bridge from the enemy. It is plausible to assume, however, that Sherman knew that it was being built or at least expected it to be built. The engineers completed the bridge about nine o'clock on the night of December 19. If it had been completed a few hours earlier, Hardee would have evacuated Savannah that night.[44]

December 20, 1864, was a day of suspense for the Confederates. The men knew that the city would be evacuated and anxiously awaited the

42 Frobel Notes on the Siege of Savannah in C. C. Jones Papers; Hardee to J. G. Clarke in Pierre Gustave Toutant Beauregard Papers, 1854–93 (Duke University Library).
43 This unusual and unstable method was adopted because the Confederates could obtain only half the number of boats that would have been necessary to complete the bridge with pontoons perpendicular to the bridge, the customary procedure.
44 Frobel Notes on the Siege of Savannah, in C. C. Jones Papers; J. G. Clarke to Beauregard, April 6, 1875, quoted in Beauregard to C. C. Jones, April 13, 1875, in C. C. Jones Papers; Hardee to J. G. Clarke, December 13, 1864, in P. G. T. Beauregard Papers (Duke); *Naval Records*, Ser. I, Vol. XVI, 484; Jones, *Siege of Savannah*, 113–34.

order. On the main defense line the Union soldiers were kept pinned
down in their trenches all day, as the Confederates fired lavishly,
using the surplus ammunition they knew would have to be destroyed
if it was not expended. Early in the day Hardee visited the South
Carolina shore and found that Ezra Carman's Union brigade had
crossed the river and engaged Wheeler's cavalry. With his communication line in jeopardy, Hardee ordered Taliaferro to furnish Wheeler
with all the men he called for. To further agitate the Confederate
commander, news arrived that advanced enemy units under Foster
had penetrated to within three fourths of a mile of the Savannah and
Charleston Railroad at Pocotalago. Fortunately for Hardee, Foster's
advance lacked the finality that Sherman wished. On this very day
Sherman had decided to reinforce Foster's troops with one of his divisions. The united force would then move on the Savannah and
Charleston Railroad and place themselves athwart Hardee's escape
route.[45]

Hardee knew only too well that he must act quickly to avert destruction of his command. His orders, based on the experience gained
in the Atlanta campaign, called for the customary night withdrawal.
Prior to moving his troops and artillery, Hardee directed that all the
army wagons and caissons be sent across the bridges.[46] A confidential
circular outlined the troop movement. The light artillery would be
pulled by hand to the bridges and sent across before the men left their
trenches. Troops at outlying posts, such as Forts Jackson and Bartow,
would assemble at 9 P.M. and move by steamer to Screven's Ferry. At
the nearer forts, such as Rosedew and Beaulieu, the men would withdraw at dusk, march into the city and over the bridge. Hardee would
begin uncovering the main line from the left, with the troops having
the longest distance to cover. This force, A. R. Wright's division,
would pull out of the trenches at 8 P.M., McLaws' division at 10 P.M.,
and Smith's at 11 P.M. The division skirmish lines would be strengthened and left in position for about two hours after their parent units
had left. After the skirmishers had crossed, Colonel Clarke of Hardee's
staff would destroy the pontoon bridge. All powder to be abandoned
would be destroyed by dousing it with water; ammunition would be
dumped into the river, and the numerous heavy guns that must be

45 Berry G. Benson Manuscript, in Benson Papers; P. M. B. Young to C. C.
    Jones, n.d., in C. C. Jones Papers; *Official Records*, XLIV, 6–7, 450–51, 973;
    Carman, *Hardee's Escape*, 26–27; Gray to Ropes, December 14, 1864, in Gray
    and Ropes, *War Letters*, 42; D. H. Poole to L. McLaws, December 19, 1864,
    in Lafayette McLaws Papers, 1861–65, Record Group 109.
46 Roy to McLaws, December 20, 1864, in McLaws Papers.

left would be spiked at the exact time their division withdrew from the line.[47]

Hardee had worked out the plans for the disposition of the naval force with Beauregard on December 18. The *Isandiga* and *Firefly* would proceed up the river to join Commodore Hunter near Augusta. The *Georgia* would be scuttled. The *Savannah* would cover the evacuation, wait two days to protect the rear of the army and the stores at Screven's Ferry, and then proceed to sea.[48]

During the morning of December 20, Union troops on the South Carolina side of the river witnessed a scene that they never forgot. Over the pontoons, it seemed, came the entire civilian population of Savannah, "wagons, family carriages, men and women on foot. . . . The stream of fugitives and number of carriages and wagons increased as the day wore on." To discourage Carman's troops from molesting this procession, Hardee strongly reinforced Wheeler's line just to the west of the line of retreat. Next he subjected the Union soldiers to a bombardment from the *Savannah,* which steamed up to their flank.[49]

While the cavalry and navy held Carman in check, the infantry in the main line began their withdrawal on schedule. Preceded by forty-nine pieces of artillery, the three divisions retired without incident. The last, Smith's division, began crossing at 1 A.M. When Smith had passed over the bridge, rockets were fired to inform the forts down by the sea that the city had been evacuated. Hardee himself, with most of his staff, crossed the river on the steamer *Swan* about 9 P.M. He left one staff officer behind with a detail "to preserve order" in Savannah until the last possible moment and to be certain that no skirmishers had been left behind. Hardee had to leave behind many of his sick and wounded also, because he could not provide transportation for them.[50]

Despite the precautions taken to ensure a minimum of noise, the wind carried the grinding and the rumbling of the wagons up the river to the Union positions. When General Carman informed his superiors, he was told "not to risk interference with the movement, as [the Confederates] would be cut off from above," that is by Foster.

47 *Official Records,* XLIV, 967.
48 *Ibid.,* 965; *Naval Records,* Ser. I, Vol. XVI, 482. The *Isandiga* ran aground and had to be burned. The *Firefly* met the same fate after doing good service in ferrying material. The several ships under construction in the city had to be burned also.
49 Carman, *Hardee's Escape,* 27.
50 Frobel Notes on the Siege of Savannah, in C. C. Jones Papers; C. S. H. Hardee, "Reminiscences"; Jones, *Siege of Savannah,* 162.

Many of the Confederates also expected to be cut off. There seems to have been some confusion, some units became tangled, and everyone appeared to be ill-humored. It was a bitter moment; many of the Savannah garrison were leaving not only their long-held military post but their homes as well. The fires of the burning ships gave the whole column a garish appearance. As one Confederate noted, "The constant tread of the troops and the rumblings of the artillery as they poured over those long floating bridges was a sad sound, and by the glare of the large fires at the east of the bridge it seemed like an immense funeral procession stealing out of the city in the dead of night." [51]

The solemnity of the Confederate evacuation contrasted sharply with the exuberance of the triumphant Federals. Sherman exemplified the attitude of his troops when he presented Savannah to President Lincoln as a Christmas present. And the Confederates had left some presents for Sherman himself. Although most of the movable war material had been carried away, the heavy guns and equipment represented a rich prize, for over two hundred guns fell into Union hands. To their amazement Sherman's soldiers uncovered an even richer prize: at least thirty-five thousand bales of cotton, negotiable anywhere at top prices. This cotton caused the pulses of merchants and speculators throughout the North to quicken and brought droves of "seekers" to Savannah. [52]

Why had Hardee failed to destroy the cotton? This the Confederate House of Representatives demanded of Davis, and this in turn Davis demanded of Hardee. [53] The cotton was of great economic benefit to the enemy, and the general who neglected to destroy it had a brother, Noble Andrew Hardee, who was a prominent Savannah cotton merchant. Hardee replied:

The cotton was distributed throughout the city in cellars, garrets and warehouses, where it could not have been burnt without destroying the city. It had not been sent off by railroad previous to the cutting of the road, because railroad transportation was monopolized for removal of ordnance, commissary, and other important Government stores. From the cutting of the road to the evacuation of the city—twelve days—every man was required to work on the lines, and every wagon, dray and cart that could be impressed was needed to keep the troops in a line twelve

51 Carman, *Hardee's Escape*, 29; J. B. Elliott to his mother, January 10, 1865, in Habersham-Elliott Papers, 1863–85 (Southern Historical Collection).
52 Sherman, *Memoirs*, II, 231; *Official Records*, XLIV, 63–65; George Winston Smith, "Cotton from Savannah in 1865," in *Journal of Southern History*, XXI (November, 1955), 495–96.
53 *Official Records*, LIII, 413.

miles long supplied with ordnance and commissary stores. Not a man nor a woman could have been spared to collect the cotton in a place where it could have been burnt.[54]

When one reflects on the use of trains by the harried Confederates during the last few weeks the road was in operation, and the necessity not only to prevent the destruction of the town but to avoid alerting the enemy, Hardee's answer seems self-evident. The suggestion that the financial interests of his brother influenced him is inconsistent with Hardee's scrupulous integrity. Furthermore, the commissary and ordnance stores salvaged from Savannah prolonged Confederate military resistance more than any amount of cotton could have.

General Josiah Gorgas and others criticized Hardee also for the sacrifice of Fort McAllister, and this criticism, too, merits closer scrutiny. Why did Hardee leave the fort exposed and fail to recall the garrison in time? Or, if Hardee knew, as he should have known, that the Great Ogeechee was Sherman's most feasible line of communication, why did he fail to strengthen the garrison and make a determined effort to hold the position? Charles C. Jones, the historian of the Savannah siege, believed that Hardee hoped that a "bold retention" of the fort might lead Sherman to hesitate, perhaps to give up the idea of establishing a base near Savannah or even of attacking Savannah. Jones admits, however, that this thin reasoning hardly justifies the loss of the garrison.[55] Two other factors should be considered. First, Hardee, who had an intimate knowledge of the terrain, probably believed, as did others, that Sherman could not maneuver a large assaulting body through the supposedly impassable area around the Great Ogeechee. Here, as later, Hardee appears to have underestimated the ability of Sherman's men in overcoming natural obstacles. Second, and most important, Hardee probably had little choice. If he abandoned the fort, Sherman got his line of communication gratis; if he reinforced the fort, he would weaken a line already bare of reserves and hardly strong enough to withstand a determined attack by a Union corps.

Could Sherman have captured Hardee's army in Savannah? It is doubtful that Sherman could have cut off this body of ten thousand men unless he had planted at least a strong army corps across Hardee's line of retreat after the siege had opened. To have attempted the movement earlier would have enabled Hardee to evade him rapidly

54 Hardee to Cooper, February 6, 1865, in Telegrams Received, Adjutant General's office.
55 Jones, *Siege of Savannah*, 107–108.

and fairly easily by going up the coast line by rail while Bragg applied pressure against Sherman's left flank. Sherman hesitated to place a body of men across Hardee's communications once the siege had begun, for he feared that Hardee might crush an isolated force with his advantage of interior lines. Sherman also worried about the Confederate ships that commanded the vital stretch of the Savannah River and the soft, marshy ground just across the river on the South Carolina side.[56]

Actually, Sherman's primary objective appears to have been not Hardee's army but a base on the Atlantic. After securing this base, he then prepared steadily for the destruction of his opponent. The real criticism of Sherman comes in the question of timing. Surely he and Foster could have arranged to attack the railroad at Pocotalago in force sooner than they did. Hardee, however, with a large segment of his pontoon bridge completed and a sizable number of steamers on hand probably could have evacuated most of the garrison as early as December 17. The methodical Sherman risked the escape of his foe so that he might establish his base. Once it had been established, he would be able to close in on Hardee with the number of variables reduced to a minimum.

Although credit for the successful evacuation must be given to Hardee, Beauregard's contributions should not be overlooked. Beauregard remained in general control of the operation throughout. It was he who made the basic decision placing the army's welfare above the city's. He sketched the general plan for the line and method of retreat, checking constantly with Hardee to ensure that the details had been worked out properly. Most important, perhaps, he gave Hardee additional troops when they were desperately needed and dispatched the men necessary to keep the line of retreat open.

In light of Beauregard's contributions and the conclusion that Sherman might not have been able to cut off all of Hardee's garrison if he had made a supreme effort, how can Hardee be justified in stating, "Tho' compelled to evacuate the city, there is no part of my military life to which I look back with so much satisfaction"? [57]

The value of Beauregard's contributions and the fact of Sherman's

56 Sherman, *Memoirs*, II, 216; Gray to Ropes, December 14, 1864, in Gray and Ropes, *War Letters*, 42; *Official Records*, XLIV, 6-7.
57 Hardee to C. C. Jones, May 14, 1866, in Georgia Portfolio, n.d. (Duke University Library); author's interview with Mrs. Howard Bowen, August 5, 1957.

slim hope of success both are based on the assumption that Hardee had immediate operational control of the Savannah forces and would conduct the withdrawal with his proven excellence in this type of endeavor. As the commander of this garrison he went beyond his traditional successful retreat in the face of the enemy. He had to. Never had he operated so close to the enemy with troops so limited in both numbers and quality. He displayed a signal aptitude in improvisation and in utilization of terrain and resources. Sherman's men marveled at the Confederate battery that had been mounted on a railroad car; it was moved from one front to another with celerity, firing accurately into exposed groups of men and generally harassing the Union army. Hardee should be credited for the novel technique of employing ships not only to hinder Union troop movements but to guard land features and to serve as mobile forts on the Confederate right flank. This close integration of naval and land forces represents one of the finest displays of joint operations by a Confederate commander during the war. The nature and location of Hardee's main defense position demonstrates his skill in using his terrain advantageously, for the flooded rice fields and canals effectively offset the disparity in numbers of men. Hardee's main line evoked admiring comments from friend and foe alike and gave great assurance to the many untried defenders.

In assembling the Savannah garrison and giving it a combat efficiency quite disproportionate to its surface capabilities, Hardee displayed once again his talent for getting the maximum yield from his human resources. His confident and decisive manner pervaded all ranks, giving his militia, laborers, clerks, dismounted cavalry, and the others faith in themselves and the troops next to them. Through two weeks of constant skirmishing and periodic attacks both officers and men handled themselves effectively. Smith and Wright exhibited a steadiness and consistency that was remarkable in light of their spotted military backgrounds. McLaws and Wheeler behaved in a manner that rivaled better performances in the salad days of their careers.

To have removed the large civilian group, the war matériel, and ten thousand men from the presence of sixty thousand veteran troops commanded by one of the ablest Civil War commanders represents one of Hardee's finest achievements. After 10:30 P.M. December 20, one enemy assault in only division strength might have disrupted the evacuation and resulted in the capture of most of the garrison. To minimize this risk Hardee ensured secrecy by destroying ordnance silently, by muffling cannon wheels, and by establishing strong skirmish lines. The orders upon which the withdrawal was based were detailed and precise, providing for the most expeditious movement of troops. This scrupulous regard for proper planning prevented the blundering, panic, and disaster that in one form or another occurred in the evacuations of Corinth, Nashville, New Orleans, and other cities. Thus in getting the maximum performance out of his nondescript force, in utilizing his terrain, and in conducting a skillful retirement in the face of an overwhelming opponent, Hardee's accomplishment could justifiably be a source of satisfaction to him.

While the infantry column labored on its way to Hardeeville, the navy remained behind with army details to forward the stores deposited at Screven's Ferry. The gunboat *Savannah* discouraged any Union attempt to molest the removal of these stores, but was unable then to escape to sea through the obstacle-choked waterways. When the last supplies had been started inland, Hardee ordered the remaining men to burn the wharf, the steamer *Firefly*, the *Isandiga*, and the *Savannah*. For the second night in succession the water around Savannah reflected the lurid glare of burning vessels.[58]

The Confederate army, followed by the navy detachments on foot, arrived at the railroad in Hardeeville disgruntled and half frozen. The first men to arrive mounted the water tanks, smashed the thick layers of ice, and formed relays to pass the water over to the locomotives' boilers. Hardee assigned priorities to the units and dispatched them toward their destinations as quickly as he could. At this time Hardee released the volunteer battalions of workers from the Macon and Augusta war factories and all the men that he had forced into the army at Savannah.[59]

Hardee departed on December 22, leaving McLaws in command and instructing him to expedite the shipment of the supplies and troops to Charleston.[60] With the garrison and supplies deposited safely in South Carolina, the troops distributed, and a new defense line being drawn behind the Combahee River, Hardee made his way to Charleston to set that house in order before the uninvited arrived.

---

58 Hardee to Beauregard, December 21, 1864, in Confederate Archives; *Naval Records*, Ser. I, Vol. XVI, 484; Pickett, *Hardee*, 42.
59 C. S. H. Hardee, "Reminiscences"; Hardee to Beauregard, December 21, 1864, in Confederate Archives; *Official Records*, LIII, 38.
60 Roy to McLaws, December 22, 1864, McLaws to wife, December 27, 1864, in McLaws Papers.

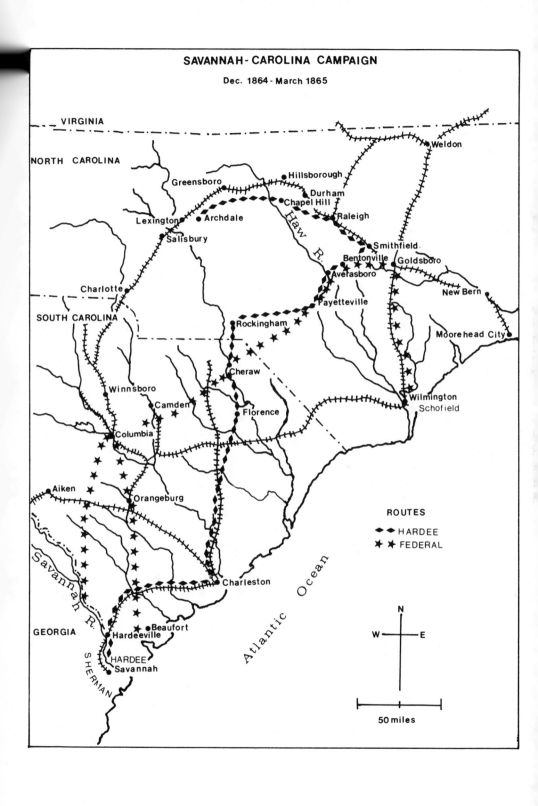

SAVANNAH-CAROLINA CAMPAIGN

Dec. 1864 - March 1865

VIRGINIA

NORTH CAROLINA

Weldon

Greensboro

Hillsborough

Durham

Chapel Hill

Lexington

Archdale

Raleigh

Salisbury

Smithfield

Bentonville

Goldsboro

Averasboro

Charlotte

Fayetteville

New Bern

SOUTH CAROLINA

Rockingham

Moorehead City

Cheraw

Winnsboro

Camden

Florence

Wilmington
Schofield

Columbia

Aiken

Orangeburg

ROUTES

◆ ◆ HARDEE

★ ★ FEDERAL

Charleston

Atlantic Ocean

Savannah R.

GEORGIA

Beaufort

Hardeeville

N

W — E

S

HARDEE

Savannah

SHERMAN

50 miles

XV

Death March of the Confederation

CHARLESTON LOOKED confident. Confederate flags floated cockily from a multitude of masts; Fort Sumter appeared stronger than ever— ready to resist a ten-year siege if necessary. Mary Hardee and the girls tried to imprison their returned hero, allowing him out of their sight only with reluctance, but they had to compete with the call of departmental headquarters. Inside that building the specter of defeat could not be dispelled. No one waited eagerly for messages coming over the telegraph. Reality whispered over the wires and stared up at Hardee from the maps and muster rolls. Even with the salvage of the Savannah garrison, the defense of South Carolina depended upon an inadequate force of about 20,000 men. Wheeler's cavalry comprised 5,000 of this number; the three infantry divisions under A. R. Wright, Taliaferro, and McLaws numbered 2,000, 4,600 and 7,000 respectively. In addition Hardee had an insignificant number bound together in demibrigades and 1,500 Georgia militia under General G. W. Smith at Augusta. In February, 1865, as the military situation deteriorated, Governor Brown of Georgia would add to the general disillusionment by resuming command of the Georgia militia and returning the men to their farms. Furthermore, Wright's division, as such, would vanish when General Cooper ordered all of the Augusta and Macon workers back to their factories.[1]

In a review of his manpower Hardee told Davis that he would need a force of fifteen thousand additional men "operating outside of Charleston's defenses"; or at least five thousand regulars to maintain the line now held. Governor Andrew G. Magrath of South Carolina had promised five thousand state troops, but Hardee doubted he could

1 *Official Records,* XLIV, 1004, 1005, XLVII, Pt. 2, p. 984.

provide them, or even any reinforcements. In his desperation for troops Hardee violated his own experience and began once again to recruit from the Union prisoners.[2]

To increase the effectiveness of his troops Hardee proceeded to reorganize his command. He placed all of the cavalry in three divisions, and he armed the Charleston artillerymen with rifles, gave them long hours of infantry drill, and then brigaded them as infantry.[3]

To further increase the impact of his small force Hardee arranged his men in what he hoped would be a deadly defensive coil. Wheeler stayed along the New River and the Savannah River, watching Sherman and acting as the outer rim of the coil. McLaws' division would constitute Hardee's main line of resistance along the Salkehatchie River. To support McLaws and to lengthen the Salkehatchie line to the ocean, Hardee used Wright's division. Taliaferro remained near Charleston, guarding that gold nugget. For his strategic reserve, Hardee had only General James Conner's North Carolina brigade, recently sent from Lee's army. To provide depth for his departmental defenses, Hardee appealed both to Governor Magrath and to G. W. Smith to begin a concentration of reserves at Branchville, a critical South Carolina railroad junction.

In his preparation for defense against an invasion, Hardee directed his cavalry to strip the countryside near the Combahee River. He re-established the navy patrols on the Savannah under Commodore Hunter. To prepare for a campaign of maneuver Hardee set up supply depots at central points in his department.[4]

To simplify the command situation in South Carolina, President Davis transferred Beauregard to the West. Before he departed, Beauregard left instructions with Hardee for the defense of the department. He emphasized that preparations must be made for the evacuation of Charleston, and he urged the War Department to extend Hardee's control to include Augusta, which was done.

2 *Ibid.*, XLIV, 1004, XLVII, Pt. 2, pp. 999–1000, Ser. IV, Vol. III, 1083.
3 Hardee to Cooper, February 8, 1865, in Telegrams Received, Adjutant General's Office; Charles Colcock Jones, Jr., "A Century at the Guns, History of the Gallant Chatham Artillery," in Savannah *Daily Morning News,* May 3, 1886; *Official Records,* XLVII, Pt. 2, pp. 980, 999–1000.
4 *Official Records,* XLIV, pp. 991, 995–1002, 1008, XLVII, Pt. 2, pp. 980–89, 999–1000.
   While Hardee and Sherman were preparing for one another's destruction, they co-operated very well in transporting the Savannah refugees to Charleston. Hardee again utilized Hunter's naval forces in this domestic combined operation.

The War Department also assisted Hardee by ordering the transfer of troops from Hood's shattered Army of Tennessee and by sending the fiery and capable D. H. Hill, who had been sitting out the war since Chickamauga. Hardee, nevertheless, had no illusions about his ability to defend South Carolina against Sherman. To Davis he stated, "I am acting strictly on the defensive, and unless heavily re-enforced must continue to do so." He added that without a mobile force of fifteen thousand men he could not conduct a reliable defense.[5]

Davis sent Hardee's letter at once to R. E. Lee for comment. Lee replied, "The dispositions made by Gen Hardee appear to me to be judicious, and as far as I can judge at this distance, the line he proposes to hold is the best. All he wants is sufficient troops." [6] Thus fortified, Davis approved Hardee's plans and told him that he was rushing help from Hood's army. He urged Hardee to "use all means to obtain men from Georgia." [7]

Georgia, however, could or would provide little help beyond the troops of G. W. Smith. Indeed, she continued to call on Hardee for help. Enemy raids in the southern part of the state resulted in keeping one of Hardee's cavalry divisions south of the Savannah River. Farther south in Florida, Brigadier General William Miller seemed preoccupied with removing railroad iron instead of trying to relieve the pressure on Hardee. To ensure competent management of affairs in that state and to gain more co-operation there, Hardee transferred the experienced Sam Jones to Florida.

While Hardee labored to strengthen and reorganize his command, his adversary Sherman remained quietly in Savannah for nearly two weeks after its capture. Then, early in January, Sherman pushed forward one division of the Twentieth Corps toward Hardeeville. He followed this movement by massing the bulk of Howard's wing at Beaufort, South Carolina, on McLaws' left flank. On January 13 Howard advanced upon McLaws at Pocotalago. The alarmed McLaws reported to Hardee that he was retiring to the north bank of the Salkehatchie River. As Howard continued to move in force, Hardee decided to have Wheeler guard the river crossings while McLaws moved along the north bank paralleling Howard's march.

While Howard moved directly across the front of the Salkehatchie

5 *Official Records*, XLVII, Pt. 2, pp. 999–1000.
6 R. E. Lee to Davis, January 10, 1865, in Robert Edward Lee, *Lee's Dispatches*, ed. Douglas Southall Freeman (New York, 1915), 314.
7 *Official Records*, XLVII, Pt. 2, pp. 999–1000.

line, Slocum had been crossing the swollen Savannah River. Howard's maneuvers masked those of Slocum nicely, and the Confederates could only guess Sherman's intentions. Hardee thought that Sherman's objective was Branchville, but McLaws believed that it was Charleston. Sherman encouraged McLaws' misconception by feinting toward the Confederates at the Salkehatchie bridge to "make Hardee believe I am coming straight for Charleston." Sherman also ordered heavy demonstrations along the seaboard near Charleston.[8]

As soon as it became evident that Sherman had mounted a major offensive in South Carolina, President Davis took action. He ordered Beauregard to hurry to bring the troops from the Army of Tennessee and to take command once again in South Carolina. Davis could not detach any more troops from Lee's army, so he turned to Georgia, but Governor Brown contended that he had no available men to send.[9] To deepen the seriousness of the situation, news came on January 17 that Fort Fisher had fallen. Wilmington's fall would only be a matter of time. The alarmed Governor Magrath, aware of Beauregard's intention to hold Charleston only so long as militarily feasible, visited Hardee in Charleston. Hardee's logic led to the stern conclusion that Charleston must fall unless heavily reinforced. Magrath then turned to Davis and pleaded with him to send Hardee more troops, stating that Charleston, not Richmond, was the heart of the Confederacy. Magrath also turned to Governors Brown of Georgia and Vance of North Carolina asking for aid.[10]

The desperation of the South Carolinians prompted a letter from Hardee to Davis: "The people of Charleston, tho' in many respects to be admired, are so entirely wrapped up in their own State and City as to be unmindful of the wants of other portions of our country—to them Charleston is the Confederacy, and to save Charleston they are willing that Lee should give up Richmond, or any other section of the Confederacy so their selfish ambition might be gratified." [11]

By February 2, Sherman's entire army had crossed the Savannah River and was advancing rapidly in two columns. Howard's column

8 *Ibid.*, XLIV, 994, XLVII, Pt. 1, pp. 18, 1067–68, Pt. 2, pp. 125, 1014–16, 1019, 1034; Cobb to Hardee, January 10, 1865, in Howell Cobb Letterbooks, 1861–65 (University of Georgia Library).

9 J. E. Brown to Beauregard, February 24, 1865, in Joseph Emerson Brown Papers, 1850–94 (Georgia State Department of Archives and History).

10 A. G. Magrath to Davis, January 29, 1865, in Jefferson Davis Letters, 1808–89 (Emory University Library).

11 Hardee to Davis, January 29, 1865, in Jefferson Davis Papers, 1851–90 (Duke University Library).

threatened Augusta and the railroad junction at Branchville; Slocum's column could strike either Branchville or Charleston, or could support Howard. Sherman had completely abandoned his base at Savannah. Beauregard and Hardee dryly noted in their dispatches to Davis that Sherman, unlike orthodox opponents, had no real lines of communications.[12]

Once Sherman's troops crossed the Savannah, they quickly outflanked McLaws' inadequate command at River's Bridge, a movement that undid the Salkehatchie line, and as a result the Confederate strong points rumbled down like stacks of toy blocks. After the loss of this primary defense line, the Confederates had to play Sherman's game and contend with fluid warfare in the Carolinas.

The second week in February, 1865, saw the continuing deterioration of the military situation. Sherman's relentless advance prevented the Confederates from concentrating to defend the South Carolina Railroad; Carter Stevenson's line along the South Edisto River, which protected Columbia, crumpled by February 9. Time and time again the Confederates took defensive positions only to be outflanked by Sherman's heavier and faster moving forces. The Confederate army in South Carolina became so stretched that it could not seriously impede Sherman. As the strain proved unremitting, Confederate communications, supply, and command broke down. Moreover, the menace of Sherman's advance was heightened by strikes near Charleston by the Union amphibious command under Foster.[13]

Finally, Beauregard and Hardee recognized the hopelessness of the situation and decided on February 14 to abandon Charleston. When informed, Davis initially refused to allow the garrison to withdraw, yet he too ultimately yielded to the iron logic of military necessity, and on February 17 the Confederates withdrew.[14]

12 *Official Records*, XLVII, Pt. 2, p. 1085; Hardee to Beauregard, February 4, 1865, in Confederate States of America Archives.
    For a detailed account of Hardee's defense of South Carolina against Sherman see Hughes, "Hardee, C.S.A.," 502–37. For a general account of the campaign see John Gilchrist Barrett, *Sherman's March Through the Carolinas* (Chapel Hill, 1956).

13 Dahlgren, *Memoir*, 497; John Johnson, *The Defense of Charleston Harbor* (Charleston, 1890), 250–51; *Official Records*, XLVII, Pt. 2, pp. 1167, 1169. The diversion at Bull's Bay represents the last of the series planned by Sherman, Foster, and Dahlgren. During February, 1865, Union amphibious forces entered the Edisto, Toogoodoo, Wadmalaw, and Combahee rivers and threatened landings in force. The feints at James Island and Bull's Bay were the most serious.

14 *Official Records*, XLVII, Pt. 2, pp. 1181, 1201–1204.

As at Savannah, Hardee conducted a successful evacuation of the garrison and most of the transportable war material, but he had to abandon great quantities of munitions, precious machinery, and raw materials.[15] The political and psychological loss of Charleston was incalculable. For many, the war was over when the city fell. Governor Magrath darkly prophesied, "I tell you now that the retreat from Charleston will be the . . . death march of the Confederation." [16]

As Hardee's men marched north from Charleston, he received news of the fall of Columbia. Beauregard, confused by Sherman's open movements that threatened several key points simultaneously, directed Hardee to hasten to Greensboro, North Carolina. The most expeditious route was by way of Wilmington, but Bragg reported that the enemy would momentarily sever the railroad there, so Hardee proceeded by way of Cheraw.[17] As Hardee's men crossed the Santee River, uncertainty, panic, and the news of Sherman's depredations caused desertions to sweep through the ranks like a brush fire. Indeed, some of Hardee's South Carolina units had to be disbanded. Further inroads into Hardee's manpower were made when Governor Magrath withdrew the South Carolina militia to repel a Union cavalry raid and when Governor Brown ordered his Georgia militia home to the "agricultural field." One of Hardee's division commanders, A. R. Wright, decided to attend the meeting of the Georgia legislature; another Georgia general officer, Hugh Mercer, had to report to Macon to General Cobb. With these personnel losses, Hardee again decided to reorganize his command. He broke up Wright's division, parceling out the brigades to McLaws and Taliaferro. Hardee's force now constituted two divisions of five thousand men each.[18]

Many of the men who deserted from Hardee's command believed that they were already cut off by Sherman, and the over-all military situation seemed to support such a view. Wade Hampton reported on February 22 that Sherman appeared to be turning eastward. If Sherman did so, Hardee would be pinned between the forces of Sherman and those of Schofield in Wilmington. No one knew Sherman's

---

15 *Ibid.*, Pt. 1, pp. 1008, 1021; Roy Diary, February 19, 1865.
16 A. G. Magrath to Hardee, January 11, 1865, quoted in Charles Edward Cauthen, *South Carolina Goes to War, 1860–1865* (Vol. XXXII of *The James Sprunt Studies in History and Political Science*, ed. Fletcher Melvin Green, Chapel Hill, 1950), 224.
17 W. D. Pickett Memorandum, February 22, 1865, in Hardee Papers (Duke); Hardee, "Memoranda."
18 Roy Diary, February 20–22, 1865.

destination, and reports like Hampton's drifted in all too seldom. Actually, Sherman had advanced north of Columbia to Winnsboro and then sharply veered to the east toward Cheraw. His army was delayed for a few days at the Wateree River by floods, but as soon as the water subsided, the men pressed on.

Working to the Confederates' advantage was the fact that Sherman did not know Hardee's location or his strength. Likewise, Hardee learned nothing of Sherman's movements for days, because his telegraph and railroad communications with Bragg, Beauregard, and "everywhere" had been broken. To hinder Hardee further, he found "the rolling stock of a half dozen R. Rs & the prisoners at Florence upon our hands. No outlet for either." Yet one note of assurance came, the word that Foster, who had been pursuing him from Charleston, had turned back. The last of Hardee's troops finally crossed the Santee on February 25, and on the same day Hardee and advance elements of McLaws' division reached Cheraw. More desertions occurred on the march from the Santee to Cheraw. The unseasoned Charleston garrison troops suffered greatly from exposure, disease, and fatigue. None of those troops would ever forget the short rations, the endless corduroying of roads, and their thirst in the pine forest.[19]

One event had occurred, however, that cheered the spirits of the veterans, at least: Joseph E. Johnston had been appointed commander of the forces opposing Sherman. Lee, who had been responsible for Johnston's appointment, ordered him to "concentrate all available forces and drive back Sherman." Johnston was a military realist. He replied at once, "It is too late to expect me to concentrate troops capable of driving back Sherman. The remnant of the Army of Tennessee is much divided. So are the other troops." But he was also a conscientious, loyal soldier. Knowing that his task was futile, he worked with great vigor.

Meanwhile, the bulk of Johnston's troops were straining to escape Sherman's clutches. When Hardee learned that Sherman had turned toward Cheraw, he rushed to assemble his troops. He pushed out McLaws to slow the enemy advance while the rear came up from Florence.

By March 2, as Sherman's two wings closed on Cheraw, Hardee's position became untenable. To his rear was the Pee Dee River, with

19 *Official Records*, XLVII, Pt. 2, p. 584; Roy Diary, February 21, 1865; Luis Fenollosa Emilio, *History of the Fifty-fourth Regiment of Massachusetts Volunteer Infantry, 1863–1865* (2d ed.; Boston, 1894).

only one narrow bridge; to the north at Chesterfield, the sound of infantry fighting; to his front, Howard's two corps moving rapidly upon him. Hardee waited until his trains and artillery from Florence arrived, but once they were across the Pee Dee, he evacuated Cheraw immediately.

On the day that Hardee left Cheraw, Sherman decided to make an all-out effort to catch him. "I want Hardee attacked rapidly and boldly, if in any position this side of the Peedee. If he makes the mistake to fight on this side we ought to catch him." Hardee did not make that mistake, and Sherman had to content himself with piles of damaged Confederate supplies left behind for want of transport.

Hardee now turned his column left for Rockingham, North Carolina. He had intended to make Fayetteville his objective, but a message from Bragg stated that Schofield was advancing up the west bank of the Cape Fear River from Wilmington. Bragg soon learned that there had been a mistake and corrected it, but by the time Hardee learned the truth, he had already burned the bridges to Fayetteville. This turn of events embarrassed Johnston, who had planned to unite Hardee's force and the Army of Tennessee at Fayetteville. In answer to Johnston's criticism, Bragg distorted the truth, stating that he had not sent the erroneous message. As a result of the error Johnston canceled his order to Hardee, and Beauregard further confused matters by ordering Hardee to Fayetteville if the enemy should head in that direction. If the enemy went north, Hardee was to go to Raleigh.[20]

Sherman crossed the Pee Dee at Cheraw and at Sneedsborough on March 7, 1865, and struck out for Fayetteville. Hardee, acting on Beauregard's order, raced with him. Hardee had the advantage, having turned in that direction a day earlier.

Hardee reached Fayetteville on March 9 and found Johnston there to meet him. Johnston gave him additional cavalry and, assuming that Raleigh was Sherman's ultimate objective, ordered Hardee to keep between Sherman and Raleigh. If Sherman did not move toward Raleigh, Hardee would proceed to Smithfield, North Carolina, to unite with Bragg's force from Wilmington and the Army of Tennessee.[21] Smithfield had been chosen for its strategic location between

20 *Official Records*, XLVII, Pt. 2, pp. 667, 1247, 1303, 1315, 1319, 1329, 1332, 1335; Roy Diary, March 2, 1865 entry.
21 *Official Records*, XLVII, Pt. 2, pp. 1356–57.
   This would be a different army from the one Hardee had known. Beneath its regimental battleflags gathered groups of men that would have made only fair-sized companies at Shiloh or Murfreesboro. Clayton's division,

Sherman's most probable objectives, Raleigh and Goldsboro, and for its proximity to the railroad.

The next day, March 10, when Sherman was within seven miles of Fayetteville, Hardee abandoned the town, leaving behind large quantities of arms and stores. He did manage to have some of the arsenal machinery removed, but the rest of the equipment, priceless in 1862, only encumbered in 1865. Wade Hampton, covering the rear, had "a close shave to get out of town," having to break through the enemy to get across the Cape Fear River.[22]

After crossing the river Hardee turned toward his supply depot at Averasboro. He moved with deliberate slowness from March 11 through March 15. Hampton's cavalry skirmished constantly, and occasionally the infantry turned and struck at the Union vanguard. Each day gained would assist Johnston's concentration at Smithfield.

Hardee halted his weary and bedraggled column on March 15 just south of the village of Averasboro. He authorized a day of rest for his men while Hampton and Wheeler gathered information about Sherman's movements. Meanwhile, Sherman, whose objective was Goldsboro, was coming up on his rear. Hardee's position blocked Sherman, so he determined to clear Hardee from his path. For this mission he selected Slocum's wing. Slocum's two corps, preceded by Judson Kilpatrick's cavalry, advanced and encountered the Confederates about six miles south of Averasboro at the Smith house. Slocum sent up a brigade of infantry under William Hawley to assist Kilpatrick and set about preparing his troops for the main effort on March 16.

Thus opened the battle of Averasboro. Hardee made his stand deliberately, "to ascertain whether I was followed by Sherman's whole army, or a part of it, and what was its destination. . . ."[23] Hardee

---

for instance, mustered only 887 effectives; the Army of Tennessee itself contained only 7,766 men. The troops of the army were scattered throughout the South, many of them unaware of the location of their organizations and having no way to rejoin them even if they did know their location. Three fourths of the Army's weapons had been lost in Tennessee, and approximately 1,300 men were without arms. The army lacked field transport and consequently depended entirely upon the railroad. The rank and file had been palsied by the successive defeats sustained under Hood. Confusion was rife, most of the men were unpaid, records had been lost, and many of the general officers lacked staffs. The army had lost many of its best generals, "its pride and ornaments," at Franklin. It had, in fact, been mortally wounded at Franklin.

22 Roy Diary, March 10, 1865; *Official Records*, XLVII, Pt. 2, p. 1444; McLaws Letterbook-Journal, March 10, 1865, in McLaws Papers.
23 Hardee, "Memoranda."

would be opposed by the four divisions of Slocum's wing and by Kilpatrick's cavalry. Discounting one of these divisions, which remained in reserve, Slocum's force totaled not less than fifteen thousand men. Hardee had about eight thousand effectives, including Wheeler's cavalry.[24] McLaws' division comprised nearly half of this force. McLaws had the brigades of Conner (commanded by Kennedy), Blanchard, Harrison, and Fiser. Taliaferro had two brigades, commanded by Elliott and Rhett. Wheeler had the two cavalry brigades of Allen and Ashby. The disparity between the size of Hardee's force at Averasboro and that of two months before is striking. Nearly half of his command had melted away through desertion, illness, and the withdrawal of various units, including a brigade of South Carolina militia in Taliaferro's division. The majority of the remaining troops had never seen field service before they left Charleston. No one could calculate their reliability.[25]

This fact influenced Hardee's choice of terrain and plan of battle. The battleground would be the narrowest piece of land between the Cape Fear and the Black rivers. This limited frontage would enable Hardee to bring all of his strength to bear but would cramp the superior numbers of the enemy. Just as at Savannah, the front would be covered with creeks and swamps and much of the field would be knee-deep in water. The flanks rested, as at Savannah, upon the two rivers, which at this point were deep and had high banks. Although Hardee lacked the Savannah canals and rice dams, the Averasboro terrain provided him with deep ravines and a dense maze of undergrowth along most of his line. The weather assisted the defenders also, supplying heavy rainfall throughout the engagement.

A year earlier Hardee would have placed three of his four divisions across this front, holding back one as a reserve. In March, 1865, he dealt with troops of a different caliber. If he massed his force on one line, he invited a breakthrough, and the Charleston troops' lack of training and confidence would turn a breakthrough into a disaster. General Hardee resolved this problem by a defense in depth. His first line stood astride the Fayetteville-Raleigh road, which bisected the battlefield. This line was in the rear of a large home called the Smith house, which had an open field to the front. In the line he entrenched his least experienced troops, A. M. Rhett's brigade, and put them

24 *Official Records,* XLVII, Pt. 1, p. 43, Pt. 2, pp. 1386–96; Hardee, "Memoranda"; McLaws Letterbook-Journal, March 14–15, 1865.
25 *Official Records,* XLVII, Pt. 2, p. 1372; Hardee, "Memoranda."

directly under Taliaferro's supervision. Two hundred yards to the rear was Stephen Elliott's brigade. Six hundred yards in the rear of Elliott, Hardee placed his main line, consisting of McLaws' veterans. McLaws had his left on a large swamp close to Black River, and his right extended by means of a skirmish line to the Cape Fear. To the rear of McLaws' line was a road junction that promised routes of retirement to either Raleigh or Smithfield. This gave Hardee about a mile of depth and, counting the infantry and cavalry skirmish lines, five defense lines. Hardee intended for this formation to be compressed by the enemy, but when fully compressed, this collapsible cone of fighting men would be able to employ its maximum firepower.

This defensive arrangement received its initial test on the afternoon of March 15. When Hawley's infantry came up, they forced back the Confederate cavalry pickets. Hardee's infantry pickets next engaged the enemy, and almost immediately Brigade Commander Rhett was lost, as he blundered into the Union line and was captured. Hawley, acting according to orders, did not press his attack, and the firing subsided after nightfall.

Kilpatrick and Hawley tested Hardee's defenses again at dawn. The Confederate pickets withdrew to Taliaferro's line. The Federals probed for and located Taliaferro's position and then sent back word that they had found Hardee in force. Twentieth Corps Commander A. S. Williams then sent up Ward's and Jackson's divisions.

The two Union divisions arrived on the field about 10 A.M., just as Kilpatrick's cavalry fell back from Taliaferro's advancing skirmishes. Williams halted Taliaferro's skirmishers and proceeded to envelop the Confederate right, just as Taliaferro repulsed a frontal attack. The surprise was complete, and the Charleston troops gave way in confusion. Between two and three hundred Confederates were lost in the rout, and the remainder fell back to Elliott's position.[26]

In the early afternoon Elliott's line collapsed in less time and from less pressure than had Rhett's line, as Kilpatrick pushed his men upon the left flank of the second line.[27]

The Confederates now prepared for their final defensive effort. Taliaferro took position on the main road. McLaws formed the left, extending to the bank of Black River. Wheeler, supported by Mc-

26 McLaws Letterbook-Journal, March 16, 1865; *Official Records*, XLVII, Pt. 1, pp. 422, 585–86, 611, 784–90, 1085, Pt. 2, p. 871.
27 McLaws Letterbook-Journal, March 16, 1865; *Official Records*, XLVII, Pt. 1, pp. 889–90.

Laws' best brigade, under Kennedy, held the right. The enemy began his attack about 3 P.M. Morgan's division of the Fourteenth Corps struck the Confederate right, but overcame the creeks and ravines only with difficulty. Morgan finally found Wheeler and Conner, entrenched behind a ravine. The defenders greeted him with a "heavy and destructive fire." "It would have been worse than folly to have attempted a further advance." In the center Taliaferro and McLaws also repulsed several Union attacks with ease. As dusk approached, Jackson's bruised division tried to turn the Confederate left. Hardee sent Rhett's brigade to resist this movement. General McLaws, however, believed that the Union troops probably would have turned this flank if more daylight had remained.[28]

At 4:30 P.M. General Hardee reported to Johnston that his line had held firm, but that he would withdraw that night. Probably the primary cause of his decision was a report from Hampton stating that Howard's wing had crossed the Black River. He soon would be in position to cut off and perhaps crush Hardee.[29] The weakness of Hardee's extended Averasboro line also influenced his decision to retire, as did the immediate threat of Jackson's turning movement.

Although intermittent skirmishing continued until 8 P.M., the battle proper ceased about 4:30 P.M. The Union commanders reported their casualties as 682, few of whom were captured. Hardee lost about 500 men, most of whom were captured in the attack on Rhett's line.[30]

In light of the casualties and numbers involved, Averasboro ranks at best as a small battle. Decidedly more than a skirmish, perhaps it should be labeled a delaying action in force, like the battle of Tunnel Hill. But in a study of Hardee it merits equal treatment with some of the larger and more important battles in which Hardee participated as a subordinate, since Averasboro was one of the two battles in which Hardee commanded the Confederates. The Confederates usually exaggerated the importance of this delaying action, and this is understandable, for it was virtually the only pin point of light in four months of gloom. Among Hardee's soldiers "the impression was general that the enemy had been decidedly checked [and] with considerable loss." Hardee congratulated his men for "giving the enemy the first serious check he has received since leaving Atlanta." "The

28 McLaws Letterbook-Journal, March 16, 1865.
29 *Official Records*, XLVII, Pt. 1, p. 1073; Howard, *Autobiography*, II, 141.
30 *Official Records*, XLVII, Pt. 1, p. 43; Roy Diary, March 16, 1865; Hardee, "Memoranda."

lieutenant-general augurs happily of the future service and reputation of troops who have signalized the opening of the campaign by admirable steadiness, endurance, and courage." [31]

Averasboro served as a tonic for Hardee's depressed, footsore troops. It climaxed the month-long retreat from Charleston—a valuable indoctrination that made the Charleston garrison into field troops and fused together a patchwork of commands. The Confederate commanders and Hardee himself seem to have been surprised at the general good behavior of the command. After the Charleston troops were thrown from Rhett's line, they conducted themselves with creditable steadiness and made possible the strong stand at the main line.

The comparison of Averasboro and the battle of Cowpens, nearly a hundred years before in the same general location, is striking. Both Daniel Morgan and Hardee had a nucleus of reliable troops, which they placed in the rear of two lines of untried troops. Both generals thus gained depth and psychological support for their weaker units. The advance lines knew that they were expected to retire and therefore retained their position a little longer than they might otherwise have done and inflicted more damage upon the enemy. This information also forced the enemy to deploy earlier, thereby disclosing his strength and intent. Both generals made good use of terrain and maximum use of their human resources. Morgan, however, approached numerical parity with his opponent and held a much shorter line, thus enabling him to keep on hand a reserve that he ultimately used as a counterattacking force. Wheeler's cavalry constituted Hardee's reserve, but this force had to be committed in the defense of the main line. Such defensive formations as Morgan and Hardee employed can usually be defeated by superior numbers in two ways: by an overpowering frontal attack against the weak first line, designed to capture or rout it, or by a flanking movement. The second is generally preferable. Bonastre Tarleton attempted the first method against Morgan and failed; Slocum tried the second method, combined with a holding attack, and succeeded in stampeding Rhett. He again utilized the flank attack to dislodge Hardee's second line and succeeded. When he approached Hardee's third line, he made a frontal attack and failed. He was beginning a flank movement when darkness ended the fight.

Hardee should be criticized for his failure to provide adequate

---

31 McLaws Letterbook-Journal, March 17, 1865; *Official Records*, XLVII, Pt. 2, p. 1411.

flank protection for Rhett's right and Elliott's left. These mistakes cost him heavily and could have been avoided. The use he made of his reserves seems to have been dictated by the enemy's mode of attack. It should be kept in mind that Slocum never launched a general attack with the four divisions he commanded. He made his offensive moves against Hardee's lines by means of limited attacks or in strong skirmisher formations. Only a few of his brigades launched determined assaults. Slocum planned a general assault the morning of March 17. In light of the number and quality of Hardee's men and the length of Hardee's line, this attack probably would have succeeded and seriously damaged his opponent. Generally speaking, however, Hardee displayed sound generalship at Averasboro. He showed ingenuity in his formations, an eye for terrain in his defensive positions, an understanding of his troops in his disposition of them, and tactical ability in his conduct of the battle.

From the perspective of the general war Averasboro assumes importance as a classic example of delaying action with an inferior force. The battle deranged Sherman's approach march by widening the distance between his two wings. It stalled Slocum's wing and gave Johnston more time to prepare for Sherman's anticipated ambush.[32]

Late in the evening of March 16, Hardee started his command toward Elevation, North Carolina, where he believed the Smithfield and Raleigh roads joined. If Sherman moved toward Goldsboro, Hardee would join Johnston at Smithfield; if Sherman moved toward Raleigh, Hardee would keep in front of him.[33] The following afternoon Wheeler became certain that Sherman's objective was Goldsboro. When Johnston received the news, he ordered Hardee to march at once for Bentonville, where they would unite. On the evening of March 18 Hardee encamped about six miles from Bentonville. He would complete the march beginning at 4 A.M. the next morning.[34]

Also on March 18, heavy columns of Union troops rapidly approached the destined battleground. Howard's right wing came down the eastern Goldsboro road, arriving at the present town of Newton Grove before dark. Howard's left wing, composed of Jefferson C. Davis' Fourteenth Corps and A. S. Williams' Twentieth Corps, encamped at the crossing of the Smithfield-Charleston road and the Fayetteville-Goldsboro road.

32 Barrett, *Sherman's March Through the Carolinas*, 158.
33 *Official Records*, XLVII, Pt. 2, pp. 1401, 1410, 1416.
34 *Ibid.*, pp. 1427-28; McLaws Letterbook-Journal, March 18, 1865; Roy Diary, March 18, 1865; Johnston, *Narrative*, 385.

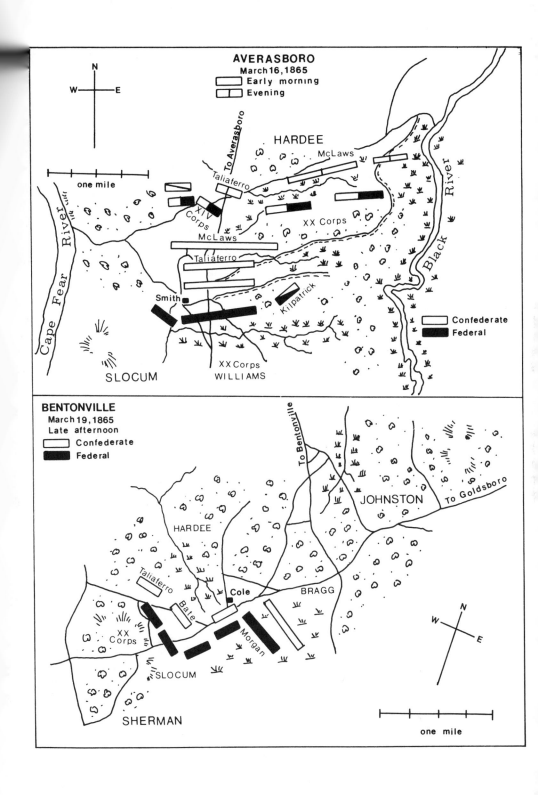

AVERASBORO
March 16, 1865

☐ Early morning
☐☐ Evening

N
W—E
S

HARDEE

McLaws

To Averasboro

Taliaferro

Black River

one mile

Cape Fear River

XIV Corps

McLaws

XX Corps

Taliaferro

Smith

Kilpatrick

Confederate
Federal

SLOCUM

XX Corps
WILLIAMS

BENTONVILLE
March 19, 1865
Late afternoon

☐ Confederate
■ Federal

To Bentonville

JOHNSTON

To Goldsboro

HARDEE

Taliaferro

Bate

Cole

BRAGG

XX Corps

Morgan

N
W—E
S

SLOCUM

SHERMAN

one mile

Joy and excitement reigned in the Union camps that night. One day's march ahead was Goldsboro. There they would discard their worn-out shoes and rotting clothing for new issues. Mail from home awaited them, as did the friendly faces of members of Schofield's army. From Goldsboro it was a short march to Virginia and the end of the war.

The end of the war came for many of them the following morning. William P. Carlin's division, of Davis' corps, developed determined resistance by Hampton's cavalry at the junction of the Bentonville and Goldsboro roads. Carlin's lead brigade attacked about noon, slowly driving the Confederates a mile through the forest and across the open field east of the Cole house. The Federals pursued to the opposite woodline, where they were met by devastating fire from thousands of concealed muskets. The remnants of the brigade fled back across the field into the forest. Carlin called up the rest of his division and entrenched. Slocum took immediate action, once he had been informed. He hurried forward Morgan's division and sent for the Twentieth Corps. Carlin's troops waited at the front for the enemy attack, spending the unexpected time allotted them throwing up breastworks. About 3 P.M. masses of Confederate infantry spilled out of their concealed lines and deployed for the attack.

At the moment Carlin's attack had struck the main Confederate line, the head of Hardee's column came up to Johnston's position. Hardee's troops had begun their march at 4 A.M. and had come up the road across Hill Creek to Bentonville. They reached the town at 9 A.M. and found the road blocked by A. P. Stewart's troops. Hardee therefore had his men fall out of ranks and allowed them to rest in the churchyard. Some time after noon, Stewart's Army of Tennessee and Hoke's North Carolina troops moved up to the deployment point. Then Hardee's troops marched up to the battlefield. When Hardee's leading division under McLaws came up, Johnston turned it to the left toward Hoke's position. General Bragg, in immediate command of Hoke's and other troops on the left, had become concerned over Carlin's attack and had called for immediate reinforcement.[35]

Johnston quickly outlined his plan of battle to Hardee. Hardee would command the Confederate right, composed of Taliaferro's division and the Army of Tennessee. Hardee would open the attack

35 Johnston, *Narrative*, 386; McLaws Letterbook-Journal, March 19, 1865; Roy Diary, March 19, 1865.

as soon as possible, charging with these troops obliquely to the left. Bragg's men would join in the attack successively from the right.[36]

General Hardee opened the attack at 2:45 P.M. In two lines his wing rushed forward through "a sparse growth of old field pines on through some thick huckleberry bushes and ponds." In Bate's division the first line received a deadly volley and was thrown into confusion. The second line, however, quickened its pace, moved through the disorganized first line, and assaulted, carrying the Union position. Taliaferro struck the enemy flank. A Union soldier on that line commented in a letter, "We were beaten and driven back about ¾ of a mile & the Div. lost 3 guns in all We however showed to the Rebs as well as our side some of the best running ever did." "It looked to me like a stampede," stated a member of the Eighty-second Illinois.[37]

As Hardee's troops attacked, they reached a covered position. To their front was a wide field controlled by enemy small-arm fire. "Franklin was fresh in their minds and they hesitated." Hardee rode up and saw their reluctance to leave the cover and cross the field. He moved his horse forward through the covered position and then rode out into the field urging his men forward. "They recognized their commander, now seen for the first time since the October before [by the Army of Tennessee] & raising a cheer, such as those old hills had never echoed before, they rose the ascent, dashed across the field & drove the enemy pell mell from those works." [38] Johnston attributed much of the initial success to Hardee's leadership. "Hardee, after commanding the double-quick, led the charge, and, with his knightly gallantry, dashed over the enemy breastworks on horseback, in front of his men." Johnston complimented him on the spot, saying, "You have done, however, what you always do." [39]

The critical moment in the battle had arrived. The Confederate right, flushed with success, could continue rolling up the Union line;

36 Johnston, *Narrative*, 387.
37 C. S. Powell, "A Confederate Soldier's Account of the Last Days of the War in Ga. and The Carolinas" (1916), typed copy in North Carolina Collection (University of North Carolina Library); *Official Records*, XLVII, Pt. 1, pp. 671, 1108; C. S. Brown to parents, n.d., in Charles S. Brown Papers, 1864–65 (Duke University Library).
38 Roy, "Odds and Ends."
39 Unidentified newspaper clipping in possession of Mrs. Howard Bowen, Birmingham, Ala.; John William Jones, "William J. Hardee," in *The South in the Building of the Nation*, 13 vols., ed. Julian Alvin Chandler and others (Richmond, 1909–38), XI, 442.

Morgan's flank lay exposed, and only one other organized Union division remained in supporting distance—a mile down the road. Hardee, however, thought it best to halt and regroup the tangled Confederate lines.

After regrouping, Bate and Taliaferro turned and advanced parallel to the Goldsboro road in pursuit of Carlin. The other divisions of Hardee's wing renewed the attack on Morgan across the Goldsboro road. Morgan had already shattered the mismanaged attacks of Bragg and now, realizing his danger, ordered a counterattack by his reserve brigade. This brigade sacrificed itself but blunted the Confederate flank attack. With only two brigades Morgan fought on, behind excellent entrenchments. Hardee led a column behind Morgan's line, while Loring and Coltart attacked in front, and Hoke moved up again on the enemy right. "The works of the First and Second Brigades were never given up, although attacked in front, flank, and absolutely in the rear, and had to fight their works in reverse." Morgan's division survived the attack because the Confederate assaults lacked co-ordination. Hardee's attack from the rear did not commence until Hoke's assault had been repulsed. The frontal attack by Loring and Coltart had been repulsed just before Hoke's.

Hardee's columns floundered in the deep swamp located behind Morgan's position, and again reorganization was deemed necessary. Once Hardee's attack from the rear commenced, it was smothered by a counterattack conducted by two of Morgan's regiments that had just returned from counterattacking Hoke's forces. The assault of these regiments stunned the Confederates, disorganized their lines, and cost the Fifty-fourth Virginia its colors. Simultaneously, Cogswell's brigade, rushed forward by Slocum, appeared out of the swamp in the Confederate rear and splintered Hardee's confused forces.

Bate and Taliaferro continued on after Carlin on the other side of the road. After beating off an attack by Hawley's brigade, these two divisions struck the line of the Twentieth Corps. Before they deployed for the attack, one of Hardee's staff rode up and ordered them to discontinue the attack. Hardee's order, when his imperiled situation behind Morgan's line is considered, is quite understandable. He probably thought Cogswell represented the spearhead of a Union counterattack in force, particularly since supporting forces could not seem to get through to him. Cogswell had attended to Hardee's reinforcements, assisted by an artillery concentration that delivered enfilade fire down the axis of the Goldsboro road. Hardee's forces behind Morgan's line extricated themselves as best they could. Over three hundred men were cut off; some of these spent nine harassed days within the Union lines before they rejoined their commands.

While the Confederates reorganized their fractured line, Slocum stitched together his forces in a crude Z. Morgan held the upper line, the Twentieth Corps the lower, and assorted commands from both the Fourteenth and the Twentieth corps the diagonal.

The Confederates made one last general effort about sunset. Their attacks on the left, center, and right all failed. During this attack Hardee operated on the extreme right, which opposed the Twentieth Corps. Here Bate and Taliaferro, supported by two of McLaws' brigades, launched a series of violent attacks just at nightfall, but the Twentieth Corps repulsed them handily; the Union reserves were never called into play. Bate contended that if McLaws had joined him even an hour earlier, victory probably could have been won. McLaws had been wandering about the battlefield since about two o'clock, obstructed by thickets. He had not reached Bragg's position until after the enemy threat had passed. He had remained quietly until one of Hardee's staff officers had summoned him to the right. The confused McLaws, hearing firing all along his left as he advanced, halted several times and deployed. Near the Cole house (where the Confederate attack had started and a long way from the advanced Confederate right) McLaws ordered his men to collect the ammunition and arms lying on the field, as he believed the attack to be over. Another rider came up from Hardee and took the two brigades from him. After the failure of the sunset attack, desultory combat continued into the night. Late that night the Confederates on the right pulled back from their advanced positions to a new line.

Thus Johnston's well-conceived and inefficiently conducted attack ended. Johnston's and Slocum's forces were evenly matched—16,895 to 16,127, but the Confederates as the attackers had suffered heavier casualties, losing nearly 2,000 men while Slocum lost about 1,500. In their few remaining weeks the Confederates would not again hold such favorable odds.

Sherman learned of Slocum's difficulties at 2 o'clock the following morning. He immediately dispatched Hazen's division from Logan's Fifteenth Corps to the scene. Next he relieved Slocum's two divisions guarding the wagon trains, ordering them to rejoin their corps. Then Sherman alerted the Seventeenth and the Fifteenth corps for an early morning march to Bentonville.

Meanwhile, Johnston consolidated his position. He brought Wheeler's cavalry over to the left and advanced them to impede Howard's approach. He also sent McLaws to the left and retired Hoke's line parallel to the Goldsboro road.

Sherman, remembering the costly lesson of Kennesaw Mountain, declined to attack after Howard came up, devoting all day March 20 to strengthening his lines and searching for weak points in the Confederate defense. Meanwhile, Johnston pushed the preparations for a general retreat. He decided not to withdraw that night, however, "in the hope that [the enemy's] greatly superior numbers might encourage him to attack."

Sherman did attack the next day but not in the way Johnston hoped for. The morning passed quietly enough; only a few Union skirmishers ventured near the Confederate works. A Union threat to the right never materialized. The situation on the left, however, deteriorated rapidly in the afternoon. Union forces pressed Wheeler's dismounted cavalry closely, and Wheeler, holding about 1,200 yards, extending from McLaws' left to Mill Creek, could not mass against them. McLaws reported the movement on his left to Hardee and sent over Kennedy's brigade to help Wheeler. Hardee, with divisions on both ends of the Confederate line, headed toward McLaws' position, bringing with him Taliaferro's division and the reserve of Hoke and the Army of Tennessee. At Johnston's headquarters he learned that Joseph A. Mower's division of Blair's Seventeenth Corps had punctured Wheeler's cavalry screen and was headed toward the Confederate hospitals and the only line of retreat. Johnston directed Hardee to take the reinforcements coming over from the left and push back Mower. Mower, however, left no time.

The only units immediately available to Hardee were the Fourth Tennessee Cavalry and eighty of the Eighth Texas Cavalry (Terry's Rangers). Hardee moved these regiments in front of Mower's advance. Roy appeared at this time, leading Henderson's brigade to Wheeler's support. Hardee also ordered this brigade to the threatened point. Henderson's brigade reached its position just as Mower appeared on the edge of Bentonville, two hundred yards from the bridge. Hardee hurled Henderson and the Terry Rangers against Mower's front, the Fourth Tennessee Cavalry struck Mower's left, Hampton attacked Mower's right with Young's brigade, and Wheeler assailed Mower's rear with part of Allen's Alabama Brigade. Hardee not only directed the attack but led it.

When Hardee motioned to the Texas Rangers to move up, he called upon the regiment with which he had the closest personal tie. Mounted proudly in its ranks was his son Willie. The confusion of the war had freed Willie from his school-prison, and he had come straight to his favorite regiment. Captain Kyle of Company D dutifully reported him to Hardee. The General saw that resistance was hopeless. "Swear him into service in your company," he said to Kyle, "as nothing else will satisfy." About four hours later Willie galloped off with the Rangers to the attack.

Hardee's combined forces moved forward with a rush. Although they were outnumbered, their charge "was so sudden and impetuous that it carried everything before it." Mower fell back nearly a mile in confusion. It was an imperative victory for the Confederates.

The major share of the credit for Mower's repulse must go to Hardee, the officer in charge. He grouped the Confederate forces, closely supervised the execution of his orders, and during the key moment in the charge, personally led the assault, "with his usual conspicuous gallantry." His tardiness on the morning of March 19 had been fully compensated in the minds of his fellow officers by his leadership on March 19 and now again on March 21. It proved an empty victory for Hardee himself, for in the charge Willie was critically wounded.[40]

While riding back with Hampton from the charge, Hardee said to him, "General, that was 'nip and tuck,' and for a while I thought 'tuck' had it." Shortly after, the two generals met two litter-bearers bringing Willie back from the front. Hardee dismounted and went over to his boy, then returned and rode off with Hampton, giving orders for the deployment of his troops.[41]

Now with his left endangered and his right stripped of troops Johnston decided to withdraw. The policy of repairing rips in one part of the line by tearing patches out of another segment could no

40 Henderson's brigade happened to be one of Cheatham's brigades that were only now arriving after their long march from Mississippi.

Official Records, XLVII, Pt. 1, pp. 486, 497, 1056, 1059, 1094, 1106; McLaws Letterbook-Journal, March 19, 21, 1865; Livermore, *Numbers and Losses*, 134-35; Roy Diary, March 21, 1865; Johnston, *Narrative*, 391; Hardee, "Memoranda"; Roy, "Hardee"; Wade Hampton, "The Battle of Bentonville," in *Battles and Leaders*, IV, 705; J. K. P. Blackburn, "Reminiscences of the Terry Rangers," in *Southwestern Historical Quarterly*, XXII (July, October, 1918), 170.

41 Walter Branham Capers, *The Soldier-Bishop: Ellison Capers* (New York, 1912), 116-17.

longer suffice. Under cover of a chilling rain and extreme darkness the army moved by echelon down the road to Bentonville, across Mill Creek, and on toward Smithfield. Union skirmishers soon discovered that the Confederates had retired and pressed forward hurriedly. Their efforts failed because of Sherman's reluctance to pursue and because of Wheeler's stout rear-guard action.

Bentonville represents Hardee's final performance as a battle commander; it was one of his best efforts. Hardee was a man who exposed himself to danger as an example, to engender confidence and perhaps to satisfy the demands of his ideal of a soldier. He was not the kind of general who leaps recklessly over breastworks to lead a charging column. Yet he did at Bentonville. The reason is found perhaps in the morale of the men he led. By the summer of 1864 many junior officers had been destroyed or incapacitated because of their zeal, as had many enlisted men. Breastworks bred caution, and the troops of 1865 needed even more of an example than before, so Confederate officers of high rank had to lead attacks that juniors would have led in 1862. The deaths of men like Cleburne, W. H. T. Walker, Gist, and scores of excellent field officers illustrate the point.

Hardee deserves criticism for his tardiness on the morning of March 19. It seems to have upset Johnston's timetable of attack, although after Hardee arrived at Bentonville, he had been unable to move forward until Stewart's troops were out of the way, some six hours later. Johnston assumed the responsibility for Hardee's late arrival, admitting that because of faulty maps he had miscalculated the distance Hardee had to march from Elevation to Bentonville. Other factors in the delay were the deplorable roads and the tender feet of Hardee's Charleston troops. Yet Hardee knew that Johnston expected him early in the morning of March 19 and undoubtedly realized that the success of the Confederate attack depended upon his promptness. By forced marches he could have covered the twenty-five miles on March 18. Hardee also demonstrated a lamentable ignorance of the roads leading from Elevation to Bentonville, an oversight that could easily have been corrected by a personal reconnaissance or one by a reliable staff officer.

The halt Hardee called when he regrouped the attacking line at the height of the opening fight is also open to question. The ensuing delay permitted the construction of stronger works by Morgan and allowed Carlin to re-form his routed division. Hardee was never one to continue an all-out assault with fragmented forces. The comparatively rigid and compact tactical formation that he employed invited disorganization in heavy terrain and in the confusion of an attack. He always believed in retaining an organized force on the offensive, a bitter lesson of Shiloh. This conviction may have cost him the chance to crush Morgan and inflict serious damage on Sherman.

On March 22 Johnston's army formed a line of battle on the north side of Mill Creek, awaiting pursuit. When Sherman declined to pursue, Johnston continued the march crossing the Neuse River near Smithfield. Hardee found the roads in terrible condition; mud sucked at wagonwheels and at shoesoles. Upset by Willie's wound, depressed at the failure of the battle, and irritated by the mud and rain, Hardee passed a fretful day. He received some solace from a wire from Beauregard, reporting that he believed that all of the wounded had been evacuated safely.[42]

Hardee halted his corps on March 23 and went ahead to Hillsboro, where at the home of General W. W. Kirkland, Willie was being cared for by Mary and Anna Hardee. Willie died there on March 24. At St. Matthews Episcopal Church in Hillsboro, Willie received the military funeral that he would have wanted; he was buried in the churchyard.[43]

Hardee stayed with Mary and Anna in Raleigh until April 3, then returned to his corps in Smithfield. To one observer the shrunken elements of the Army of Tennessee were "the saddest spectacle of my life." [44] Some regiments consisted of only a handful of men commanded by a lieutenant. Johnston reorganized the army for the last time, breaking up many regiments and divisions that numbered less than a hundred. For his corps commanders Johnston appointed Hardee, S. D. Lee, and A. P. Stewart. Lee had D. H. Hill and Carter Stevenson for his division commanders; Stewart had Loring, Walthall and Patton Anderson; Hardee retained Hoke's North Carolina Division and resumed command of Cheatham's and Cleburne's divisions, the latter commanded by John C. Brown. McLaws, who had never proven satisfactory to Hardee or to Johnston, was sent to Georgia for a territorial assignment and his division given to Walthall. Talia-

---

42 *Official Records,* XLVII, Pt. 2, p. 1451.
43 Roy Diary, March 24, 1865; Howard, *Autobiography,* II, 152; *Official Records,* XLVII, Pt. 3, p. 722; Hillsborough (N.C.) *Recorder,* March 29, 1865.
44 Ridley, *Battles and Sketches of the Army of Tennessee,* 455–56; Samuel W. Ravenel, "Ask the Survivors of Bentonville," in *Confederate Veteran,* XVIII, 124.

ferro was also relieved and his division given to Patton Anderson. The army, once again labeled the Army of Tennessee, numbered about thirteen thousand effectives. Hardee commanded about half of these troops.[45]

While the army rested and reorganized at Smithfield, the Virginia front collapsed. Johnston left Hardee in command and went to Greensboro to confer with Davis. There Johnston received confirmation of Lee's surrender. If the Army of Tennessee continued to resist, the future looked ominous. General Henry Halleck wrote to Sherman: "If Johnston will surrender as Lee has I presume you will give him the same terms. Beauregard, Bragg, and Hardee deserve no consideration." [46]

Sherman now set his army in motion for Raleigh. Hardee marched through Raleigh toward Greensboro according to instructions. Stewart and Lee moved via Hillsboro, while Hardee's corps passed through Chapel Hill and continued toward the Haw River. Mary, Anna, and Mrs. Kirkland accompanied Hardee's corps. Hardee crossed the Haw on April 15. The next day, in New Salem, he received an order from Johnston to halt the army and to await further orders.[47]

The following week proved to be one of the most difficult in Hardee's career. As acting commander of the Army of Tennessee, he had the responsibility of maintaining it as an effective combat instrument, yet he seemed unable to prevent it from melting away. He wrote Beauregard, "We are all agog respecting the object [of the halt], and surmises are that negotiations are afoot between Johnston and Sherman. If such be not the case, it would be well for me to know it as soon as practicable, that I may contradict it. The report, as you may well conceive, can do our troops no good." [48] The report did nearly destroy the army. "*Nothing*—but Rumors of capitulation very demoralizing to troops." "Thousands under pretense of not being willing to remain to be surrendered, stole mules . . . and horses . . . & deserted their colors, endeavoring to get home." [49] Elsewhere in

45 *Official Records*, XLVII, Pt. 1, p. 1083, Pt. 2, p. 1460, Pt. 3, pp. 757–59, 773–74, 779.
46 Roy Diary, March 11–12, 1865; Johnston, *Narrative*, 396; *Official Records*, XLVII, Pt. 3, p. 151.
47 Gordon Diary, April 14, 1865, in William M. Gordon Collection, 1820–1904 (Southern Historical Collection); *Official Records*, XLVII, Pt. 3, pp. 804–805; Roy Diary, April 16, 1865.
48 *Official Records*, XLVII, Pt. 3, p. 807.
49 Roy Diary, April 17, 1865; Gordon Diary, April 17, 1865; *Official Records*, XLVII, Pt. 3, p. 811.

North Carolina chaos prevailed. Deserters, soldiers returning from Lee's army, and some organized Confederate units pillaged supply dumps, commandeered trains, and in various other ways demonstrated that army discipline was breaking down.

Johnston ended the "suspense and uncertainty" when he returned to the army on April 19 and declared that an armistice would be in effect while negotiations continued. Many of the veterans believed that they faced dreary months in Union prison camps or worse. Men of Hardee's old Arkansas brigade came to him and asked his advice and help. He assured them that if they would remain with the army, "he would see them across the Mississippi." To implement this promise he had wagons filled with supplies and sent to South Carolina. There the wagons could be bartered to provide the necessities for the march. He declined, however, their offer to escort him and his family to Alabama.[50]

When the armistice ended on April 26, Hardee moved west as far as Trinity College, near Archdale, North Carolina. There the army halted again, and Hardee established his headquarters at Dr. Braxton Craven's home, reserving the second floor for Mary, Anna, and some of the wives of other officers. He pitched his own tent in front of the college building, and his troops camped around the college and along the road.[51] Earlier that day Johnston and Sherman had concluded their negotiations, and the Confederates had surrendered, receiving liberal terms. Sherman appointed Schofield as the officer to put the military convention into effect. Schofield announced that he would give ten days' rations to the Army of Tennessee if the latter would provide transportation. To work out these and other details Johnston appointed Hardee as his representative. On April 30, 1865, Hardee, accompanied by Roy, left Trinity College and went to Greensboro to receive his instructions. The next day Hardee and Roy boarded a special train for the trip to Raleigh to see Schofield.[52]

50 Roy Diary, April 19, 1865; Johnston, *Narrative*, 410; *Official Records*, XLVII, Pt. 3, pp. 810, 842–43; Roy, "Odds and Ends."

51 *Official Records*, XLVII, Pt. 3, pp. 835, 837; Roy Diary, April 26, 1865; Jerome Dowd, *The Life of Braxton Craven* (Durham, 1939), 100–101; Nora Campbell Chaffin, *Trinity College, 1839–1892* (Durham, 1950), 248; W. T. Gannaway, "Trinity College in War Times," in *Trinity Archives*, VI (May, 1893), 328–29.

52 *Official Records*, XLVII, Pt. 3, pp. 320, 321, 366, 857; Roy Diary, April 29–30, 1865.

A correspondent for the New York *Herald*, Theodore C. Wilson, had been at Kilpatrick's headquarters in Durham Station, awaiting an opportunity to get to the Confederate camp. General Johnston had agreed that he might come if he could find means of transportation. It was to be expected then that Wilson would carefully watch the arrival of Hardee's train in Durham Station. After a short visit to Kilpatrick's headquarters Hardee proceeded to Raleigh, where he and Schofield completed their transactions that night. Early the next morning he returned to Durham Station and had breakfast with Kilpatrick. Wilson had somehow managed to secure a seat in the car with Hardee and Roy, and now he headed off to Greensboro with them.[53]

Exploiting his opportunity, probably as Hardee breakfasted, Wilson asked him for an interview, which Hardee granted, receiving him "in a very cordial, generous, unreserved manner." In reply to a general question about the war and slavery Hardee said:

. . . I accept this war as the providence of God. He intended that the slave should be free, and now he is free. Slavery was never a paying institution. . . . For instance, my wife owned about one hundred negroes; forty of the hundred were useless for work, yet she had to feed these forty, in order to get the work of the other sixty. The negro will be worse off for this war. Will any of your abolitionists . . . feed and clothe half-a-dozen little children, in order to get the work of a man and woman? Sir, our people can pay the working negroes a fair compensation for their services, and let them take care of their own families, and then have as much left at the end of the year as we had under the old system.

General, do you think we will soon have real peace?
I do. I think the people of the South are anxious for it. They wanted it two years ago. I then saw that our cause could not succeed.

Will we not have guerilla warfare?
So help me God, sir, if we do I am willing and ready to fight to put an end to it. . . . Let me impress it upon you that the people of the South want to live in peace with the people of the North, and you will find they will do it. They will do it cheerfully, provided your government does not resort to harsh measures. If it does resort to such measures, I cannot answer for the consequences. We staked our all on the success of our arms, and they failed us, and now we are willing to return and live under the laws of the United States as we find them. . . .

Your officers have no money. What are they going to do?
They must go to work. The prospect before them is most gloomy indeed.

53 New York *Herald*, May 9, 1865.

It will be very hard on old men like me. I cannot now commence a profession.

Do you think Jeff. Davis was pleased at the assassination of President Lincoln?

I do not think he was. The people of the South do not like Andy Johnson. How can they, compared to Mr. Lincoln? Lincoln had been in office for four years, and knew who he could trust. He had also learned to govern. He had made a name. He could have done many things for the South that Johnson cannot. I do not believe that Lincoln was a party man—that is, that he was particularly so. Johnson is a party man. He is new, and the fear is he will be radical. I hope he will not, for the good of the country and the welfare of the people.[54]

The train jerked to a halt at Hillsboro to refuel. Soon another train came up behind, bearing Generals Schofield, Cox, and Kilpatrick and some Federal troops. Hardee excused himself from Wilson and together with Roy went back and boarded the other train. When he entered Schofield's car, he found the Union generals nervous about the number of Confederate cavalry hovering about the station. The two trains pulled out of Hillsboro and headed for Greensboro. Schofield and Hardee swapped tales about the "old army" and discussed the late campaigns. To further ease the situation the two older officers began to tease Cox about having denied an old woman rations at Atlanta. Hardee intensified the joke with the statement that this lady confirmed Hood's idea that Sherman had retired across the Chattahoochee. Cox was "taken in" by Hardee's personality. ". . . The time ran rapidly away. Hardee was in person and bearing a good type of the brilliant soldier and gentleman. Tall and well formed, his uniform well fitting and almost dandyish, his manner genial and easy, his conversation at once gay and intelligent, it would be hard to find a more attractive companion, or one with whom you would be put more quickly at ease." Cox had nearly as many questions as had the *Herald* reporter. In answer to a question about the war Hardee replied,

I confess . . . that I was one of the hot Southerners who shared the notion that one man of the South could whip three Yankees; but the first year of the war pretty effectually knocked that nonsense out of us, and, to tell the truth, ever since that time we military men have generally seen that it was only a question how long it would take to wear our army out and destroy it. We have seen that there was no real hope of success, except by some extraordinary accident of fortune, and we have also seen that the

54 *Ibid.*

politicians would never give up till the army was gone. So we have fought with the knowledge that we were to be sacrificed with the result we see to-day, and none of us could tell who would live to see it. We have continued to do our best, however, and have meant to fight as if we were sure of success.

In answer to Cox's question about his future plans Hardee said that he thought he would leave the country "till the heated and exasperated feeling at the North should subside, and then return to his home and his private affairs." [55]

Upon their arrival at Greensboro, Hardee went with the Union officers to see Johnston. With official business virtually completed at Raleigh, little remained but to exchange pleasantries. Johnston provided amusement at Hardee's expense when the officers reminisced about the war. Hardee had once assured Johnston that Sherman could not maneuver his army through the Salkehatchie swamp, and had lived to repent these words. Hardee laughed at Johnston's remark and admitted that when he "learned that Sherman's army was marching through the Salkehatchie swamps, making its own corduroy roads at the rate of a dozen miles a day or more, and bringing its artillery and wagons with it, I made up my mind that there had been no such army in existence since the days of Julius Caesar."

The bouquets continued to be tossed around for several hours. The light conversation of Hardee and Johnston belied their sense of depression, much more openly expressed by many of their fellow Confederates. Their attitude, however, made a marked impression on the Union officers and probably accomplished a great deal for the men of the Army of Tennessee and for the South.

Following the meeting at Johnston's headquarters, Hardee and Roy returned to Trinity College. The corps had already moved on toward Salisbury, having received its paroles. Colonel Roy decided not to follow the army. He said good-by to Hardee and his friends and headed back to Virginia, in company with Irving A. Buck and others. After parting with his chief of staff, Hardee had his wife and Anna get their belongings together and prepared to catch up with his troops.

The North Carolina soldiers still remaining at Trinity College refused to let him go without a ceremony. Anna, accompanied by some of the staff, furled the flag in front of his headquarters, where the men were lined up in formation. Hardee and his wife came out, and emo-

55 Cox, *Military Reminiscences*, II, 525, 526, 532.

tion fought its way to the surface. He first told his North Carolina troops good-by; then as he prepared to enter his carriage, he stooped down and picked up young Emma Craven and kissed her. As he drove away, a North Carolina soldier tolled the college bells.[56]

56 Society of the Army of the Tennessee, *Report of the Proceedings of the Society of the Army of the Tennessee*, 45 vols. (Cincinnati, 1866–1922), XIV, 115–16; Roy Diary, May 2–3, 1865; *Official Records*, XLVII, Pt. 3, p. 873; Dowd, *Craven*, 101; Chaffin, *Trinity College*, 248.

XVI

The Corps Commander

THE SOLDIER who started back home was a different man from the colonel of the First Georgia Regiment. He had entered the war as a lighthearted, debonair professional soldier, ambitious enough to seek glory wherever it might be found. His friend William Preston Johnston recalled him in glowing terms: "His personal appearance was striking. In form he was tall and sinewy, and his bearing was eminently military. His features were somewhat harsh in repose, but his frank and genial smile lit them with a most winning expression. He was good tempered, friendly, and intelligent in conversation with men, and very charming with women. His deference and gallantry were of the old school. His social success belonged to this perfect poise, in which were mingled frankness, amiability, and tact-qualities. . . ." [1]

By 1865 the war had transformed him into a grim, disillusioned old man. The profession that had been his life had destroyed its own illusory grandeur; members of his family had fallen prey to it, and his country itself. Before the war his life had followed a pattern; he had mastered the rules of military science, and he set himself to apply them on behalf of the Confederacy. As this pattern fell apart, he sought another. He developed the spiritual side of his life; he remarried; he even considered resigning from the army, abandoning completely his chosen way of life. But none of his efforts restored the old confidence. He had discovered that he had limitations as a military man. The once-ambitious professional soldier refused the offer of army command.

Following the Atlanta campaign the changes in Hardee became increasingly obvious. At Atlanta he met his nemesis, trench warfare.

1 W. P. Johnston, *Albert Sidney Johnston*, 353.

301

Now his greatest skills were obsolete, the corps that he had trained so thoroughly was ineffective, and his tactics manual was irrelevant. After three successive and costly attacks, Hardee led a beaten army once more against the enemy breastworks at Jonesboro. Here he and his men gave a remarkably bad performance. His corps had lost its efficiency, and he made as many tactical errors as he had made in the entire course of the war—perhaps more. As defender of Savannah Hardee did not—probably could not—effect any combination to halt Sherman. The immediate defense of the city, however, was conducted with skill and manifested Hardee's excellent use of available resources. In South Carolina Hardee again was helpless before Sherman in the open field. At Charleston, as at Jonesboro and Savannah, he called for his superiors to come and take command.

After the evacuation of Charleston he regained much of his lost prestige. He retired north like a dangerous wounded animal, fighting well on the defensive at Averasboro and with savage desperation at Bentonville. These last battles are a true measure of Hardee's devotion to the Confederacy. Knowing the cause was futile, he continued to fight to the limit of his abilities.

In many respects, then, Hardee's Civil War career is a record of discouragement and disenchantment. According to Albert Sidney Johnston's definition of a successful general—one who wins—Hardee was a failure. He never led an army to victory; he never participated in a successful campaign; indeed, he never fought with an army that drove the enemy from a battlefield and held its gains.

His men, however, would remember not the man who was a failure but the man they called "Old Reliable." The nickname that they gave him reveals not only his soldiers' affection and respect but also their insight, for it encompasses his finest qualities as a military man.

He earned the sobriquet slowly. In Arkansas and Missouri he showed little promise beyond the organizational aptitude that he had already displayed in the United States Army, at Savannah in early 1861, and at Fort Morgan. In Kentucky and during the retreat through Tennessee he did not distinguish himself. Then came the flurry of campaigns punctuated with Shiloh, Perryville, and Murfreesboro, and Hardee was at his best. Now he proved to be an outstanding tactician and battle leader. At Murfreesboro Hardee gave one of the greatest performances of any corps commander in the Civil War. In the summer of 1863 in Mississippi he chafed because of the limited scope of his command. Here he himself accomplished little, but his corps and his army fought their greatest battle. When he returned to the army in November, 1863, Hardee continued his earlier successes at Missionary Ridge. At this point Davis offered him the command of the army, and the offer was refused.

After the spring of 1864, attacks with formal, heavy lines of infantry could be indulged in only by armies that could replenish the staggering losses that resulted. Even the Union army, with its preponderance of force, abandoned such methods soon after Kennesaw Mountain and Cold Harbor. To attempt them with an inferior force was suicidal. Recognizing this fact may help to explain why the Confederacy kept an effective fighting machine in the field longer in Virginia than in the West. The Army of Northern Virginia stood on the defensive during the summer, fall, and winter of 1864 and did not experience a disaster similar to the fatal series of Peachtree Creek, Atlanta, and Jonesboro, where the Army of Tennessee attacked. As a corps commander Hood had realized the threat of a superior entrenched enemy and had refused battle on a number of occasions. Yet in his and the Confederacy's desperation for a success in the summer of 1864 he ignored his experience and expected others to do what he himself had refused to do. Unfortunately for Hardee, Hood generally chose him as his instrument.

As long as the old rules of warfare applied, Hardee had few superiors. He is recognized as one of the finest corps commanders the Civil War produced. Among his contemporaries, Jefferson Davis held that "in his various high commands my . . . estimate of him was confirmed and increased, but never diminished." [2] Joseph E. Johnston claimed that he had no superior as a corps commander.[3] The Union commanders agreed generally that he was one of the most capable soldiers in the service of the Confederacy. A great number of the men who followed Hardee during the war reinforced or went beyond these remarks—particularly men who were close to him.

These tributes are based on Hardee's accomplishments in organization and in battle tactics. He was probably the ablest drillmaster in the Confederate army. "His corps was always a unit, all inspired with the loftiest patriotism and with the utmost confidence in their commander." [4] It was the toast and mainstay of the Army of Tennessee and earned the respect of its foes as well.

Traditionally, the kind of training that Hardee could give had

2 Davis to Roy, February 29, 1880, quoted in Roy, "General Hardee," *loc. cit.*, 377.
3 Edward Alfred Pollard, *Lee and His Lieutenants* (New York, 1867), 829.
4 Pickett, *Hardee*, 3.

paid high premiums on the battlefield. He understood terrain and used it to the greatest advantage. He liked to maneuver his corps into a good position and then match his exposed line of battle against that of the enemy, and his men developed wonderful proficiency in this type of fighting. They held their ground obstinately under fire and could sustain the heaviest losses. If their fire succeeded in overpowering the enemy line, they then pursued. In this mode of fighting, the force that marched most rapidly, in the best-controlled formations, had a great advantage. Hardee's men, particularly Cleburne's division, could make complicated wheeling or flanking movements beyond the capacity of other divisions in the army. His corps was known for its vigorous and sustained attacks. Hardee worked well with cavalry when it was assigned to him, and he seems to have mastered the employment of artillery. He was noted as an offensive fighter throughout most of the war, and army commanders usually assigned his corps as the element of maneuver or used it to assail the critical point in the enemy line. On the defense Hardee frequently held the most important position.

Moreover, Hardee's leadership consisted of more than the mastery of battle formations. While developing and using his corps as a unit, he retained the perspective to recognize individual leadership within its numbers. Forrest first achieved recognition under his command, as did John H. Morgan, Cleburne, Hindman, Bushrod Johnson, and Bate. He led his subordinate generals without friction, at least until late 1864, and his personal gallantry on the battlefield was an example and an inspiration for his men.

The Army of Tennessee was vital to the Confederate war effort, and Hardee should be remembered as an integral and able part of it. Albert Sidney Johnston, Bragg, Joseph E. Johnston, and even Hood placed great reliance in him as a battle commander and consulted him in strategic matters. Jefferson Davis valued him highly—perhaps too highly—and considered him capable of any assignment. Limited by his reluctance to abandon outmoded military techniques in which he was expert, Hardee never rose to first rank. His star shone brightly enough during most of the war, flickered in 1864, and dimmed in 1865. As a corps commander Hardee found his proper command level and his niche in history; there he became "Old Reliable." Whatever changes the Confederates might make if the battle of Shiloh could be refought, the first line would still be assigned to Hardee.

XVII

Civilian

THE DEATH of the Army of Tennessee occurred in North Carolina in April, 1865. The funeral procession of its once proud brigades and regiments was slow and long, winding its way through the lower tier of Southern states. Hardee, leading the units of the army from the states west of the Appalachians, rode south into Georgia and then turned west toward Alabama.

Union officials watched the procession carefully, but no incidents worthy of record hindered the march. The larger units kept fairly close together for physical and psychological security. In central Alabama the procession fragmented. Troops from the Gulf and Trans-Mississippi states proceeded down to Mobile on Federal steamboats. Accompanied by a group of his men, who had vowed not to leave him until he was safely home, Hardee passed through Montgomery and finally arrived at his wife's home near Demopolis about May 20, 1865.[1]

Near Demopolis were Mary's plantations "Ash Place" and the "Hermitage," and those of her brother, Ivey Lewis. Hardee, of course, was familiar with the Lewis plantations and had controlled by correspondence the operation of Mary's two plantations for over a year. Unlike many of his unfortunate compatriots, Hardee returned to lands that were in relatively good condition.

For approximately nine months Hardee lived on and supervised Mary's two plantations. He and Mary and his daughters lived in a modest log cabin that had been occupied by the overseer. After they had set up housekeeping, guests began to arrive. The guests who re-

---

1 Josiah Gorgas Journal, 1857–78 (microfilm copy, Southern Historical Collection), May 23, 1865; *Official Records,* XLIX, Pt. 2, p. 833; Roy, "Odds and Ends."

corded their impressions found Hardee interested and active in his new work. The Hardee dwelling they found crude and filled with assorted furniture from other homes. Mary provided good dinners "served on all sorts of odd China." [2]

To work the plantations Hardee had about seventy-five former slaves from the Lewis, Foreman, and Hardee families. To organize the Negroes into a profitable labor force Hardee installed the share-cropping system. He provided for medical care through annual payments and gave authority and extra pay to his Negro foremen, but he found dealing with free Negroes a different experience from controlling soldiers. Once as guests were departing, a shower came up and the Negro driver fled to the cover of a barn. Hardee raced after him, caught him, and "shook him soundly." [3]

"Ash Place" and the "Hermitage" had been highly profitable cotton plantations before the war, and Hardee immediately set to work to produce a crop. His farms prospered from the first, largely because of 160 bales of cotton he had on hand at the end of the war. Cotton prices were high, and Hardee placed his cotton on the market at opportune times. Although so-called "Confederate cotton" was subject to confiscation, Hardee was able to dispose of his cotton at a high profit. As time went on and the financial condition of the plantations improved, Hardee began to raise hogs and mules and planted corn. [4]

Instead of applying all of the money from the sale of the stored cotton to build up his badly needed capital, Hardee used a sizable portion to help relieve President Davis' financial embarrassment. Hardee sent Mrs. Davis a check for $522, telling her that this money was unused secret service funds that remained in his hands at the time of the surrender. Hardee also wrote William Seward in Davis' behalf. [5]

After a year of plantation life, the Hardees moved to Selma, Alabama. Before the war this town of 6,500 people had been a great Alabama cotton center with some manufacturing. During the war it became one of the largest arsenals and munitions centers in the Confederacy, employing some 4,000 workers. As the war closed General James H. Wilson's cavalry made a devastating raid through Selma,

2 Gorgas Journal, June 10, July 12, 1865; author's interview with Mrs. Howard Bowen, August 5, 1957.
3 DuBose, "Chronicles of the Canebrake," *loc. cit.*, 540.
4 Lewis Plantation Record Book and Lewis-Hardee Cotton Book, both in Lewis Family Papers.
5 Hardee to W. H. Seward, August 14, 1865, and Hardee to Mrs. Davis, August 15, 1865, in Hardee-Roy Letterbook (Alabama Archives).

leaving it in ruins. The returning Confederates found the commercial property wrecked and piles of rubble where once homes and business houses had stood. Some fine homes escaped, however, and the Hardees purchased one of them, on the corner of Dallas and Lapsley streets.

Hardee did not now commit himself to a single occupation. He had an interest in a warehouse and became one of the original board members of a new company, the Selma Fire and Marine Insurance Company. He also helped organize the Central Agricultural and Mechanical Association. This group, commonly known as the Fairgrounds Committee, proposed to stimulate the economic growth of Selma by means of publicity and fairs. They purchased a site for the fairground and constructed the necessary buildings to house the exhibits. Hardee, as vice president, seems to have taken an active part.[6]

Hardee moved to Selma primarily because he had been offered the position of president of the Selma and Meridian Railroad. This company began operation in 1856. By 1861 the road had not been completed, but it had fine prospects for success. Its route would provide the east-west link between several of the major railroad systems of the South. During the war there was considerable talk of completing the line, but it remained unfinished, perhaps the most critical missing link in the Confederate transportation system. In 1864, when Hardee moved his troops west to support Polk in Mississippi, the lack of a railroad between Selma and Meridian made troop concentration so slow that it could not be effective.

By 1865 the once-promising railroad had been virtually destroyed. With few exceptions its employees, shops, rolling stock, and locomotives were gone. Key bridges that had been built at great cost had been dismantled. Most of its liquid capital had been invested in Confederate bonds and these were gone.[7]

This, then, was the railroad of which Hardee became president on February 7, 1866. His first concern was to get the trains running again. His immediate needs were six engines and fifty-six freight and passenger cars. Temporary bridges had to be built, and many sections of the eighty-one miles of worn track had to be replaced. To build the bridges, replace the track, and purchase the engines he required capital. He first went to New York and sought loans from the lead-

6 Walter M. Jackson, *The Story of Selma* (Decatur, 1954), 252, 278. In 1870 this company was absorbed by the Cutt Bank of Selma.
7 These conditions, however, were shared by all of the Alabama railroads and all nine had to be reorganized financially after the war. Only three succeeded.

ing banking houses. Having failed there, he turned to the United States Army, which was still heavily engaged in railroading, and purchased, for $142,000, six locomotives, fifty flatcars, and other equipment. Hardee failed to obtain a long-term note from the army and had to agree to repay the loan within a year.[8]

After procuring this essential equipment, Hardee negotiated the lease of the Northeast and Southwest Alabama Railroad. This lease expanded the operational range of the Selma and Meridian considerably. Hardee also raised the rates on freight.

Hardee seems to have enjoyed his new profession. He had been interested in railroad management for several years, and doubtless, as he had complained repeatedly about the gross mismanagement of lines in Tennessee, North Carolina, and elsewhere, he thought that he could ensure competent management and dependable service. As president he proved to be authoritative and energetic. He openly rebuked members of the board when they were inattentive to their duties. He made trips to New Orleans to stir enthusiasm for a prospective railroad chain stretching from New York to Mexico and made other trips around the country to raise additional capital.

Hardee succeeded in having the short-term government notes extended for a year. He negotiated several new loans by using his own and Mary Hardee's property as collateral. In 1867 he instituted an economy drive, slashing the number of passenger trips, cutting labor costs, increasing rates even more, and reducing his own salary from $4,500 to $2,800.[9]

In spite of his efforts to reorganize the Selma and Meridian and to operate it efficiently, the company fell deeper and deeper into debt. The section that it served was economically depressed and hardly could be expected to support a railroad that still needed major investment to complete its basic facilities. By 1868 the end was in sight. Colonel W. James Robb inspected the company and found that a complete financial reorganization was again necessary. The Selma and Meridian "has no available means nor can it by any process of arrangement, command either money or credit, beside it is in default in its engagements to bondholders, creditors and employees." [10]

---

8 *House Executive Documents,* 39th Cong., 2nd Sess., Doc. 34, p. 857.
9 Minute Book, Selma and Meridian Railroad, 1860–77 (Southern Railroad Archives, Washington, D. C.); *House Executive Documents,* 39th Cong., 2nd Sess., Doc. 34, pp. 181–90.
10 Minute Book, Selma and Meridian Railroad.

In 1868, because its payment of rent was four months in arrears, the company had to give up its lease of the Northeast and Southwest Alabama Railroad. The following year the United States District Court placed the management of the company in the hands of Hardee's old associate, "railroad troubleshooter" Sam Tate.[11]

With the appointment of Tate, Hardee's active part in the management of the railroad ended. Several years of litigation followed, and the railroad was sold finally to a New York syndicate whose agent was the same Colonel W. James Robb who had inspected the railroad earlier. Robb purchased the road for about one and a half million dollars. In 1882 the railroad was absorbed by the East Tennessee, Virginia, and Georgia Railroad and eventually became part of the Southern Railway System.

While he was being considered for president of the Selma and Meridian in 1865–66, Hardee realized that he must receive a pardon from the government or be seriously hampered in managing the railroad efficiently. He took the prescribed loyalty oath and sent in his petition, backed by an impressive list of names, including those of nearly all high state officials and as many as sixty of the Alabama House of Representatives. The petition met with snarls and slowdowns, and Hardee turned to his old friend Sherman for help. Sherman endorsed his application, but the government took two years to grant Hardee his pardon. Mary also applied, receiving hers without delay.[12]

It is difficult for one living in the era of total war to comprehend Hardee's profession of loyalty to a government that had just overwhelmed his nation, but his was the limited point of view of a classical professional soldier. As a military man and a pragmatist he believed that the issues between the North and the South had been settled conclusively on the battlefield, and he accepted the outcome. To one reporter he declared that if the United States went to war against any foreign foe he would volunteer his "services to the United States Government in any capacity, even as a private." [13] Northern professional soldiers understood his attitude. He renewed his membership in the United States Military Academy Association of Graduates, and his fellow officers who had fought against him for four years

11 *Ibid.*, John Hardy, *Selma: Her Institutions, and Her Men* (Selma, 1879), 110.
12 Hardee to A. Johnson and Mary Hardee to Johnson, December 8, 1865, R. M. Patton and others to Johnson, January 20, 1866, Hardee to Sherman, February 9, 1866, Sherman to Johnson, February 17, 1866, in Amnesty Papers, Record Group 109.
13 *Senate Executive Documents*, 39th Cong., 1st Sess., Doc. 43, p. 4.

received him warmly. Immediately after the war Hardee and his wife went to Mobile and, as always, stayed at the Battle House. When Union army officers learned of his presence, they promptly sent their regards and arranged a dinner party for him. With boldness in his step Hardee appeared, wearing the first civilian suit that he had owned in years, a suit of cadet gray, and was the center of attention. For their participation in such festivities, however, the Union officers were sharply upbraided by the New York *Herald*.[14]

Hardee's "old army" friendships helped him and his section during the postwar years. General George G. Meade, who commanded the military district in Alabama until 1869, was asked for favors on several occasions by Hardee. Often Hardee, respected both by local officials and by army officers, acted as an arbitrator and mediator. The Ryland Randolph case, for instance, was settled to the satisfaction of local citizens and of the government, at Hardee's dinner table.[15]

To have been a guest of Hardee's was the boast of Selma's society for several years. His friends included of course the former Confederate general officers, "more numerous in Selma than privates." Among the members of this group were C. M. Shelley, E. W. Pettus, John T. Morgan, and Joseph E. Johnston. Johnston, while he was President of the Alabama and Tennessee Rivers Railroad, lived in Selma and (according to Josiah Gorgas' diary, at least) camped out at the Hardee's.

Hardee usually spent his evenings at home, playing whist with Johnston, the ever-present T. B. Roy, Sallie Hardee, and often Gorgas. Among his close friends in Selma and Demopolis were Nathan B. Whitfield, Congressman F. S. Lyon, and N. H. R. Dawson. Frequently old friends like Longstreet and General William N. Pendleton, whose daughter tutored Mary Hardee's nieces, visited there.[16]

At Sewanee, Tennessee, was another cluster of Hardee's friends. Among the many former Confederates at Sewanee were Edmund Kirby Smith, Jason Fairbanks, one-time Hardee staff officer, and Francis A. Shoup, once Hardee's chief of artillery. General Josiah

---

14 DuBose, "Chronicles of the Canebrake," *loc. cit.*, 541; United States Military Academy, *Annual Report, Association of Graduates of the United States Military Academy* (West Point, 1872); New York *Herald*, October 10, 1865.
15 John Witherspoon DuBose, *Alabama's Tragic Decade* (Birmingham, 1940), 242–44; Walter Lynwood Fleming, *Civil War and Reconstruction in Alabama* (New York, 1905), 499; Gorgas Journal, June 7, 1868.
16 Gorgas Journal, August, 12, 1865. Hardee commented to Gorgas after their visit with Longstreet that he thought him "too self-sufficient and engrossed with himself." Gorgas agreed "that Longstreet seemed to think that he rather than Lee had made the Virginia victories possible."

Gorgas, after his ill-fated industrial attempt at Brierfield Ironworks, had been recommended by Hardee as the headmaster of the Junior Department at Sewanee. There is no evidence that Hardee ever visited Sewanee himself, but the Hardee baseball club still exists. The Hardees and the Sewanees have been traditional rivals at the University since 1870. There was also a "cherished relic" in the Gorgas home known as the "Hardee bed." In the University of the South Library one may see portraits of many of Hardee's comrades in arms, and in the old chapel, there still hangs the battleflag that Hardee's corps carried into the battle of Shiloh.[17]

Not only did Hardee have close ties with the leading Episcopal educational center, but he took an active part in the life of the church. He and his family belonged to St. Paul's Episcopal Church in Selma, along with his friends Johnston, N. H. R. Dawson, E. W. Pettus, John T. Morgan, and his sons-in-law N. R. Chambliss and Roy. Hardee was elected to the vestry of St. Paul's in 1868 and served until the time of his death. Although he was frequently absent from vestry meetings, the minutes reveal that he was interested and articulate when present. He served on a number of committees and went as a deputy to the Diocesan Convention in 1871 and 1872.[18]

The conversion of Hardee from soldier to civilian necessitated changes, but many aspects of his old way of life remained the same. Among these was his obsession with neatness. The epitome of good grooming and propriety, Hardee never left his room without his coat. He demanded that his children show similar care, remarking to Elizabeth and Sallie that it was their "duty" to dress as nicely as possible. One might not be beautiful, but careful dress could certainly enhance one's endowments. The only time that Hardee seems to have violated his own dictum was when, as a civilian, he became an avid gardener. Like most gardeners he had his favorite outfit, "a disreputable hat and impossible clothes." His amused family, eager to turn his advice back upon him, continually chided him about it.[19]

As in prewar years, Hardee read a great deal, particularly in the

17 Frank E. Vandiver, *Ploughshares into Swords: Josiah Gorgas and Confederate Ordnance* (Austin, 1952), 278n., 288.
18 Parish Records, 1863–72, St. Paul's Episcopal Church, Selma, Ala.
19 For details of Hardee's last days, the author has drawn once again on his interview with Mrs. Howard Bowen, August 5, 1957. See also T. B. Roy to Dr. E. L. Drake, November 8, 1878, in Hardee-Roy Papers (Alabama); W. J. Hardee to Mrs. Caroline Russell, December 25, 1871, in Hardee-Zacherie Papers; Dallas County, Alabama, Record of Wills, Book C; and DuBose, "Chronicles of the Canebrake," *loc. cit.*, 542.

field of history, and demanded that his family read often and widely. As a result the Hardee family circle, led by the General and the omnivorous reader Roy, frequently had long discussions about various authors and topics. The General was also very interested in French and seems to have instructed Roy and other members of the family.

Always horrified by the thought of debt, Hardee insisted on strict economy even in regard to minute details like matches. He kept himself well informed on the state of the companies in which he held stock and frequently received reports on the value of his property in Florida and Texas.

He also kept in close contact with his brothers and sisters around Savannah. He felt a particular obligation toward his widowed sister, Caroline Hardee Russell, supporting her and her family for years before his death and providing an annuity for her in his will.

Hardee made frequent trips to Savannah and St. Augustine to visit his many relatives. He also visited White Sulphur Springs, West Virginia, to escape the summer heat in Selma; it was during one of these trips that he fell critically ill.

Without adequate medical records, it is impossible to know exactly the nature of the disease that caused Hardee's death. From his youth, however, Hardee had suffered from dyspepsia, and by 1872 Hardee's friends knew that he was seriously ill with cancer of the stomach. To relieve his suffering he desperately tried changes of climate and did find that oranges from his groves in Florida made him more comfortable.

In the summer of 1873, Hardee and his family made their annual trip to White Sulphur Springs. This year Hardee was particularly anxious to go, for the Southern Historical Society was to be organized. The Hardees reached White Sulphur Springs by train, but when they arrived, Hardee became ill and had to be confined to his bed for the remainder of the summer.

The Southern Historical Society learned of the nature of his illness and sent a delegation composed of Fitz Lee, Jubal Early, Governor John Letcher, and Admiral Raphael Semmes to express the society's regret at his absence. In the early fall Hardee rallied, and though he was in great pain, he was placed on the train for the return trip. On the way General Johnston entered his car and was greatly moved by the sight of his dying friend.

Hardee was carried as far as Wytheville, Virginia, where he became too feeble to continue the journey. He was carried from the train to the Buck Hotel near the station and died there on November 6, 1873.

His physician, who had known him for years and who admired his war record, was so impressed by Hardee's courage in enduring the intense pain of his final illness that he named his son Hardee Johnston. The old soldier went to his death as nobly in peace as he would have preferred in war.

When Hardee's body was brought home, he received "the greatest public demonstration known at a funeral in Alabama." In the procession came Black Auster, with the General's boots inverted, led by a veteran of Hardee's corps. Above his grave is a large cross, simply marked: William J. Hardee, Lieutenant-General, C.S.A.

XVIII

Postscript

DURING THE few years between the end of the war and Hardee's death, two of his daughters married. On April 24, 1867, his oldest daughter, Anna, married her old beau, Nathaniel R. Chambliss. He had been the captain of the cadet corps when the Hardees were at West Point. He had asked then if he could marry Anna but Hardee discouraged him. During the war Chambliss served as one of Hardee's staff officers and afterward became a professor of mathematics at the University of Alabama. He soon gave this up, however, to become a planter. One of his children, Dr. Hardee Chambliss, possessed his aptitude for science and mathematics. He became a chemist and Dean of the Catholic University School of Science. He taught also at Columbia and at Oklahoma Agricultural and Mechanical College.

Sallie Hardee married Colonel Roy in Hardee's home in 1871. The wedding delighted Hardee, of course, and he built them a home adjoining his own. Roy had been in Selma for four years as a law partner in the firm of Brooks, Haralson, and Roy. Like his father-in-law he became a member of St. Paul's vestry and also served as a director of the Commercial Bank of Selma.

In the 1880's Roy and Sallie moved to France and then to Berlin, primarily because of Roy's health. They lived in Berlin until the time of Roy's death. Roy remained to the end a stanch defender of his friend and idol, General Hardee. He wrote several articles defending Hardee's actions in the Atlanta campaign and began a biography. The Roys had no children of their own, but they adopted a daughter of Anna and N. R. Chambliss. This daughter married a German and had no children. After Roy's death, Sallie returned to Alabama and died at her niece's home in Birmingham.

Hardee's youngest daughter, Elizabeth, or "Bessie," did not marry until after her father's death. On October 24, 1877, she married Dr. Fanning F. Gage of South Carolina, who died at an early age. The Gages had one child, Elizabeth, who lived in Birmingham, Alabama, at the time of this study.

Mary Lewis Hardee outlived her husband by only two years. She died on April 6, 1875, at the age of thirty-five from tuberculosis. Her death provided one of those odd coincidences that appear periodically in history. She died of the same disease, in the same town, in the same house, with the same attending physician, as Hardee's first wife, Elizabeth Dummett.

Critical Essay on Authorities

Prefatory Note

THE GREATEST problem in the study of William J. Hardee was locating material. He was never a voluminous correspondent, and even the letters that he did write have largely disappeared.

To be sure, Hardee the lieutenant general appears frequently in the official documents that have been preserved. Yet these records usually deal with him obliquely. The records too are often arid and are written in a studied, defensive manner. As for his personal military papers, they were carefully arranged and sent to Macon, Georgia, for safekeeping in the spring of 1864. In the confusion of the late summer they were lost. Following the Atlanta campaign Hardee left his papers at army headquarters, but they too were subsequently lost. In early 1865 more of his papers were abandoned in South Carolina. After the war, fire destroyed what was left.

William J. Hardee the father, husband, and friend is even more elusive. Some seven hundred widely scattered collections and sources were investigated and employed in the course of this study. This researcher found useful information in Texas, New York, California, Barbados, and France. The nature of the material is as varied as its location. Only a handful of family papers exist, but these papers were invaluable. Interviews with descendants and with specialists familiar with phases of Hardee's life proved of great assistance. The impression of a private who saw Hardee at a review, the record of a traveler who met him, the memory of an ill-tempered subordinate who quarreled with him, and the memory of a son-in-law who worshipped him had to be fitted together to form a meaningful mosaic.

Most of the sources consulted, however, yielded only small fragments, and including such sources in the bibliography seemed unwarranted. Readers interested in particular phases of Hardee's life may refer to the footnotes.

Manuscript Collections

The bulk of the manuscript material pertaining to Hardee's military career, beginning with his application to West Point and ending with his application for a pardon, is to be found in the records of the Secretary of War, the Judge Advocate General, and the Adjutant General in the National Archives. Regimental returns, histories of his regiment, court-martial proceedings, and sometimes a personal note are to be found in this treasure house.

At the United States Military Academy one can find numerous records covering Hardee's life as a cadet and as commandant. Even the house he lived in and the books he read are to be found at "The Point."

The following collections contained Hardee correspondence essential to recreating the prewar phase of his life: at the Georgia Archives, the W. J. Hardee Papers; at the Library of Congress, the Felicia Shover Letters; at the Southern Historical Collection, University of North Carolina, the Edmund Kirby Smith Papers; in possession of Hardee Chambliss, Jr., Fairfax, Virginia, the W. J. Hardee Collection; at the New York Public Library, the Clara K. Paige Papers; at the North Carolina Archives, the Pitt County Records; and at the St. Augustine Historical Society, the Dummett Papers.

Indispensable correspondence for Hardee's life after 1861 were found in the following: at the Duke University Library, the Hardee Papers and the Charles C. Jones Papers; at Emory University Library, the Savannah Squadron Papers; in the Southern Historical Collection, University of North Carolina, the Lewis Family Papers and the Leonidas Polk Papers; at the Historical Society of Pennsylvania, the W. J. Hardee Letters; at the Henry E. Huntington Library, the W. J. Hardee Papers; at the Western Reserve Historical Society, the J. Stoddard Johnston Diary; in possession of Mrs. Howard Bowen, Birmingham, Alabama, the Thomas B. Roy Diary; and the Southern Railroad Archives, the Selma and Meridian Railroad Minute Book.

Printed Official Documents

It would be virtually impossible to attempt a biography of a Civil War military figure without *The War of the Rebellion: A Compilation of the Official Records of the Union and Confederate Armies,*

73 vols. in 128 parts (Washington, 1880–1901). A great deal of useful prewar material appears in Allen D. Candler, *The Revolutionary Records of the State of Georgia*, 3 vols. (Atlanta, 1908); and *Regulations of the U.S. Military Academy at West Point, New York* (New York, 1832, 1853, 1857). A number of Senate and House Documents also provided a quantity of information regarding Hardee's *Tactics* in particular and his prewar career in general.

Newspapers and Periodicals

Although forty-five newspapers and periodicals were used, the most important prewar yields came from the files of the following: The *Army and Navy Journal;* Savannah *Daily Morning News;* St. Augustine *Ancient City;* the New Orleans *Bee;* and the Washington *National Intelligencer.* The above contained fragments of factual data, along with personal accounts of events, such as the raids of Indian villages in the Seminole war. For the Civil War era, the author found the *Confederate Veteran* (Nashville, 1893–1932) replete with information, most of it surprisingly accurate, considering that most of the material was written after the war.

Diaries, Memoirs, and Collected Correspondence

References to Hardee are to be found in thousands of these sources. Samuel G. French, *Two Wars, an Autobiography* (Nashville, Tenn., 1901), is exceptional in that it gives insight into Hardee's activities at different stages of his career. Other fruitful sources of this nature are William W. Bailey, "My Boyhood at West Point," *Personal Narratives of Events in the War of the Rebellion*, 12 vols. (Providence, R. I., 1891); Jefferson Davis, *The Rise and Fall of the Confederate Government*, 2 vols. (New York, 1881); Basil W. Duke, *Reminiscences of General Basil W. Duke, C.S.A.* (New York, 1911); Anna Marie Dummett, 'Remembrances of the Old Plantation," in *Literary Florida*, V (February, 1949), 9-15; A.J.L. Fremantle, *The Fremantle Diary* (Boston, 1954); Oliver Otis Howard, *Autobiography*, 2 vols. (New York, 1907); Joseph E. Johnston, *Narrative of Military Operations* (New York, 1874); George F. Price, *Across the Continent with the Fifth Cavalry* (New York, 1883); Dunbar Rowland (ed.), *Jefferson Davis, Constitutionalist*, 10 vols. (Jackson, Miss., 1923); Morris Schaff, *The Spirit of Old West Point* (Boston, 1907); William T. Sherman, *Memoirs of General William T. Sherman*, 2 vols. (New York, 1875).

Tactics Manuals

The manuals consulted extensively other than Hardee's *Rifle and Light Infantry Tactics*, 2 vols. (Philadelphia, 1855), were Samuel Cooper, *A Concise System of Instructions and Regulations for the Militia and Volunteers of the United States* (Philadelphia, 1847); Winfield Scott, *Infantry Tactics*, 3 vols. (New York, 1835); United States War Department, *Cavalry Tactics*, 2 vols. (Philadelphia, 1855); and Ministre Secrétaire d'Etat de la Guerre, *Ordonnance du Roi sur l'Exercice et les Manoeuvres des Bataillons de Chasseurs à Pied*, 3 vols. (Paris, 1845). A great deal of information about the controversy over publication may be found in Hardee's *Memorial to the Congress of the Confederate States* (Mobile, 1863).

Military Studies by Contemporaries

Among the many studies of particular episodes and campaigns the following contributed much to understanding Hardee's role: Ezra Carmen, *General Hardee's Escape from Savannah* (Washington, 1893); Basil W. Duke, *Morgan's Cavalry* (New York, 1906); Clement A. Evans, *Confederate Military History*, 12 vols. (Atlanta, 1899); Robert U. Johnson and Clarence C. Buel (eds.), *Battles and Leaders of the Civil War*, 4 vols. (1884–87); Charles Colcock Jones, Jr., *The Siege of Savannah in December, 1864* (Albany, 1894); John Berrien Lindsley (ed.), *The Military Annals of Tennessee* (Nashville, 1886); Thomas B. Roy, "General Hardee and the Military Operations around Atlanta," in *Southern Historical Society Papers*, VIII (August, 1880), 337–87.

Secondary Works

Although there exists a mass of historical literature about the Civil War, the amount relating to the Army of Tennessee is relatively small and the coverage uneven. The classic work is Stanley Horn's *The Army of Tennessee* (2nd ed., Norman, Okla., 1952). The best monograph is Thomas Robson Hay's *Hood's Tennessee Campaign* (New York, 1929). Hay also published his studies of some of the problems of the Army of Tennessee. These proved invaluable to the author: T. R. Hay, "The Atlanta Campaign," in *Georgia Historical Quarterly*, VII (March, June, 1923), 18–43, 99–118; "The Battle of Chattanooga," in *Georgia Historical Quarterly*, VIII (June, 1924), 121–41; "Braxton Bragg and the Southern Confederacy" in *Georgia Historical Quar-*

terly, IX (December, 1925), 267–315; "Davis, Bragg and Johnston in the Atlanta Campaign," in *Georgia Historical Quarterly*, VIII (March, 1924), 38–48; "The Davis-Hood-Johnston Controversy of 1864," in *Mississippi Valley Historical Review*, XI (June, 1924), 54–84.

In addition to the works of Horn and Hay, the author relied upon the following secondary studies; Thomas Conn Bryan, "General William J. Hardee and Confederate Publication Rights," in *Journal of Southern History*, XII (May, 1946), 263–74; John Witherspoon Du-Bose, "Chronicles of the Canebrake," in *Alabama Historical Quarterly*, IX (Winter, 1947), 471–613; Joseph Idus Lambert, *One Hundred Years with the Second Cavalry* (Fort Riley, 1939); Theodore F. Rodenbough, *From Everglade to Cañon with the Second Dragoons* (New York, 1875); James T. Vocelle, *History of Camden County, Georgia* (Jacksonville, Fla., 1914).

Biographies

Many of these studies of individual participants provided a great deal of information about Hardee. Most fruitful, of course, was William Douglas Pickett's short study, *Sketch of the Military Career of William J. Hardee, Lieutenant-General C.S.A.* (Lexington, Ky., 1910). Irving A Buck's *Cleburne and His Command* (New York, 1908) has captured Hardee's beloved and most capable lieutenant. Other biographies of primary importance were: Nathaniel Rives Chambliss, "Lieut.-General Hardee," in the *Confederate Veteran*, III (May, 1895), 142–43; John Witherspoon DuBose, *General Joseph Wheeler and the Army of Tennessee* (New York, 1912); Charles Winslow Elliott, *Winfield Scott* (New York, 1937); Gilbert Eaton Govan and James Weston Livingood, *A Different Valor, The Story of General Joseph E. Johnston, C.S.A.* (Indianapolis, 1956); William J. Hardee, "General Pat Cleburne," in *Southern Historical Society Papers*, XXI (1903), 163–65; Charles Edward Nash, *Biographical Sketches of Gen. Pat Cleburne and Gen. T. C. Hindman* (Little Rock, 1898); Joseph Howard Parks, *General Edmund Kirby Smith, C.S.A.* (Baton Rouge, 1954); William Mecklenburg Polk, *Leonidas Polk, Bishop and General*, 2 vols. (New York, 1915); L. V. Reavis, *The Life and Military Services of Gen. William Selby Harney* (St. Louis, 1878); and T. Harry Williams, *P. G. T. Beauregard: Napoleon in Gray* (Baton Rouge, 1954).

Index

Adairsville, Ga., 204
Adams, D. W., 129, 130, 139
Alexander, E. P., 58
Allen, W. W., 282, 291
Anderson, Archer, 163*n*
Anderson, E. C., 261
Anderson, Patton: 120, 121, 137, 234, 238, 294; at Perryville, 124–33
Arista, Mariano, 25, 27
Arkansas regiments, 115
Army of the Mississippi, 119, 135
"Ash Place," 305, 306
Atlanta, battle of, 225–32
Atlanta *Appeal*, 163
Augusta *Constitutionalist*, 224
Averasboro, battle of, 281–86, 302
Aztec Club, 35

Bailey, Jacob W., 9
Baker, L. S., 257
Baldwin, W. E., 181
Ball, Charles P., 72
Ball, Eustace H., 105
Banks, Nathaniel P., 197
Barnard, John G., 56
Bartlett, W. H. C., 9, 63, 66
Bate, William B.: 174, 176, 177, 190, 191, 201, 204, 237, 289, 304; as division commander, 191, 194; at New Hope Church, 204–206; at Kennesaw Mountain, 209–13; at Peachtree Creek, 220–25; at battle of Atlanta, 225–32
Beall, Lloyd J., 19
Beauregard, Pierre G. T.: 11, 12*n*, 13*n*, 35, 70, 71, 90, 93, 97, 99, 100, 103, 107–109, 111, 186, 215, 248, 250, 254, 257–60, 263, 270, 274, 276–80, 295; defends Corinth, 115–19
Beckwith, Bishop John W., 177, 186, 188, 208
Beech Grove, Tenn., 155
Bell Buckle, Tenn., 151, 152
Benet, Stephen V., 46

Benjamin, Judah P., 83
Bentonville, battle of, 287–93, 302
Black, Samuel L., 117, 209, 221
Black Auster, 113, 313
Blair, Francis P., Jr., 73, 228–30
Blanchard, Colonel, 282
"Bleak House," 187, 188
Bowen, John S., 160, 161
Bowling Green, Ky., 81–91
Bragg, Braxton: 97–99, 138, 156, 157, 164, 183, 186, 190, 191, 215, 240, 243, 245–47, 257, 278–80, 287, 290, 295, 304; at Shiloh, 99–112; at Corinth, 118; assumes command of Army of the Mississippi, 119; and Kentucky campaign, 120–35; at Perryville, 125–33; fails in Kentucky, 134–35; at Murfreesboro, 139–47; asks for support, 148–49; asks for Hardee, 163; as a leader, 165; at Chattanooga, 167–78; his opinion of Tennesseans, 168; leaves Army of Tennessee, 179; and removal of Johnston, 216–17; is ordered to halt Sherman, 254
Breckinridge, John C.: 93, 99, 101, 108, 110, 118, 136–38, 144, 145, 148, 156, 191, 193, 241; at Murfreesboro, 140–47; at Chattanooga, 166–77
Bridgeport, Ala., 165
Brookes, George M., 38
Brown, John C., 130, 131, 156, 173, 175, 176, 178, 193, 237
Brown, Governor Joseph, 68, 70, 181, 273, 276, 278, 294
Brownlow, William G., 96
Brown's Ferry, 165
Buchanan, James, 60
Buck, Irving, 171, 172, 189, 299
Buckner, Simon B., 81, 82, 87, 120–22, 124, 129, 133, 134, 137, 138, 164, 169
Buell, Don Carlos, 86, 87, 89, 91, 96, 98, 100, 110, 121, 137
Bullock, Governor Archibald, 4